Interpretation of Jesus Christ's Gospel according to St. John

EUREKA
RESEARCH AND GLOBAL SOLUTIONS COOP

via Ferrovia, 70

33033 Beano di Codroipo (Udine) - ITALY

info@dimensione-eureka.it – http://dimensione-eureka.it

EUREKA is dedicated to the study of the factors that contribute to a high quality life in the fields of agriculture, environment, nutrition, medicine, veterinary, architecture, spirituality, and applied science. We publish results obtained from our research to educate people on creating new and healthy lifestyles.

Our work is based on the spiritual scientific work of Rudolf Steiner and the action of the Christ on all life..

EUREKA's activities focus on the promotion and creation of centers for study, research, development and dissemination of information and research results.

To further this effort, EUREKA creates products that are prepared using techniques of homeopathy which support the natural kingdoms, water depuration and water vitalization systems, environmental depollution, furniture design, protection from electromagnetic fields, etc. For more information about these concepts, please visit our website.

EUREKA is also active in planning farms, parks and gardens, various environments, buildings, and furniture where there is a need to create a vital environment following organic laws.

Originally published in English by Viva la Vida Foundation
www.vivalavidafoundation.org

This edition published by Lindisfarne Books
an imprint of SteinerBooks/ Anthroposophic Press, Inc.
www.steinerbooks.org

ISBN 978-1-58420-927-0

Printed in the United States of America

Interpretation of Jesus Christ's Gospel according to St. John

Text translated from ancient Greek and commented on from a spiritual-scientific point of view

Curated by Enzo Nastati

Thank you to everyone who participated

in this work. Thanks to their devotion,

we were able to create it.

A special thank you to Renzo Miotti

who helped with the translation process.

An additional thank you to Jessie Melison for the English translation.

SUMMARY

Interpretation of Jesus Christ's Gospel according to Saint John

INTRODUCTION

In the path of inner awakening there is a moment in which we perceive with our whole being the importance to find Truth, which brings us to Faith, in relationship with the Divine. This yearning of our soul corresponds to the moment in which we find the Gospels, which are the "Good News" that Christ brought to us. If, in this path of searching, we use our whole heart, our whole soul and our whole mind (Mc 12, 20), then we can start to perceive John's Gospel in comparison to the other three, like a monument of incomparable greatness, harmony and truth.

This moment corresponds to the transition from "Simple" Faith to "Conscious" Faith.
The same thing happened to us. After translating and studying the Gospels, we dedicated our time in particular to John's Gospel. This work was able to happen only after we went from the Latin translation to the Greek one. The spiritual study of the terms used by Saint John allowed us to lift the veil that was covering this immense treasure of knowledge and wisdom. In addition, we had the chance to get ahold of the most ancient text, called "Codex Sinaiticus" which goes back to the fourth century after Christ.

Instead of doing what all the other translators did, we decided to add our own interpretation of the text, which is a commentary that absolutely does not give a definite and complete meaning, but instead hopes to encourage a deeper and more profound reading of the text.

The reader, who is accustomed to the Latin version of the text, will struggle with the version that we are giving. We apologize already, but the language used to express spiritual truths doesn't always go with the common language used to express terrestrial things.

To help with the comprehension of this text, we suggest you read our "Scientific-Spiritual Glossary", "Ancient and New Ways to Initiation", and also "The Sacraments: Ancient Mysteries and Christian Initiation" in which you will be able to find the basic and fundamental keys to spiritual readings.

FUNDAMENTAL ELEMENTS OF JOHN'S GOSPEL

John's Gospel primarily revolves around the Greater I, and the process that helps us with the conscious birth of it within us.

The Gospel begins speaking about Logos, and so in the peculiarity of Jesus, in which in the moment of birth the Logos descended. In Luke's Gospel (verse 2, 6-7), he describes with extreme clarity this particular episode. Because of its importance and the little knowledge about it, we think it is important to talk about it.

> *2,6 and so it was, that while they were there, the days were accomplished that she should be delivered*
>
> *2,7 and she brought forth her first son, and wrapped him in swaddling clothes, and laid him in a manger; because there was no room for them in the inn.*

After this event, we have the other fundamental event, the baptism at the Jordan when Jesus-Logos received within him the Christ. Only John gives us the completion of the Being of Jesus, bearer of the Logos first, and then of the Christ. Within this viewpoint, we can start to comprehend the reason why only John brings back the episode of the Washing of the Feet of the Last Supper, but he does not bring back the institution of the Lord's Supper.

With John, we have the beginning of the Greater and Conscious I in the new relationship with the Divine, a relationship that can be called "direct worship" or "upside-down worship," since it flows from "below" to "above" without the help of mediators.

Lastly, in Saint John's Gospel, we find the beginning of the institution of the New Community which is based on love, and it is an event in which the metamorphosis surrounds all of his Gospel. It begins with the episode of the Marriage at Cana (which is talked about only by John) ,and it ends with the famous "*Woman, see your child*". And then he said to the disciple: *"See your mother"*. From that moment on, the disciple took her with him (John 19,26-27). With this we can follow the transformation of the community from the blood (family members at Cana), to love (John and the Mother at the cross).

The importance of the articles

Connected to this, we find the presence or lack of **articles in front of the nouns** (of people, places, populations, animals, etc). Within the occult meaning, the presence of the article indicates that the one who is speaking or writing wants to express the greater aspect of the person or the thing that is being talked about. Sadly, the Latin language doesn't contemplate articles, and so only by studying the Greek version can we understand this aspect. We are going to cite, as an example, the name "Jesus": when it is not cited with an article, "the man Jesus" is spoken about, the "Nathan" Soul reincarnated on Earth; but with the article, it becomes "the Jesus", which means Jesus with the Christ within him. The deeds that these two different aspects of Jesus accomplish, are different.

The internal resonances in the Saint John's Gospel

Just as we have already demonstrated regarding the four Gospels, within each one of them there are internal resonances that determine a hidden architecture, the comprehension of which helps with the "metamorphic" approach to the text.

In the case of Saint Matthew, in general, each chapter "resounds" with the following octave according to the logic of **1-8-15-22; 2-9-16-23.....up to 7-14-21-28**

In Saint Mark, each chapter resounds with the following fourth, and so we have **1-5-9-13, 2-6-10-14.... Up to 4-8-12-16**

The resonances of Saint Luke recur every eighth verse, so we have **1-9-17, 2-10-18, up to 8-16-24.**

In Saint John, we have a peculiar resonance, precisely direct **1-12, 2-13, 3-14, 4-15, 5-16, 6-17, 7-18, 8-19, 9-20, 10-21. The main chapter, the one which the Gospel revolves around, is chapter 11, the chapter of the resurrection of Lazarus John.**

In regards to Saint John's Gospel, it is articulated in the I, so within this there are two cycles of the I present (the cycle relative to the number 10, just like the 10 Commandments), with the resurrection of Lazarus at the center (which is the Evangelist himself). Therefore, we have the "old" I, its metamorphosis, and the birth of the "new" Christic I.

Little dictionary of Saint John's Gospel

During the translation process, we bumped into some words (especially verbs) for which the customary translation was not enough to give the true value of what John wanted to express.

Here is a list of the main words which need an in-depth translation so that we understand the spiritual value of the text. In the text, the Greek terms are indicated with parenthesis and italics.

"TO SEE"

GREEK	TRANSLATION
• Theaomai	to see God with the Incorruptible Body. Concise Translation: to see God in the new etheric body.
• Theoreo	it is the spiritual vision; one activates the spiritual part of seeing with the third eye. Concise Translation: to spiritually see
• Opsomai	it is the future of *horao*, it is the Etheric vision through the Incorruptible Body Concise Translation: to see in the new etheric
• Idein Idon(part.pres) Ide(te) (imperative)	it is the infinite form of eidon, it's an expansion that allows us to understand if we have the strength, the laws of Logos. Idein: "to see" Idon: "seeing, the one who sees, Seeing". Idete: "see!" Concise Translation: understand (the Logos).
• (ide)	"here" (let. See!) Concise Translation: see (just like above with the spiritual meaning)

• Blepo	it's the "soul" vision, the soul sees the aura of things or people. Concise Translation: Soul Vision
• Blepo(2)	to see the spirit participating in his life Concise Translation: to see the life of the Spirit
• Anablepo	to regain vision, to lift the eyes, to lift the tunic of skin that covers the eyes.
• Hora Heoraka Ophthe	it is the etheric vison *heoraka(perf)*: "I saw" *ophthe(aor.pass.)*: "it was seen" Concise Translation: to see etherically
• Eidon	it's the past (aorist) of horao, the etheric "dies" and from the sacrifice the physical vision, that expands on all superior levels, comes to life. Concise Translation: to physically see on all levels. True bodily vision.
• Deiknymi	to indicate, point out.

"TO DO- TO ACT"

GREEK	**TRANSLATION**
• Poieo (I create)	to create, to make with art, generate, to shape, to mold, to operate.
Poeie (he creates)	Concise Translation: to create
Epoiesa (I created)	
Epoiesen (he created)	
Poiein (to create)	
• 'ergazomai' (I accomplish)	to accomplish, to work, to practice.

	Spiritual Fulfillment: from the spiritual plane to the terrestrial one.
Ergazetai (he accomplishes)	
• Ktizo	to substantialize.
• Teleo	to accomplish in the etheric spatial plane.
• Teleioo	to accomplish spiritually in the spatiality.
• Ergon	accomplishment, fulfillment.

'TO TAKE'

GREEK	TRANSLATION
• Bastazo	to understand in the spiritual plane.
• Lambano	to take in the spiritual plane or in general in the subtle planes, depending on the context.
• Katalambano	to completely win, to fully take, to imprison, in the spiritual plane or in general in the subtle planes, depending on the context.
• Paralambano	to take, to receive or embrace within ourselves, to assume, in the spiritual plane, or in general in the subtle planes, depending on the context.

• Syllambano	to close, in the spiritual plane or in general in the subtle planes, depending on the context.

'TO BELIEVE AND HAVE FAITH' (listed according to the different levels of "importance").

GREEK	TRANSLATION
• Pisteuo(I believe)	present/imperfect/perfect/future : I believe/ I believed/ I have believed and will keep believing/ I will believe.
Episteua(I believed) Pepisteuka(I have believed) Pisteuso(I will believe)	Concise Translation: to believe
• Episteusa (I believed)	past (aorist): "I believed". Concise Translation: to have faith
• Pisteusete ('believe!) Pisteuso	believing and having faith (generic). Concise Translation: to be believers/ followers.
• Apeitheo	to be incredulous, to refuse to believe. Concise Translation: incredulous.

"TO SAY"

GREEK	TRANSLATION
• Eipon	it's a blocked saying, done. Concise Translation: I said.
• Eipon(2)	it's a categorical saying, irrevocable and unappealable. Concise Translation: I said.
• Eipon pros	to answer, reply.
• Lego(I say) Leghei(he says) Elegon(I said)	it's a saying that keeps going with time. Concise Translation: I say, he says, I said.
• Ephen(I uttered) Ephe(he uttered) Phemi(I utter)	he uttered. Concise Translation: to utter.
• Eireka(I said)	I said, and the effect continues. Concise Translation: I said.
• Krazo	to say with force; literally to yell

• Laleo	to speak with a stutter; to express the simplest things, the initial things. Concise translation: to stutter.
• Apokrinomai	to reply. to discern the Truth. Concise Translation: to reply (to discern the Truth)
• Apokrinomai pros	to react, to discern the Truth Concise Translation: to react (to discern the Truth)
• Kerysso	annunciation on the spiritual plane Concise translation: to announce

"TO HEAR"

GREEK	**TRANSLATION**
• Akouo	to learn spiritually through clairvoyance. Concise translation: To hear.

"TO COME"

GREEK	**TRANSLATION**
• Heko Hexo(future)	to arrive, to arrive as a result of a spiritual journey. Concise Translation: I have arrived.
• Erchomai(I come) Elthon(I came)	to come, to return spiritually.

Elelytha(I came)

GREEK	TRANSLATION
• Anabaino	to ascend spiritually
• Katabaino	descend spiritually
• Hypago	to descend below, on a lower plane.

"TO GO"

GREEK	TRANSLATION
• Aperchomai Apelthon(aor.) Apelelytha(perf.) Apeleusomai(future)	to go (generic)
• Poreuomai	head towards spiritual paths.
• Hypantao	Descending/ Going down. Concise translation: to descend.

"HOUSE"

GREEK	TRANSLATION
• Oikia	home, descent, lineage, race
• Oikos	home, residence, abode, room, apartment, space, room or chamber of the temple (also internal).

• Tameio	room, little room or chamber (also internal)
• Hieros	internal temple
• Naos	external temple

"DEATH"

GREEK	TRANSLATION
• Apokteino	to kill (within one's inner being)
• Thnesko	it's the "normal" death
• Apothnesko	it's the death that divides, it's a deeper death that creates a greater estrangement than "normal" death. This deep death expresses the condition of the one being initiated (or of the Child) which is stopped in the evolutionary spiritual process even for multiple reincarnations.
• Ho thanatos ho deuteros	"the second death", the one that represents the exit of the evolutionary process. It corresponds to the death of the etheric body, death that will prevent the future Zeus to proceed.
• Sphazo	to bleed dry, to slit someone's throat for sacrifice, the kill in general.
• Teleutao	to completely die. To reach the depth of death.

On the "REBALANCING/RENEWAL" (in general)

GREEK	TRANSLATION
• Katharizo	to make pure, but evil (the "unclean" spirit) can still return. Concise Translation: to purify.
• Iaomai	to free oneself from evil, to heal spiritually from an "unclean" spirit so that he will never come back. Concise Translation: to heal, to cure.
• Therapeuo	to be made servant, so to ascend to the Sun and reach the spiritual self. Concise Translation: to be healed.
• Hygies	strong and healed
•	
• Nosema	moral (ethical) suffering, bad habit, foolishness, madness.
• Kompsos	raised, graceful, clever.

"TO STAY"

GREEK	TRANSLATION
• Histemi	to stay unmovable (it's extremely physical), to place, to establish

- Anistemi — to lift oneself up, to resuscitate, to rise, to rise from being in an unmovable state.

- Tithemi — to impose (as a command or order, for example laying on of the hands, of a name, of a title).

"TO SAFEGUARD"

GREEK	TRANSLATION
• Tereo	to safeguard, to observe in the sense of guarding.

"TO SAY" AND "TO SEE"

In the Saint John's Gospel, there is an abundance of "to say", and within this, we can capture the dimension of "Word-Logos" in his Gospel. The continuous back and forth, between "he said and he says" is a quality of time used by Saint John so that we can free ourselves from the verbal tenses and also from their forms.

INTERPRETED TEXT OF JESUS CHRIST ACCORDING TO SAINT JOHN'S GOSPEL

PROLOGUE[1]

[1] The prologue represents the entrance to the Gospel, and it represents a summary.
The whole structure is articulated in "waves": John expresses a concept and then, just like a wave on the beach, he resumes it and brings it to the next level.
PROLOGUE

1. As a[2] First[3] Cause there was[4] the[5] Logos

---

[2]Normally, the first two verses are translated like this: *"In the beginning was the Word, and the Word was with God, and the Word was God"*. The translation that we suggest is the result of an in-depth analysis of the Greek idiomatic expression *"En archei"*, which is usually translated as "in the beginning" and on the term *"en"* which represents the present perfect of the verb to be, which is normally translated "was".

[3] This "First" does not refer to a term of time but it instead represents the *Arche'*. The First, "the First Cause", the Prince (in Italian the Archon: which is the ruling "ruler" of the seven Heavens), the "Natural Authority" which "rules" and whose command is recognized from the others *arche'*. This "First", exactly because it is such, connects to the Father of the Holy Trinity, which is indicated in Judaism with the name of Adonai. John speaks to the Jewish people first, and he helps them see that Logos was already within Adonai, and so there is continuity between the message of the Christ and the revelation of the Jewish Law (it is a continuity that the Jewish people did not recognize).
Some writings also translate the preposition "in" with "in the", we suggest that this translation is even more incorrect since the preposition "in the" is "in" plus "the" and so it brings us back to the First Father of the Holiest Trinity and not of the Holy one. In the esoteric Greek language, the article raises the subject to its highest dimension.
It's important to remember that Greek words were often acronyms, which means that each letter had a meaning "within itself", and the union of these letters would determine the concept that the word was expressing. So the expression *en archei* means: *E* the expansion, *N* of the mind (the law of God as a project, as Logos), *A* (that) begins, *R* (Ra) as the father, *CH* here where we are at, *E* (to) expand, *I* (in the) connection between spirit and earth. If we then look at the Hebrew word *berish,* which is the expression with which the Bible begins, it also usually gets translated "at the beginning". The difference with the Italian language is extreme. The word *berisch* can be divided in three words: *be,* the beginning, *-ris*, the change, the transformation; *-ch*, the Christ who will arrive at the end. So, now we have three expressions of the same concept but they evoke three extremely different spiritual realities.

[4] The conjugation of the verb "to be" acquires a particular aspect in the Prologue. Since Logos is the aspect of the "Son" of the Holy Trinity, this is the corresponding aspect of the "Son" in the Holiest Trinity and so to the Christ. In other words, it corresponds to the " I am the I am" or the " I am the one who is". So, from what we just stated, this "was" (in Greek *en)* does not refer to the past, but instead to our "there was": so "As the First One there already was the Verb-Logos". In the Greek language, the imperfect tense is called "durative imperfect" and it refers to something that began and it continues (in English this would be the present perfect tense).
In an even more dynamic aspect, this verb becomes *ghighnomai* which means "to be born, to be, to become". And so this is the verb of the Life that begins and doesn't die, of the Spiritual Life (read verse 1,3).

[5] In the esoteric Greek language, the presence of the article indicates the raising of the subject to a higher plane. When it is referred to a man it indicates his higher spiritual aspect, but when referred to Jesus it refers to the Christic aspect within Him; when referred to Logos it specifies that He is a God.

[6],[7]

And the Logos remains[8] near the God,[9]

and God[10] is[11] the Logos[12].

2 These being[13] as the Primary Cause near the God[14].

---

[6] The Logos, First Father of the Holy Trinity, acts as the central Spirit of the Holy Trinity, and so as a Solar Spirit. The Christ (First Son of the Holiest Trinity) reveals Himself through the Verb-Logos. In John, it means that the essential Word of God, the wisdom in unison with God, his ministry in creation and governor of the universe, the cause of all forms of life in the world both perceivable and not, had to descend in order to obtain human salvation. He descended in human nature in the body of Jesus the Messiah. Heraclitus used the term logos around 600 B.C. to explain the reason, or the divine plan, that coordinates the universe which constantly changes.

[7] This is the first "wave".

[8] Just as we said earlier about the first "was", this second "was" can be better translated with "remain/ continue".

[9] This is the God of the Holiest Trinity, because in the esoteric spiritual language, the article in front of a name indicates its higher aspect. The Holiest Trinity created the Holy Trinity. The Holiest Trinity corresponds to the whole Universe, whereas the Holy Trinity corresponds to the evolutionary system, the solar system, and it goes up to the belt of the Zodiac (Zodiac constellation). This is the second "wave".

[10]Without the article, and so it is of the Holy Trinity.

[11] This "was" is correctly translated with our "is" since it now "is". John accentuates the verb *to be* because his Gospel wants to testify the "birth of the Being", of the I Am within the man.

[12] Third "wave".

[13] This is the fourth reference to Being (to the I am): now it "exists" in a meaning that is not related to the passing of time. It's as if this path is closing within itself as John reunites the three subjects mentioned: the Verb (these), the First, and God. Therefore, we have: the Verb-Logos "there was", then "remains", and the "is" near the God of the Holiest Trinity.
From what we just said, the "spiritual conjugation" of the verb "to be" is completed, and it appears three times (in the first verse) "plus" one (in the second verse). Let us remember that the logic of the spiritual world is the logic of the three "plus" one, which means of the One and the Triune (three).

[14] The Verb-Logos is God (of the Holy Trinity), he exists as the First factor of our evolution, and he exists in the Holiest Trinity, as he was created by it. Fourth (3+1) "wave".

3 Everything[15]through the same[16] had become (alive)(*ghighnomai*) and without him no One became (alive) of what become (alive)(*ghighnomai*).

4 Within the same Spiritual Life (Zoe)[17] was (from always)[18] and the Spiritual Life (Zoe) was (from always)[19] the Light[20] of men (*antropos*)[21]

---

[15] This "everything" means the beginning of our evolutionary system where "everything" was "one" and it was enclosed in the enormous caloric sphere called "Old Saturn" as a non-material substance. Now (verse 1,3 and 1,4) a second concept is exposed by John: the Logos is Light (which means Spiritual Love) and it's Eternal Life.

[16] This is usually translated as "by means of the Same". With this verse, the evangelist wants to express that what has "gone by" Him has become alive (maintaining the connection with Him). This anticipates the words of Jesus to Gethsemane: *"My father, if there is strength, pass the Cup (goblet) through me, but this, not how I want, but how you want."*(Mt 26 39).

[17] In Greek, Zoe. Zoe is the eternal spiritual Life and it differs from Bios, which is Life as a transient existence on Earth. Bios is limited to time and space, whereas Zoe is unlimited. The man formed by God was in Zoe, but with the Fall from the Terrestrial Paradise he entered the terrestrial existence: in Bios. "Spiritual Life" refers to the second evolutionary phase of planet Earth: after Old Saturn came the phase air-Light and to the non-material substance, and so the etheric body was added: Life.
From what we just said, we can look at this spiritual Life as the "plus One" of the verb *ghighnomai*: the Evangelist conjugated this verb in the logic of the Spirit.

[18] The particular conjugation of the verb "to be" can be translated in Italian with this "from always/since always".

[19] See the note above.

[20] Now the evangelist is recalling the third evolutionary phase of the Earth, the so-called Old Moon. This is the phase where the astral aspect, the Light, is added to the forming cosmic body. At the same time, the Light is, and continues to be, the manifestation of the Eternal.

[21] The Light "was" outside of the man, but now it is getting closer to the man: it's barely touching him; it's touching him, it makes him visible and alive. So God is not "in the heavens", he is close to all of us.

5 and the Light in the darkness[22] revealed itself, and the darkness didn't completely apprehend it (receive it/take it in) (*katalambano*)[23].

---

[22] The "dual" aspect begins here in the Prologue: the light is in contrast with the Darkness.
With this we are re minded of how in the times of the Old Moon, Evil came into evolution as the demonic entities refused to respond to their calling of giving the gift of Light to men (Lucifer means "Bearer of Light"). From then on, the luciferic principle came between men and God; when man will transform it in Good, then he will become the helper for humanity, he will become the Paraclete Spirit, which is spoken about at the Pentecost. For the complete vision of the "Paraclete" see John 14, 16.
The evangelist summarizes all of the action of the Logos in the first five verses: from Logos that donates Life to Verb-Light, which then wins the opposing forces of the ahrimanic darkness with the mystery of Golgotha. This happens because with the exiting of the Sun from Earth, a part of the Light evolves in spiritual Light and another part evolves in terrestrial light in which man descended. The action of the Darkness, in the moment of the descent of Jesus in the center of the Earth, was, as always, to attempt to surround and constrict the Light and overshadow it. However, the Light of Jesus Christ won because He came to guide humanity to the era of the spiritual Light. This darkness has a maximum period in the dark Era (or *Kali Yuga*). This era lasted 5000 years and it ended in 1899. When the Chosen Ones, which are the people of Israel (or people of God, or the Chosen people), the ones that "are in the world but not of the world", will appear in white clothing (see the Apocalypse).
These first verses can have a higher level of reading. Who "studied" the theme of the divine with courage knows that it's articulated in 3+1 levels (and this finds correspondence in the One and Trine). If we look from the point of view of the man, we find the Holy Trinity as a reigning divinity of our evolutionary system (from Earth to the Zodiac), divinity articulated in Original Father, Son and Holy Spirit. Then we have the Holiest Trinity, which is the divinity that governs all of creation (all the stars) which is portrayed by the Light. Cosmic Life penetrated all of creation (which finds image in the stars and the interstellar space), and finally there is the "plus One", the Infinite One, the purest divine Love. If now we follow this path by "descending" we can see that all of this is expressed as an extreme summary in the verse 1,4: the Divine which was Life, which was Light, of the men.

[23]

6 He became (*ghighnomai*)[24] a man (*antropos*) (in Life[25]) sent from God, whose name (interior[26]) was John[27].

---

[24] In many codes it is "*eu*"=was, was in the sense of verse 1. Here begins the third concept that John wanted to bring with his Prologue: the arrival of the Baptist and the fact that he was not the Light, but only a witness of the Light. Maybe this statement, which can have a light adversarial taste, has been made necessary for the ones that continued to follow the Baptist and have not recognized (or followed) Jesus Christ. After all, the Church still practices the Baptism of water, but not the one of Fire nor the one of the Spirit.
This man (in Greek *antropos*, which means the "normal" man, the one moving towards the spirit and not *Aner* which is the one already Enlightened by the Spirit) enters Life.

[25] "The man in the Life" is the one who has "changed mind", and so he brought his conscience in the flowing of the divine Life.

[26] It is clear here that the title "John" is a spiritual title.

[27] John the Baptist was the reincarnation of Elijah, the prophet who was kidnapped with a wagon, in the Sun (home of the Higher I, of the Son of the Man) by the horses of fire (the *Merkaba*). Elijah reincarnated as John the Baptist, and the molding solar force shaping his body became, exactly, the head of John the Baptist. Thanks to these forces, he was able to preach the "changing mind". He was then "beheaded" because his head completed its task: the one of indicating and straightening the Way, of making men "change mind". John the Baptist is known to wear leather (and hide) and this brings us back to "wear leather garments" of Adam and Eve after the transgression. John is the "man of leather" who, with his death, anticipates the emancipation of Adam, the first "man of leather".
John's favorite disciple was Eliseo (cfr II Re), and he left him his cloak (which represents the forces of his astral body). Following some clues, we can assume that Eliseo came back as Elisabeth, the mother of the Baptist, to give back the forces that he received as a gift.
The entity of John the Baptist-Elijah was also part of the Nathan Soul, precisely its aspect of thought (always for the invitation that worked to "change-mind"). The will aspect of this Soul was incarnated in Nathan Mariam (*"it will be done to me according to Your will"*), which is an entity that descended for the first time on Earth. We find within the Nathan Jesus, who was also incarnated for the first time, the aspect to Feel, the Sun, the connection, the central strength between the two. Within him, the Christ will then manifest. The three aspects of the Nathan Soul will meet for the first time on Earth when Marian, pregnant with Jesus, goes to visit her cousin Elisabeth who was 6 months pregnant with the Baptist. Thanks to this encounter, the physical body of the Baptist "turns/flips" in Elisabeth's womb: which means that "it becomes animated": the three aspect of the Nathan Soul re-found each other here, on Earth.
Let's remember the esoteric meaning of the name (from Latin *nume*, that is God) John. In Greek it's written *Ioannis* and it can be spiritually interpreted as follows: *I* as the connection between above and below; *N* as the connection with God's mind, a new light expands, the Sophia expresses herself; *N* when it's repeated it's interpreted as the opening of a second veil, of a second level in this spiritual journey; *I* as the beginning of a new connection between above and below; and *S* as bringing inside, to make fruitful, fertile.
"John" is not truly a "name" but a "title", a spiritual title given to the ones that develop a double connection with God (that is the highest initiation). This double connection corresponds to the metric anapestic rhythm (unstressed-unstressed-stressed) and the anapestic rhythm is the rhythm that is used to write John's Gospel and the Apocalypse (also of John's). Dante's Divine Comedy and Shakespeare's works were also written with an anapestic rhythm.

7 He came to be a testimony, so that he would testify about *(peri)* the light[28], so that everyone [29] would believe[30] through him[31].

8 He himself was not the light, but (he came) so that he would testify around the light.

9 He became *(ghighnomai)*[32] the light, the true[33], the one that enlightens every man (*antropos*), that comes in the world (natural) (*cosmos*).

10 In the world he was[34], and the world (natural) through him became (living)[35], and the world (natural) did not know him[36].

---

[28] Both the interior one (of the Incorruptible Body) that is present within each one of us and the development of our spiritual work (the "Son of the man") allow it to manifest, and also the Light that is Life.

[29] All the men, including the non-Chosen ones.

[30] There is an extreme difference between having faith and believing. Faith is a virtuous motion of the soul towards a purpose that deems to be full of value, so it is directed towards something or someone. Believing is the next step that unites us with that purpose; we enter it. Since we initially just love our own selves, the moment we walk into this higher entity we begin to love him. To believe in God, in the Christ, implicates the complete acceptance of our higher I to His Word. Loving him is what allows Him to love us. This starts the process that will take us to John's step: of the disciple that He spiritually loved. God responds to our faith with His benevolence (the mercy), with believing he can gift us His Love. It's interesting to see how John does not use the word "faith" in his Gospel, he only talks about "believing".

[31] That is as they received from him: and precisely the teaching (aspect connected to Thinking), and the example of life (aspect connected to Will) and he would preach in Samaria-feeling.

[32] Now we are at the fourth phase, at the 3+1. Now the Christ appears (who is Light), the Christ who became flesh (the duality with the Darkness) for us and he entered us (the three) to bring us back to the Father.

[33] This is the light brought by Jesus with the Christ within him. For the Jewish people the light came from the Law but it did not have Life within itself.

[34] The subject is logos.

[35] In him, the world comes back to life because he has renamed it, as it was full of Holy Spirit from the maternal womb (as Luke says). Moses received the "fixed" and static Law; John the Baptist, within himself, permeated it with Life and so he entered a process of change (the "change mind"), and thanks to this gesture, the Christ was then able to transform it in living Grace and Truth (see v.17)

[36] The theme of rejection appears here, of the Evil that enters evolution. With this, another theme is presented that interests John: all of his Gospel can be seen as a big process: testimonies, accusations, convictions, and tortures.
The Christ is now in the world (his), the darkness didn't recognize him nor discerned him (*ghignosco*). This verse is the paraphrase of the verses1-3.

11 He came to the personal[37] things, and his[38] didn't receive[39] him.

12 But to all the ones that welcomed[40] him he gave them the power to become sons (*tekna*)[41] of God[42], to the ones that believe in his name[43],

---

[37] From Greek *taidia*: personal property, all of the given Cosmo since He made it alive (John 1,3)

[38] Generally the Chosen People, the ones who are called to enter the Kingdom. The Chosen People, the Eternal Israel descend directly from the Nathan Soul, and the Baptist, together with Mariam and Jesus, are the Leaders. To be more precise, the ones that didn't receive him are represented by "his" crowd, which will then be partially healed by Jesus with the curing of the Moody Child, that is the Son of the One of the crowd.

[39] The verb is *parelabon*, which means "close to receiving him". Receiving him within one self, within the soul.

[40] Now the verb *elabon* appears, which is the same as verse 1,5 but now it's in a positive form.
For example, the welcoming that was given to him in Samaria (John 4,39), from the pagans (John 12, 20). It's interesting to see how He came for the Chosen People ("his") but he was especially recognized by strangers. It is important to understand that He does not ask to accept a particular creed, instead it is about welcoming Him, his message of love, his teachings, his Guidance towards Resurrection.

[41] The term used for "sons" is *tekna (*=terrestrial sons, the adoptive ones) which is a term that is "colder" than *hyos*, which is the term used to portray the Son of God. This is used because yes, we will become God's sons, but we are Adoptive Sons and not sons *de jure*.

[42] God's sons correspond to the First Son and First Father within us. The anthroposophic reading calls them Vital Loving Spirit and Spirit Man.

[43] The term used for "name", which is *onoma*, is the "name" that is given to the person we love. His Name is the "first Name" of God, which corresponds to the Holy Spirit of God in the Trinity. This is the 'I am' that manifests itself in the man. With this affirmation, John states for the first time in Hebrew the principle of the Holy Spirit. It will be this aspect that will descend in Jesus at the Baptism at the Jordan, and within Jesus it will manifest as "first Son", as Christ.

13 who not from blood[44], nor from the will of the flesh[45], nor from the will of the enlightened[46] man, but they were born from God (in the spiritual Life).

[44] The term "blood" used here relates to its Jewish meaning. The child was conceived by menstrual blood and male sperm. This is the ancient strength and power of blood that wants to remain "united", or better, does not want to accept any other type of blood. Throughout time, it became a luciferic force which subtracts us from freedom. When the blood combines, the human I can incarnate itself, better defining a higher possibility of freedom forces. With what has just been said, the consanguinity connects us to the domain of the sphere of the soul with the I.

[45] The will of the flesh to reproduce itself: just like cellular reproduction (or worse cloning). The Greek term (*sarx*) is usually translated as "flesh" but it's a lot richer and deeper. It already appears in the Bible when God puts Adam in an "initiation sleep" and he took from him the famous rib and then filled the empty space with "flesh". After this, Adam began to talk (*Genesis 2:21-24: And so God the Lord had a deep sleep fall on the man, who fell asleep; he took one of his ribs, and put flesh in place of it. 23: The man said: "This, finally, is now bone of my bones and flesh of my flesh. She shall be called woman because she was taken from the man". 24: That is why a man will leave his father and his mother and is united to his wife, and they will be one the same flesh).*
The term *sarx* can be better translated as "red meat moistened with blood", and so permeated with the "first I"... and Adam began to speak, becoming a bearer of logos. When God "divides" Adam from Eve he inserts the first "three": the logos.
It will be on the Golgotha that Jesus, the new Adam, will receive a wound on his ribs exactly in the intercostal space that was opened by God in the first Adam. The "first" I contained in the blood will be poured until its last drop, until it will be "mixed with water" so that the redemption of Adam can be fully completed.
In Greek *sarx* means: "flesh", "man", "human nature", "corrupted nature", "mortal life" and also "king", "queen", "strength", "sovereign ruler": all of this depending if we are capturing the aspect of "matter" or the aspect of the "I" that flows from the blood.
If we follow the spiritual meaning of each letter we can find: *S* (within us, in the cave from which we enter); *A* (beginning, primordial beginning); *R* (the Father, the higher aspect); *X* (the casket, the coffin, what is below). So the "flesh" is the tool for the manifestation of the divine principle in the "lower" ground.
In Hebrew, flesh is called *basar* which means "primordial ground/earth", and in the center of this word we find the syllable *sin* which means 300. It is the number of movement, of dynamism: the number 3 (the principle of trinity of God that overcomes the luciferic duality) descended on Earth (*basar)* as a seed (logos) for the change of the flesh (the Incorruptible Body) of the man, to achieve the ultimate marriage, the interior marriage. The flesh becomes the space of the total fulfillment, the one of the most intimate union with God. Always from the Hebrew language, we find that *basar* comes from *basorah*: the Good News, the Gospel. Lastly, *basar* is the abbreviated version of *berisch*, the "principle" of the Genesis, so *basar* becomes the Christ's Principle that manifests, while *berisch* is the Non-manifested Principle, the one that hasn't yet manifested itself.

[46] The human desire of the conscious I. This man in Greek is *aner*, the groom, the Enlightened, the one that does not need to follow his own will but the one of the Spirit. If his "will" falls into the luciferic Initiation, he will leave the Verb and Life.

14 and the logos became[47] living[48] flesh, and it lived[49] within us[50] and we contemplated

---

[47] Normally translated as "it became flesh". This, though, implies a process of falling, of downfall, of degradation. However, "He became flesh" indicates that he consciously wanted it.

[48] The flesh now can enter the spiritual Life; it can go from biological existence (Bios) to divine Life (Zoe). The Verb became living flesh to bring it back to its spiritual dimension. This event corresponds to the moment of the Gethsemane in which Jesus sweats blood, which is the action that determined the complete transformation of the flesh thanks to the principle of the Christ present in Jesus' blood. Now the flesh can return to Light. The Incorruptible Body has completely permeated and transformed the physical material body.
All of this was and still is blasphemy for the Hebrew Law and for the Koran. The logos, the divine Light became flesh. Darkness: the two extremes are united.

[49] This "lived" should be literally translated "placed the Curtains". This expression refers to the Sacred Curtains of the Tabernacle, the curtains of the Temple: the human heart. This term is also connected to the Tent of Meeting, where the "Glory of the Lord" appeared. The Greek term is *eskenosen* and it contains the "strong" consonants *skn*, the same found in *shekinon* which in Hebrew means " the living presence of God".

[50] "Within" us (in the heart) but also "in the middle of us" (where two people are united in His Name..). "Us" means the Chosen People, the Eternal Israel. It can also be translated as "has taken root".

[51] the glory[52] (his), glory as of only-begotten Son of the Father

---

[51] To contemplate means both "in the same temple" and "in the same time": that is "here and now". This means that now the eyes can see; these are the eyes of the Incorruptible Body to which the Christ gave the spiritual sight back (see the born blind, John 9,1). From the chakra with two petals, it permeates in the temple of the temples and it permeates in the time-memory (Turkish saddle/sella turcica of the sphenoid bone).This is so we remember our divine origin and the fact that our Incorruptible Body was built for immortality. The fact that "remembering our own divine origin" means to "know" that God exists and that we are part of Him, we belong to Him, we are called to come back to Him and so we need to make His Will. To refuse this is the sin of impiety. Even in this case, we are not in front of a new Law, but instead we are in front of an event, and this is "contemplated". As we have already seen, some words used by the Evangelist need a deeper study, and this is one of those cases.
The word *theaomai* comes from the Greek *thea*, which means Goddess. We are now in front of a feminine aspect of Mary: the veneration (action of Venus), the devotion and contemplation that we have in front of the Sun, of the Christ-Sun. This action comes from the Purification process of the soul, so it is connected to the forces of Mariam-the Virgin Mary. The suffix *omai* indicates that the term *thea* turns into a verb, so it can be translated "to make Godlike". So, John says that when the human soul elevates itself with veneration and devotion it "acquires a God-like aspect" and thus it contemplates God's Glory: to be specific, Glory "as" the Only-Begotten. In the spiritual contemplation, the man develops clairvoyance and clairaudience. This brings us back to John (the search for the Christ, the initiated) and Mariam (the purified soul, the one that "is God-like") to the cross and the entrusting from one to the other on behalf of Jesus. Mariam and John unite and the Incorruptible Body can be born again within each man thanks to the multiplication of the Incorruptible Body in the Resurrected. They represent the new Christian Community.
In the Old Testament, the expression "Glory of God" means the direct irradiation of the Divinity within the human soul, which would extend itself to the etheric body, and it would enlighten it. To this meaning, in the New Testament, there is a new meaning added: vivification (connected to the Son). The First Son donates Life to what is created by the First Father and it is manifested from the First Spirit.

[52] The term "Glory" has uncertain origins. In Greek *kleos* means "of good name"; but in the Sanskrit origin *klu* means to hear, echo. There is also the origin *slovo,* which in the ancient Slavic language, means "the owners of the word". In the Old Testament, the word "glory" means Light, Fire and the Word of the Lord who enlightens (men, people, tents, etc) (Isaiah 60,1): "*Arise, Shine, for your light has come, and the glory of the Lord rises from you!*" And in Ezekiel (1, 28) we find: "*Like the appearance of a rainbow in the clouds on a rainy day, so was the radiance around him. This was the appearance of the likeness of the glory of the Lord. When I saw it, I fell facedown, and I heard the voice of one speaking.*" So we found both aspects: of light and of word, so of logos, of Christ-Son. The Glory can then mean the fullness of spiritual contemplation (clairvoyance and clairaudience). To get to this point, it is necessary to reach the highest quality of love: the one that only death and resurrection can give.

[53] in fullness[54] of grace[55] and truth

---

[53] We have the whole Trinity: the Holy Spirit with the "name" of the verse 1,12 and now also the Only-Begotten and the Father. To this, the "plenitude" will follow: the +1.
The Father of the Holiest Trinity "generated" his Son, the Christ, who "created" the cosmos in His image and likeness, and in which our evolutionary system is included, and also the Zodiac circle which is called by the Jewish people "Adonai", or "God the Lord". He "formed" Adam in His image, but not in his likeness. By saying this, it means that the interior quality of Adam is not the one of Adonai (Adam means "from the earth"). Adam would have to conquer Love and Freedom through a process of internal transformation. From this "formed/shaped" Adam, men were "originated". With the Fall from the Terrestrial Paradise, "another" Adam was given, we who are the image of the image of God, like in a game of misleading mirrors (and luciferic). In this case, he appears "as" the Only Begotten, that he manifests himself in the aspect of the Son who has not fallen. John takes an extremely important spiritual step here: he goes from the concept of a unitary God (the one the Jewish people had) to a God of Trinity that is found in Christianity. As we already saw in verse 1,12, we have understands " His name" (The Holy Spirit), and now the aspect of "Son of the Father". After this (verse 1,16) we have Plenitude: the +1.

[54] The word plenitude comes from "pleroma", which indicates the action of multiple spiritual Entities that collaborate for a specific project. While the action of the single spiritual Entities is indicated with masculine nouns, "pleromas" are feminine nouns. In our spiritual culture of these "pleromas", the only noun left is Mary, which has to be seen as a "container" for several different "pleroma". In this case, we find ourselves in front of Celestial Sophia, cosmic wisdom, the Holy Mary Mother of the God of the Holy Mary. It's important to see how He appears "in" plenitude; that is His plenitude derives from the one of the Father. In verse 16, we will talk about "his" plenitude.

[55] Grace from Greek *charis* as Charity, Gift, and so " free and operating Love". The operating Love is the love that is completely donated as grace to the ones who receive it. This corresponds to divine Love, while *agapao* corresponds to spiritual Love which differs from *fileo* (family love or marital love) and *eros* (sensual love). It's important to point out how in the Old Testament, grace was always connected to "God's eyes" (for example *Noah found grace in the eyes of God* (Gen. 6,8)). In the New Testament, grace takes on the aspect of Gift brought to us by God, Gift that we can access first with faith and then believing.
In the Epistles to the Ephesians (2,8), we find: *"for it is by grace that you are saved through faith; and this is not of yourselves, but it is the gift from God"*. And in Titus (3,7): *"so that being justified by his grace we might become heirs according to the hope of eternal life"*. This is how the "new" grace becomes the gift to receive eternal Life, in the House of the Father through the entrance of the Kingdom.

[56].[57]

15 John testifies[58] around *(peri)* him[59] and he declares by saying: "He was (all along) the one I spoke about: the one who came after me has become (living) before[60] me, because he was before[61] me".

---

[56] Literally "to unveil" *(a-letheias)*, or also "loyalty". We need to remember that "truth" also translates as "amen", which is the word Jesus uses when he wants to express a truth. When the word "amen" is singular, then it means that the truth that he is speaking is valid only for the person to whom it's attributed. When it's repeated twice, it means that it is a universal truth. We also need to remember that the "truth will set us free". Grace-*charis* and Truth-*aletheis* are the attributes of God and our soul. Contemplating them, they turn "god-like", and from *antropos* we become *aner* (Sons of the Man and then Sons of God).
The word "*amen*" is the Latin form of the sacred syllable "*aum*" and it indicates the action of the therapeutic forces, the *mercur* of the world: the first Child. Precisely, the three letters of the syllable indicate the first Father (Brahma), the Son (Vishnu) and the Holy Spirit (Shiva). The word *amen* also comes from Hebrew "*aman*", which means "to be sure" (to be sure of the truth) from which the ending of prayers come "so be it".
The word *alatheia* means "without forgetfulness", in which *letheia* comes from *lete*, which is the river of the afterlife, the crossing of which would imply (for the conscience of the Greeks) the loss of the memory of our own spiritual essence: the I. Christ brings us the fullness of the forces of the memory of the divine plan relating to our spiritual evolution: Christ brings us the Initiation through the I. This is a Truth. The word *aletheia* can also be interpreted as *al-etheia*, where *al* means God and *etheia* means dear, loyal, and intimate. So, "completely united within God".
We can enclose the meaning of this word with: *when the purified and "God-like" soul unites completely to God, our eternal spiritual principle (the I am) ascends to the House of the Father: and this is a Truth to believe in, and this is brought to us by the operating love (Grace) of Christ.*

[57] The explaining of these two words (Grace and Truth) might seem extreme, but these are the two words that John uses to portray the whole Being of the Christ. And if the man does not "change-mind", these two words can easily degenerate in their most material aspect: precisely Grace in "pretty", or "graceful" and so "beautiful", and pure beauty is an attribute of Lucifer, the most beautiful one amongst all angels; and Truth in "loyalty" (and some biblical people translated it as such, like J. Mateos and J. Barreto). The bearer of Grace and Truth would turn into a "loyal pretty"!

[58] Let's remember that "witness" means literally "the one who is in the three", in Trinity. So John vouches for his understanding of the Trinitarian aspect of God and of "being" a witness.
This John is NOT John the Baptist or the Evangelist, but the Being of John, the "John-like essence" in which we all ascend step by step and that, with the growth of consciousness, it keeps raising.

[59] Around plenitude, at +1.

[60] In Time and in Space-Light, because he is "before" John, it's of a higher degree: it's the Guide outside of Time.

[61] This "before(first)" is *protos* in the sense of "prototype". With Jesus (Christ) the new human prototype rises, the New Adam, the Risen One who donates to us His body of Resurrection to let us ascend as Sons (adoptive) of the Father. From the fallen Incorruptible Body, to the new one who is made Glorious.

16 and from his plenitude[62] we all received grace[63] for grace[64].

[62] Plenitude as "Pleroma", which is a union of multiple spiritual entities. When multiple spiritual entities work together to fulfill a project, they determine the forming of a Pleroma and they acquire a feminine noun (see the feminine divinities of Greece). From this we understand that Mary is the Pleroma of all Pleromas. This brings us back to the "contemplation of Mary" of verse 14.

[63] For the word "Grace" see the comment of verse 1,14. Here it is said that to grace a new grace corresponds, and so when we give love we receive it back in a higher extent. This is because Love "operates".

[64] We are then translating the constant exchange between love and love, between proven love (from Jesus with the gift of His life) to the one that is communicated (the gift of the Holy Spirit from God), these are represented with the blood and the water which will flow from Jesus' rib cage. This will be repeated in John 13, 32.

17 Since the law was given through[65] Moses, grace and truth (living) became (*ghighnomai*)[66] through [67] Jesus Christ[68].

---

[65] The first time God wrote directly with his "finger" the tablets of Law. Then, after Moses broke them, they were given "through" Moses, that is through his mental, psychic, soul-like and social forces. So, they are the "true" Law.

[66]The Law becomes Life. We can make a correlation between verse 1,3 and this one. In both cases it is a matter of a creative activity that is now completed.
We also find a polarity between the Law that "was given" and then it's "finished", and grace and truth "become alive" and so they continue to be.

The fact that the law goes "through" Jesus Christ means that it was purified from the human-terrestrial aspects inserted by Moses and then it was transformed.
Through Jesus the new exodus takes place: not in the old Law, in the old Alliance, but in the perfecting of Love. Jesus can then bring the man that believes in His Name to the Father, to Eternal Life and so he accomplishes the last Exodus: from flesh, through the blood, to the Light which is Eternal Life. The "Exodus" are: 1. From Atlantis (from the Manu) to India (and here we have the 7 Rishi Saints); 2. From India to Persia (and so we have Zoroaster); 3. From Persia to Egypt (and so we have Moses); 4. From Egypt to Palestine (and here we have the Priests); 5. From the Law to Love (and here we have Jesus, from the heart of stone to the one of "flesh"); 6. The resurrection (the blood) of Jesus Christ, the New Alliance; 7. From flesh to Light, (Incorruptible Body) to the Father (Etheric Christ).

[67] It's important to notice that the expression "Jesus Christ" recurs only twice: in the Prologue (1,17) and in the Priestly Prayer (17,3). The term "Jesus" here means the human being who hosted the logos and the incarnation of the Chris; and the term "Christ" here means the divine entity. "Jesus Christ" here means the one sent from God in his completeness and perfection of the human and divine nature. Bearer of Life, Grace and Truth through which He will completely regenerate us in the body, soul and spirit as he donates his Body of resurrection

[68] The fact that the law goes "through" Jesus Christ means that it was purified from the human-terrestrial aspects inserted by Moses, and then it was transformed.

18 No one (since always) has seen God; Only Begotten God[69], who is in the breast[70] of the

[69] This passage ends the Prologue and so, metaphorically, the man's path in which the Divine Mission is completed, ends as well. Its importance and magnificence can be understood only when we experience it, because no human word is appropriate to describe it.
Some codes report "the Only-Begotten Son". The first "God" means the Infinite One, or better, the purest Love that hugs everything and from which everything descends. The "second" Jesus (metaphorically the man) refers to the man in whose heart the Christ was born and then the Father. With these events the man is ready to receive the "plus One" of the Sons, the "son" of the Infinite One, which is the Purest Love from which everything descends. This happens after trials that recall the ridicule, the mocking Jesus Christ had to go through, in addition to the misunderstandings and the abandonment from the Apostles and the Disciples.
The Only Begotten means to ascend to the Infinite One, to be embraced in his hug, where He generates with us the Only Begotten.
The Infinite One is the Only Begotten of the Only Begotten ones. He gave this gift to His Son, the Christ, and now he wants to give it to us as well. What will determine this birth-Title is the **complete acceptance of his plan**, of what he has foreseen for us. This entails bigger trials, because the one that will ascend to his Title will not have exterior peace, but he will instead have the Peace of all Peace, the interior Peace that comes from Him.
He will never leave us alone in these trials of life now that our heart beats with His in the Love that unites us all.
With the birth of the Only Begotten, we become DELEGATES. Christ was sent from the Father, so he was plenipotentiary in order that the plan of the Father would come to life. He so acted as a "descending bridge" from the Father and also as a "bridge" for our ascension to Him. So now we also are Delegates, that is other people through which we can ascend to the Father so that the plan of the plans can be fulfilled, the plan in which all humanity goes back to the One in the Purest Love.

[70] In the breast, which means in the heart's forces. In the same breast from which Mariam conceived Jesus (as a Body of Heat): the breast from which Children can be conceived within us.

father[71], the one who brought us to understand him[72].[73]

[71] In the old scripture, it was written in lowercase. It probably refers to the first Father within us. It's important to see how in verse 13, 23 it will be John (so the man) to lay his head on the breast of Jesus Christ.

[72] This means that only the Christ gave us " explanations", the clues with words and with miracles to get to the Father, and then from the Father we ascend to the Infinite One.
This clarification might seem secondary but it is of extreme importance since it summarizes the whole work of Jesus Christ on Earth. Before Moses received for the second time the Decalogue of the Law, he addressed some of his requests to God and he fulfilled all of them. But when he asked to see God's Glory (Es 33,18 and ss.), God told him he would let His Glory pass in front of him, but he would put him in a crevice on the ground so that he could see God's back but not His Face. This was because no one could see His Face and stay alive. So the Lord, full of Grace and Truth, passed above him. From this we understand that "to see the Face" is "to see the Glory". Like the Light identifies with Life, Glory identifies with Grace and Truth. Now the man who hosts the Christ and the Father in his heart, can look at the Face of God, which is the fullness of the operating love, without dying. This is because Jesus has won over death for all of us. Rudolf Steiner translates this expression with: "*he became Guide within looking".*
This is the gift from Christ to humanity: to guide us to the vision of the Glory-Face of God and to remain alive (and so win death). In other words, the entering of God's Kingdom, then the entering of the House of the Father, to then become Only-Begotten.

[73] With the ending of the commentary of the Prologue, we can now grasp its entirety.
John is talking to the Jewish people and so his goal is to help them go from a consciousness of the God-Jahve which Genesis talks about, to the consciousness of the God-Christ. We can see how in the first verses (1,1-5) there is a summary of the first five days of creation. On the sixth day, God created man and on the sixth verse, John appears, as a "new" man sent from God. The "new" sixth day goes up to verse 1,13, to when the new man finds the path to become Son of God.
Verse 1,14 is the verse of the Verb that becomes flesh and so we are on the seventh day. In Genesis, on the seventh day, God "rested" within man, and now the seventh day becomes the door for the Christ to descend; and for man, it is the door of reunification with God (to become his Sons) by entering the Kingdom.

JOHN'S TESTIMONIES (Is 40,3; Mc 1,3; Mt 3,3; Lc 3,4)

19. And this is the testimony[74] of the John[75], when the Jewish leaders sent[76] to him from Jerusalem's[77] priests and Levites[78], to question him: "Who are you?[79]"

20. He agreed in the logos and he did not deny and he agreed[80]in the logos[81]: "That I am not the Christ".

---

[74] As we can deduce from the text, this is the testimony "of the" John, and to this it will follow, in verse 1,34, the one of John (without the article).

[75] Read the note on the verse 18 where John testifies in his higher dimension.

[76] The I of Jesus progressively opens up to the action of the Christ within Him, which is permeating him from the I in the Man-Spirit to the lower body: the I in the Physical Body.
So we have:
The **first** passage corresponds to the Prologue: the descending of the principle Christ in the Human Spirit of Jesus;
The **second** passage corresponds to verse 1,19: the descending of the principle Christ in the Loving Vital Spirit of Jesus, which is an event that the Baptist perceives;
The **third** passage corresponds to verse 1,29: the descending of the principle Christ within the Spiritual self of Jesus, which is an event that the Baptist perceives even more;
The **fourth** passage corresponds to verse 1,35: the descending of the principle Christ in the egoic principle of Jesus which is an event that the disciples perceive as well;
The **fifth** passage corresponds to verse 1,43: the descending of the principle Christ in the principle of the I in the astral body of Jesus, which is an event that also Nathanael perceives;
The **sixth** passage corresponds to verse 2,1: the descending of the principle Christ in the principle of the I in the etheric body of Jesus, which is an event that the Mother and the Teacher of the room perceive;
The **seventh** passage would correspond to the descending of the principle Christ in the principle of the I in the physical body of Jesus, which is an event that cannot yet happen.
Within the 4 Gospels, the 6 days are repeated 3 times: now (before Cana) to the Transfiguration it enters the physical body starting from the head, to the holy Week it reaches the bone-flesh, and then to the victory over death.
The sixth day corresponds to the birthing of man: it's like saying that in the Gospel, we assist the preparation, the gestation and the birth of the New Adam within ourselves..

[77] In the text it always refers to "Jerusalems", in the plural form, because it's "one" of the locations of the Sacred word.

[78] The Levites were the tribe that had the task to help the priests in the celebration of the ritual.

[79]Therefore, the knowing of which spiritual entity was present within him as a reincarnated entity.

[80] Here, the verb *homologeo* is used (in Italian "*omologare*") which means "to speak in harmony with the logos". So John was speaking inspired directly by the logos.

[81] "to agree in the Verb" is repeated twice. This happens to indicate that what he is about to say is a cosmic truth and this truth corresponds to the Being and the will of the Verb. John stands in the logos; he agrees the type of response with the Verb.

21. And they questioned him: "Therefore who? Elijah is it you?[82]" And he says (*lego*): "I am not[83]". "Are you the prophet?[84]" and he answered: "No".

22. And so they told him (*eipon*): " Who are you? In order that we give answer to the ones who sent us. What do you say (*lego*) around yourself?[85]"

23.He said: " I (am) voice[86] of who screams in the desert[87]: *Straighten up (within yourselves) the path of the Lord[88],* like the prophet Elijah said (*eipon*)".

24. And the ones who were sent were from the Pharisees[89],

---

[82] Since Elijah was dead for almost 500 years, we can deduce that the priests knew about the process of reincarnation. Elijah represents the spirit of the Jewish people, the undifferentiated spirit (not yet "Holy").

[83] The response is extremely interesting since the Baptist was the reincarnation of Elijah (Sun). Let's remember that Jesus says: *"All the prophets and the law that they prophesied up to John, and if you want to receive, he himself is Elijah who is the one established to come. Who has ears to understand, let them hear"* (Mt 11,13-15). But now, it was not at the spiritual level of Elijah-Sun anymore, since it ascended to the one of John (Saturn).

[84] The Levites descend to another level in their question: from Christ, to Elijah the Prophet (Sun).

[85] "around yourself", which means they are asking about the entities that are around him.

[86] He speaks inspired by the logos. With him, the era of the Law brought by the prophets ends, and the era of the Word-Logos begins, which speaks within every man that opens up to it.

[87] The desert that is being spoken about is referring to both the intuitive consciousness, and the area of the spiritual seeds which is found in between the Zodiac and the Milky Way: the area of the Spiritual Seeds of the Man for the birth of the new Man

[88] This is the path of the internal path. The path that was usurped and distorted by Lucifer-Kundalini within the man. From the fig to the vine and then to the olive tree. With Jesus Christ, instead of the fig, the vine will raise (to ascend to the heart) and then to the olive tree to get to the Garden of the Olive trees, the top of the head. These three trees will find their synthesis, their "+1", on the Cross: the fourth tree of the initiatory path.

[89] The Pharisees want to verify if the teaching of John complied with their interpretation of the Law. They were part of a religious and political movement of big influence, which was extremely connected with the Hebrew traditions and customs. They believed in the resurrection of the dead and of angels; but they hid their vices and their pride under the appearance of a religion that was hypocritical and formalist. The Pharisees were the "separated ones" because they would follow the Mosaic Law meticulously and they would identify themselves as the best amongst the Jewish people. They had an initiation that would take place in the warmth ether, which corresponds to the upper part of the brainstem. Jesus always invites us to a higher level of comprehension of the facts above ground. The first level of comprehension belongs to the Apostles; the second one to the Chief Priests (or the Pharisees and Sadducees); the third level to the Romans. To these three levels there is an additional one, the "+1", which is given to the Devout Women. They are disciples (and so they correspond to the apostles), they are priestly (since they are connected to the lineage of Abel and so of the priests), they are Romans (since Pilate's wife was amongst them). For these reasons, they will be the ones to grasp the range of the action of the Christ in Jesus and they will be the first ones to greet him after the crucifixion.

25. they questioned him, and they told him (*eipon*): "then why are you baptizing[90], if you are not the Christ, nor Elijah, nor the prophet[91]?"

26. John answered them saying (*lego*): "I baptize in water[92]: but amongst you there was[93] someone you do not know,

27. (he is) the one that comes after me (who was before[94] me): the straps of whose sandals I am not worthy to untie[95]".

---

[90] The Baptism of John was a baptism of water and the disciple would be held under water for a sufficient time so that he would not spiritually experience all of his gone life, since it would reconnect to the spiritual reality. When the disciple would come out of the water, he would know of the reality of this dimension and so he would "know" that within him existed a part (the I am), that can live without the support of the physical body. This would transform the dominant mentality of identification with the material physical body. Within him, he would feel as "one" with the spiritual body and he would perceive that the first I Am was descending from the spiritual world upon Earth; and thanks to His forces of spiritual love, all the various egotistical "I's" would be overcome and he would be brought to union (in the dimension of love).

[91] They understand that the baptism of John was a new purification of the man and they believe that it could only come from God.

[92] John still does not satisfy the Pharisees' curiosity, but he makes it clear that his baptism acts out on the soul-like level.

[93] The transition from past to present is interesting: variation of the concept *egheneto*: to be born, to be, to become.

[94] This also corresponds to the "First" of me (see verse 1,1).

[95] Sandals were the symbol of a man that was ready for marriage: in this case, the Groom-Christ that marries the Chosen People-Sophia Mariam. Additionally, with marriage, a new bond would be achieved and only Christ can dissolve terrestrial bonds.
In the Hebrew tradition, when a wife would become a widow, it was the job of someone that was related by blood to the deceased to help her procreate (and the son would take on the name of the deceased). If this man would refuse, then it would be another one's turn to do so who was still blood related but not as close. Before doing so, he would grab the sandal of the one that dropped out, and he would spit on it in front of the crowd. And in this way he would acquire the right to get the widow pregnant.
John is saying that he is not the one that has to make the sterile human soul fertile (the widow, the soul of the Chosen People), because that is Christ's job.

28. these things became in Bethany on the other side of the Jordan[96], where John was baptizing.

---

[96] It is specified that it is not Bethany close to Jerusalem. Bethany means "Healing Home", therefore the place where the spiritually ill would heal. They were the ones that got sick along the Way: they lost strength. This Bethany is therefore along the way to the Path of the Baptist; the other one will be along the Path of the Christ. The Jordan represents the strength of the I that flows within the man through his spinal cord. The Jordan connect the lower waters (amniotic fluid- womb) with the higher ones (Dead Sea-head). Within the man, the lower waters stopped reflecting the higher ones and so they are flowing towards death. And so the divine seed awakens within us, the wound of the fall (feet) closes up and the stream reverses (the emerods) and we begin the cosmic Life. Jesus will also immerse himself (in the sphere of what is still incomplete) to then immediately re-ascend. He travels through Adam's path again; he descends in the aspect of shadow-feminine-darkness that he needs to marry to become complete. It is important to know that Jesus will immerse himself up to his calves. This is to indicate that only the feet- which are the organ of "listening" for Mother Earth- were yet to be purified. This action will find a resonance with the Washing of the Feet with which Jesus will purify the apostles at the Last Supper. The expression "on this side of the Jordan" represents the man whole with his consciousness and so, for esoteric movement, the Chosen People. From these we can deduce that the expression "on the other side of the Jordan" represents the human condition of the one that finds himself outside of the Chosen People, close to the Dead Sea, the maximum depression of the Earth, an expression of the Ahrimanic forces (also of Gomorrah and Sodom). So Jesus is baptized in the place that represents the abyss in which men fell. In the other Bethany, "on this side of the Jordan" (and close to Jerusalem), the resurrection of Lazarus will take place, and so his Baptism of Fire with the spiritual awakening to which the entering of the Kingdom will follow (Loving Vital Spirit).

29. The day after[97] (John[98]) sees the Jesus coming close to him[99] and he says (*lego*): "Here is the Lamb[100] of the God[101], the one who takes away[102] the errors of the world[103](natural).

30. He is the one I meant when I said (*eipon*): "After me comes an enlightened[104] man that became before me: because he was my principle[105].

31. And I did not know[106] him, but, in order that he was manifested to Israel[107], that is why I came to baptize the water[108]".

---

97 For "the day after" read the notes on verse John 1,19.

98 The article is not present, and so John-man has completely permeated in the higher impulse that he received.

99 John corresponds to Aquarius, he looks towards Pisces-Christ and he sees the Lamb-Aries.

100 According to the ancient forces, the initiated would still see through the forces of the soul and so they would understand the gods with animal shapes.
Let's remember that the blood of the calf would be offered by the high priest on the day of the great fast (or day of the penance) within the holy place of the temple to asperse, and so purify, the one who has to be propitiated. In this specific case, the blood of the calf would purify the subject from his personal sins and also his family sins. After this followed the blood of the ram (the male sheep) to purify the mistakes of the people (community tied through blood and territory). As a third offering, they would offer the blood of the buck (male goat from which comes "scape-goat) for the sins of the nation (ethnic group with cultural homogeneity). In the end, one last male goat, on which they would place (destined) the sins of Israel, would be sent in the desert, which is oblivion (this it the "+1").

101 Of the Holiest Trinity

102 In some texts they would say, "he would take on himself" (and so he does not take away). He takes it upon himself because he is offering himself to support the man in his process of resurgence, of ascending, of going back up.

103 The luciferic error resulting from the Fall (it is not a "sin"). We can also interpret this expression with the action that the Christ prepares himself to execute: to descend from the sphere of the Father- the elements- and unite with the sphere of the ethers in which the luciferic entities were found and they would bring chaos to humanity.

104 This is Jesus. This definition is probably referring to a Man who ascended various spiritual levels.

105 From the Greek *protos*. Or "to the higher me". Let's pay attention to the progression: the enlightened man is Jesus, within him the Christ is present (generated from the Father) and he is compliant to the First, to the logos whom John also complies too (see John 1, 20).

106 In this tri-spiritual dimension. John was Jesus' cousin but he didn't capture the aspect "Messiah". When he will see the Spirit descend on him as a Dove, then he will recognize him.

107 To the Chosen People. The Christ has come for the Chosen People that will then testify of him amongst other men.

108 To prepare them.

32. And John[109] testified by saying (*lego)* that I saw (*theaomai*) the descending spirit[110] as a dove[111] from the sky[112] and it stayed above him[113].

[109] It's the Man-John that testifies.

[110] The Spirit in his purity: John testifies the Trinity of God. For us this Spirit is "Holy", as a part of the Spirit of God descends in us and it makes us Holy, which means separated from everything that is not perfect. John testifies that "the Spirit" has descended and it "stayed": and so it is not "Holy".

[111] The Spirit can descend as Dove only on a man who is completely pure and there "he can make a nest". If the man is not as such, the spirit descend as tongues of fire to purify what is still impure.

[112] He refers to the Holy Trinity. Only he has this vision because of the purity of his soul. John is the first man that completely respected the 10 Commandments.

[113] During the Baptism, the Spirit would descend on the one being baptized and then it would go back to the sky. With this event, the Christ unites for the first time the sphere of the Father (or of the "original" Gods working through the elements) with the sphere of Lucifer (or the "conceived" God working through the ethers).
With this Baptism, the I of Jesus distances itself to leave room for the first I of the Christ that will act transforming the three lower bodies of Jesus and individualizing the Incorruptible Body, up to the physical (I am the Good Shepherd, and the awakening of Lazarus).
In that moment, the voice of the First Father says again: *"You are my Son, the spiritually loved, within you I am well received."* With this, the complete union between man and God is established as well as Jesus becoming Son of God even though he will keep announcing himself as Son of the man to indicate that what he does, he does as a man and every man can take the same path. As said, the first time the Father spoke at the Baptism on the Jordan (*this is my son the spiritually loved*); the second time at the Transfiguration (*Listen to him!*); the third time at the announcement of "His time" (John 12, 28). In the end, there will be a fourth "conversation" between Jesus and the father: at the Cross when Jesus will "speak" to the Father (*Eli, Eli, lamma sabactani*).
In the light of this, it is understood that the first Christians would celebrate Christmas on January 6th, the day of the Baptism at the Jordan.

34. And I did not know[114] him, but who sent[115] me to baptize in water, told me (*eipon*): "The one on whom you will see (*edein*) the spirit descend and remain[116] above him, he is the one that baptizes in the Holy Spirit[117].

34. And I saw (*horao*) and I testified[118] that this is the Son[119] of the God[120]".

---

[114] In verse 31 he did not know Jesus-Messiah; now he states that he didn't know in Jesus-Messiah the First Christ that entered him.

[115] Now John is "sent". He probably was a "mandate" and not a "delegate". Jesus is a delegate.

[116] From that moment on, the First Christ remained united with Jesus in a permanent way.

[117] Now the Spirit is called "Holy" and this is the first time it happens. In the Bible, only the Spirit is talked about. With Holy Spirit we interpret the tri-articulated action of the Spirit. The tri-articulation that is formed by the Holy Spirit, Lucifer (who will be redeemed) and Mariam. He will donate to us a baptism that will make us Saints, which means separated from the world.
And so we have three baptisms:

- Of water, to purify the soul part tied to the past; it's a baptism to "reorganize" which allows us to understand that the only way to salvation is the reunion with the Divine;
- Of fire, operated by Jesus and that purifies the soul from all of its passions, instilling a sacred fire towards the Spirit and allowing us to experience the Grace;
- Of Spirit, it comes from Jesus Christ and it allows us to capture the reality of our higher dimension (the Holy Spirit within us) and reestablish the conscious communication with the creator.

[118] It's always the Man-John that testifies that Jesus Christ is the direct manifestation of the living God.

[119] From the Greek *hyos*, which means son of "law" (*son de jure*) or spiritual son.

[120] Therefore, the Christ, the First Son of the Holiest Trinity. Let's remember that in the moment of the baptism of Salomon Maria (Maria Salomonica) "descended" the Nathan Maria (Maria Natanica), who was stopped on the sphere of the Sun and the Salomon Maria physically went back to being a virgin.

THE CALLING OF THE DISCIPLES (Is 53,7)

35. The next day[121] the John was once again[122] straight, with two of his disciples[123].

36. And looking (*blepo*)[124] in the Jesus that was passing by[125], he said: "Here is the Lamb of God[126]".

37. And the two disciples heard him speak and followed the Jesus.

38. And so the Jesus turned around[127] and, observing (*theaomai*)[128] that they were following him, he said (*lego*) to them: " What are you looking for?" and they told (*eipon*) him: "Rhabbi (that is said (*lego*) to be interpreted as Teacher[129]) where do you stay[130]?"

---

[121] For the "next day" see the note on the verse John 1,19.

[122] And so in the fullness of the I, of the Spirit.

[123] John puts himself in the three; here is the correspondence between the birth of the three in the second day and John who puts himself in it.
With his testimony, John the Baptist convinces two of his disciples to follow Jesus: we are talking about Andrew and another anonymous disciple. After Andrew, three more come that are originally from Galilea: Peter, brother of Andrew and Philip, who were from Bethsaida, and Nathanel, who was from Cana (21,2). This would prove that the first five of Jesus' disciples were from the same area as the disciple John the Baptist.

[124] From the Greek *blepo* which means to spiritually look. He "sees" on three levels: terrestrial, solar, stellar. Just how he said in verse 1,18, he "saw".

[125] We are at the "ring around", which means John sees Jesus with the unsettledness overhead.

[126] John captures the bright Zodiac aspect when he says "Lamb", as "of the" God captures the aspect of the Holiest Trinity.

[127] In which direction? Probably in "vertical": from the stars to the sun.

[128] He "sees" with the Incorruptible Body the divine part within them that was following him.

[129] The clarification helps us understand that in reality, Rhabbi does not mean Teacher. Rabbi means the *nirmanakaya* of Buddha present in Jesus: his aspect of preacher and prayer.

[130] Just as the Spirit remains on Him, he also remains in the "higher levels" and from there he can operate. The disciples therefore ask him where his Home is.

39. He said (*lego*) to them: "Come and see (*opsomai*)[131]". They came and they saw (*eipon*) where he stayed and they stayed near him for the day, that[132]: it was almost the tenth[133] hour.

40. Andrew[134], the brother[135] of Simon Peter[136], was therefore One[137] of the two who listened to John and followed him.

41. The first brother find him, the[138] ones, Simon and he says: " we have found the Messiah (who is interpreted as Christ[139]).

---

131 As always, He never answers directly. He instead puts himself on the level of the interlocutor and so he lets him evaluate His spiritual level.

132 The second day: they entered the three.

133 Since it's without an article, it indicates the time frame from 24 to 02, which correspond to Capricorn. The substance associated with Capricorn is clay, the *mercur*, the one that overcomes the duality and determines the forming of the three.

134 Andrew means "courage" and this is the virtue of the *aner*. As a disciple, Andrew represents the prayer.

135 Andrew has the article: he is Enlightened.

136 Without article, Peter is not Enlightened. In Italian *Pietro* (Peter) sounds like *pietra* (which means stone). So, the assonance with "*pietra*" brings us to the Hebrew way of saying "*pietra*" which is *even*. This word is formed by *av*, the Father, and by *ben* the Son. And so it's the symbol of the man in whom the awakening of the consciousness happened. The awakened man become Son of the Father.
Peter always proves himself to be a pioneer amongst the Twelve and Jesus will gift him the keys to the Kingdom (Mt 16,19). These keys, in the microcosmic way, are the collarbones, or better the "little keys" that shut the gateway to the entryway to the door on the east of the terrestrial Heaven. The Cherub with the flaming and rotating sword guards this door. In Hebrew, Peter is said *Petros'*, which means "the one who opens": and now he "opens the way for the others".

137 Number, and so Andrew represent the "Number one" of courage, the champion.

138 Two more articles for Andrew.

139 Messiah means delegate; Christ means anointed, or better "the one upon which the Spirit descends". They are not the same thing.

42. And he guided him to Jesus. And so the Jesus seeing (*blepo*) in him, said (*eipon*): " You are Simon[140], son of Giona[141]: you will be called Cefa (who is interpreted as Pietro[142]).

43. The next day[143] he wanted to go out towards the Galilea[144] and he found Philip. And the Jesus told (*lego*) him: "Follow me![145]"

44. It was Philip from Bethsaida[146], of the city of Andrew and Peter.

---

[140] He is not Enlightened.

[141] Now he has the article. Giona represents the initiation process and Simon worked within himself to reach that point (he is a "son"), but he still did not complete the process: he is still immature.
Giona spent the three days of Initiation inside the whale. This is the experience of three days of darkness, after which man receives the internal Sign. The era of teachers, prophets or sibyls is done; today the Spirit begins to answer to us and to speak to us starting from our inner being. The "sign" is the fact that Giona is "thrown up" by the fish, and he reaches the seashore (the imaginative consciousness). To vomit is a gesture which from the metabolism, from the yearning, we ascend to the head, to the consciousness, and so it corresponds to the purification of Kundalini, of the ancient luciferic initiation. This ahrimanic and luciferic generation will be "given" to be in the storm, to enter the fish, etc. and so it will be given the trials to allow it to purify. The whale represents the animal-like forces that possess the first feminine forces (the Black Mother) that are present in our depths, the parts that need to be redeemed to then unite with them in the initiation marriage. This will be possible with Golgotha, the "sign" given by Jesus to all humanity, which opened the way for all of us to go back to the Home of the Father.

[142] Cefa means head: now Jesus gives him the new name; now he is Enlightened. The term Cefa (which is Peter) indicates the tenacity of the world of ideas, and their eternity. In our case, it indicates that Simon "changed-mind", the way of thinking, he entered the living thought and so he became a Peter and he enters the Chosen People. R. Steiner indicates how Jesus, in Peter's name, wanted to underline also the "man of stone", meaning a different dimension in the elementary world, like *Boanerges*. *Boanerges* means Sons of Thunder, which is a nickname that he will give to James and John indicating this elementary world under the forces that govern the physical terrestrial world act upon.

[143] For the next day see the note on verse John 1,19.

[144] Galilea is lush and so it represents the world of plants: the third day.

[145] For Philip this statement is enough. Philip represents the decision.

[146] Bethsaida in Aramaic literally means "home of fish". It is the city that represents the forces of the Virgin: the first three disciples come from the current of Mary.

45. He found Philip the Nathanael[147], and he told (*lego*) him: "We found the one that Moses talked about in the law, and the prophets[148]: Jesus, son of Giuseppe[149], the one from Nazareth[150]".

46. and Nathanael said (*eipon*) to him: "Can there be[151] something good from Nazareth?" And Philip told (*lego*) him: "Come and see (*idein*)".

47. Jesus saw (*eidon*) Nathanael[152] coming towards him, and he said (*lego*) around him: "See (*idein*) a true Israelite[153], in whom there is no deceit[154]".

48. Nathanael told (*lego*) him: "From what do you know me?" Jesus answered and said (*eipon*): "Before the Philip called you, when you were under the fig[155], I saw (*eidon*) you".

49. Nathanael replied: "Rhabbi, you are the Son of the God[156], you are King of the Israel[157]".

---

[147] Natan-el, which is the divine Nathan, the enlightened representative of the priestly path (the Nathanic current).

[148] Nathanael knew the Bible really well and so Philip turns to him with the knowledge that he has.

[149] It's interesting that the article is on Giuseppe and not Jesus: Nathanael presents the line of descent as a "guarantee" for Jesus. Giuseppe was a well know initiate in the Temple.

[150] City founded by Nazarathos- Zarathustra. This city becomes Jesus' cultural cradle.

[151] Nazareth is in Galilea and for the Jewish people, Galilea was heretical (Galilea means "land of the hybrids", which brings us back to the lineage of Giuseppe-David). Additionally, he knew that the Messiah was supposed to come from Bethlehem, from David's lineage.

[152] Nathanael means "gift of God" and it is thought that it's the same person as Bartholomeus.

[153] Fifth level of Persian initiation. The Name of the People, which is the freeing of the power of the spirit of the People within us. Recognizing this Nathanael, Jesus declares to have this level of initiation, and then he will act in the elements (Marriage of Cana) and then He will be in the elements (Samaritan's Water).

[154] "Deceit" is also translated as "falseness/untruth". From this, we have the comparison between Nathanael and Jacob, the founder of Israel that "stole" Esau's birthright with a trick.

[155] The fig represents the first tree of initiation. The fig brings the Son of man within us to birth, the vine will bring the first Son of God, and the olive tree will help us reach the Garden of the Olive trees, the top of the head. These three trees will find their synthesis, their "+1", in the Cross: the fourth tree of the initiated path that will eternally bear fruit.

[156] Contradictory indication: as Rabbi in the Holy Trinity, and as "of the God" in the Holiest Trinity.

[157] Of the Chosen People. It's important to underline the "quickness" with which Nathanael recognizes Jesus' level.

50. Jesus replied and he told (*eipon*) him: "Why do you think I told (*eipon*) you that I saw (*eipon*) you under the fig[158]? You will see (*opsomai*) bigger things than this".

51. And he tells (*lego*) him: "Amen, Amen[159] I say (*lego*) to you all, you will see (*opsomai*) the open sky and the angels of the God ascending and descending above the Son (*hyos*) of the man[160]".

---

[158] Lunar tree that represent the old path of initiation which develops starting from the awakening of Kundalini in the sacrum. It's the spirit's old path. The Bodhi tree where the Gautama Buddha received enlightenment was also a fig (in those times it still produced fruit). With the Jesus Christ in place of the fig, the vine will rise (to ascend to the heart), and then the olive tree to reach the Garden of the Olive trees, the top of the head. These three trees will find their synthesis, their "+1" in the Cross: the fourth tree of the initiating path that will eternally bear fruit.
It's also a symbol of the Egyptian initiation: Chaldean for her connection with the forces of the Moon that are refined through the fertilizing love of bees. The mature fig becomes the higher step of the old initiation. From the spiritual composition of the word (in Greek *syke*) we understand that, in an older setup, the "fig" represented the manifestation of the renovation of the spiritual forces of Kundalini. This corresponds to the process of Transfiguration, which is the event with which the transformation of the old initiated path begins on behalf of Jesus. Let's remember how R. Steiner indicates in the Transfiguration, the continuation, on behalf of Jesus, of the actions of the Buddha (enlightened under the "old" fig). The transformation of the fig, once renewed, becomes the olive "passing through" the vine.
It's interesting to see how the word "fig" comes from the Latin word "ficus" which means liver. And so from this, we can see the connection between this organ and the Light that it can accumulate in relation to the spiritual work that has been done. So the fig-liver can relate to the desires of the world or the ones of the spirit: Jesus will curse the first of these.
Botanically, the fig, is a *moraceae*, and so it's a plant that is deeply connected to the forces of the Moon. This is apparent in many of its characteristics (sap, bark, type of fruit, and shape of the leaves). And so we have a memory of the Jahvetic Initiation, in which Jahve is a Spirit of the Solar Form that used to act through the Moon to connect the Jewish people with the spiritual world.
Another interesting fact of the fig is given by its milky sap, which reminds us of the "lower waters", the ones that have not been purified by Light yet. Finally, the fig is not naturally sweet, but thanks to the process of caprification that is done by the wasps, it develops a sweet taste, and so sugar, which is connected to hydrogen and so to the Spirit. The process of caprification corresponds to the transition from egotistical love to selfless love; it's interesting to learn that this process was historically practiced for the first time in Jericho, which is the city that represents the darkest point, the most egotistical point of humanity (see Mc 10, 46).

[159] Jesus now expresses a universal truth (and so it's higher than the various limits of consciousness of the ones listening to him).

[160] Antropos. This brings us back to Jacob and to his "scale" that is formed by the celestial hierarchy. Jesus offers himself as a new sanctuary of God by which we can ascend to God.
It's important to see how in John, the expression Son of Man appears 12 times: 1, 51; 3,13-14; 6,27-53-62; 8,28; 9,35; 12,23-34-34; 13,31. The Son of the Man is the one who possesses the fullness of the Spirit: Of the I am.

THE WEDDING AT CANA[161]

[161] This Wedding is the archetype of all the internal Marriages, both between the left side and the right side, and between mind and breast. With the wedding, the man's spirit and mind return to being one, just like it was at the beginning when God made them "male and female" (John 1,27). To this we add that the Infinite One, which is the "plus One" of the Divine, is expressed in Groom and Bride, in Harmony and Sweetness and from their union, the Everything is conceived, the Life that permeates all of creation.
With this miracle, the transubstantiation is anticipated when Jesus Christ will say:" *this is my body (Spirit)... this is my Blood (Soul).."* and so the human nature that fell with the original sin will be healed. This miracle is to be seen as an anticipation of the transubstantiation, the transformation of the body of flesh into spiritual light. This is why he will say it is still not His time.

1. And on the third[162] day, they became[163] the wedding at Cana[164] of the Galilee[165]: and the mother of the Jesus[166] was there[167].
2. Jesus and his disciples were also called to the Wedding.

---

162 According to the way time is spoken about, "the third day" indicates "after two days". And so we should ask ourselves "after" what does the dating begin? It corresponds to verse John 1,35: the descending of the first Christ in the egoic principle of Jesus. This was an event that even the disciples were aware of, and so He will be able to act in unison with the forces of the disciples (the transformation of water into wine does not happen through the old blood forces anymore).

163 Now time is mature.

164 A town of Galilee, where Jesus did his first and second miracle. Galilea means *land of the "hybrids"*, that means the overcoming of blood ties. It was the town of Nathanael (John 21,2). It is located about 4 kilometers northeast of Nazareth.
Cana means "to acquire": in Cana, the forces for the completion that the married woman (the soul that unites to the Spirit) represents are acquired.
The word "Cana" is connected to "dog" (in Italian it's "*cane*"), which is an animal that represents the dark-luciferic forces of the Sun. It's also the name of a constellation in which there is the brightest star of the cosmos: Sirius (Lucifer) with her twin dark dwarf star (Ahriman). The "exterior" Sun gets closer to this constellation in the middle of summer (summer heat wave), which is also the time when the sun manifests its luciferic forces at its maximum.
In Hebrew, dog is *keleb*, which is a word that comes from *kol*: the totality. Its anagram is *kebel* which means the tie, the chain. And so the dog, the forces of the Obstacle, the Cerberus of Dante's hell, is the dark obstacle that needs to be overcome so that the fallen man can be freed and he can be brought back to his magnificence in his Body of Incorruptible Light.

165 Cana represents the Canaanite forces and so the luciferic ones: "of the" Galilea (pay attention to the article) represents the forces of the Father that act in the metabolism. We are in a situation of redemption of the sexual-matrimonial forces so that we can reach the forces that arise from the mystical Marriages.
The fact that the evangelist specifies that Cana of Galilea is being spoken about, signifies that only in that place Jesus was able to find the right people to fulfill his first miracle. The Christic action is not enough, the right people are also needed to allow it and to receive it. In Judea, where the Jewish blood was purer, He could not have fulfilled the miracle. Galilea was needed because the blood there is mixed (hybrids) and so the force of Lucifer was lesser and the one of the I was greater.

166 The forces of the two Marys are together. Only John remembers the presence of Mariam at the beginning and at the end of the Gospel, and he does this because he wants to indicate her continuous presence as an aid and support to the endeavor of humanity's redemption at the events in Palestine.
According to the Apocryphals, the bride and groom were Mariam's relatives and it looked like the groom was the same Nathanael that Jesus described as a "true Israeli", an initiate. Additionally, the bride-soul is described as the "daughter of a rich Israeli". We are now in front of a mystical union between two initiates, a union that finds its highest resonance in the one between Jesus and Mariam.

167 The mother represents the forces of the soul: they are already ready. Mother is the term to indicate the seventh level of feminine initiation. The act of transformation starts from the sentient soul, which is represented by Magdalen (the Black Holy Mary), and she acts in the metabolic sphere. Mariam-soul invokes the Spirit-Groom to act within her. They "are there" as delegates. With this we can see how Jesus respects our freedom, and he comes to us only when he is called by us.

3. And, running out of wine[168], the mother[169] of the Jesus told (*lego*) him: "They have no wine[170]".
4. And Jesus says (*lego*) to her: "What is there between you and I, oh woman[171]? My time has yet to come"[172].

---

[168] The forces of the Initiation connected to the Vine. The wine was used in the old mysteries (ceremonies) under the guidance of the priests in order to break old blood ties.

[169] The mother was not just part of the events: she was also an inspiration, as a cosmic Wisdom, to the actions of the Son.

[170] Without the article. It is referring to the fact that the formal observance of the Torah, the ceremonies of sanctification, the Mosaic Law in its complexity, weren't enough to guarantee an intimate relationship with God. With the arrival of Jesus Christ, the third path of Initiation starts, the one of the Olive tree (and of the oil). The wine, and so the "ferments", finished their role as the connection (etheric) with the spiritual world, just like the fig before them: Now the era of the Word is beginning: after this one (1413) there will be the one of the consciousness soul and so of the I am.
It's important to see that the Mother does not say: "they have no *more* wine"; instead she says "they have no wine". This is to indicate that it is not the time to renew the ferments, but instead it's the time to open a new path, the one of the oil, of the Spirit.

[171] In Jesus, at the Baptism at the Jordan, Christ descended on him; in Mary Salomonica, the Nathanic Mary descends on her. Therefore, both find themselves in a phase of deep transformation and they ask themselves what they need to do now that is new, different. R. Steiner translates this passage with these words: "*Oh woman, this goes from me to you*" and so he accentuates the intimate force that goes from His soul to the one of the Mother: this is the force that he will use to do the miracle. As we said, at the moment of the Baptism, Nathanic Mary (who was "stopped" in the sphere of the Sun, giving up on ascending to higher spiritual levels) "descended" on Mary Salomonica ". With this union, the Salomonica Mary physically went back to being a virgin and so now she has within herself the forces of the sprouting virginity.
This nickname corresponds to the redemption of the fallen feminine part, the redemption of Eve. The Woman represents the higher feminine aspect within us, the soul that generates the Spirit. It is the Mother's job to initiate this path of redemption, since another woman (Eve) started the one of the Falling.

[172] The first Christ permeated only one part of Jesus, and that is where the expression "my time has yet to come" comes from. This means that it was not the time of the Christ. Instead, coherently with the sign of the sixth day, the time of the Father was still active. The time that has to come will be the time of the Last Supper when Jesus sends the disciples to look and follow the man that has an urn on his shoulder. The drawing that was started in Cana, in the sign of water and the six recipients, ends in the sign of water and the seventh water jar. With this, the evangelization of the Son (started in the sign of water and of the six vases in the house of the Wedding at Cana) finds its ending and its perfection in the sign of water and in the seventh pitcher in the house of the Last Supper, where wine will be transmuted into blood. This seventh pitcher, the pitcher of the perfection in the mysteries of Time, will be represented by water of the Washing of the Feet.
It can also be seen as: He says that His time, when he will act with only His strength, has still yet to come. Right now the connection between Him and the Mother is still extremely important. The Mother is extremely conscious that He is also the new Spirit of Nature, of Earth and so he can fulfill the transformation.

5. His mother[173] says (*lego*) to the ministers[174]: "*Create (poieo) everything that he will tell you (lego)[175]*".

6. There were six water jars[176] made out of stone[177], for the purification of the Jewish people, laying on the ground[178] each one of them holding two or three "metrete"[179]. (metrete in Italian indicates about 39 liters).

To prepare humanity he will have to make some spiritual healings and before that he will have to purify the Temple by sending the merchants away (John 2,13).

[173] Mary represents the feminine part of the seventh water jar, jar of wisdom; Jesus Christ the spiritual part. We are at the seventh level of Initiation.

[174] Venus level.

[175] Jesus Christ begins his Work by "speaking"; with this we have the evolution of the process of the transubstantiation from the "ferment" phase connected to the etheric-element water body, to the "word" phase in which the divine descends.
The spirit (the Christ) can act when the soul (Mariam) asks the questions. Mariam knows that now the Christ is operating within the Jesus and so the Father is operating as well. This is the third and last time that Mariam speaks: from now on, she will follow all of the events in silence.
Once again, Mariam represents the complete Faith in the divine, this Faith will also act on the disciples by helping them to believe (John 2,11).

[176] They can represent the Davidic hexagram (Solomon's seal). It's really interesting to compare the 6 water jars with the 6 days of creation: the forces were almost consumed (there was not much water-wisdom-knowledge in the internal): it will be with the purification of the temple that the seventh water jar, the seventh day, will begin to reveal itself. Since we are still in the 6, we are still in the forces of the Father (consequently the active force was the one of Moses).

[177] The heart's petals were "still". In Hebrew, stone is *even*, which is a word composed by *av*, the Father, and by *ben*, the Son. Therefore, it's a symbol of the man in whom the awakening of the consciousness happened. The awakened man becomes Son of the Father.

[178] It's important to pay attention to the clarification that expresses the fact that the water jars are laying on the ground, and so they are not "vertical" and that indicates the lack of force of the I am.
They can also represent the six petals of the heart *chakra* of 12 petals.

[179] A *metreta* equals 38-39 liters. They are two or three to indicate the trinity of the body and the one of the soul that the Jewish people knew really well: now the third trinity is missing, the one of the Spirit, the one in the Holiest Trinity that the Christ brings to us.
The *metreta* is a unit of measurement that contains the word "metro". If we do the math, six jars of two or three measures, equals to 12-18 metrete; they contain between 480 and 720 liters; and so a big quantity! What was being offered is a huge gift that cannot be measured. It goes beyond any need, and it goes beyond anything anyone could expect. This should not be odd, because it's always been said how God does not measure His gifts with a measuring cup. Instead he gives them in overabundance (cfr. Zc 1, 17; Tb 4,21). He is now preparing himself to be the "seventh jar" for the whole humanity. When the Lord will multiply the bread for the crowd, 12 baskets will be left over (cfr. Lc 9, 17). This is to say that what he was gifting, he did not measure, and he instead gave it in abundance. This is to express God's typical abundance: the abundance of Life that God possesses, and because he has it, he is capable of donating it to men.

7. Jesus tells (*lego*) them: "Fill the jars with water[180]". And they filled them with water to the brim[181].
8. And he tells (*lego*) them: "Now draw it out and take it to the master of the banquet[182]". And they did so.

---

[180] As we said earlier, Jesus Christ begins his Work by "speaking" and so the evolution of the process of the transubstantiation from the "ferment" phase connected to the etheric-element water body, to the "word" phase in which the divine descends. After this, the phase of the "consciousness of the I am" will begin, and only John was able to grasp it. He will not speak to us about the transubstantiation made "in *memory* of Me". We need to follow the Mosaic Law, and only in this way we go from the Initiation of the Fig to the one of the Vine.
He needs water that is freshly drawn from the springs of the Earth, water that is still full of Nature's forces: He needed this quality of water to fulfill his miracle. In the vine, the Earth knows how to transform water into wine, and now the Christ, that is united with the Earth, becomes Spirit of the Earth and so he can operate and go beyond the work that the Earth can do. The presence of the Christ will keep improving the present forces within Jesus.

[181] From this, we gather that the jars are straight: in the I am.
The Law is not being abolished (with its empty regulations) but it is being completed with the Law of Love.

[182] The master of the banquet (*architriclino* in Italian) is formed by the *arche'* (the first cause, the principle), *tri* (three) and *kline* (the bed of the initiation), and so "the spiritual principle of the three initiation beds", of the three internal births. This is Michael, the guardian of the door of the Sun and of all the solar initiations. We are now assisting the transformation of Michael's forces, the one who saw the Christ getting further away from the Sun and getting closer to the Earth, and now he can recognize him as the bearer to the initiation in the I am. Michael "goes" from Face of Jahve to Face of the Christ.
In the interpretation where "wine" corresponds to a "secret", he represents the custodian of the knowledge that the rabbis had. Under this aspect, we find Michael as the bearer of the cosmic intelligence, the Protector of Mary-Sophia.
The argument of Michael as the bearer of cosmic intelligence is the cornerstone of Michael's current regency. In fact, he is the bearer, and Mariam as Celeste Sophia is the subject and at the same time the force with whom to investigate and penetrate the cosmic intelligence. The cosmic intelligence fell in the human brain and it often turned into superficial intellectualism; Michael's mission is to bring the human brain back to working in harmony with God's thoughts, and to then make them descend into the heart. Therefore, go from "the mind that lies" to its spiritualization (from which the invitation to "change mind" comes), and then to understanding the big plan of the spiritual evolution of humanity and of the cosmos, and so to understand the laws of the Father. Only then will we be able to become His partners; only then will we be able to "do His will" like the Our Father prayer says.

9. As soon as the master of the banquet tasted[183] the water that turned into wine[184], and he did not know where it came from[185], but the ministers that drew the water[186] knew; and the master of the banquet called the groom[187]

10. And he said (*lego*) to him: "Every man (*antropos*)[188] puts the best[189] wine first, and when they are drunk the worst one: but you kept the good wine up to now[190].

---

[183] The Jesus acted on the etheric body of the present men by allowing to flow within them the forces of his etheric body: with the following healing of the Son of the Functionary, the forces of the Jesus Christ will act in the soul.
The sense of taste is connected to the chemical ether, the ether that is in order, and where there is order the Christ can manifest. The fact that the master of the banquet "tastes", allows us to understand that the water is still water, but the intimate quality of it has changed and it is being perceived as wine. Taste is connected with chemistry and so the world of "ferments". This can also mean the beginning of the transition from the Baptism of water (of purification and reorganization) to the one of Fire through a renewal of the ferment-wine. At the Last Supper we will have the overcoming of the mysteries of the ferments and the beginning of the mystery of the I, of love; and all of this is described by John and not by the other evangelists that still think of the sphere of the ferments as a link to the Divine.

[184] The transition from water to wine also represents the transition from individual memory to a cosmic one (the memory of our own origin and destination). A second meaning connects the word "wine" with the word "secret": it is like saying that in the wine there is the secret, the higher hidden truth that is usually reserved for the rabbis.

[185] To be a "teacher" is not enough to know these mysteries: the union of the divine with the man is a mystery that belongs to God. Only the I am will say about itself: "I know where I come from and where I am going to" (John 8,14).

[186] The ministers-Venus brought the water to the Sun.

[187]Jesus Christ is the spiritual groom; but in the manifesting level, the groom was a rich Israeli (spiritually rich). The master of the banquet-rabbi-Michael now becomes the "Face of the Christ".

[188] Non- Enlightened man.

[189] At the beginning, he shows the best of him.

[190] You kept the highest secrets up until now, up to your arrival. However, the jars remain six, to indicate that not everything has been done. It will be Jesus that will bring the force that transforms Evil into Good, and he will embrace them. He will bring us beyond the thought of duality from which the vision of the world of Good and Evil come. All is One; both Good and Evil come from God and so they both have lineage. It is our conscious job to go beyond and overcome this duality and to meet the One, the Infinite One, the God of the purest Love from which everything arises and it is expressed within himself as Groom-pulsing principle-Harmony and in Bride-principle of realization-Sweetness.

11. The Jesus created (*poieo*) this as the first[191] of the signs[192] in Cana of the Galilea, and he manifested his glory[193] and his disciples believed[194] in him.

12. After this he himself descended to Capernaum[195] and his mother and his brothers and his disciples and they stayed there not many days[196].

---

[191] This "first" is *archei*, which is the same as the one in the Prologue. So to have a crescendo from the action of the Jesus-*Logos* to the one of the Jesus-*Logos*-Christ.

[192] The initiated Jewish people on the fifth level (Name of the People, like Nathanael) could transform water so that it would taste like wine, and they would do so when all of the clan was reunited for particular events and this could happen thanks to the force of the blood that would magically act from one soul to the other. Just as we will see in the next verse, Jesus operates the sign without the help of the blood; but instead he does so thanks to the presence of the Mother (the two Marys), the stepbrothers and the disciples, all of whom are part of the spiritual family. This sign becomes a miracle.

[193] In verse John 2,14 we have the first aspect of the glory, the "celestial" one; so the glory, which is the complete clairvoyance and clairaudience, has already descended on Earth.

[194] The transition from having Faith to believing in Him begins here, in His Divine descending. There is a profound difference between having faith and believing. Faith is a virtuous motion of the soul towards a goal that is full of virtue, so it's "towards" something or someone. Believing is the next step that allows us to unite to that thing; we enter it. Since at the beginning we only love ourselves, from the moment we enter this higher entity we start to love him. To believe in God, in the Christ, implies the complete acceptance of His Word, of loving Him, and this allows Him to love us. The process that will bring us to John's step begins here, and John was the disciple that He spiritually loved. God responds to our faith with His benevolence (mercy), when we begin to believe he can gift us His Love. It's important to see how in his Gospel, John does not mention the word "faith" but instead he only uses "believing".

[195] After He left Nazareth, Jesus and the Mother go to Capernaum in the house of Peter. Capernaum is below sea level and that indicates His descending in humanity.
Let's remember that Capernaum means "village of *Naum*" or "village of the consolation". It was the village located on the Lake of Genezareth, where Jesus lived during the three years of His public life. It corresponds to the forces of Cancer because the lake of Genezareth can be associated with the Zodiac belt and the seven constellations of the bright Zodiac that are represented by the seven cities that arise on the northwestern bank. The last syllable "*aum*" from Latin "*Copharnaum*", in Sanskrit, represent the Hindu Trinity.

[196] He stayed two days, and so it corresponds to the 4th and 5th day of Creation.
4th day: creation of the lights of the sky. Light is being determined through the visibility of the celestial bodies. This corresponds to the era of Lemuria, when the luciferic rejection towards the Gift of the Light began (which the Light would go through it). The "greater light" represents the Spiritual Solar Self that illuminates the "day", which is the fullness of the consciousness; the "lesser light" is the egoic lunar principle that illuminates the "night", which is the slumber of the consciousness.
5th day: the creation of animals, of the forces of the soul.

THE PURIFICATION OF THE TEMPLE (Mt 21,12-13; Mc 11,15; Ps 68,10)[197]

13. And next was the Easter[198] of the Jewish people and the Jesus ascended[199] at Jerusalems[200].

[197] The text immediately follows the first miracle of the Jesus at Cana of Galilee (2,1-12). There are some expressions and sentences that are being repeated in these two scenes and this makes us think that the author wanted to create a contrast between these two scenes. During the celebration of Easter in Jerusalem, the Jewish people refuse to believe in Jesus and they do not embrace his word. Jesus did his first sign in Cana (2,11). Here the Jewish people ask Jesus to give them a sign (v.18), but then they do not accept the miracle that is being given to them by Jesus (2,20). While the synoptic translation places the episode of the banishment of the peddlers from the temple at the end of Jesus' life and ministry, John places them at the beginning. Reading the two tales of John and Marcus, we can see that both of them take place in the same location: in the temple of Jerusalem. In John 1,14 we found that "the logos became living flesh, and he lived within us (also "he placed his tents within us"); and we contemplated his glory, glory as of the Only-Begotten Son of the Father in plenitude of grace and truth". In other terms: Jesus declares that with his flesh and with his body, he is replacing the mosaic *tent of the meeting*; Jesus becomes the new *meeting* with God, the new temple where the believers contemplate the *glory* of the Lord and they meet the living God.

[198] In John's Gospel, three Easters are mentioned: *the first one* is being mentioned now (John 2,13), and it is a little bit after the beginning of Jesus' work; the *second one* will be before the multiplication of the bread and the fish for 5000 (John 6,4); and the *third one* will be after the resuscitation of Lazarus (John 11,55). There are "three" "normal" Easters, and then a fourth one that is "special": the one of the resurrection. So the Christ's action happens for three years and 4 months (3,3 in the decimal system), the number of days Lazarus remained beyond before being resuscitated; and so was Jesus resuscitated after three days and a third (80 hours). In a broader spectrum, the Christ remained for three years and four months in the grave which is represented by the physical body of Jesus. In Matthew and Marcus, this episode happens at the end of Jesus' public work, but with John it is at the beginning. John's Gospel begins where others end.

[199] He went to the spiritual level. See the note John 2,23.

[200] Jesus goes from Cana to Cafarnao and now to Jerusalem: in the cubic bone (sella turcica) under the pituitary gland, under the thalamus where the spiritual weddings happen of the "change mind".

14. And he found in the temple (internal) (*hiero*)[201] the peddlers[202] of oxen and sheep and doves[203] and the money-changers were sitting down[204]

[201] In the sacred spiritual aspect. The whole passage refers to the transition from the exterior old temple to the new temple (the internal one): the man. The temple symbolizes the man in whose inner being there is the House of the Father. In the human's inner being there isn't just the spark of divine origin of his Higher I, the one that was given to him at creation (Gen. 1,27), instead there is also the true presence of the Creator that rested within the man on the seventh day (Gen. 2,2).
There are various "temples". The main one is Jerusalem's temple, which represents the forehead between the temples, and so the chakra with two petals, the so-called "third eye". The second one is in Samaria-heart, and the third one is in Galilee-perineum. In general, the temple is the place in which we can find the manifestation of the spiritual forces.
The Greek language uses two different terms for "temple". They are "*hiero*" and "*naos*". "*Hiero*" is the most sacred part of ourselves, the *sancta santorum*, where we are in our I am and so in perpetual communion with the Christ. "*Naos*" is the external temple, and the first one was the one which, during the exodus, the Jews erected in the desert and so it represents the Tent of the Alliance.

[202] From the Greek *poleo* that also means "to betray".

[203] The peddlers are the ones that "trade" out of egoism, the human possessions enmeshing them in materialism and not towards devotion to the conscious development of the Incorruptible Body. Oxen as in metabolism-will, sheep as in rhythm-rumen-to feel, dove as in head- to think; they are the three parts of the man seen in their animal aspect. The fourth part, the man of the Aquarius, is represented by John the Baptist and he will have to come for all humanity in the Last Supper when the disciples will follow the man with the water jar to prepare the new Easter.

[204] They represent the ones that change the value in things. They are sitting down, they represent men that work internally.

15. And having made[205] a scourge of ropes[206], he expelled everyone[207] from the temple (internal), the sheep and also the oxen[208] and he poured out the coins[209] of the money-changers[210] and he flipped the tables[211].

16. And to the ones that were selling doves[212] he said (*eipon*): "Take these away from here, (and) don't create (*poieo*) out of the home of my[213] Father a house of negotiations[214]".

---

205 In Latin "almost" is added to it. In the occult sense of the fact, the word is there.

206 It represents the astral body that is harmonized once again. It is connected to the central nervous system, through which it express itself: the ropes are the images of the nerves. Let's remember that the Dragon within us is represented also in the image of the central nervous system. The word "almost" indicates the similarity but not the identity between the physical plane and the "subtle" plane. We can think that in front of His harmonious integrity, the peddlers, felt lashed.
This episode shows us the moment in which new spiritual forces entered the man to make him more apt to become the Temple of the Spirit.

207 Only His presence, the presence of an astral body that is completely renovated, can produce this effect of expulsion. Let us remember that the chemical ether is within us, the ether that orders everything and it acts expelling impurities.
This expulsion regards "everyone", and so also the ones that "were buying": this is to show us that the path that he was seeing in the sacrifice of an animal to repair possible mistakes, ended.

208 The animals that are representing the will and feeling, are being added to "everyone". This is to say that the soul-like forces that were connected to them and that were being practiced in an "old" manner, which is through "mediators", have no space to be in the new Temple.

209 Literally, "copper coins", metal that is connected to Venus, the planetary headquarters of the luciferic forces and of the religion/shape.

210 Inside of the temple there was an "internal" value, not contaminated from the relationship of the world; it was the old way of purification to which Jesus put an end to. The money-changers are the ones that change the value on things, they represent the force of lies.

211 Also the "canteen". In reality, Jesus didn't flip anything: it's his soul-like presence that is re-harmonized (the "scourge of ropes") that generates the disarray.

212 They represent the Holy Spirit, the truth, that is being sold to sustain personal interests. They are not being sent away since they bring an aspect of truth.

213 This Home is the inner being of the man. In a "adolescent" phase of the human conscious, it was allowed to create external buildings (temples).

214 Of a market. This reminds us of the market of the indulgences or the begging that happens during Mass right before the Communion.

17. His disciples remembered[215] that it's written: "The zeal of your house is consuming me[216]".

18. The Jewish people replied and they told him (*eipon*): "Which sign[217] are you showing us, why are you creating (*poieo*) these things[218]?"

19. Jesus replied and said (*eipon*) to them: "Dissolve[219] the temple (external)[220], this, and in three days I will raise it up".

20. The Jewish people then said: "The temple (external)[221], this, was built in forty and six years[222] and you will raise one up in three days[223]?

---

215 The "remembering" indicates the sphere of the heart (ri-*cor*-dare).

216 The internal warmth towards the matters of the spirit is insatiable and it does not make compromises.

217 Also "prodigy".

218 They want to understand where he is wanting to take them. They ask for a sign; Cana was not enough for them.

219 Mercurial action of metamorphosis, which has nothing to do with destruction. The human body is "melted" by the forces of love and then the I Am rebuilds it in the New Adam, thanks to the individualized Incorruptible Body.

220The term being used now is *naos* and it is not the same that we see in verses 14 and 15. *Naos* indicates the external temple, the Tent of the Alliance that accompanied the Chosen People in the Sinai Desert. So here it's referring to the material temple that needs to be "taken down" and then rebuilt within ourselves. It's being called to be the temple of the I am.

221 For "temple", see the note on verse 2, 14.

222 Meaning of the number 46. Adam is present in the whole world, and the initials of four Greek words show this to us. They are the four parts of the world: East, West, North, and South. So, they are the whole universe [*and so the Lord says that when he will come to judge the world, he will find his four chosen ones from the four winds:* cf Mc 13, 27]. If we write these four names in Greek, from their initials, we obtain the name "Adam", and we also find the number forty-six because the flesh of Christ comes from Adam and the Greeks (and John) write numbers using the alphabet letters. Considering the numbers that correspond to the letters of the name "Adam", we find the temple that was built in 46 years. In "Adam", there is the *alfa* that is one, there is *delta* that is four, and so now we have five; and then there is another *alfa* that is one, and so we have six; and finally, we have *my* which is forty, and all of this equals 46. It's important to know that only John talks about these events, and he is also the only one that brings the number 46 up.

223 It's the temple of Initiation, the time of Easter.

21. But he was saying (*lego*) about the temple (external) of his body[224].

22. But when he was raised from the dead, his disciples remembered that he said (*lego*) so and they believed[225] in his scripture and in the verb that the Jesus said (*eipon*).

---

[224] *Soma*, which is the living body. The transition from the sixth day (the creation of man), to the seventh day: the resurgence.. It corresponds to Mc 14,1, the beginning of the Passion and the establishment of the New Man. The Gospel talks about "*naos*", which is the external temple, but after what we just said, we believe that is was a mistake made by the transcriber.
This "body" is the *soma*, which means the body that is permeated with life in opposition to *ptoma*, the corpse.

[225] For the difference between "having faith" and "believing", see John 1,7. John himself "saw and believed" only at the sepulcher (John 20,8). He also did not quite have the complete Faith.

23. And while he was in the Jerusalems[226], in the Easter[227], in the festivities[228], many believed in his name[229], by spiritually seeing the signs that he was creating *(poieo)*.

24. But Jesus himself did not believe them, because he discerned everyone[230],

25. and because he did not need someone to testify around man: he himself would discern what was within the man[231].

---

[226] In Jerusalem's Apocalypse (the New One) it's in the singular form. In the Gospel, the "terrestrial" Jerusalem is one of the many headquarters of the Sacred Word, and so it is in the plural form.

[227] This one, in the Gospel of John, is the first Easter. It has the article in front of it, and so "it's" the Easter, it's like saying that Easter is dedicated to make this transition happen.
It's the main holiday of the Jewish people, and it celebrates the exodus, the liberation of Israel from Egypt. It's also called the Holiday of the Unleavened or the Unleavened Bread (because they couldn't eat bread that had yeast in it before they left Egypt). In reality, the Holiday of the Unleavened used to refer to the holiday of the whole prior week, in which the day of Easter was the last day of the holiday. All the Jewish people used to have to go to Jerusalem every Easter. However, the holiday itself was not necessarily observed.
Initially, Easter indicated the lamb that was sacrificed by the Israeli in Egypt; they would put its blood on the two door jambs and the epistyle of the doors and they would eat its meat. Thanks to this *Easter* (term that comes from the Hebrew verb *pasach*, which originally means to go beyond, in the sense of saving, protect, spare), the destructive angel went over the Israelis, without harming them, while the firstborns of the Egyptians were beaten to death. Hereafter, the Easter holiday was the commemoration of this event and of the event of leaving Egypt. Now, Jesus Christ is our Easter; he was sacrificed on the cross and he frees us from sin and condemnation.

[228] It's Saturday. We can find a correspondence with the Holy Saturday (the fourth Easter), when Jesus will descend to the underworld and he will free Adam. Now he talks about rebuilding the body that is hosting the Spirit and purifies it.

[229] In the Spirit that is within him. In the next passage, we will find that the Spirit is like the wind...(John 3,8). To believe in the Name is bigger than to believe in the Words. This means to recognize the spirit present in the being: in this case in the Christ present in the Jesus.

[230] He knew of their little Faith.

[231] He knew human nature, with its light and its darkness.

NICODEMUS

This chapter can be seen as a chapter in which Faith is the main subject. There are three episodes in which Faith becomes the main idea and the key element, and the verb “to believe” is repeated seven times (in the prior chapter it was mentioned only 4 times).

The *first* episode is the meeting with Nicodemus, prince of the Jewish people, who represents the act of believing within the act of thinking. After this *follows* the Samaritan, who had some precepts of faith that were different from the ones of the Jewish people, and so she represents the believing within feeling. *Finally* comes the noble man, the man of command, that even though he was a pagan, he believed in Jesus and so he represents faith within will.

1. There was a man[232] from the Pharisees[233], by the name of Nicodemus[234], he was the archon of the Jewish People[235].

---

[232] In the text he is denominated as an *Anthropos*, and so someone who is not enlightened. However, if we pay close attention to what we are reading, we see how we are actually in front of an *aner*, who is the enlightened one. Therefore, this is a transcription error.

[233] They were part of a religious and political movement that had an extreme influence, and it was extremely connected to the Hebrew customs and traditions. They believed in the resurrection of the dead and of the angels; but they would hide their vices and their pride under the appearance of a hypocritical religion. The Pharisees were the "separated" ones since they would observe the Mosaic Law and they felt as if they were better than the Jewish people. Their initiation would take place in the ether of heat that corresponds to the upper part of the brainstem. Jesus always invites us to a higher way of understanding the facts that happen above ground. The *first* level of comprehension and understanding should belong to the apostles; the *second* one belongs to the chiefs of the priests (or the Pharisees and Sadducees); and the *third* one belongs to the Romans. A *fourth* level is added to these ones, a "+1", that is given by the Pious Women. They are disciples (and so they correspond to the apostles); they are priestly (they are connected to the lineage of Abel and therefore of the priests); they are Romans (amongst them, there was Pilate's wife). For all these reasons, they will be the ones that will grasp the range of the action of the Christ within Jesus, and they will be the first ones to greet him after the crucifixion.

[234] Nicodemus means "winner of the people", which means the one who went beyond the bond with the people: from the Greek *nike* (victory) and *demos (*people), the "winner of the people" is the one who achieved the sixth step of initiation (after the "name of the people", the fifth step). This means he arrived to the dimension of the "Son" which is connected to Jupiter. The Nicolaitanes of the Apocalypse (they are a group, there is no individual) are won over by the mass (*laos*) of what gets agitated in the man in an unconscious manner. In Nicodemus (he is an individual), the forces of freedom that are present in the man win the ego over. The Greek language does not support the different interpretation that we find in the aspect of group-individual.
The Nicodemus of the Gospels was a Pharisee. He was a ruler, which means he was the highest magistrate in the Sanhedrin. After, he defended Jesus in front of the Pharisees and in front of the priests because they didn't hear him (John 7,50-51), and he helped Joseph of Arimathea to bury Jesus (John 19, 39-40). From all that was just said, he is more than an *aner*, more than an enlightened one; he was "almost" an Initiate. Jesus will initiate him in the "night". Together with Joseph of Arimathea, he was the owner of the room (which was "above") in which Jesus celebrated the Easter.

[235] This is his title. Archon (in Greek *archon*) is a component of the highest board of the magistrates, and so, in this case, of the Sanhedrin, which is the highest Hebrew council that administrated public and justice affairs.

2. He went to him during the night[236], and he told him (*eipon*): “Rhabbi[237], we know from what we saw (*eidon*)[238] that you came from God (as a) teacher[239], no one has the strength to create (*poieo*) the signs, that you create (*poieo*), if the God is not with him”.

---

[236] He goes to Jesus, and he does it in the astral plane (during the night).

[237] He recognizes in Jesus a higher teacher than he is, and he refers to the “Buddha” aspect that lived in Jesus.

[238] As an initiate he “sees” and so he “knows”. This “us” refers to those who, just like him, had the fifth step of initiation.

[239] He only sees two aspects of Jesus: first the Rhabbi-Buddha and now the Teacher-Zarathustra (*didaskalos*).

3. Jesus[240] answered and said (*eipon*): "Amen, Amen[241] I say (*lego*) to you: if one is not born again from above[242] he does not have the strength[243] to grasp (*idein*)[244] the Kingdom[245] of the God[246]".

4. The Nicodemus tells him (*lego*): "How does a man[247] have the strength to be born when he is old? Does he maybe have the strength to enter once again the womb of his mother and then be originated[248]?"

5. Jesus replied: Amen, Amen[249] I say (*lego*) to you: if one is not originated by water and spirit[250] he does not have the strength to enter the Kingdom of God[251].

---

[240] Not "the" Jesus, since Nicodemus only grasped the Rhabbi within him.

[241] He says a universal law.

[242] Here we have the 7th day. The Greek term *anothen* means both "again" and "from above". Up to this point, the initiations had a luciferic characteristic and so they would not be allowed to enter the Kingdom: for this level, it's necessary to "be born from above" and only with His arrival this is now possible.

[243] The forces of Mary.

[244] *Idein*: expand the capacity to grasp (to see) the laws of the Logos. In this passage, we find the expression "Amen, Amen" three times. Now it is relating to "seeing" the Kingdom. But afterwards, with the Baptism of the Spirit, we will "enter" it. Finally, "it will testify" in regards to the world.

[245] Let's remember how the Kingdom is the dimension of the Vital Loving Spirit. Thanks to the conscious I, the man can enter it. In the sense of the Sefirot *Malkhut*, it's the terrestrial Kingdom, including the terrestrial sensitive world in which the man consciously acts. To enter the celestial Kingdom before the Christ, the initiate needed to dim his I, with the Christ the human I will be the one to enter, with its fullness, in the Celestial Malkut.

[246] Up to the Holiest Trinity.

[247] *Anthropos* in Greek.

[248] Nicodemus is aware that this transition needs to happen but he can interpret it in the sense of returning to a prenatal condition, which means before the descending of matter (and the entry of the double ahrimanic), and so he does not understand how this can happen.

[249] This is the second universal truth.

[250] There is a hint here of the difference between the two Water Baptisms (for the reorganization of the human bodies) and the one of the Spirit (to go back up, thanks to the help of the Father). The Fire Baptism is missing, which is the one that allows us to reach the solar dimension of "Jesus" and this can happen because he already achieved this.

[251] At this point, it is not about "seeing" the Kingdom; the birthing within the Spirit allows us to "enter" it.

6. What is originated by the flesh, is flesh[252]; what is originated by the spirit, is spirit[253].
7. Do not be surprised because I told you (*eipon*): you need to be originated from above.
8. The spirit blows[254] wherever it wants to; and you hear its voice, but you don't know where it's coming from or where it's going. This is how it is for the ones that are originated by the spirit as well.
9. Nicodemus replied, and said (*eipon*): "How do these things have the strength to become?"
10. Jesus answered and he told him (*eipon*): "You are the teacher of the Israel[255], and you don't have clarity upon these things[256]?
11. Amen, Amen[257] I say (*lego*) to you that what we know we pronounce[258] and what we have seen (*horao*) we testify, and you are not welcoming our testimony.
12. If I told you (*eipon*) about the terrestrial things and you don't believe[259], how will you believe (*pisteusete*) if I will tell you (*eipon*) about the celestial[260] things?

---

[252] This reminds us of John 1,14: "*And the logos became living flesh, and it lived within us..*". The flesh is also a principle of life (the biologic one) within us, but it can only produce more biologic life (the terrestrial existence, the physical and etheric body: the hereditary current).

[253] The Spirit is free like air and wind.

[254] The Mary force.

[255] Here we comprehend how his level goes beyond the one of Enlightenment (Sun), but he has yet to be an Initiate.

[256] Nicodemus, since he belongs to the old Hebrew path of initiation, can reach the spiritual worlds only through the Moon; he does not have the new complete Initiation, the new connection with the Spirit (that would blow wherever it wanted to). Nicodemus also has the name of the winner of the people (teacher of Israel); therefore, he is on the sixth step of Initiation, the one of Jupiter, the one of wisdom, of discernment.
Jesus helps him understand that there was a reference to the "birthing from above" in the Old Testament. Both Jeremiah and Ezekiel referred to a New Alliance and to a Law that was written on the heart.

[257] Third universal truth

[258] To see and pronounce (the Word) are One in the Trinity. Jesus is now speaking as the Christ and also as the Father. The fact that the testimony was not believed, reminds us of discernment, which is an act that is given to us by the Holy Spirit.

[259] For the difference between "having faith" and "believing", see John 1,7.

[260] This teaching, projected into the future, corresponds to our era in which the Christ manifests himself in the etheric plane.

13. And no one ascended to the sky if not the ones that descended from the sky, the Son (*Hyos*) of the man[261].

14. And just how Moses lifted up in the glory[262] the snake[263] in the desert, it is necessary that the Son of the man is lifted up[264] in the glory:

15. So that everyone that believes in him can have eternal spiritual Life.

---

[261] The man descends from the Sky having within himself the seed of the offspring from God and then he goes back up as the Son of man, which means as the conscious I with the Jesus within himself. He donates the "similarity" with God, which is the perfection that he had as a created man.
From this plane, we then ascend to Son of God, which means to have the operating Christ within ourselves, and we can enter the Celestial world (the sphere of the Holiest Trinity: the Milky Way).

[262] This glory has a luciferic aspect since Lucifer gave the old path of initiation to us.

[263] He lifted up to the Sun (glory as a complete clairaudience and clairvoyance) the force of Kundalini (the "snake of fire" that sleeps in our womb, as a luciferic force that fell with the Fall), and so he purified it and he prepared it for the Glory (that Jesus Christ will do). To be precise, he lifted up the first ten vertebras (the 5 sacral ones, which are the ones of the sacrum, and the 5 lumbar ones). These vertebras were "built" through the 10 commandments but they were not "made" yet, they were not yet "accomplished" by the man. These vertebras lead to the generation of a son within us: the Son of the man, the superior I. The "gestation" of these 10 vertebras is represented by the 10 plagues of Egypt where the tenth one, the crossing of the Red Sea, indicates the opening of the waters for the birth of the Promised Land, towards the Kingdom. The Baptist will be the first man that interiorized the law and so respected the 10 commandments (The Law).
This is not a matter of lifting up the snake-Kundalini anymore; now it's about becoming Sons of the Light (John 12,36), and so to be born from Above.
When the Son of the man (born from below) will be lifted up and will be united with the Son of God (born from above), the two will become one and the forces of death will transform into forces of resurrection.

[264] The Son of the man (*Hyos and Antropos*), represented by Jesus, unites himself completely to the Christ and he becomes the "I am" like Adonai (the secret name of God), which means "God is". Only John uses the expression "to be lifted".

16. This is how the God spiritually loved the world[265], so much to gift his Only-Begotten[266] Son: so that whoever believes[267] in him will not be lost[268], but instead he will have eternal[269] spiritual Life.

17. God did not send the Son into the world so that he could judge the world, he sent him to save the world through him[270].

18. Who believes in him is not judged[271]: but who does not believe, is already being judged[272], because he did not believe in the name[273] of the Only-Begotten Son of the God.

19. This is the judgment: that the light came to the world[274] and men spiritually loved the darkness more than the light; they were their evil[275] deeds.

20. Everyone who acts evil hates the light and does not come to the light, so that their deeds will not be repelled[276].

---

[265] The world that God loved is the world He created in His image and likeness. He also loves our world since the man is in it, which is the most elevated fruit of creation and since this man got lost, He sent his Son to save him.

[266] The Christ, Son "of" God.

[267] For the difference between "to have faith" and "to believe", see John 1,7.

[268] Also "lost" or "in ruins"; that will not get lost in the consequences of the Fall.

[269] That will arrive to the mysteries of Eternal Life, the mysteries of the Father that we can comprehend on Easter Monday.

[270] Thanks to the gift of the victory over death and the liberation of Adam.

[271] The Spirit does not judge us, we are the ones that judge ourselves once we find ourselves in front of our true spiritual image.

[272] From himself.

[273] The name that is being evoked is Jesus' name, or better the form He took on so that he could be more accessible to humanity. With "name" we are referring to the spiritual essence. The action of not believing in him condemns us to spiritual paralysis.

[274] At the time of the Old Sun, part of us decided to stay in the light and others decided to stay in darkness. From this, the Chosen People came to life and also the humanity that is now in "the" world.

[275] Also "heavy, painful, grievous, suffering, wicked".

[276] Also "accused".

21. Who creates (*poeio*) the truth[277] comes to the light, so that his deeds can be manifested, because they are executed in God".

THE JESUS IN JUDEA, TESTIMONY OF JOSEPH (Mt 4,12; Lk 3,19)

22. After these things, Jesus and his disciples came to the land of Judea and here he stayed with them[278] and he was baptizing[279] .

23. John was also baptizing[280] in Aenon[281], close to Salim[282]; because there were many waters[283] there; and they would become there[284] and they were baptized[285].

24. The John was yet to be thrown in prison[286].

---

[277] To act in a bad way (verse 20). He contrasts the "operating of truth". Truth is not just to be known, it also needs to be put into practice.

[278] The Christ would "move" casting a shadow, from time to time, above the Disciples. From this, we can understand that He himself was not directly baptizing, but he was baptizing through the Apostles.

[279] The Jesus would baptize in Fire and Spirit (just like he told Nicodemus- v John 3,5).

[280] Also "he was baptizing" indicating the static element of the action of the Baptist.

[281] Aenon (in Greek *Ainon*) means "springs", the "rebirth". Others say it means "the Springs (water springs)". The "land of many springs" (Aenon) was situated on the eastern shore of the spot where you could cross the Jordan, and so it corresponds to the spiritual world. From what we just said, microcosmically it corresponds to the space behind the heart: the spiritual heart from which many waters of life come.

[282] The identification is not certain, but it could be in the region of Scitopoli, on the Decapoli side (which corresponds to the constellation of Aquarius) to the west of the Jordan. Let's remember that the Baptist brings the Initiation of Aquarius.

[283] Depending on the person, John would choose what type of water to use to purify that specific person. In the Hebrew baptism, the priest was the one that would address the soul of the one being baptized (through the "helmsman") towards the soul-like region wanted.

[284] In that place, they would grow internally.

[285] It's important to see the difference between the baptizing of the Jesus and the one of John. John is more static and it happens in a limited environment. Jesus, on the other hand, is more dynamic and he directs it to all Judea. John's Baptism is mainly directed to the vital forces (the waters) and it's about reorganization; Jesus' Baptism is of the soul-spiritual and it's also about salvation and "going back up": it's the baptism of Fire and Spirit.

[286] Blocked from acting in the physical plane. John the Baptist is characterized by dressing in leather and this brings us back to "dress with leather" of Adam and Eve after the transgression. Therefore, John is "the man of leather" that, with his death, anticipates the liberation of Adam, the first "man of leather".

25. It so became (*egheneto*) a research[287] of John's disciples with some other Jewish people on purification[288].

26. And they came to John and said (*eipon*): " Rhabbi[289], the one who was with you, on the other side of the Jordan[290], the one you testified[291] about, see (*idein*) he baptizes[292] and everyone goes to him"[293].

27. John answered and said (*eipon*): "A man (*Anthropos*) does not have the strength to receive unless it's given to him from the sky[294].

28. You all are my witnesses that I said (*eipon*): 'I am not the Christ, but I was sent in front of him'.[295]"

---

[287] They ask an inner question.

[288] It's without the article. For the Jewish people, the purification would happen through the various ablutions. With John, the inner purification begins.

[289] It's part of the Nathan Soul, within him the Buddha would act and preach. He was also part of the Buddha current.

[290] Behind the spinal cord: in the spiritual world. The Jordan represents the forces of the I that run through man's spinal cord. The Jordan connects the underneath waters (amniotic fluid-womb) with the waters that are above (Dead Sea-head). Within the man, the waters that are below stopped reflecting the ones that are above and so now they flow towards death. As the divine seed reawakens in us, the injury from the fall (the feet) closes (heals) and the flow is inverted (hemorrhage) and we begin to participate in the cosmic Life. Jesus will also immerse himself in it (in the sphere of what is still unfinished), and right after that he will re-ascend. He travels through Adam's path; he descends in the shadow-feminine-darkness aspect that he needs to marry so that it will be finished.
The expression "on this side of the Jordan" represents the whole man with his consciousness and so, by esoteric transposition, it refers to the Chosen People. From this, we have the expression "on the other side of the Jordan" which represents the human condition of the ones that are outside of the Chosen People.

[291] The "path" of the previous passage is picked up again: from seeing, to entering, to testifying. Here we start again from the testifying of the Fire Baptism.

[292] In the Spirit.

[293] In all of this, there is a sense of malice with which they try to counter-pose John to Jesus.

[294] Also the power "to receive", which is the permeation of oneself with the spiritual gifts; it's a Gift from the sky. Precisely, it's a gift from Mary: it's the bride that opens up to the groom. It's thanks to the enlightenment that he received (John 1,32) that the Baptist can say this.

[295] With this he makes us understand how Jesus is the Messiah that we have been waiting for.

29. Who has the bride[296] groom[297] is, but the friend[298] of the groom that stands tall[299] and hears him will be full of joy[300] when he hears the voice[301] of the groom. In this manner, the joy, my own joy, has reached its fullness[302].

30. It's necessary that he becomes greater and I become less[303].

31. Who came from above[304] is above[305] everyone, who comes from the earth[306], to the earth he is and he speaks from the earth. The one that comes from the sky above everyone[307] is.

32. And what he saw (*eipon*), and what he heard, this he testifies; and no one embraces his testimony[308].

33. Who embraced his testimony, confirmed that the God is truthful[309].

---

296 The promised or tender bride.

297 The spouses are Mariam-soul and Jesus Christ-spirit.

298 The one that loves him, in this case John the Baptist and so all the ones that rise to John's plane.

299 He is in the I.

300 Joy is the presence of the spirit in the soul.

301 The voice is the expression of the logos. The throat, with the collarbones (little keys) that will keep going with the arms and the hands, represent the eagle in us: the Guardian of the Door of the Gods, of our higher trio.

302 The one that receives the joy of the groom will embrace it within himself, and so he will become groom and bride.

303 Like the sun after Saint John's Day descends, while the sun of Christmas increases. The man that is in the Law (the Baptist) needs to decrease while the new man rises, the one that created himself in the new likeness with the Creator: in Freedom and in Love.

304 It's not a matter of lifting the snake-Kundalini up anymore, but to become the Sons of the Light (John 12, 36), and so to be born from Above like Jesus did.

305 Also "before" everyone else. The Nathan Jesus was born "from above".

306 This is a John that was "born from a woman".

307 To the two categories that we mentioned up above. There is the earth, and then the above (the seventh step of initiation), and then "the" sky of the Holiest Trinity. It refers to the Christ.

308 As always, "his" do not recognize him.

309 Within Him, there is the whole truth.

34. The one that God sent[310], speaks (*lalein*)[311] the words[312] of thee God: for he gives the spirit[313] with no limit.

35. The Father spiritually loves the Son (*Hyos*) and he gifted everything in his hand[314].

36. The believer (*pisteuo*)[315] in the Son has eternal spiritual Life, but the one that refuses to believe (*apeitheo*) in the Son will not see (*opsomi*) spiritual Life but instead the wrath of God will remain on him[316]".

---

310 The one that was sent is Jesus.

311 The verb being used is *lalein*, which means to "stutter". It's basically like saying that everything needs to be said in truth and with simplicity. Jesus could not say more to the disciples, he could only say the basic and initial things of the spiritual path: from this comes to "stutter".

312 The term being used is "*rema*" (exactly "*remata*"), which is the term that expresses the word as a part of the Logos, in this case as a Law.

313 The spiritual world gifts to us all of its graces with no limitation, especially without looking at the "human" limitations.

314 The hand, in Hebrew *yada* represents the consciousness but it also means, "I love". This consciousness is a wedding, it is a spiritual love.
Here he is telling us how the Father entrusted the Son with the task of saving humanity.
The tri-articulation of the whole arm represents the Holy Spirit (while the forearm represents the Son and the arm represents the Father). In the Psalm's tradition, the right hand represents the Holy Spirit that brings to life, and the left one represents the Son that structures, molds, shapes. The hands put together represent the union of the force that structures with the consciousness that brings to life.
The fingers of the hand also have a meaning: the thumb-Venus-head; the index finger-Jupiter-gall bladder; the medium finger-Saturn-spleen/pancreas; ring finger-Sun-liver; pinky-Mercury-heart.

315 Once again we have the difference between the having Faith and the believing, which means "to put" (inside) the Faith and so they have the complete adhesion to His Word. For the difference between "having faith" and "believing" , see John 1,7.

316 It's always John that is speaking: he understood extremely well who Jesus Christ is. The wrath is the feeling that comes to life in the ones that oppose the plan of divine love. The man will be the one that will judge himself and will condemn himself in the moment death comes (the moment of the crossing).

THE LORD IN SAMARIA

1. When the Lord[317] found out that the Pharisees[318] heard[319] that Jesus baptizes and creates (*poieo*) more disciples that John,
2. –even though Jesus himself wasn't baptizing, but his disciples[320]-
3. He left Judea and he went once again to Galilee[321].
4. He had to go through Samaria[322].
5. He then arrives to a city of Samaria, called (*lego*) Sychar[323]: close to the field that Jacob gave to Joseph, his son (*Hyos*).

---

317 The Lord corresponds to the step of Saturn, to the Persian Father.

318 The Pharisees were the "divided" ones, they would follow the Mosaic Law very carefully and they were believed to be the best amongst the Jews. Their initiation would take place in the ether of heat, which corresponds to the upper part of the brainstem.

319 Since Jesus wouldn't baptize directly, this "to hear" happens in a non-physical plane. Therefore, he perceives that they spiritually "heard" the echo of what He was doing through his apostles.

320 It is now being clearly said that Jesus was not baptizing.

321 Towards the will pole, where he will achieve free actions.

322 The Samaria is located between the Judea-head and the Galilea-metabolism. Therefore, it represents the sphere of feeling and here he will meet the Samaritan woman. The name comes from *Semer*, it's a city of Palestine, which is 11 kilometers north-west of Sichem (the place where Joshua gathered the twelve tribes of Israel and he renewed the alliance). The Samaritans were people that weren't completely Jewish because of various deportations and they were despised by the Jewish people. They adored the same God of Israel, but they also adored other Gods.

323 The name means "inebriation" in the sense of intense feelings. Sicar is located in the heart of Samaria. Jacob from Egypt (where he died), was taken to Sichem, and there he was put in the sepulcher that Abraham acquired and where he rested with Isaac. Joseph's clothes were there too, and one of Jacob's sons.

6. And Jacob's well[324] was there. The Jesus, who was internally tired of the journey[325], was sitting upon the well[326]: it was almost the sixth[327] hour.

7. A woman[328] from Samaria comes to draw water[329]. Jesus says (*lego*) to her: "Give me a drink[330]".

8. His disciples went to the city[331] to buy some food[332].

---

[324] The fountain represents for the Hebrew world the number 70, sixteenth letter of the alphabet. The 70 is *hain* (or *ahin*) which is a word that means "eye" or "fountain, springs of living water" and it indicates the principle of time, which gushes from what is hidden. It also indicates the disappearance, the death, the nothingness, but also the return, the rebirth on the plane of the terrestrial incarnation. The Samaritan will sense to be in front of the Messiah since she will grasp within him the capacity to know her life, to spiritually "see" the reality that is within her.

[325] This tiredness is not physical, it's internal and it's coming from the task of giving life to faith (the "believing") within the Chosen People.

[326] The Jesus is experiencing the swamp (pond) of the spiritual human life. By sitting down, which symbolizes the internal meditation upon the well, is the symbol that He is the spiritual master of both the human soul (the Samaritan) and of the ancient Hebrew knowledge (Jacob's water).

[327] Since this "hour" is without an article, it refers to the "esoteric" hours, so from 12 to 13: the hour of Gemini and so of the forces of Lucifer that act through the solar disc.

[328] The nickname "Woman" corresponds both to the step of Venus (the third one) and the one of the Sun (the fourth one). Let's remember that this nickname corresponds to the redemption of the fall on behalf of the feminine, at the redemption of Eve within her. The woman represents the higher aspect of the feminine within us, the soul that, united with the Spirit, generates the Child.

[329] In this case, the water represents both the forces of the ancient knowledge, and the forces of the soul.

[330] Jesus begins the process of reawakening of the soul of the Samaritan through the path of dialogue. He is thirsty, just how he will be on the Golgotha. He is the "thirsty" and with this we understand the condition (for Him) to go through the sphere of the Zodiac to get to the one of the Milky Way. This means that he is feeling a strong desire (just like thirst) to be recognized by the Chosen People. The Samaritan, a woman, will be the one to recognize him as the Messiah. His request indicates His request of hospitality (to the guests, water was always offered), and in this case we are talking about "internal" hospitality and this will become the opportunity to "give" (in the end, he will not drink but instead he will offer the water of Life). Amongst the disciples, the condition of being "thirsty" is the condition to go from the step of the Moon (Raven) to the step of Mercury (Hidden).

[331] Probably the heart *chakra*. From the text, we can understand how the disciples have yet to understand the will of the Christ and so they are looking for material food and not the spiritual one.

[332] Jesus looks for spiritual nourishment, and his disciples are looking for material nourishment. Jesus is not being recognized by "his own" and so he is "thirsty" along the path. It will the Samaritan woman, the one that is from the region in which the Baptist had already preached, the one that will recognize him: the soul is ready.

9. And so the woman, the Samaritan[333], tells (*lego*) him: "Why is it that you, a Jew as you are, ask for a drink from me, a woman from Samaria?" (The Jews have no relations with the Samaritans[334]).

10. Jesus replied and said (*eipon*): "If you knew the gift of God[335] it is him that tells (*eipon*) you: 'Give me a drink', you would have asked him[336] and he would have given you spiritual living water."[337]

11. The woman says (*lego*) to him: "Sir[338], you have nothing to draw water with and the well is deep[339]: where do you get the water, the one that is spiritually alive[340]?

12. Maybe it is you that is greater than our father Jacob[341], the one that gave the well to us and drank from it himself, and his sons and his descendants[342]?"

---

[333] Now it has the article. It conquers the step of the people: the one of Mars.

[334] Both with no article: the Jews considered the Samaritans as heretical because they would only recognize the first 5 Books of the Old Testament as sacred, and they wouldn't accept the one of the prophets. This is why they hated each other and they went to war for 700 years. The Jews destroyed the temple of the Samaritans that was built on mount Garizim.

[335] This gift is the eternal spiritual Life. This concept was lost and the consciousness was limited to the terrestrial existence.

[336] Here is the encouragement to keep going in the search of the Messiah.

[337] Jesus gets her ready to know him. He is the spring of living water, and it can be assimilated with His vital impulse, with His moral ether that renews the other four ethers, the Word that brings life.

[338] The Samaritan is amazed but she begins to predict the truth and she calls him "sir", the level of Mars that she reached.

[339] At the bottom of the well, there is the stagnant water, and it is this way for the old knowledge. The only way to reach it is with a bucket, and so it's a limited form (thoughts connected to the materialistic world) and it is also limiting (the quantity).

[340] The woman is still stalled in front of Jesus.

[341] Now she sees the level of the Sun.
Abraham, Isaac and Jacob prepared the entrance to the Promised Land. Abraham "looked" at it (spirit), Isaac "raised" altars (soul), Jacob "dug" wells (physical). The question of the woman manifests the soul's difficulty in changing secular beliefs that created preconceptions and false beliefs.
Therefore, we have the comparison between Jacob and Jesus. The people of Israel began with Jacob ("Israel" was his second name), the Chosen People. With Jesus a new population begins: the one "of the" Chosen Ones, the ones that are looking for the Truth.

[342] The Chosen People.

13. Jesus answered and told (*eipon*) her: " Whoever drinks this water, will still be thirsty[343];

14. But the one that will drink the water that I will give to him, will stop being thirsty; but the water that I will give to him will become within him a source of water that ascends to the eternal spiritual Life[344]".

15. The woman tells (*lego*) him: "Sir, give me the water, this one, so that I will no longer be thirsty, and so that I won't come here to draw it[345]".

16. He says (*lego*) to her: " Go, call your enlightened[346] man and come here".

17. The woman answered him and told (*eipon*) him: "I don't have an enlightened (*aner*)[347] man. The Jesus tells (*lego*) her: "You are right in saying: I have no enlightened[348] man;

18. You had five enlightened[349] men, and now the one you have is not your enlightened man; so you stated the truth[350]".

19. The woman says (*lego*) to him: "Sir, I spiritually see that you are a prophet[351]".

---

343 The old knowledge will never be able to completely satisfy the deep desire of knowledge of man; it's a desire that leans on his soul. The old initiation would also keep them connected to the terrestrial teacher and so it would not give us the true freedom.

344 The water that He gifts to us is the Spirit of Truth that quenches our thirst and it makes us source of life for the ones that want to listen to the Word. We are still on Mars level.

345 We assist to the awakening of the soul to the Word, to the Guide that sets us free.

346 Like a new Eve that calls her Adam, the woman is sent to look for her husband (the enlightened man). She was yet to reach the level of wife and so she was looking here and there but she still could not find her husband: she will find him within Jesus.
In the evolution of humanity there are seven evolution cycles, all threatened by the temptation that is represented in the Apocalypse of Babylon. Five have already happened; the sixth one is the current one that sees the division between Babylon and Celestial Jerusalem. The seventh one, the last one, still has to happen and it will "stay" (Ap 17,9).

347 She states to have not gotten to the level of Wife.

348 The higher I, the I am.

349 These can be the five books of the Mosaic tradition in which the jewish people were connected, and that are being connected to an element of adultery (of the Truth).

350 Saying the truth makes her overcome the challenge and so she will be able to know the real Truth: the water of Life. The constant affirmation of truth is the safest path to reach the Christ.

351 The step of Prophet is on the Sun. she begins to understand but she yet has to grasp the real dimension of the Jesus.

20. Our fathers bowed on this mountain[352], this one, and you say (*lego*) that in Jerusalems there is the place where you need to bow[353]".

21. The Jesus says (*lego*) to her: " Woman[354], believe (*pisteuo*) in me, that a time will come in which nor on the mountain, this one, nor in Jerusalems you will bow to the Father[355].

22. You bow to what you do not know[356]; we[357] bow to what we know, because the salvation is of the Jews[358].

23. But a time will come, and it is now, in which the ones that truthfully bow, will bow to the Father in Spirit and in Truth[359]. The Father also looks for them, the ones that bow to him.

24. Spirit (is) the God: and the ones that will bow to him is necessary that they will bow in Spirit and in Truth[360]".

25. The woman tells (*lego*) him: " I know that the Messiah is coming, the so called (*lego*) Christ. When he will come he will announce everything".

---

352 It's mount Garizim of Samaria that was "opposing" to the mount of Jerusalem.

353 Literally to "bow down", or "to bring a reverent kiss to the mouth".

354 Also "feminine" or "wife". Jesus gives her back the title of wife, of soul united with her I. this corresponds to the redemption of her fallen part, of the redemption of Eve within her.

355 Jesus announces the ending of every external Temple, of every eye-catching ritual, and of particular places. Now we meet God within ourselves. In John 2,13-25 we already saw the purification of the Temple.

356 The Samaritans adored other Gods as well.

357The disciples of the Christ.

358 The Jews had the knowledge of what they adored (they were not idolaters like the Samaritans), the Chaldean knowledge flowed within them (through Abraham and the stay in Ur) and also the Egyptian knowledge (through Moses). With this, we understand that a faith that does not understand is not needed; instead, what is needed is an internal effort to understand.

359 With the enlightenment given to us by the Holy Spirit and within the truth given to us by the Christ. By testifying and obeying to this, we will reach the Father.

360 This is the big change brought by the Christ to humanity: to not look for God in the temples but instead in every place, in every moment, and looking for him by looking for the Truth that unites us to the fact that everything is eternal and divine. Lucifer wants to be adored in the abstract and formalist religiousness, Ahriman in the material world.

26. The Jesus tell (*lego*) her: "I am, that I announce (*laleo*)[361]".

27. And in that moment his disciples came and they were amazed that he was speaking to a woman. But no one said (*eipon*): "What are you looking for?[362] Or "You talk to her?"

28. The woman[363] left her water jar, and she went towards the city and she says (*lego*) to the men[364]:

29. "Come, see (*eidon*) a man[365], who said (*eipon*) to me all that I created (*epoisa*): maybe he is the Christ?"

30. They left the city[366] and they were coming to him.

31. In the meanwhile the disciples were praying to him by saying (*lego*): "Rhabbi[367],eat[368]".

32. And he said (*eipon*) to them: "I have food[369] to eat that you do not know[370]".

---

[361] We are in front of the first I am that is being pronounced by the Jesus: He (Jesus and not the Christ within him) declares himself bearer of the Logos.
This is the only time that Jesus will announce His identity and His mission. The verb being used is *laleio*, which means "to stutter", and it indicates that the woman is only at the beginning of the comprehension of the mystery of the Word.

[362] He who "seeks" finds but their soul is not ready, it's not open. They are the ones that still have doubts, they are the ones that haven't understood the teaching of Jesus. They do not ask: maybe in their own pride they are waiting for Jesus to fall in contradiction.

[363] The water jar is the old form with which the soul would connect to the old knowledge. For the Christic knowledge, forms and shapes are not needed anymore, what is needed is freedom, and the predisposition of the heart.

[364] The soul full of spirit becomes "joyful" and it wants to make everyone part of her joy.

[365] She does not qualify him in a certain way (Jew, prophet, Messiah…) and she invites others to make that internal step so that they can recognize him within themselves.

[366] From their habitual spiritual dimension.

[367] They do not see higher than that.

[368] They now want to offer their spiritual nourishment to Jesus, the fruit of their reasoning and their "human" explanations: the nourishment that "perishes".

[369] This is a food that is eagerly eaten.

[370] They got so far from the knowledge of spiritual truths; the real food is the knowledge of the Truth and the knowledge of their own internal reality.

33. The disciples were then saying (*lego*) to each other: "Maybe someone brought him some food[371]?"

34. The Jesus says (*lego*) to them: "My food is to create (*poeio*) the will of the one that sent me here to accomplish (*teleioo*) his work[372].

35. Do you not say (*lego)* that there are still four months, and then comes harvest[373]? Here I say (*lego*) to you: lift your eyes[374] and you will see (*theaomai*) the fields[375] that already are bright[376] for harvest.

36. Already the one who reaps receives a compensation and he receives fruit in eternal spiritual life, so that the sower[377] can rejoice with the reaper[378].

37. In this the logos is true: one is the one that sows and the other one is the one that reaps[379].

---

[371] The materialistic vision of the apostles is horrible. They now fear that others brought to Him the fruit of their "human" knowledge and they they have conditioned him.

[372] When we make the Father's will, we will receive our spiritual daily Bread. No human will can condition the Spirit.
The making of the Father's will is articulated in three aspects or phases:

- Respect the Commands that he gave us (aspect "Father");
- To do what He tells us to do internally with the internal Word (aspect "Son");
- To be at his complete disposition, to be at His service (aspect "Holy Spirit").

This also represents a transition from a condition of "obligation" to one of "Freedom". From this the fourth aspect comes to life, the "+1", the "prize": to reach the eternal spiritual Life.
The Work of the Father comes to its completion when the man, who is the successful completion of His creation, reaches the reason why he is created: to become a Creating Principle (in unison with the Christ).

[373] The moment of reaping of what was sowed within ourselves, in our four bodies.

[374] To the sky, from the material to the spiritual. The eye indicates the necessary death for the process of resurrection.

[375] From the Greek *Chora*, which means region (zodiacal spiritual region).

[376] It's the same term used in the Apocalypse.

[377] The Father with his Hierarchies.

[378] The man.

[379] It is not important that the one who sows also reaps: the importance is to seek the Truth, to have within oneself the seed of the spiritual search.

38. I sent you to reap that for which did not tired you: others got tired and you have entered into their tiredness[380]".

39. Many Samaritans from the city, had faith (*episteusa*)[381] in him for the logos that the woman was testifying for: "She told (*eipon*) me all that you created (*poieo*)[382]".

40. When the Samaritan came to him, they prayed him to stay amongst them. And he stayed there for two days[383].

41. And many more had faith (*episteusa*) in him for his logos.

42. And they said (*lego*) to the woman: "We believe (*pisteuo*) not because of what you said: we ourselves heard and we know that he truly is the savior of the world[384]".

---

[380] The Truth was sowed by the prophets and the initiates, and now they have to reap through their testimony.

[381] For the difference between "having faith" and "believing", see John 1,7.

[382] Jesus understood all the experiences within her, also the deepest ones.

[383] Symbol of the necessary time to nourish them in the soul and in the spirit, which means to bring the nourishment to the Husband and the Wife.

[384] Because he gifts to the man the possibility to grasp the true knowledge and so the Truth. The Samaritans understood the message of the Christ.

THE RETURN TO GALILEE, THE SON OF A ROYAL OFFICIAL

THE RETURN TO GALILEA, THE SON OF A ROYAL OFFICIAL (Mt 4,12; Mt 113, 57; Mc 6,4; Lc 4,24).

43. And after the two days[385] he left for Galilee[386].

44. Jesus himself testified that a prophet[387] does not receive honor in his homeland[388].

45. When he arrived to Galilee, the Galileans welcomed[389] him, they had seen (*horao*) all that he did in Jerusalems in the feast day[390]: they also were there.

THE RETURN TO GALILEA, THE SON OF A ROYAL OFFICIAL

[385] These are the two days of the verse 40, which are the symbol of the necessary time to nurture them in the soul and in the spirit. This is also to testify how much Jesus gave to those people.

[386] From Samaria, he goes to Galilee.

[387] Fourth step: the Sun.

[388] This is because each prophet, teacher, or founder of a spiritual movement, when he returns to the spiritual current that he is connected to (his Homeland), he finds it (when it's still going good) blocked in the form with which he brought his teachings. But he spent a period of time in the higher worlds where he re-elaborated his message and so now he brings it with new features that are not being understood by "his own" (see verse John 1, 11). Furthermore, there is a certainty that God is "far" from man and so when someone wants to bring his teachings in a direct way closer to man, he does not recognize it.

[389] The welcoming is good after what was done in Judea.

[390] The feast day is Saturday, the *sabbat* that means "the day of the Graces". This is the day of "resurgence" to the Father and Jesus acts "leaning" on the strength of this day of prayer, of grace and gratitude.

46. So he came back to the Cana of Galilee[391], where he created (*poieo*) the water wine[392]. And there was a royal official[393] whose son (*hyios*) was without strength[394] in Capernaum[395].

---

[391] It's the town of Galilee, where Jesus made his first miracle (John 2,1-11). It was the town of Natanaele (John 21,2). It's located approximately 6 kilometers north-east of Nazareth.
Cana represents the forces of Cana which are the luciferic forces; "of the" Galilee represents the forces of the Father that act on the metabolism. We are in a situation of redemption of the sexual-matrimonial forces. After the wedding at Cana (which indicated the arrival of the new Husband-Jesus Christ and his union with the Wife-Israel) and after sending the merchants away from the temple, which is an act that antagonized him to the priests (the "administrators" if the divine did not welcome him), He goes back to Cana which symbolizes a new beginning to His Work. He will here meet the Royal Official, who is a mediator of the political power. Therefore, a new cycle is starting, a cycle that is based on the opposition between infirmity-death and health-life. This cycle will keep going up to chapter 11,54: the resurrection of Lazarus.

[392] With the transformation of water to wine that happened in the Wedding at Cana, the Jesus acted on the etheric body of the men that were present, and he allowed his forces of his etheric body to flow through them: with the healing of the son of the Official (always in Cana), the forces of Jesus Christ will act in the soul to win over the luciferic death.

[393] The King corresponds to the fourth step of initiation that in that era was usually "black" (because it was gained with force and it was connected to power): the one of the anti Sun (while the Prophet is of the "true" son). The fact that they are talking about an official can lead us to think that he was on the third step of initiation, the one of the Venus-altar boy.
It's important to take note of the blood tie between the Official and the son. However, this sign is not in the Jewish context nor in a blood context.

[394] It's like saying that in the path of development of the Child, he had no spiritual forces, or better yet the forces of Mary. The Child represents the transition from Venus to the Sun. To be "with no strength" is the Incorruptible Body in his process of individualization by the I am.

[395] City in which Jesus lived with Mary. Macrocosmically it corresponds to the constellation of Cancer and microcosmically it corresponds to the ribcage. The fact that Cana is mentioned helps us to understand that we are in front of the second sign made by Jesus. At Cana he healed the forces wife-husband, which refer to soul-spirit, and now he is healing the forces father-son, old man-new man. The miracle of Cana is directed to the future (the wine that will become blood at the Last Supper), the royal official is mainly directed to the past, so that the hereditary forces of the father will not be passed on to the son. In this case, the official is used to obeying and so he is used to not making free and autonomous choices that require the strong presence of the I. The son (spiritual) needs to be healed from the weakness of the I (paternal).

47. When he heard[396] that Jesus came from Judea towards Galilea, he went to him and begged him to come[397] and heal (*iaomai*) his son (*hyios)*[398]*:* he was at the point of death that would do them part (*apothnesko*).

48. The Jesus told (*eipon*) him: "If you do not see signs and miracles, you will not believe (*pisteusete*)[399] and you will not have faith".

49. The royal officials says (*lego*) to him: "Sir, ascend[400] before my little child[401] enters to the death that does us part".

---

[396] On the contrary from the wedding at Cana, what is needed is that the Christ comes closer and the physical presence is not necessary. It's important to see that the official does not express his acceptance of the Christ's message: instead, he express the necessity of it. He is a commander, a man of power, at the most he can "beg" the Christ.

[397] The healing force of the I am has to *descend* from the faith in the depths of the human soul.
This is what he beg Jesus for, to descend within him.
At the wedding in Cana it was the Mother that interceded.

[398] *Hyios* is the term used for the spiritual son.

[399] The man needs to start "walking" and so the spirit can help him (verse 50).
Another analogous aspect with the wedding at Cana, now he expresses the disagreement upon acting.

[400]He goes back to the invocation of the I am to descend.

[401] From the Greek *paidion* which indicates the Child within us in the phase of the Spiritual Self.
The official calls the son "child" to indicate the filial connection that united them, Jesus will call him "son" to indicate the individuality that acts within him.
This term refers to the fruit that comes to life within us from the union between the right rational-empirical-masculine side and the left-intuitive-creative-feminine side. To the union right-left, the union above-head-sky and below-metabolism-earth is added. From these unions the "girl child" comes to life, and she indicates that it is not feminine nor masculine. We have three children: the Spiritual Self (the principle of the Holy Spirit within us that comes to life thanks to the transformation of the astral body); the Loving Vital Spirit (the Son within us that is born from the transformation of the etheric body); and the Spirit Man (the Father within us that comes to life thanks to the transformation of the physical body).

50. The Jesus[402] says (*lego*) to him: "Go[403], your son (*hyios*) spiritually[404] lives." The man (*antropos*) had faith (*episteusa*)[405] to the *Logos* that the Jesus told him (*eipon*), and so he went[406].

51. While he was ascending, his servants[407] went towards him saying that his young man[408] spiritually lives.

52. So he was questioning them upon the time that he was lifted[409]. They told (*eipon*) him that yesterday, on the seventh hour[410], the fever[411] left him.

---

402 Another correlation with the wedding at Cana. Now he acts even if he said he would not.

403 Also "to begin walking the path of life". The spiritual world desires this from us as well" that we keep searching for Truth. This "walking" is what matters to the Spirit and this because whoever yearns for this will meet the Christ eventually.

404 This is the second miracle (after the wedding at Cana) and once again two souls need to harmonize. The Christ acts so that within the soul of the official, the force of Faith can come to life and he can believe. If the official wouldn't have believed, the miracle couldn't have happened. We are in front of a strengthening of the forces of the Jesus: now it's not about harmonizing with the soul of the Mother, but instead with a stranger.
It's important to see how the Christ is not going to Capernaum, and he heals always by bringing (with the Word) the internal spiritual life to the ones that are ill.

405 He is not being identified with his public power, but instead as a "man".

406 He starts a spiritual path.

407 They represent the one that reached the solar sphere, and so the forces that are part of the Higher I. This allows us to understand the social rank of the official.
Another correlation with the wedding at Cana, the servants are a tool for the work that just happened.

408 Now he is a "young man", which still indicates a dependency with the father.

409 From the Greek word *kompsos,* which can also mean "clever, graceful". His Higher I was lifted.

410 From 18 to 20, corresponds to the Libra, the door between Light and Darkness within us. The son reached this point, he completed the purification and now he can be born. Jesus will be the one to cross the threshold of the Libra to bring consciousness in all the Dark Zodiac, within the unconscious forces of the man (see note John 13).
This also reminds us of the rhythm of seven, the rhythm of the human soul.

411 Manifestation of the luciferic forces in which the father was the bearer towards the son.

53. So the father[412] had clarity that (he was) in the time, that one, in which Jesus told (*eipon*) him: " Your son (*hyios*) spiritually[413] lives, and he[414] had faith (*episteusa*) and his whole house[415].

54. This second sign[416] was created (*poieo*) once again by the Jesus, coming from Judea towards Galilee.

---

412 Here is the completed transition: from Official to man, and from man to father: now he can generate the inner son in his life, the I am.

413 It's important to understand that the son wasn't only healed from the luciferic action, but he also received a new inner life. This is how great the action of the Christ is to the ones that open up to Him and his true Faith.

414 He thinks that the healed one is not his "child" anymore, but his "Son".

415 They spiritually are the higher auric bodies. In some texts, instead of "house" there is "family". This is to indicate that where there is unity, the faith of one person spreads to everyone else that partakes in the process of inner rebirth.
Another correlation with the wedding at Cana, now everyone believes in Him.
There is also the comparison with "his" (the "house" of Israel) that didn't welcome him in Judea: but now they welcome him: so now every "house" can accept him and welcome him.

416 Last correlation with the wedding at Cana, another sign, another start.

HEALING OF A MAN WITH NO STRENGTH

1. After these things[417] came the holiday[418] of the Jewish people, and Jesus went to Jerusalems[419].

[417] To indicate the concatenation of the events that are acted by Jesus.

[418] It's a Saturday, day that is dedicated to the relationship with the Spirit, day in which the forces of love dominate amongst men: these will be the new conditions needed to make the third miracle. This is the first Easter of John's Gospel.
In John's Gospel, three Easters are mentioned: *the first one* is soon after the beginning of Jesus' work (John 2,13), the *second one* is soon after the multiplication of the bread and the fish for the 5000 (John 6,4), and *the third one* is soon after the resuscitation of Lazarus (John 11, 55). This brings us to "three normal" Easters. Following these, there is a "special" *fourth one*: the one of the resurrection. The action of the Christ within Jesus is prolonged for three years and four months (3,3 in the decimal system), just how Lazarus stayed beyond the 3,3 days before resuscitating and just how Jesus was resuscitated after three days and a third (80 hours). Furthermore, the Christ also stayed in the grave that was represented by the physical body of Jesus for three years and four months.

[419] It's the second time that Jesus goes to Jerusalems, but this time he does not go to the Temple, instead he goes to the wounded ones, the sheep that have no shepherd.

2. In Jerusalemns on the Probatic[420] there is a pool, which is called Bethzatha[421] in Hebrew, and it had 5 covered porches[422].

[420] From the Greek *probatike* which relates to the sheep (*probation* means sheep). It also comes from *probaino* that means "to go forward, to proceed, to advance, to make progress". It was the pool in which the sheep that were destined to serve as a sacrifice would get washed. The "*probatio*" is the recognizing as good. It was also called "The Gate of the Sheep", which means of the Faith: but in this case the term "gate" is being omitted to indicate the static aspect of the sheep, the devoted ones with no shepherd.

[421] *Bethzatha* means "ditch, crevice, crack". It is located north of the Temple (and so amongst the elements of Water and Earth, in the quality of "cold") and it would separate a new neighborhood from the rest of the city. Bethzatha can be better translated as "home of grace or reverence or mercy" and it's beyond the valley (the Ditch) of Kidron. Nowadays it's called the Fountain of the Virgin and it's not too far from the Pool of Siloe. In a microcosmic sense, it finds a correlation to the dip that is find on the seven cervical vertebras and that is more noticeable when we bend our head back. The Pool of Siloe corresponds to the base of the cerebellum (John 9,7).

[422] To have 5 covered porches, 6 columns are needed. So now we are in front of the fifth and sixth day of Creation and now a man on the Path, that is left with no spiritual strength, can become a real man, entering the seventh day and overcome the luciferic obstacle.
The five covered porches of the pool come from the fact that it was trapezoidal and it was divided between east and west by a central wall. These walls formed an arcade where the ones that were ill could stay. From its depths, a few times a day, water would gurgle on the surface of the tanks and from there it would go to the pool and the baths.
The five covered porches (a superficial specification for our consciousness), indicate an opposition between the porches of the Temple and the remaining suffering people. In this case, the five porches indicate the five books of the Law of which Jerusalems was the custodian of the theological interpretation.
The second pool that we will encounter will be the one of Siloe where the Blind Man will receive the mud that was kneaded with Jesus' saliva which activated the process of re-formation of the man that will make him say " I Am". In both cases, it will be a Saturday, the seventh day, the day of the going back up to God.

3. Within them there were many[423] people with no strength[424], blind[425], crippled[426], paralyzed[427], that would receive the movement of the water.

4. An angel[428] of the Lord was descending at the right time[429] in the pool and the water was stirred up[430]. And who would descend (in the pool) first[431], after the stirring up of the water, would become strong and healed from any illness[432] that took over him[433].

---

423 The first stage of the formation of the illness.

424 Spiritual strength to continue the path of rebirth.

425 The one who, with an excess of egoism (of luciferic origin), can only see himself. In Hebrew, blind is said *iwer*, which pronounced *aor*, means a "tunic made out of skin", which refers to the skin that Adam was covered with after the Fall.

426 It's the second step (Mercury) of Initiation. The crippled is the one that struggles with going from familiar love to spiritual love. He represents the one that still hasn't married his own totality (one of his feet is still hurt), but he began this step towards "verticalization", the conquering of the 12 dorsal vertebras.

427 They lost the forces of the Holy Spirit, the forces that act on the right hand, the active hand, the hand that donates Life. They went through a process of Ahrimanization.

428 That brings the forces of the Higher I (the Angel within us); the Angel enters and mixes the water, the Higher I connect to the water and it heals the physical. For the born Blind, they talk about the Angel (the Delegate) but in the case of the one with no strength, the Angel is the one that acts with discretion, in the case of the Blind it will be him going to the pool and he will be the one calling the Angel.

429 It's the *"kairos",* the current of time is "full" (30 years) and the Light can burst into it in a metamorphic way. This action "descends", probably from the Pool of Siloe, which is the Angel within us, the I am.

430 From the Greek word *tarasso*, which means "moved from below to above". Also "to loose aplomb". A "hurricane" of spiritual forces would form and heal only one man.

431 From the Greek *protos*, first as a force of a light that creates.

432 From the Greek *nosema*, also "moral suffering, psychic illness, vice, dementia".

433 From the Greek *katecho*, plagued and held back in the spiritual path.
The healing is spiritual (Angel) but it's not Christic. It is not an increase in consciousness, which is the process of the I Am. It's important to see how only the "first" one is healed and this "first" one can be seen as the "first" part of ourselves. It's the individuality that is still in the embryo, the one that is activated to connect to the Divine and so it can create the requirements that the other components (physical body, etheric body and astral body) need to reconnect to the Divine.

5. And there was a certain man, that lived thirty-eight[434] years with no strength[435].'

6. And the Jesus, seeing (*idein*)[436] him lying and discerning that he already had much time, tells (*lego*) him: "Do you want to become strong[437] and healed[438]?"

7. The one with no strength replied: " Sir, I don't have a man[439] that, when the water is stirred up, puts me in the pool; while I arrive[440], another one descends before me".

8. The Jesus tells (*lego*) him: " Get up[441], grab your little bed[442] and go on[443]!"

---

[434] It was on its second "lunar node". The "lunar node" corresponds to the moment in which in the sky the same configuration of the stars that was present when we were born is showing, and this happens every 18 and half years. This showing again of the "initial conditions" of our life helps us to use this moment as a "new birth", a moment of extreme importance and change in our life. The clarification of the date means that the illness was in relation to its sin. Now Jesus has the strength to pour his inner strength out to the moral-soul like nature of man.
The number 38 corresponds to the period in which the Chosen People stayed in the desert before they arrived to the border of Israel (Dt 2,15).

[435] The term is *astenia* and it will show up again in John 11,4 and it refers to Lazarus.

[436] The ability to understand the laws of the Logos.

[437] It's the transition from *antropos to aner*: which means Enlightened. It's interesting to see how the one that is ill doesn't ask for anything, but it's in his *Kairos* and so it's as if he is asking since the same stellar conditions of his life plan reappeared.

[438] From the forces of the Obstacle.

[439] He is alone, no one is with him in time of need. The Christ will take care of this shortcoming since he is his *Kairos*. He sees and rewards his perseverance (*...knock and it will open up...)*.

[440] It's in the lower I, and since it has no spiritual strength he cannot connect to the angelic sphere of the Higher I.

[441] With this exhortation, he brings him to the seventh day.

[442] In the whole passage, "little bed" can also be translated as "burden". The little bed represents the test from which we spiritually grew. This is what characterizes us in our path. He will never be lost, even when we will be in heaven he will identify us.

[443] Literally "to walk around", observe your karma (burden) from different points of view so that you can conscious of the test you had to go through. Don't stop in your past, even if it was difficult. Instead take initiative and go through life! The presence of the Christ help us to overcome the need to lean on exterior things.

9. And, in that moment, the man became strong and healed[444] and he grabbed his little bed and went on[445]. And that day, was Saturday[446].

10. So the Jews said (*lego*) to the one that was cured[447]: "It's Saturday, it is against the law to take your little bed[448]".

11. And he replied to them: "Who created (*poeio*) strong and healed, he said (*eipon*) to me: "Grab your little bed and go on".

12. They questioned him: "Who is the man, that said (*eipon*) to you: Grab it and go on?"

13. But the one that was healed[449], didn't know who he was[450]. The Jesus left the crowd, that place[451]

---

444 From the greek *ughies*, represents the possibility for the Higher I to act on the interior and exterior plane.

445 To indicate the path that he still needs to go through to reach the I Am (just how the born Blind will do).

446 The seventh day, the day that God left to the man so that he can be fulfilled by ascending to Him. It's important to see how in the process of incarnation of the principle Christ in the Jesus, He still needs the external conditions of "help". In this case the day of prayer and devotion of Saturday.

447 Literally "*made servant*", and so taken to the step of the Sun.

448 Saturday was the day of the Grace. The Jews wouldn't let him work independently to his karma, of making him conscious and taking him. It's interesting to see how they are not amazed that he is healed, instead they are focused on the fact that is happened Saturday. Saturday was a sacred day for the Jewish people and so the priests would "manage it" as power.

449 Healed is the precise expression for the ones that are free from the luciferic force (also the castrated ox is a "healed one").

450 Even though he was healed, he didn't fully comprehend the merciful action of the Christ within him.

451 And that he mixed the water. He does not look for the approval or clamor of the world.

14. And then the Jesus find him in the temple (internal)[452] and he said (*eipon*) to him: "Look, you became strong and healed, don't do wrong[453] again, otherwise worse[454] will happen".

15. The man[455] went, and he announced to the Jews that it was Jesus that created (*poieo*) him strong and healed.

16. And for this reason the Jews persecuted the Jesus, because he would create (*poieo*) these things on Saturday.

17. And the Jesus replied to them: "My Father works (*ergazomai*) to this day and I also work (*ergazomai)*[456].

18. For this reason the Jews wanted to kill him[457] even more so, because not only was he dissolving (the bond) of Saturday, but he also said (*lego*) God was is Father, creating (*poieo*) himself equal to God[458].

---

[452] Grace manifest itself at the right time within the inner part of the man.
There are various "temples". The main one, the temple of Jerusalem, represents the forehead between the temples, and so the *chakra* with two petals, the so-called "third-eye". The second one is in Samaria-heart and the third one is in Galilee-perineum. In general, the temple is the place in which the spiritual forces can manifest.

[453] Jesus sanctions the relationship between the illness and the human error that came from the Fall. The wrongdoing is meant as "not giving testimony". The error is of the one that loses his way in the etheric plane, the plane of "debts", of habits and unilateral temperaments. It is the current of time and now, for the man, time is "full".

[454] He received a grace, to give thanks and walk the Path with no repercussions that would be worse than the first fault.

[455] He is no longer someone with "no strength", he is now a "man" (*Anthropos)* because he began to be aware of what happened to him. But he is not "saved", he only is "healed". This is because he still has not completely accepted the Word of Jesus within himself.

[456] In Latin "to work/to operate" is passive, so through us He can operate, He can work (we are His instrument).
The work of the Father now consists in the completion of the third part of man (the Spirit) even though he is continuing to maintain in the life of the other components (soul and body). Now he is the Verb incarnated that is being declared to the Jewish people so that our darkness can accept his light (John 1,5). This makes us go from his image to his likeness.

[457] From the moment that the Jewish people don't want to recognize him, in fact they kill him within themselves.

[458] The man will never be able to be exactly like God, but he received the task to grow and multiply the fruit of this growth so that he can become a new creating principle (always in unison with the Christ).

THE SPEECH OF THE SON: THE WORK OF THE CHRIST THROUGH THE LOGOS[459]

19. Jesus replies and said *(leghei)* to them: "Amen, Amen[460], I say (*lego*) to you[461]: the Son (*hyios*) has no strength[462] to create (*poieo*) by himself if not what he sees (*blepo II*) the Father creates (*poieo*). The things that he creates (*poieo*), the Son (*hyios*) also creates (*poieo*) these things[463] in a similar way.

20. The Father loves the Son (*hyios*) in a brotherly way, and he shows to him everything that he creates (*poieo*)[464], and he will show to him bigger accomplishments than these ones[465], so that you will be amazed[466].

---

[459] This passage has a therapeutic value that is extremely important, John's meditative reading, united with the one of the prologue, allows us to "ask" the Therapist that an object (or some water) becomes therapeutic to a certain person. It should be obvious that who wants to act in this way had to receive some sort of "special approval" from the Therapist.

[460] It's the fifth time that the Jesus says Amen-Amen, which is a universal truth and it is not limited to the specific time that he has someone in front of him. In this passage, he will repeat it three times. The first one is primarily directed towards the Father, the second one to the Son-Logos, and the third one to the Spirit within ourselves.

[461] And not to your old blood ties, people, etc. He speaks to the individuality, he speaks to the ones that began their spiritual path.

[462] He himself, as Son of man, as Jesus, is with no strength if he does not do the will of the Father and he is not united with Mary-Mother. To operate the forces of Mary-Mother are needed (who followed him) and to do the will of the Father is needed as well. This applies to us as well, and it concerns our inner wedding. Let's remember how in the previous verses, we spoke about the ones "with no strength" that He heals.

[463] The Father acts his work in the pure Spirit (the Spirit that is not manifested, the purest one, the inconceivable and the immeasurable essence of Love), while the Son acts (the same things) in the formed Spirit (or the manifested one).

[464] It cannot be given differently since they are one within the other.

[465] It refers to the victory upon death. Transform the matter in a new Spirit. To this, more work will be added that will have a greater impact,m but the humanity of that time was not ready to understand it.

[466] Amazement is the feeling that structures the soul to veneration; it's the feeling that opens us up to the higher level. From this, the feeling to elevate oneself to God can come to life, the feeling of rising up to a higher dignity.

21. Just how the Father raises the dead[467] and creates (*zoopoieo*) in spiritual life, the Son (*hyios*) also creates (*zoopoieo*) in spiritual life the ones he wants[468].

22. The Father judges no one, but he gave (*dedoka*) to the Son (*hyios*) full[469] judgment,

23. In order that everyone honors the Son (*hyios*), just how they honor the Father: who does not honor the Son (*hyios*), does not honor the Father, who sent him[470].

24. Amen, Amen[471], I say (*lego*) to you that the one who listens[472] to my logos and believes (*pisteuo*)[473] to the one that sent me, will have eternal spiritual life, and he does not come in judgement, but he went from death to spiritual life[474].

25. Amen, Amen[475], I say (*lego*) to you that a time will come and now[476], when the dead will hear the voice of the Son (*hyios*) of God, and the ones who will hear (*akuou*) it will spiritually[477] live.

26. Just how the Father has spiritual life within him, he gave (*edoka*) spiritual life to the Son to have within himself;

---

[467] The ones that do not believe in the existence of the Spirit are dead and so they have no spiritual life within themselves. The higher work will be the one of the resurrection of the ones who do not believe.

[468] The life given by the Father is the divine spark within man; the one of the Son is the new Spirit generated after the terrestrial experience. He gifts life basing it to His will, which is always right and merciful because it is connected to the perfection of the Creator.

[469] The Son does not utilize this "power", instead he mirrors us so that we can judge ourselves and we can educate ourselves. This is because He has within himself the synthesis of the masculine and the feminine. Since he is incarnated, the Son experienced the human condition (which fell within matter) without being contaminated by Evil. Therefore, the Father gave him the "power" of judgement upon each "flesh", which means upon every state that is denser than the spiritual one. This means upon the spiritual, soul-like, etheric and physical plane (this is the "whole"). From this, "to eat his flesh" means to adapt to His way of living in the terrestrial form. He is completely pure even though is spirit is a prisoner of the flesh.

[470] To honor the Son means to conform to His Word while recognizing his Justice and Truth.

[471] Now he is referring to Jesus himself: the Son.

[472] The one who uses his ears for spiritual listening.

[473] For the difference between "having faith" and "believing", see John 1,7.

[474] He is conscious of his spiritual reality; he has awaken from the dead.

[475] Here we have the third amen, amen. Now he is referring to us.

[476] This is the *Kairos*, outside of time and space. The time is also a petal of a *chakra*.

[477] The arrival of Jesus (and Christ) on Earth is the big (and last) opportunity given to the "dead" to wake up and recognize the action of the Spirit.

27. And he gave (*edoka*) him the power to create (*poieo*) a judgment, because he is the Son (*hyios*) of the man[478].

28. Don't be amazed by this, because a time[479] will come in which everyone that is in the memories[480] will hear (*akouo*) his voice[481],

29. And they will go, the ones who create (*poieo*) for the better, in resurrection of spiritual life[482]; the ones who practiced (*poieo*) evil, will resurrect in judgment[483].

30. I do not have the strength to create (*poieo*) on my own anything[484]. Just how I listen (*akouo*), I judge; and the judgment, my own, is right, because I do not look for the will, my one, but the will of the one who sent me.

31. If I give testimony around myself, my testimony will not be true[485].

32. Someone else is testifying about me, and I know the testimony he testifies about me is true.

33. You sent someone to interrogate John, and he testified the truth[486].

---

[478] Because the Christ is also Son of man. In the Jesus Christ there is the Jesus component, human, and so he can judge men. This is why he is Jesus Christ the Lord of karma. Jesus manifests how man should have been if he wouldn't have welcomed the luciferic impulse.

[479] The time is the moment in which the individual consciousness wakes up, so that one can judge oneself and one can welcome the impulse of the Christ thanks to the seed of individual consciousness brought by Jesus.

[480] The ones who walked the Path up to the head, up to the inside of the cranium and they experimented the memory of their own divine origin. The fact of "remembering our own divine origin" means to "know" that God exists and we are part of Him, we belong to Him, we are called to Him to return and so we have to do His will. To refuse to do so, is the sin of impiety.

[481] This voice will be heard in the internal also by the ones who are still in darkness.

[482] It's the Holy Spirit that gives life. Death is only a transition towards a resurrection within the Spirit. Within Jesus, this can be seen to the highest expression because He did not abandon the physical body, instead he made it spiritual.

[483] He will have to reincarnate. We are now in the level of Everything of the Everything.

[484] Jesus speaks as a pure instrument of the Father.

[485] For the Hebrew Law, a testimony was real when brought by two people. He announces himself free from this condition and he revokes the consciousness of people.

[486] The Baptist is part of the Nathan Soul and so he was able to testify. Strictly speaking, this "John" represents the Spirit that manifests itself in the ones who rose to this initiation step. Jesus is testifying for all humanity.

34. But I do not welcome the testimony from man; instead I say (*lego*) this so that you will be saved[487].

35. He was the burning and shining lamp[488]. But you decided to be excited about his light for a brief period of time.

36. But I do have a higher testimony of the one of John. The tasks (*ergon*) that the Father gave to me so that I could achieve them (*teleioo*), the same tasks (*ergon*) that I create (*poieo*)[489], will testify about me, that the Father sent me.

37. And the one who sent me, (who is) Father; he himself testified about me; and you never heard his voice[490], nor seen (*horao*) his shape[491].

38. And you do not have his logos that remains within yourselves[492], because you do not believe (*pisteuo*)[493] in the one whom he sent.

---

[487] Salvation consists in reconnecting to the Christ who is the Life. This happens through Faith (the Path), and so from this, this is possible. After this, the man's spirit needs to transform his soul to make it conscious of the Truth and so it can bring the whole individual being to his eternal salvation, which means to a full consciousness, to perfection, to Life. Jesus accomplished all of this in only one existence.

[488] Just like in the "Prologue", it was the Light. John is not yet the "true Light" (John 1,8). Instead, he represents the light of discernment that gives us the possibility to see within ourselves and to straighten up the path of the spirit.
The "lamp" or "torch" or "reflected light" (in a lunar sense). It represents the inner light that each man has, but it gets turned on by our inner work. It is a gift of the Spirit (see verse 25). It represents the forces of the Spiritual Self that came to life from the transformation of one's own soul; this transformation happens in the mysteries of Light. It also represents the "horn", which is the organ to perceive the Spirit. It comes to life from the transformation of the lower bodies. The Jewish people perceived the Spirit through the forces of blood. But now everything changes, the Messianic "horn" completes its deployment in the person of Jesus Christ: from seed born into a family, it becomes seed of People and then seed for the whole humanity.

[489] His fruit.

[490] The voice of Logos.

[491] Also "image", which is the creating Word that finds form in the image. This "form" is the Christ himself.

[492] In the inner part of the man, in his "I Am".

[493] For the difference between "having faith" and "believing" see John 1,7.

39. Inspect the scriptures, because you believe to have within them eternal spiritual life[494]: and those are the ones that testify about me[495];

40. And you do not want to come to me to have spiritual life[496].

41. I do not welcome the glory from men[497],

42. But I discerned within you, that you do not have the spiritual love of the God[498] .

43. I came (*elelytha*) in the name of my Father, and you are not welcoming me: if someone else would come in his name, you would welcome[499] him.

44. How do you have the strength to have faith (*pisteusai*), that you welcome glory from one another, but you do not seek for the glory that is close only to God[500]?

45. Don't think I will accuse you near the Father; there are the ones that will accuse you, Moses in which you trusted[501].

46. If you believed (*pisteuo*) in Moses, maybe you will also believe in me; he wrote about me.

---

494 The letter kills, but the Spirit gives life.

495 The reason for the testimony comes back. John's whole Gospel is permeated by it. From the three testimonies of John, to the ones of the Christ and now the ones of the Scriptures.

496 This is because the man often is detached from thoughts and feelings of the world and he does not seek the divine.

497 The term "glory" means the highest clairvoyance and clairaudience, which is the complete vision and the complete listening of God.

498 The main strength that man needs to cultivate within himself is the one of true love, the love that takes us to perfection.

499 Because he would come with human logic.

500 He encourages us to have Faith, Faith that takes us to a true Spiritual Life.

501 This is because Moses was the Great Guardian of the Threshold and he judges the human karma. After the Golgotha, this function will be one of the tasks of the Christ, who will be in mercy and not in the Law. The Christ will have this rule because, through Jesus, he went through the complete experience in the human plane (and also in the human condition).

47. But if you do not believe (*pisteuo*) in his writings[502], how will you have faith (*pisteusete*) in my words (*rema*)[503]?"

---

[502] The word that is dead now.

[503] This passage is correlated to chapter 17, 1-26: the priestly prayer of Jesus. The term used is *rema*, which is part of the Word-Logos; it is like saying that they cannot comprehend even a small part of what He came to bring to humanity. To want to examine in depth the Logos, represents the Divine aspect that he leads, that everything leads to the conquering, from the man, to Freedom and Love. After the luciferic fall, it was necessary to determine new evolutionary conditions for humanity. It was necessary to operate the redemption (or freedom) or Adam, and so also of humanity. The Christ, who is the Logos of all Logos, descended in Jesus-Logos to carry out His plan of salvation for us.

THE MIRACULOUSLY NOURISHED CROWD[504] (Mt 14,13-33; Mc 6,30-522; Lc 9,10-17)

[504] A well-rounded vision of the multiplications.
The first one is for the 5000 and there are 12 baskets (the number 12 is the number of the "celestial" things). This multiplication happens soon after the Easter and it happens to give to the Enlightened ones the spiritual nourishment that will prepare them to deal with the Holy Death. After this, Jesus will appear as the one walking on water and Peter will descend on water but he will not sink. Philip will say that 200 coins are not enough to feed the people: the 12 will reply to the Gift of multiplication with no Faith.
The Second multiplication (that is not reported by John) is for the 4000 and there are 7 baskets (number of the planetary things). After this, the disciples forget to take the bread: they will respond to the Gift with a lack of Consciousness.
The Third multiplication takes place at the Last Supper and it is for the 12. After this, they won't pray (lack of Faith) nor will they guard (lack of Consciousness) the Gethsemane. This corresponds to receiving the strength for the transformation of the physical body into the Body of resurrection, and the corresponding virtue is Hope.
The Fourth one (the "+1") is the miraculous Fishing (John 21,1) and it is for the 7 disciples. The 7 are on a boat and they toss the nets on the right side as the Risen Again (Faith) commanded. Peter wraps his hips and he jumps in the water ("descending"), and then he ascends ("going back up") and he carries the net on the earth (to descend and then to ascend means to broaden the multiple consciousness, and to then bring them here on earth from which the boat was apart by 200 cubits: the number of man's bones) with 153 big fish. After this, Peter will not manifest spiritual love (*agapeo*) for Jesus (he already lost consciousness). Elijah (the entity that is now acting as an illness of the Baptist in unison to Jesus) also multiplied the bread and he did this at Sarepta (Phoenicia) in the home of a widow. He then resuscitated the son (2R 4:1-7, 42-44; 2 Co 9:8-10). This widow did what Elijah said; her family and Elijah, and she had food for a long time. The flour in the vase and the oil will not run out (first King Chapter 17). Therefore, the spirit Elijah-Baptist is participating in the multiplication that is being done by Jesus.

60. After these things, the Jesus went on the opposite side of the Sea[505] of Galilee[506], of the Tiberias[507].

61. And a great crowd followed him, because they could see (*theoreo*) the signs that (He) created upon the ones that had no strength[508].

62. Jesus went up the mountainside[509]: and he secretly[510] worked with his disciples[511].

---

505 The Sea of Tiberias represents the soul sphere in relation to the zodiacal forces. From the soul point of view, one "side" of the Sea of Tiberias (the Western side), represents the part that is being lived in and so it is connected to the things of the world (fishing men, traffic, etc.). The other side, the Eastern side, represents the deserted side, the silence of the Spirit that illuminates the soul. In Luke's verses, it is said that Jesus goes to Betsaida (and so on the western shore, in the region of the Virgin). From the spiritual point of view, the western side represents the Bright Zodiac (from Aries-head to Libra-hips), which is the part of us that is already conscious. The Easter side represents the Dark Zodiac, the part within us that still needs to be conquered (from Libra-hips to Pisces-feet). In this case, Jesus is in Capernaum (north part of the western shore) and so he is headed towards the eastern shore, towards the spiritual Life. It's the desert behind Bethsaida-Virgin, where at the end of it, there is the accumulation of 2500 galaxies. These galaxies, as a macrocosmic placenta, nurture and feed our zodiacal system through the constellation of the Virgin and through the star Spica. The "fallen" constellation of the Virgin represents the rigid and formal interpretation of the Scriptures (materialistic intellectual mindset of the scribes).

506 Represents the forces of the Father connected to Judaism.

507 A city on the western shore of the Sea of Galilee, which was founded on 20 A.D. in honor of the Emperor Tiberio. It was a nice city, and it seems like Jesus always avoided it. He would always go to the Jewish cities around the Sea. The Gospels do not describe a visit to the city, but only some boats of the city (John 6,23). The Sea of Tiberias is the Sea of Galilee. The fact that the lake is both called of "Galilee" and of "Tiberias" (which is the religious- Judaic name and the political name connected to the emperor Tiberio), indicates that it acts for both the Judaic world and the pagan world. Given the spatial indication, the evangelist captures the events in the mysteries of Space-Light-Soul.

508 He is manifesting is higher self: the Christ. He gifts the strength of spiritual healing to the souls that have no strength who followed him from the western side to the eastern side.

509 It represents the inspirational consciousness. Jesus is preparing himself to give new teachings. The teachers of the Temple, when they were conscious about these teachings, kept them a secret.

510 Literally "you could see", therefore it stopped the will to fulfill the inner spiritual work. Given the high level of consciousness from which John was observing the events, we rather translate the expression directly into its esoteric meaning.

511 This is the fourth miracle performed by Jesus and he accomplishes it by using the souls of the disciples, which were maturing more and more towards his Greatness. The Christ can now awaken within them a healthy soul-like force, and His force flows within the disciples. The force of the Christ flows in the man that was ill for 38 years, and now this force also flows within the disciples: what lives within the soul of Jesus Christ can now live within the disciples.

63. Easter[512] was near, the holiday of the Jewish people[513].

64. As Jesus lifted his eyes, he saw (*theaomai*)[514] that a big crowd was coming towards him, and he said (*lego*) to Philip[515]: "Where will we but bread, so that they can eat?[516]"

65. He said (*lego*) this to test[517] him; he already knew what he was about to create (*poieo*)[518].

---

[512] The entering of the ether of Light within Earth. Within the course of the year, it corresponds to the Enlightenment in the mysteries of Light. See note John 2,23. The theme of the "transition" comes back (Easter means transition). It's always the divine intervention that helps us and supports us through these "Transitions".
Let's remember that in John's Gospel, three "+1" Easters are mentioned.

[513] Citizens of the desert Of Judea, which recalls the intuitive consciousness. The passage will describe the ascension of consciousness to the macrocosms, with the Christ being the guide for the Apostles.

[514] From the verse can understand how it's a spiritual turmoil and not a crowd of people. The verb used is *theaomai*, which means "to spiritually contemplate".

[515] Philip represents the will, determination, the decision. He is the first apostle that Jesus invites to "follow him", which means to become active (John 1,42). This could mean that the strong will to follow the Teacher, is the soul-like quality that we need to receive the spiritual nourishment and to go back to the Father.

[516] He asks Philip (who incarnates the Decision amongst the Twelve) a "materialistic" question, and this is to test him. We need to remember that man first needs to assimilate on earth (sitting on earth) the spiritual consciousness and then he will be able to find direct nourishment in Heaven.
The bread (Eucharistic) feeds and nourishes our I, but mostly in the sphere of feeling and thinking. The wine, on the other hand, in the wanting.

[517] He tests them to see what the level of inner comprehension of the disciples is.

[518] He acted the will of the Father (this is why he talks to Philip who represents the will).

66. Philip replied: "The bread of two hundred[519] coins[520] is not enough[521] for them so that each one can get a little piece".

67. One of his disciples, Andrew[522], brother of Simon Peter, says to him (*lego*):

---

[519] Number of the bones of the physical body. What develops from the material corporeality (the bread) cannot nourish the crowd. In hebrew, the twentieth letter is the 200 and it's "*res*" which means "head" and it indicates the receptivity on the cosmic plane, just like the "you" created receives the cosmic creator "I". It's connected to the constellation of Pisces.
The 5 pieces of bread represent the part of the Bright Zodiac that is completely in light, and the two fish represent the two constellations that border with the Dark Zodiac (Aries and Libra). From these 7 forces, 12 baskets will appear, from the inner world that still is luciferic, the astral aspect of 7 (heredity, the time) goes to 12, to space, to fraternity based on Freedom (see page 137-138 of "The cycle of the year as a path of initiation" of S.O. Prokofieff). The passage represents the complete victory upon the luciferic forces (and the Ahrimanic ones) of the astral boddy; the Ahrimanic forces are represented by the reference of the 200 coins.

[520] It was the pay for a day's work. 200 coins represent the work of a year and so, metaphorically, of an incarnation.

[521] Philip does not do the mistake to "explain" to Jesus what to do, instead he just states how humanity has a great need for material and spiritual nourishment. He allows divine mercy to intervene.

[522] Andrew, from the Greek *andreia*, is courage, virtue of *aner*, of the Enlightened one. The spiritual quality that he incarnates is the Prayer. He talks to Jesus on his own initiative, he goes deeper into the reality of the moment and he prepares himself for prayer.

68. "There is a little child[523] that has five pieces of barley[524] bread[525], and two fish[526]; but how far will they go for so many[527]?"

---

[523] It's the Child of the Loving Vital Spirit, of the principle Son within us. Since the bread was made out of barley and so represents the Old Testament, this Child can represent the Son of the Old Testament; therefore Jesus himself came to do the will of the Father and he also brought the fruit of his incarnation. Barley does not rise on its own, an enzyme is necessary, a yeast: the spiritual nourishment brought by Jesus.
With the term "Child", the fruit that comes to life within us from the union of the right rational-empirical-masculine and the left intuitive-creative-feminine is intended. To the union right-left, the union above-head-sky and below-metabolism-earth is added. From these unions, "the child" comes to life to indicate that it's nor female nor masculine. We have three children: the Spiritual Self (the principle of the Holy Spirit within us that comes to life from the transformation of the astral body), the Loving Vital Spirit (the Son within us that comes to life from the transformation of the etheric body) and the Spirit Man (the Father within us that comes to life from the transformation of the physical body).

[524] Barley is also the grain of Mars, and so it offers us the forces for inner transformation. From Latin "*hordeum*", "order of God", the chemical ether connected to Mars and the Law. In Arabic it's called *sabar*, "desert"; in Greek *arista*, the better part.

[525] Bread", in Sanskrit, is said "*budhi*", old name of the Loving Vital Spirit. Here they represent the spiritual nourishment. They are not made out of wheat, they are made out of barley because they represent the nourishment of the Old Testament. Barley has a panicle that can be taken off but with a lot of work and this is why it is the letter of the Old Testament: it's wrapped up with the shell of many different meanings. But if you can reach the inner part, it nourishes and it fills you up. Jesus brings the wheat, which is easy to open and it gives a greater nourishment. The child that brought them could also represent the "Son" of the People of Israel, the one that was bringing the bread exactly like a child would do, without eating them. As we said earlier, this Child is Jesus himself, the one who represents the "Holy Birth".

[526] It's *opsarion* which meaning is exactly "fish".
Often it gets translated as "small fish". If this were the case, fish are also symbol of what lives in our sub consciousness and needs to be brought into our consciousness, and from this we have the various miraculous fishing. Its scales represent the Ahrimanic aspect, and its foul smelling insides represent the luciferic aspect. Its being with "no neck" represents the lacking of the word, of *Logos*. Let's remember that they were created by God on the fifth day (and so they are less evolved) while the other animals were created on the sixth day. The fish has the characteristic to absorb oxygen from water (through its gills) and by doing so it releases the atoms of hydrogen. These two atoms are the representatives of the cosmic Life and the earthly life. Furthermore, hydrogen is the door, the force that dematerializes matter, and brings everything back to the Spirit. Additionally, the Greek word for fish was an acronym for the first Christians. The greek term *ichthus* was for *iesus christus theu uios sother*, which means "Jesus Christ Son of God the Savior".
In this case, given their importance, they can represent Jesus himself (the big fish) and the Baptist (the small fish). Since they are cold-blooded animals, they represent that to perfection the soul, we need to overcome all passions and material desires.

[527] It's interesting to see how Andrew (the Enlightened One) uses the *parlar coverto* with Jesus. He asks a question that will have an extremely deep answer.

69. Jesus then said (*eipon*): " Create (*poieo*) the men[528] (in the position of) laying down[529]". There was a lot of nourishment[530] in this place. And so the enlightened[531] ones laid down, and the number was about five-thousand[532].

70. Jesus grabbed the bread and, giving thanks[533], he distributed it to the ones that were still standing[534], and he did the same with the fish[535].

---

528 The *anthropoi,* and not the initiated ones. He makes their lower part "lay down" because the first nourishment needs to come from earth. Also for the spiritual path, first we need to study, research, analyze what the world offers us (book, studies, experiences) and then we can be directly nourished by the Spirit.

529 Create the spiritual conditions so that the *antropos* can receive spiritual nourishment. Take note that by laying down, you "look up above".

530 Or "hay", which is dried grass (etheric), united with the Sun. It's the etheric transformed by the Son-Spiritual Self into Loving Vital Spirit. With this expression, they are talking about the new spiritual nourishment that He gifts us. In Luke's Gospel He makes them lay down on "higher beds", precisely (from *klisia*, which is a variable of *kline*), the bed of initiatic death which means "hut". Luke captures the solar origin of this new nourishment.

531 The *android*, the Enlightened ones that accomplished the internal marriage between soul and Spirit.

532 The number five-thousand represents the fifth era of culture (the present one) that began n 1412 and that will end in 3572, which is spiritually characterized by the development within humanity of the conscious soul, which is the aspect of the soul that feeds itself of the spiritual ideals of Truth, Good, and Right. The conscious soul is the soul that can develop within itself the Son of the man, represented by the bread that the men of the fifth era receive as nourishment. This "Bread of Life" contains within itself the seed of the Upper Limbs. The fifth era of the post-atlantean culture is the era in which the Christ manifest himself in the etheric plane; and it's the era in which humanity can accomplish the complete zodiacal initiation. The children were then nourished to expand to the Loving Vital Spirit.
The five-thousand also represent the part of the crowd that had the forces to access the new spiritual nourishment. Time wise, this will happen with the fifth era of culture.

533 By doing this, he consecrate what humanity can offer to the Spirit. This anticipates the moment of the establishment of the Eucharist, when the Christ himself will become Bread of Life for humanity.
It's important to see how Jesus "gives thanks" before the distribution, or better, before the miracle. By doing this, he anticipates the "prayer of certainty" that he will fulfill at the resuscitation of Lazarus.
We can also think that he had a certain way of breaking the bread, a way that would allow to recall the I Am of the observers and to allow it to descend within them. He blesses (from the Greek *euLogos*, the "good-*Logos*") the bread, and so he recalls with his hand the descending from Above of the forces of the Father, and then he breaks the bread. By doing this, the I Am of the people descends in an "open" form of their bodies and it unites with them. The "open" form of the physical body is the form that our physical body ""had" before the Fall, therefore when it was still "not material": the I Am descends in the Incorruptible Body and it personalizes it. From this we gather that the Grail Cup is the Incorruptible Body before the Fall.

534 Which means sacred, chosen.

535 The man begins to nourish himself by accepting to lay down, which means to place his will in harmony with the Divine One.

71. Once they all had enough to eat[536], he says (*lego)* to his disciples: "Gather the left overs, so that nothing goes to waste[537]".

72. So they gathered them[538], and they filled up the twelve[539] baskets of left overs with those five pieces of barley bread, which ended up being more[540] than expected.

73. Those men (*antropos*), capturing (*idein*) within the *Logos* the sign that he created (*epoiesa*), said (*lego*): "He truly is the prophet[541] that comes to the world".

74. But Jesus, knowing that they were about to kidnap him to make (*poieo*) him king[542], he retreats up the mountain once again, by himself[543].

---

[536] Nowhere it is said that they ate in the physical sense, instead it is said that they were full. The nourishment was in an etheric form thanks to the interpenetration of the Christ within the sphere-etheric body of Jesus. The disciples "distributed" this christic force to the ones that were present (force that interpenetrated them) and they allowed each one to take in the appropriate "nourishment" depending on his or her level of spiritual maturity. The "nourishment" consists in perceiving the force that came from the etheric body of Jesus Christ. They nourished themselves with the prayer (the giving thanks) with which Jesus took the bread.

[537] It's the Bread of Life, it cannot be left to die. This is the cosmic law of the universal economy: nothing can be lost. Therefore, the crowd did not have the strength to "eat" everything that was gifted to them.

[538] They rebuilt the connections of life, brought by the inspirational consciousness (they are on the mountain) and by the Loving Vital Spirit.

[539] Twelve is also the number of the dorsal vertebrae through which the man can be erect (after the "formation" of the 10 sacrum-lumbar vertebrae that represent the Law). The Zodiac surrounds the rhythmic man through the 12 doors of the 12 vertebrae: entering the mysteries of Light.

[540] Each and every spiritual entity is nourished depending on its level of consciousness, and they're still in spiritual nourishment and this is sacred and it cannot be lost.

[541] The ones who did not receive Enlightenment , only see the "prophet" aspect of Jesus and not the Son of God that is within him.

[542] The crowd wanted to make Jesus king so that they could take advantage of the material benefits of his action, just how the Church of Rome is doing now. But others (the apostles) recognize the spiritual value of his teachings and they recognize the fact that he is King of a higher world. To get away from this, he goes up the mountain once again, which is a spiritual region in which they cannot reach him.

[543] Comparisons between these events and the Easter of resurrection can be made.

- The Multiplication corresponds to the Last Supper;
- In the next passage (John 6,22-41) He declares himself to be "Bread of life" and this corresponds to the celebration of the Eucharist of the Last Supper;
- "now he retreats" corresponds to retreating to the Getsemani and to the descending of the Father with the crucifixion;
- Now they want to "make him king", corresponds to the appearing to the 11 on the Sunday evening (and they still do not recognize it, Lk 24,7);

THE DISCIPLES SEE JESUS WALKING ON WATER (Mt 14,22-33; Mc 6,45-52)

75. When the evening[544] came, his disciples came down to the Sea[545].

76. And, once they got on the boat[546], they reached the opposite shore of the Sea, in Capernaum[547]; and the darkness came, and Jesus was still not with them[548].

77. And, a strong wind[549] was blowing, and the Sea was getting higher[550].

---

[544] The active forces of the Sun end, and now we are entering the luciferic darkness, and the forces of Virgo are helping us which act at 6 pm.

[545] They go from the inspiring consciousness of the mountain to the imaginative one of the Sea.

[546] The term boat (or small boat) corresponds to the Hebrew *Merkaba,* which is the part of us that is transformed (or the part of the upper limbs that is conquered), the one that helps us move in the astral world (the Sea).

[547] The city of "consolation" where Jesus has lived since the second year of his public life. It's subsoil is made of basalt. It corresponds to the constellation of Cancer. It is not said that they "descend on earth"; they probably rise to the level of Capernaum and then they wait for Jesus to "descend" to them when the Sea is unleashed against them.

[548] Jesus puts them to a little test so that they can be conscious of the new spiritual forces that they accomplished through the feeding of the 5000.

[549]The wind expresses the luciferic forces. They were not able to connect with the forces of Virgo-night and so they fall into the Scorpio-Lucifer forces.

[550]From the Greek *diegheiro*, also to excite, to animate.

78. Rowing for about twenty-five or thirty stadium[551], they saw (*theoreo*)[552] Jesus walking[553] above the Sea[554], he was approaching the boat and they were afraid[555].

79. But he said (*lego*) to them: " I am[556], don't be afraid".

---

[551] Stadium is the measurement of space-Light: 30 stadium correspond to the development of the I am; 25 stadium indicate that they are on that path and that they have almost arrived to destination (represented by the number 30). Now the Jesus can help them, now that they have given the best of themselves. Now the Incorruptible Body of Jesus dominates the sphere of the Water element: the I Am is ready.

[552] It is here clearly said that they "spiritually saw" (*theoreo*) Jesus walking on the waters and not Jesus "walked" on the waters. The Apostles were in the "small boat" and the action of the Christ was increasing more and more within their souls, so much that they could see his action even if He was far away from them.
The Christ establishes a soul connection even when we are far from Him. It is typical of this spiritual vision to capture the spiritual image of the ones that are far just as if they were close. With this affirmation, we have an additional reinforcement of the action of Jesus within the human souls (obviously for the ones that are suitable).

[553] From the greek *peripateo*, the initiation walking "around".

[554] The Jesus manifests his capacity of "walking", and so to dominate, above the Sea of passions that unsettle the soul.

[555] When a higher reality manifests itself to us we always feel fear.

[556] **This I Am is not connected to the path of the 12 I Am**, but it is its introduction: to win over fear. This is the true regality of Jesus, which it's the capacity of the I to dominate the lower elements. Jesus calls the I am of the disciples so that, with his strength, they can win the test.

80. They were willing to take him on the boat[557] but right away[558] the boat reached[559] the earth[560] to which they were headed to.

EUCHARISTIC SERMON (THE BREAD OF LIFE) (Ex 16,13; Ps 77,24; Sap 16,20)

81. The day after[561] the crowd[562], the one that was on the other side of the Sea[563], saw (*eidon*)[564] that there was only One[565] boat[566] and that Jesus did not enter the boat with his disciples, instead only the disciples had left;

---

[557] From this we can understand how the boat is the part within us that is transformed (or the part of the upper limbs that is conquered) with which we move in the astral world (the Sea).

[558] Just as the Apostles become aware of the reality of the spiritual vision, they "immediately" reach their destination.
This reinforces the fact that the vision was spiritual and so it was out of space and time.

[559] Now the verb is in a past tense to indicate that the test exists and it does not exist depending on whether we are in the I Am or not.

[560] Now they descend to the objective consciousness.

[561] After having elaborated through the night all that they perceived on the day of the multiplication.

[562]The one Jesus gave bread to nourish them.

[563] We are on the mountain side of the Sea where the multiplication took place, and so we are on the eastern-desert-spirit shore. This is the side of the crowd-humanity which is still not aware of possessing the I Am. They assisted the multiplication and they were amazed by it. Now they are alone and they are starting the path in search of the Truth.

[564] This is also a spiritual vision like the one of the disciples that "saw" Jesus walking on water.

[565] The term boat (or little boat) corresponds to the Hebrew *Merkaba*, which is the center of our higher consciousness (connected to the transformed part of us or the part of the upper limbs that are conquered) with which we move in the astral world (the Sea). It corresponds to what was individually developed by the Son of man and God. "Boat" is also "Ship", which in Italian contains The Ave (Hail). It's also *Bar-arche'*, the principle Son. In Greek, it comes from *Pleiadi* (force of Michael). It's the Principle Son that is within the soul, from which the seed of the Loving Vital Spirit comes. "*Navis*" in latin contains *avis*, which in latin is "bird", which is the animal that is connect to the Old Saturn and so the future Volcano, the conquering of the Spirit Man. There is also "*vis",* Mary's force. The "Boat" is the Principle of the Son of man and of God. The "little boat-*Merkaba*" is personalized. It also corresponds to the mean of "navigation" for the internal waters: from the "below waters", through the spinal fluid, up to the cerebro-spinal fluid.

[566] It's the archetype of the small boat.

82. Then other boats came along[567] from Tiberias[568], near the place where they ate the bread, having the Lord[569] giving thanks[570]

83. When the crowd saw (*eidon*)[571] that Jesus[572] was not there[573], and neither his disciples, they spiritually descended into the boats and they went to Capernaum in search of the Jesus[574].

84. And by finding him on the other side of the Sea, they said (*eipen*) to him: "Rhabbi[575], when did you become[576]?"

---

[567] They came from above.

[568] It represents the constellation of Aries-head, and so the beginning of the path of spiritual comprehension.

[569] The one who dominates the astral sphere (Sea) and the elements (wind), and so it refers to multiple levels, just how the crowd is at different levels. Given the reference of the Lord in the astral plane, it could be that it is the crowd that is acting on this level, in the plane of the ego. "The Lord" indicates the sphere of Saturn.

[570] To give thanks in Greek is *Eucharisto*.

[571] It's always about an inner spiritual vision.

[572] Without the article. They see the man-Jesus, the one that dominates the astral-Sea.

[573] The crowd is looking for him.

[574] They are not autonomously moving, and so they are not being led by a chief but from their own I. This act of "good will" will make them find Jesus and they will be directed by him.
So we have the crowd that finds itself (from the day before) in the location of the multiplication. From Tiberias-Aries-Head they descend on the "little boats" that represent the "change mind" and they lead the crowd to Capernaum-Cancer/Ribcage-changing of the heart. From this union-wedding, the crowd will meet Jesus-the Child son of the wedding.

[575] They are talking about, on the sea-astral plane, about the pure soul of Nirmanakaya of Buddha. It is on Jupiter's level.

[576] This "became" (in the location, in the plane) is the *egheneto*, so they are asking when this happened, but they yet have to have a full comprehension about it.

85. Jesus replied and said (*eipon*): "Amen, Amen, I say (*lego*) to you: You look for me not because you saw (*eidon*) the signs[577], but because you ate the bread and you were nourished[578].

86. Work (*ergazomai*) (to look for) not the food that goes to waste[579], but the food that remains for eternal spiritual life, that the Son (*Hyos*) of the man will tell you[580], this the Father confirms[581] (by being) the God[582]".

87. So they said (*eipon*) to him: "What will we create (*poieo*) to fulfill (*ergazomai*) the works (*ergon*) of the God[583]?"

88. The Jesus replied and said (*eipen*) to them: "This is the work (*ergon*) of God, that you would believe (*pisteuo*) in the one that he sent[584]."

89. And so they said (*eipon*) to him: "What sign are you creating (*poieo*) so that we can grasp (*idein*) (the Logos) and so that we have faith (*episteusa*) in you? What will you accomplish (*ergazomai*)[585]?

90. Our fathers ate the Manna[586] in the desert, just how it's written: *He gave them the Bread from heaven to eat*".

---

577 That they already knew; see John 6,2.

578 It's not a scolding, but an exhortation to go spiritually deeper in what they have received from grace; to go deeper in the fact that within Jesus, the forces of eternal spiritual Life descend.

579 The food that goes bad is not only the material food, but it also is the truth that we listen to but that we do not capture within ourselves. The true food needs to be produced by us with the in depth examination of the Truth. Here we have the difference between three different foods: the material one, the spiritual one that is not examined in depth within ourselves, and the "procured" spiritual food which is extracted and then analyzed through inner work. This last one is the one that is also never externally forgotten.

580 Only in the future will it be given to us (and not "gifted"): when we will be ready to welcome it without distorting it to our own liking and or measure. It will become an acquired possibility.

581 From the Greek *Sphraghizo* which means to seal, to hide, to confirm.

582 To ascend to Bread of Life, the Son of man is not enough; we need to ascend to the Father. This is the Father of the Holiest Trinity.

583 The step taken from them is remarkable: they immediately associate the listening of the Word with the doing the will of the Father.

584 Here we have the task of our era, the first step for the spiritual path: Faith.

585 It's the old aspect of the crowd, the one of the Fall, that asks to transition to the new.

586 The *manas*, the Son of man, the Higher I. The fathers of the crowd received nourishment for their Spiritual Self, and now they cannot understand why they should nourish themselves with something different.

91. And so the Jesus said (*eipen*) to them: "Amen, Amen, I say to you, not Moses gave the bread from heaven[587] to you, but my Father gives to you the real bread from the sky, the real one.

92. The bread of God is the he[588] who descends from the sky, and he who gives spiritual life to the world[589]".

93. Therefore they said (*eipon*) to him: "Sir[590], always give to us this bread[591]".

---

[587] They are referring to the Manna, the celestial gift that would appear every morning and they could not take more than the daily dosage. Manna becomes the image of the *manas*, of the Higher I, of the Son of man with his daily rhythm. Manna means "to think", and this means that a nourishment that was inclined to thought was given to the Jewish people of the desert, and this means that they were given a chance to think differently about the relationship with the divine (the change mind). Let's not forget that the crowd comes from Tiberias/Aries/head.

[588] Jesus Christ.

[589] He is the true celestial nourishment.

[590] Here they refer to Him as the Sir of the astral sphere (fifth step, Mars' sphere).

[591] They now believe but they still act passively.

THE BREAD OF LIFE

35. Jesus said (*eipen*) to them: "I am the bread[592] of spiritual life[593], who comes to me[594] will have no hunger[595], and who believes (*pisteuo*)[596] in me, will not be thirsty[597].

36. But I told (*eipon*) because you saw (*horao*)[598] and you do not believe (*pisteuo*).

THE BREAD OF LIFE

[592] The first I Am: it corresponds to the level of the Sun.
We can think that he had a particular way of breaking the bread, a way that would allow to recall the I Am of the people that were present and allow it to descend on them. He blesses (from Greek *eu-logos*, which means to express the "good" Logos) the bread, he recalls with his right hand the descending from Above of the forces of the Father, and then he breaks the bread.
By doing this, the I Am of the people descends in an "open" form of their physical body and unites with it. The "open" form of the physical body is the form that our physical body "had" before the Fall, which means when it was still "non material": the I am descends in the Incorruptible Body, and it personalizes it.

[593] This means that we need to nourish ourselves from the source, which is the I Am. This corresponds to the *chakra* of the Sun, the door of the heart. This Bread is the one that he etherically multiplied thanks to the prayer to the Father. Nourishing oneself of the " I Am" means to begin to identify with it and not the ego, and by making the spiritual "flesh" become the "flesh" of Jesus himself (John 6,54). This nourishment molds the Incorruptible Body by personalizing it and making it ready for the Resurrection.

[594] The connections between "coming to Him" and hunger, and "believing in Him" and thirst are important. "Coming to Him" means ascending to the solar dimension, given the "original" connection of Jesus with the solar sphere and the one of the Christ when he "descended" from the cosmos to Earth. The "coming to Him" means to ascend to our Spiritual Self. "Believing in Him" indicates a Path, a path that sees Him as the Guide and it will take us where we no longer be thirsty for knowledge, for Truth: in other words from the Sun we will ascend to the Zodiac and beyond, up to the Holiest Trinity.

[595] Because He will have nourishment for each and every material, etheric, soul and spiritual necessity. This concept is expressed another three times (John 6,41-48,51) to indicate that He feeds all four of man's bodies.

[596] For the difference between "having faith" and "believing", see John 2,11.

[597] The thirst of spiritual knowledge, from the Holy Trinity to the Holiest Trinity.

[598] The verb of spiritual vision comes back.

37. Each and every thing that the Father gives to me[599], will be attained by me and I will not send away[600] the one who comes to me.

38. Because I descended the sky, not to create (*poieo*) my will, but to create the will of the one who sent me.

39. and this is the will of the Father who sent[601] me: that I do not waste[602] all that He gave me, but instead I resuscitate it in the last day[603].

40. This is the will of my[604] Father, that whoever sees (*theoreo*)[605] the Son (*hyios*), and believes (*pisteuo*) in him[606], shall have eternal spiritual life, and I will resuscitate him on the last day".

41. the Jewish people started whispering about him, because he said (*eipen*): I am the bread, the one that came from the sky,

---

599 He underlines that the intimate essence of Jesus is the Father himself. He is open to helping every man even if he does not have the full knowledge of the higher reality of Jesus Christ. By welcoming him within ourselves, which means to take the first step towards Him, we are welcoming a seed within us, a seed that will then develop more and more and it will help us to adjust our thoughts, feelings and actions to His teachings up to the awakening of the consciousness of the I Am.

600 He doesn't reject anyone, not even the evil ones, but the evil ones themselves are getting away from him.

601 Of the Father of the Holiest Trinity, who sent the Jesus so that within humanity and within Earth he could imprint the seed of Spiritual Love.
This passage, from verse 39 to 41, **represents the true Eucharist of the Spirit** that only John captures. At the Last Supper, he does not report the act of the Eucharistic celebration; instead he reports the Washing of the Feet. For John (that is for the one that recognizes and believes in Christ and therefore is united to Him in the operating Love), this is enough so that the Father calls him, through the path or resurrection, to become his Son.

602 See John 6,12. Also "to disperse", which is "*diaballo*". The Son wants that everyone is One with the Father.

603 This is the day in which the divine Work within man will be completed and humanity will reach the level of evolution needed to enter the spiritual Kingdom from which even greater perfection can be reached.
The last day corresponds to the seventh day of Creation.

604 Doing the will of the Father has three aspects or phases:

- Respect the Commands that He gave us ("Father" aspect)
- To do what He internally tells us to do with the inner Word ("Son" aspect)
- To put ourselves at His complete disposition, at his Service ("Holy Spirit" aspect).

This represents a transition from the condition of "duty/obligation" to a condition of "Freedom". From this the fourth aspect can come to life, the "+1", the "prize": to reach the eternal spiritual Life.

605 Literally "meditates in God".

606 Again "believing" as a tool to ascend beyond the Son, towards the Holiest Trinity.

42. and they said (*elegon*): "Is this not Jesus, the son of Joseph, whose father and mother[607] we know? How can he now say: I came from the sky?"

43. Jesus replied and said (*eipen*): "Don't whisper amongst each other[608].

44. No one has the strength[609] to come to me if the Father who sent me does not draw[610] them and I will resuscitate him on the last day.

45. It's written in the prophets: *And they will all be taught by God*[611]. Each and every one who heard the Father and has learned[612], come to me[613].

46. Not because someone say (*horao*)[614] thee Father, only who is from God, he [615] saw (*horao*) saw the Father.

47. Amen, Amen I say to you who believes (*pisteuo*) (in me) has eternal spiritual life[616].

48. I am the bread of the spiritual life[617].

49. Your fathers ate the manna in the desert and they deeply died (*apothesko*).

---

[607] They refer to the hereditary-biological aspect of Jesus; they do not capture the spiritual aspect in Him, the descending from the sky.

[608] Do not judge with human forms the Divine.

[609] From the Greek *dynamis*, the force that moves.

[610] Through an inner calling.

[611] Of the things pertinent to God. The verb is *didaskalo*, and so it is a spiritual-scientific instruction. It's not from the formal observance of the teaching that we become disciples of God. It's God himself that instructs us through thoughts, intuitions, sensations, feelings, symbols, etc using the various spiritual Hierarchies.

[612] As knowledge of the disciple.

[613] The Father is the Spirit that lives in each man. Everyone who will walk the spiritual path will reach Jesus Christ and the Father.

[614] To see the Father means to be and to rest within the perfection of the full knowledge of Truth. Only Jesus and Mariam reached this destination.

[615] The Son (Him), that can see him.

[616] Who believes in the I Am and from him he draws and through Faith he can come to life to the real Truth. Each man is destined for eternity, also his Incorruptible Body is destined for it, but he needs to re-ascend with consciousness to this through the meeting with the Christ. And by doing so, we will go back to being God's image and liking.

[617] Only by accepting the I Am (and it's action in the Incorruptible Body), we will go back in being connected with the creating forces that will take us to eternal spiritual Life.

50. This is the bread that descends from the sky[618], so that someone will eat it and he will not deeply die.

51. I am the bread, the one that spiritually lives, the one that descended from the sky. If someone will eat this bread, he will spiritually live in eternity[619]: and the bread that I will give is my flesh[620] that I will give for the spiritual life of the world[621]".

52. and so the Jewish people were fighting amongst each other, and said (*lego*): "How does he have the strength to give us the flesh to eat?"

---

618 It's important to see how the Bread "descends", and so the process continues.

619 We "eat" the Christ when we believe in Him.

620 This word has deep and complex meanings. From the Greek *sarx*, it has two meanings: "flesh", "man", "human nature", "corrupted nature", "mortal life", and also "king", "queen", "strength", "sovereign ruler". If we follow the spiritual meaning of each letter that form the word, we find that : S (within ourselves, in the cave in which we enter), A (beginning, primordial beginning), R (the Father, the highest aspect), X (the coffin, the grave, what is below). Therefore, the "flesh" is the tool for the manifestation of the divine principle. In Hebrew, flesh is *basar* and it means "primordial earth" and the word contains the syllable *sin* right in the middle which means 300, which is the number of movement, of dynamism. The 3 (the ternary principle of God that overcomes the luciferic duality) descended on Earth (basar) as a seed for the change of the human flesh, to achieve the ultimate wedding, the inner wedding. The flesh becomes the location for the total completion, the one of the most intimate union with God. Finally, always from Hebrew, we find that *basar* comes from *basorah*: the good News, the Gospel. *Basar* is the abbreviated form of *beresit*, the "principle" of the Genesis, and so *basar* represents the Christic principle that manifests itself, while *beresit* represents the un-manifested Principle.
This "flesh" is the spiritual essence of the Christ which was manifested through his works, and it was understood by all humanity thanks to His Word. This nourishment that He offers to humanity is the first spiritual Body created in the celestial Paradise by Jesus himself, who is the Creating God, and it corresponds to the Body of resurrection. By coming to Earth, he transformed it according to man's needs, and he made it apparent and visible even though its spiritual perfection remained intact.

621 This flesh-Body of Resurrection is live nourishment since, He has won each terrestrial tie and everything was regenerated through Him by imprinting the image of the divine Man. He who allows these forces of will of Jesus Christ to flow through him, will be nourished and made strong. He uses the future tense to indicate that he still needed to accomplish the transformation work of His body, which will only happen to the Getsemani. The world represents all that was created and all that will need to be transformed.

53. Jesus said (*eipen*) to them: " Amen, Amen, I say (*lego*)[622] to you: if you will not eat[623] the flesh of the Son of the man[624] and you will not drink his blood[625], you will not have within yourselves[626] spiritual life.

54. Who eats[627] my flesh, and drinks my blood, has eternal[628] spiritual life, and I will resuscitate him in the last day[629].

55. my flesh is real[630] food, and my blood is a real drink.

56. who eats[631] my flesh, and drinks my blood, will stay[632] within me, and I will stay within him[633].

---

[622] The Cosmic I says to the human I.

[623] It's a subjunctive and not a future.

[624] Principle of the Higher I, who nourishes himself with it will then be able to develop the Loving Vital Spirit (the spiritual Life) and the Spirit Man (eternal Life). This means to allow all of Jesus' works to become within ourselves.

[625] To allow the direct knowledge of his manifested Spirit to flow within us.
The eating of the flesh and drinking of the blood corresponds to the **Bride-Groom Relationship** since the "red" flesh is moistened with blood and the blood moistens the flesh.

[626] All of this corresponds to the establishment of the Eucharist. This is why John does not speak about it at the Last Supper: within his knowledge, the event had already started and it never ends. The phrase could be said this way: If you eat the heat (the meat corresponds to the bread, fruit of the heat of the Sun), the fire that comes out of me which is the operating Love, and you drink my Light (the blood corresponds to the wine, fruit of the solar light), which is spiritual consciousness, then you will have eternal Life because these gifts will regenerate you, and they will transform you in becoming Sons of God. The flesh-body and the blood-life/energy/consciousness are two poles to which man can connect and draw by putting himself in communion with the Christ.

[627] The verb is *trogo* and it indicates the cavity of the mouth. We can also think that the interatomic spaces that are "free" from the matter of the body (and so only the substance remains), get "filled" from the Resurrection body of Jesus. This finds a correlation with the so called "black matter" that permeates the cosmos, "matter" that in reality does not exist, but it is the Sea of the forces of the cosmic Life that surrounds everything.

[628] This is because he who eats his flesh and drinks his blood, is welcoming within himself the thoughts and the impulses of love of the Christ and he is making them his own. Therefore, he becomes more and more independent from the body and the matter and so he can be eternal.

[629] The last day corresponds to the seventh day of Creation.

[630] From Greek *"aletheia"* (see the Prologue).

[631] See how the verb is in the present tense.

[632] Therefore it's "in the now".

[633] The true disciple of Jesus lives within Him, he abides by His Word, he lives in the love and in truth and so within him, living Love and Truth live. At the same time, he has within himself Jesus Christ Himself.

57. Just how the spiritually living Father sent me and I spiritually live through the work of the Father; the one who will eat me, will also spiritually live[634] through my work.

58. This is the bread that came from the sky. Not like the fathers that ate the manna, and deeply died. Who will eat this bread will spiritually live[635] in eternity.

59. He said these things (*eipen*) teaching in synagogue in Capernaum[636].

DOUBTS AND DESERTIONS

60 Many listeners, amongst his disciples, said (*eipon*): "This verb (*logos*) is hard[637], and who has the strength to listen to it?[638]

61. Since Jesus knew within himself that the disciples were whispering about this, he said (*eipon*) to them: "This shocks you?[639]"

62. If you will see (*theoreo*)[640] the Son of man ascend where he once was[641]?

63. The spirit is the creator of spiritual life, the flesh[642] does not benefit from anything. The words (*rema*) that I said to you are spirit and spiritual life.

---

[634] The verb is in the future tense: the times are not yet "full" for this transition.

[635] The verb is still in the future tense.

[636] Even though it was informal, the title of 'Rhabbi" was recognized and so he could teach in the synagogue.

[637] Also "hard". The term "dry" reminds us of the "dry path" of the alchemist, which is the direct transition from Earth (physical body) to Fire (Spirit). It comes from Jesus Christ; they grasp the harshness and incisiveness of his essence. At the beginning, they just grasp the empty exterior formality, as if it was a dogma. With the opening of their consciousness, they will be able to understand the teachings, and they will be able to follow them through their inner initiative.

[638] They understood that "eating the flesh" and "drinking the blood" would have led to a complete transformation (to welcome within themselves the thoughts and impulses of love of the Christ and making them their own) of their "old" being and so they do not accept it.

[639] Which stands for: "is it your obstacle?" Is it that hard to unite Spirit and matter? Is it that hard to welcome within yourself the divine Word?

[640] Like "meditating in God".

[641] In the Etheric Ring. He pre-announces His Second Coming/Arrival when he will donate to men the possibility to ascend to the spiritual plane and transform the material body into the Body of Incorruptible Light. This also happens every time we formulate a pure and creative thought (even if we are not conscious about it. The transformation of the material body can be defined as "Work of the Holy Spirit".

[642] As physical body, shell. It's only a part of the creature, and it's on its way to being perfected. It receives everything and it cannot gift life.

64. But there are some amongst you that do not believe (*pisteuo*)". Jesus knew from the beginning who the non-believers were, and also the one that was going to deliver[643] him.

65. And he said: "this is why I told (*eireka*) you that no one has the strength to come to me, if it wasn't given to him by the Father[644].

66. Since then, many of his disciples pulled back, and they did not go around[645] him anymore.

67. So Jesus said (*eipen*) to the twelve[646]: "Do you want to leave too?"

68. Simon Peter[647] replied: "Lord[648], near whom[649] will we go? You have words (*rema*) of eternal spiritual life[650]!

---

[643] With these words, he confirms that listening to the Word and being close to Truth are not enough to have Faith. Only operating in rhythm and in coherence with them will prove that one has Faith.

[644] The only way to understand the divine Word is by welcoming the divine impulse that lives in the depth of the I Am of each one of us. However, this has to have the blessing of the Father (which is the direct Spirit that is above every form). This a blessing that He gives only after he has verified the effective inner progress of the disciple.

[645] They do not follow him because they do not want to practice the teaching.

[646] All the various levels of the Twelve, from the Apostles to the Milky Way.
Twelve is also the number of the dorsal vertebrae through which man can be vertical (after the "formation" of the 10 sacrum-lumbar vertebrae that represent the Law). The Zodiac surrounds the rhythmic man through the 12 doors of the 12 vertebrae: we are entering the mysteries of Light.

[647] The Apostle has two names. Tt's like saying that his whole being (old and new) believes in Christ.

[648] It's the Lord, the God of the various planes, and this reinforces the interpretation that he speaks to the Twelve on all levels.

[649] "To whom" indicates movement, an ascesis.

[650] Now Simon Peter recognizes that through Jesus Christ, the words of the Father are manifesting.

69. And we believed[651] and we have known[652] that you are the Saint of the God[653]".

70. Jesus replied to them: "I did not choose you the twelve[654] and One of you is the devil".

---

[651] Now they believe because they got to know. To believe we need spiritual will and courage.

[652] They know, thanks to the forces of the purified intellect. Here Jesus Christ is being recognized as "Saint of God", which is as a being that came to the world, but he remained completely uncontaminated by the world. We now have three transitions connected to the forces of Mars: Lord (v.68), You have words (v.68) and now the knowledge-discernment.

[653] With this phrase, Simon Peter recognizes the Christ within Jesus, and he recognizes that the Christ is operating to the transformation, to the personalization of the Incorruptible Body of Jesus into the Body of Resurrection: he recognizes that he is working to form the "Saint of the God". The path of ascension to the Father goes through a first phase of Faith, which means that we rely on things that are still not completely known, but we consider them good and right. After this, we have the phase of "certainty", which is of the direct knowledge of these things: the "believing".
The third phase is to become "one" with these truths.
To recognize the Jesus in the "Saint of the God" means that Peter arrived to perceiving the presence of a new Spirit, a Spirit that was created by Jesus as a man-God, and it can be defined as "the Holy Spirit of Jesus" (or the Spirit of the Spirit of God), and then it was left by Jesus himself for humanity (John 7.39): this is the physical body permeated by the Incorruptible Body and then again personalized by the I Am. This process has yet to come to completion, but it advanced to the point of being able to be perceived from the Apostles. This Spirit is the Spirit that the Risen Again breathes upon his disciples on Easter Sunday and it has to be seen as the "third Paraclete".
The **first Paraclete** (which means "lawyer" or "mediator") is Mary the Helper, who assists the soul in the path of
The **second Paraclete** is Jesus himself, the "exterior" Comforter: "*Come to me, all of you who are tired and oppressed, and I will restore you*" (Mt 11, 28).
The **third Paraclete** is the Spirit of Truth that Jesus breathed upon his disciples on Easter night and he said: "*Receive the Holy Spirit*" almost by begging them to accept his gift (John 14,16).
The **fourth Paraclete, the "+1"** is the redeemed Lucifer that will descend on Mariam during the Pentecost **(the first Paraclete)**, on the disciples that ascended to the step of Jesus **(the second Paraclete)** on which the Risen Again had already blown His Spirit (**the third Paraclete**).
This whole sentence recalls the passage in which Jesus asks to the twelve "Who do you think I am?" (Mt 16,15 and others) and the Peter replied "You are the Christ, the Son of the God, the one that spiritually lives". But now Jesus does not reply to Peter.

[654] He did not choose all the 12; in fact Judah was brought to him and He welcomed him. It is not said in the Gospels when he welcomes him, and he always appears to be the last one amongst the 12.

71. He was referring to the Judah of Simon Iscariot[655]; he was about to deliver him, (since he was) One of the twelve[656].

THE JESUS AT THE FEAST OF THE TABERNACLES

1. And after this Jesus was going around Galilee[657], and he did not want to go around Judea[658] because the Jewish people wanted to kill[659] him.
2. They were close to the feast of the Jewish people, the one of the raising of the Tents (the Tabernacles[660]).

---

[655] Judah was the apostle that was majorly connected to the specific Hebrew element. He is not able to find the transition to the Christian element and for this reason, he needs to go through the hard test of betrayal.
Jesus tells them that even though they grasped that within Him there was a new Spirit, they still have a part of themselves that is not holy and that is contaminated by the devil.

[656] Judah is presented through the hereditary lineage that is united with the old initiation. Judah incarnated the force of Scorpio, of division, of death. When each one of us "deliver" the forces of the Spirit to passions and egotistical impulses, we act like Judah. Within this, Judah is the One of this principle within us.

THE JESUS AT THE FEAST OF THE TABERNACLES

[657] Esoterically, Galilee represents the House of the Father and the human metabolism, the area of darkness in which the Christ brings Light.

[658] Esoterically, it represents the House of Holy Spirit.

[659] From the Greek *apokteinai*= "*apo*" means "to distance, to reject". *Kteina* means to kill. The compound word means that the Jewish people wanted to distance him- to reject him, and this determines the fact that the principle Jesus dies (it is killed) within them. This happens because of the luciferic force that entered in (through Judah-Scorpio). Jesus does not want to go to Galilee, not because he was afraid of getting killed, but because He does not want to force His presence on the ones that are not ready for it; the ones that are not ready to perceive him and understand him. This is because the strength that He gives us could be misinterpreted and misunderstood by man and it could become his conviction. Killing him implies an ahrimanic action.

[660] This feast (celebrated in autumn) reminds us of the escape from Egypt of the Hebrew population, during which the temples were being set up as mobile tents. During this feast, the Hebrew people would spend 7 days in a tent to remember the 40 years in the desert in which the Christ himself nourished them. In this period of time, they would try to perceive the mystical presence of the long-awaited Messiah. The Hebrew festivities were three: Feast of Tabernacles, Easter and Pentecost.

3. His brothers[661] said (*eipon*) to him: "Leave from here and go towards Judea, so that your disciples can see (*theoreo*) within God the work that you create (*poieo*)[662]".

4. No one creates (*poieo*) something in secret[663] and searches for freedom for being in action[664]: if you create (*poieo*) these things, then show yourself to the world[665]!"

5. Not even his brothers[666] believed (*episteuo*) in him[667].

6. So Jesus says (*leghei*) to them: "My appropriate (*Kairos*) time is not here[668] yet: but your appropriate (*Kairos*) time is always here[669].

---

661 Esoterically corresponding to the sixth step. His brothers were still connected to the blood ties and so they though that they would gain prestige if He would reveal himself as the Messiah to the priests.

662 There are some of His works that he does not do; those are the ones for which their time has yet to come.

663 By saying this, they are trying to incite Jesus' ambition. This entails a luciferic action.

664 No one can actively engage in spiritual matters while being in the matters (actions) of the terrestrial world. But nowadays things are a little different.

665 They represent the ones that, because of arrogance or something else, want to explain to God how He needs to behave.

666 It is odd that his brothers, (apostles and disciples) send him to the disciples. These "brothers", are religious "brothers", which are the ones that belong to the current of the Therapists, an undercurrent of the Essens in which He formed himself.

667 Regardless of the physical closeness, they did not comprehend who He was, they did not comprehend His inner perfection, His mission on Earth.

668 He is still not available, he still has to arrive. In this vision, it's the appropriate timing that gets closer to man and not vice versa. Man's task is to always be ready.

669 It's already written. In Greek *Kairos*, "the right/appropriate time" or "time of truth": it is up to them to recognize Jesus' being. Additionally, since they do not have the strength to win over death, they can die at any given point, and their death will have no chance of resurrection.
This whole phrase tells us that the time of the higher Good has yet to come (thanks to the Cross of the Golgotha everyone will be able to access the power of achieving his own whole divine nature) since there they have a low capacity of comprehension, while the time of Evil is always present and ready to act out.

7. The world does not have the strength[670] to hate you[671]: but it hates me[672], because I testify about it, that its works are evil[673].

8. Rise to the festival[674], but I do not rise to this festival, because my appropriate (*Kairos)* has not yet fully[675] come.

9. After he said (*eipon*) these things, he stayed in Galilee.

10. Since his brothers rose[676] to the festival, he also rose; not in an apparent way, instead in secret[677].

11. The Jewish people were looking for him at the festival and they said: "Where is he[678]?"

12. And in the crowds[679] there was a widespread whispering about him. Some said he was good. Others said: "No, but he deceives the crowd[680]."

---

[670] From the Greek *dynatai*, from *dynamis*, the force that moves.

[671] Since they were still connected to the old Initiation, they did not have the strength to transform and redeem the Earth and the matter did not "bother" Ahriman (see the further notes). Jesus' brothers are not hated because Ahriman (the bearer of hate), at the time had just started getting closer to humanity, but he always hated and knew the Christ, who is the bearer of Love. The Christ is the One that brings us the strength to transform the Ahrimanic hate and fear into Love, so that we can become beings that irradiate Love freely, after rejecting the concrete possibility of becoming source of hatred.

[672] It's Ahriman that hates Him.

[673] The Greek term for "evil" is "*ponera",* meaning "heavy" or "weighed down". Jesus does not judge men but he verifies that men's works are "heavy"; they are weighed down by the heavy materiality and so they are far from spiritual perfection, far from the divine law.
For this reason the spirit of the world (Ahriman) hates him, because He makes the unworthiness of certain actions clear. Likewise, he does not hate Jesus' brothers because they are still at his mercy.

[674] The verb "to rise" indicates that this feast had the task to internally raise men.

[675] The feast reminds us of the wait for the Christ; but now He arrived, and so he has no reason to go to the feast.

[676] They spiritually rose and so they purified themselves (at least partially) from the luciferic impulse.

[677] He is God and so He is present everywhere. He does not manifestly rise but He is with them, in "secret".
He goes to accompany his brothers, probably moving with the forces of the Incorruptible Body.

[678] They looked for him externally: Jesus does not show himself to them.

[679] The plural form indicates both the crowds of Good and the crowds of Evil.

[680] The crowds of Evil are receiving another teaching. and not all Jewish people are happy about it.

13. But no one was openly speaking about him for fear[681] of the Jewish people[682].

DEEDS AT THE FEAST (Mt 13,54; Lk ,47)

14. But, being already at the peak of the feast, Jesus rose to the temple (internal)[683], and he taught.

15. And the Jewish people were amazed and they said: "How does he know about letters[684], when he never studied?[685]"

16. Jesus replied and said (*eipon*): "My doctrine is not mine, it is the one of the One who sent me[686].

17. Whoever wants to create (*poieo*) his will, will know whether this doctrine comes from God[687] or if I speak[688] on my own[689].

---

[681] Spiritual.

[682] Of the magical actions that they could "move".

[683] There are various "temple". The main one, the temple of Jerusalem, represents the forehead between the temples, and so the *chakra* with two petals, the so-called "third-eye". The second one is in Samaria-heart and the third one is in Galilee-perineum. In general the temple is the place in which the spiritual forces manifest themselves.
The Greek language uses two terms for "temple". They are "*hiero*" and "*naos*".

[684] From Greek *grammata* which are the letters of the alphabet, which are the alphabetical "signs" that we use to write. The Hebrews used to only write consonants and the Scribes and the Rabbis knew how to "read" the letters. The term grammar is correct in which the Hebrews used to write only with consonants and no punctuation. From this we have the difficulty to "know how to read" and so to know "spiritual grammar".

[685] In the rabbinic schools. This makes them even more so suspicious towards him.

[686] His teaching is not written in books; instead it is in the Spirit and in man's consciousness that heads towards Good, and so man can listen to the Spirit and recognize him.

[687] Only by practicing the will of the Father, can man learn to distinguish the divine teaching from the human one, because this way he receives the inner light that allows him to recognize the Truth and have the certainty that Jesus; teaching has a higher origin.
This also represents a transition from the condition of "duty" to one of Freedom. From this the fourth aspect can come to life, the "+1", the "prize": to reach eternal spiritual Life.

[688] "If you think I want to create something of my own, you will know through the doctrine if I am talking about myself or if what I am telling you is coming from the Father".

[689] He himself, as Son, conformed all of his will to the one of the Father, even though he had a different will from the one of the Father. He was "Father" within his inner being.

18. Who speaks on his own, searches for his own glory; but he who seeks for the glory of who sent him, is a truthful[690] man and within him there is no injustice[691].

19. Didn't Moses give you the law? And none of you creates (*poieo*) the law[692]: why are you trying to kill me?[693]"

20. The crowd[694] replied: "You have a demon[695]: who is trying to kill you?[696]"

21. Jesus replied and said to them: "I created (*ergon*)[697] a[698] unique work, and you all are amazed.

22. This is why Moses gave you the circumcision[699] not because it is from Moses, but from the Fathers, and you circumcised a man on (the day of) Saturday.

---

690 Truth substantiates our body of faith (soul) and the truth will set us Free.

691 Justice presumes discernment of the heart and therefore of Love. To have discernment, man needs to have free and conscious thoughts, and he needs to reflect the spiritual laws within his heart.

692 He works to create the living law, which is the 11th commandment.

693 Not recognizing it within themselves. Through these consecutive questions, Jesus wants to make the ones that are present conscious of their inner contradictions and their lacking of coherence. The Law: they do not comprehend the deep spirit, and they limit themselves to the exterior observance.

694 Of the Jewish people representing the humanity that is still dimmed by Evil.

695 They are still prone to the forces of evil, and they attribute to Jesus their own limit.

696 They did not consciously say that they wanted to kill him, but without recognizing him and without wanting to do the Father's will, they killed him within themselves. They believed they were right and Jesus exposes their illusion.

697 One: numeral.

698 Forever. It refers to the paralytic at the pool. This sign went beyond their comprehension capacity: what would they do if He would do everything that is in his power? Do they not understand that the whole world was "*made through him*?"

699 With circumcision, the child was consecrated to the spiritual journey. It represents the "pruning" of the flesh (of the tree of life) that will allow us to penetrate the inner journey, and it will take us to the inner wedding. The "tunic of skin" that get taken away represents the tunic of skin with which Adam and Eve were dressed with after the expulsion from Paradise. The three phases of the ceremony (cut, exposure of the skin, suction from the priests which connects the soul to the blood) will find their "+1" in the blood that Jesus will gift to the Passion by becoming the "circumcision of the world" (respectively: flagellation, the emptying of the subtle bodies and the sponge of vinegar.

23. If a man receives circumcision on Saturday, to not break Moses' law, why do you get mad at me for creating a strong and fully[700] healed man on Saturday?

24. Do not judge based on appearances, but judge with the right judgment[701].

25. Some of the Jerusalemites said: "Isn't he the one they are trying to kill[702]?"

26. And here he is talking with freedom of action, and they do not say anything. Maybe they really know the principles[703] that he is the Christ[704]?"

27. But we know where he is from: the Christ, on the other hand, when he will come, no one will know where he is from[705]".

---

[700] In the sense of "complete". If the Law considered the exception of circumcision to the prohibition of work on Saturday, it should be even more so to heal the whole man.

[701] Jesus invites them to perceive the Truth within their inner being, the Truth that will set them Free.

[702] They perceive this desire to kill Jesus' impulse within their inner being and they believe it to be a clue that He is not the son of God because they believed that who is in God should not fear anything.

[703] Of the priests and of the crowd.

[704] In Jerusalem, "some" begin to reflect on the divine presence of Jesus. They are not internally free yet and so they delegate to the "principles" the discernment upon Jesus.

[705] Or "where he comes from". The ones who haven't internally examined the spiritual research with humility and patience, will not be able to comprehend where He comes from.

28. Jesus said with strength[706], teaching in the temple (inner)[707] he says (*lego*): "And you know[708] me and you know where I come from[709], and I did not come (*eleytha*) on my own, but he who sent[710] me is true, and you do not know him[711].

29. I know him: "because I am from him, and he sent[712] me."

30. They tried to seize him: and no one laid a hand[713] on him; because his hour had not yet come.

31. Many people from the crowd had faith (*episteusa*)[714] in him and they said: "When the Christ will come, will he not create (*poieo*) more signs than the ones that he created (*poieo*)?[715]"

---

[706] The term *ekraxen* contains "*krato*", the strength, and so the force of Mariam. When Jesus speak in this particular way, Mariam is supporting him.

[707] For "temple" see note on the verse 2.14

[708] In Greek *iodate*, which means I know because I saw.

[709] Because he is manifesting in the Incorruptible Body, and so his paradisiacal origin.

[710] He received a task that he needs to fulfill.

[711] Because you did not see the Father and because you did not accomplish the necessary inner transformation.

[712] The delegate was sent to accomplish the task, and he is doing it. He maintained the connection with his origin and he conserved the consciousness even after incarnating himself in a physical body. We, carnally conceived, loose this consciousness. Jesus, conceived in the Holy Spirit, maintained it.

[713] This term is usually translate as "hand", but it can also be translated as "maniple", which is the combination of the negative entities evoked by the Jewish people upon Jesus.
The hand, in Hebrew *yada*, represents knowledge, the wisdom; but it also means "I love". This knowledge is marriage, and it is spiritual love.
In the sense of the tri-articulation of the whole arm, it represents the Holy Spirit (while the forearm represent the Son and the arm represents the Father). In the psalms' tradition, the right arm represents the Holy Spirit that gives life, and the left one represents the Son that structures, shapes, molds. The two hands put together represent the union of the force that structure with the knowledge that gives life. They cannot own the Spirit of Jesus, which is absolute Truth and Freedom. They cannot do this because they have not achieved the Spirit within themselves.

[714] For the difference between "having faith" and "believing", see John 1,7.

[715] The most naive part of the people recognized Jesus from his works, thanks to the forces of good feeling.

32. The Pharisees[716] heard the crowd whispering about him; and they sent the principles of the priests and the Pharisees[717] and the chiefs[718] to take him[719].

33. Jesus said (*eipon*): "For a little bit more time I will be with you and I go to the One who sent me.

34. You will search for me, and you won't be able to find me, and where I am, you will not have the strength to come to[720].

35. The Jewish people said: "Where is he headed to, that we won't be able to find him?" maybe he is leaving for the diaspora of the Greeks[721] or to teach the Greeks?[722]

36. What logos is this, that he said (*eipon*): You will search for me, and you will not be able to find me: where I am, you will not have the strength to come to?"

---

716 They were part of a religious and political movement of great influence, extremely connected to the Hebrew traditions. They believed in the resurrection of the dead and in angels; but they would hide their vices and their pride under the appearances of a hypocritical and formalist religion. The Pharisees were the "divided" ones since they would follow the Mosaic Law word by word, and they believed they were the best ones amongst the Jewish people. Their initiation would take place in the ether of heat which corresponds to the upper part of the brainstem.

717 Jesus always invites everyone to a higher level of comprehension of the matters that are above ground. The first level of comprehension should belong to the Apostles, the second one to the chief priests (or Pharisees and Sadducees), the third one to the romans. There is another level, the "+1", which is given to the Pious Women. They are disciples (and so they correspond to the apostles), they are priestesses (since they are connected to the lineage of Abel and so the priests), they are romans (since amongst them there also was Pilate's wife). For all of these reasons, they will be the ones to grasp the meaning and depth of the action of the Christ within Jesus, and they will be the first ones to meet him after the crucifixion.

718 Third step, Venus.

719 All of this because they are afraid that man will understand that the divine is within him and so they will not need mediators.

720 Man can ascend to the I Am only after transforming himself. In that dimension, there is no room for the element that is being represented by the Pharisees that look for him while maintaining their own prejudices, their terrestrial ties and mental forms. The Jewish people don't even have the feeling that they need the Marian force.

721 The Jewish people that are scattered in the world: with the term "Greeks" they mean all the people, from which we have the term "Pagans".

722 The Jewish People were looking for answers to their questions amongst themselves, without asking Jesus, and they were relying on their own (limiting) capacities.

JESUS REVEALS THE HOLY SPIRIT (Lv 23,26; Is 44,3; Is 55,1; Is 58,11; Mi 5,2)

37. The last[723] day, the greatest day, of the feast[724], Jesus[725] stood up and said with strength (*krazo*) and kept saying (*lego*): “If someone is thirsty, come to me and drink.

38. The one who believes (*pisteuo*) in me, as the scripture said (*eipen*), will have rivers flowing from within them[726] of spiritual living water”.

---

[723] From *echatos*, which is the last one, the extreme, the greatest.

[724] Of the Tabernacles. The seventh is the last day, day in which God rested within man, and now Jesus gifts himself to man and he fulfill what was symbolically expected at the Feast: the arrival of the Messiah. At the end of the Feast, a gold water jar was carried from the pool of Shilo to symbolize the transition of the Red Sea and the water flowing from the stone by Moses through his wandering towards the Promised Land where he was going to wait for the freeing Messiah. Jesus completes the waiting and he offers himself to the ones that are thirsty, to the ones that are searching, and he is not full of himself while doing so. Only the ones that renounce themselves can be reborn, and they can rise within themselves all of the virtues.

[725] Feet represent the kingdom of Earth, *Malkut*, the terrestrial Kingdom and so the Mother, the Virgin Mother, the Black Virgin Mary, the Mother of every terrestrial existence. This is why in spiritual symbolism, the feet are represented as the “wounded” and so the ones to heal. Eve was also bitten by the snake on her foot. The wound is represented by the “false” (arch) of the foot and it is the other “half” of the other wound, the one on the head represented by the fontanel. This is because man is created in the image and likeness of God, the Zodiacal Man or First Adam who is represented by the zodiacal circle that was then “cut” between Aries-head and Piesces-fish and so it lost its “likeness” with the Creator. From this we have the episode of the unction of the feet by Mary and the Washing of the Feet by Jesus, who completely purifies the Apostles and he heals the wound that came from the Fall. Magdalen will also try to touch him by the feet on Easter Sunday but the Risen One will not allow her to do so since after healing the feed and after descending in Mother Earth’s wound, he needs to ascend to the Father to complete the spiritual wedding between Mother Earth and Father Sky. Now Jesus is “standing up” to symbolize the force that he receives from the feet since they are now healed. After this gesture of “standing up”, which is the new relationship with the earth, there will be the gesture of “writing with the finger”.

[726] Who drinks from him will produce Water of Life (and not dirty water anymore), which is flowing spiritual life that will then rise up to the head to reunite with the cerebral-spinal fluid to give birth to the Child of the Spirit Man.

39. This is what he said (*eipon*) about the Spirit[727] that the believers were about to receive (*pisteuo*) from him[728]; the Spirit was yet to be there, since Jesus was yet to be glorified[729].

40. (Some) of the crowd after listening to these verbs, were saying (*lego*): "He really is the prophet".

41. Others would say (*lego*): "This is the Christ[730]". Others[731] said (*lego*): "Maybe the Christ comes from Galilee?"

42. Didn't the scripture say (*eipon*) that from the seed of David[732], and the village of Bethlehem[733], where David[734] was, the Christ came from?"

43. Because of him, the crowd[735] became split.

---

727 This is the Spirit of verse 6,69: the "Saint of God". The Apostles got to the point of perceiving the presence of the new Spirit, which was create by Jesus as man-God an that can be defined as "the Holy Spirit of Jesus" (or the Spirit of the Spirit of God). And it was then left Jesus himself as an inheritance to humanity (on Easter Sunday): this is the physical body permeated by the Incorruptible Body and then personalized by the I Am. This process was yet to be completed, but it got to the point in which the Apostles were able to perceive it.

728 There is a deep difference between having faith and believing. Faith is a virtuous movement of the soul towards a goal that is filled with value, and so faith is "towards" something or someone. Believing is the next step in which we unite with that thing, we enter it. Since we initially love only ourselves, the moment we enter this entity we begin to love it. To believe in God, in the Christ, implicates loving Him, and this allows Him to love us. This allows the beginning of the process that will take us to the step of John: of the disciple that He spiritually loved. With faith, God can only show us His Benevolence, but with believing, He can gift us His Love.

729 "Glorified" means "to made apparent/ to manifest" by Jesus, who at the Golgotha freed the Incorruptible Body of Adam.
The Spirit did not have the chance to effuse yet because man did not accept it yet. And so Jesus' gory sacrifice was necessary to win over Satan and the death with which Satan took his physical body away through which He was able to manifest himself.

730 They meant "Anointed", and so the consecration that a man would receive God to be His living testimony through men.

731 Here we understand how there are different kinds of crowds.

732 David means "by the powerful hand". Let's remember that with the expression "Son of David", the Jewish people were talking about the Messiah.

733 "House of the living Word"; see the passage of the donkey-Child. They thought that Jesus was from Nazareth.

734 David was from Bethlehem.

735 Who is in harmony with Him, cannot be divided. Therefore, they listened to him with egotistical reason, and they were being divided. And so we have two crowds: the "good one" that will follow Him, and the "evil one" that will throw itself to Him during the Passion.

44. And some of them wanted to grab him, but no one put hands[736] on him.

45. And so the chiefs of the principles of the priests and of the Pharisees[737] came. And they said (*eipon*)[738]: "Why did you not bring him (here)?"

46. The chiefs replied (*apokrinomai*): " Never did man (*antropos*) speak like that, like the man[739] speaks".

47. The Pharisees replied (*apokrinomai*): "Maybe you have been diverted as well[740]?"

48. Maybe someone amongst the princes or the Pharisees had faith in him?"

49. But this crowd[741], which does not know the law, is execrable[742]".

---

[736] This sentence is normally translated as "put hands on him". Our interpretation is literal and it means that the Pharisees were not able to throw/toss a part (the hand piece of 44) of the crowd upon him (just how it happened to the Gethsemane).

[737] They were part of a religious and political movement of great influence, and they were extremely connected to the Hebrew traditions. They believed in the resurrection of the dead and in angels; but they would hide their vices and their pride under the appearances of a hypocritical and formalist religion. The Pharisees were the "divided" ones, since they would follow the Mosaic Law, and they believed themselves to be the best amongst the Jewish people. They had an initiation that would take place in the ether of heat which corresponds to the upper part of the brainstem.

[738] It refers to the hand-piece of 736 above.

[739] The chiefs are on Venus level, and they courageously testify towards the priests since in front of the Word, and the I am, they overcame their limits.

[740] Which is:Did you follow the positive crowd?

[741] From the context, it can look like this crowd is the "good" one, the one that follows him. But if we read carefully, we can see how it actually is the evil one that puts itself at the service of Evil, and it is the one that the priest will evoke on Jesus during the Passion.

[742] Normally translated with "cursed/damned". The crowd, being evoked by the principles of the priests, will be the one to descend on Jesus and grab him. This helps us understand the disgust of the priests towards the crowd-people and towards the ones that can perceive the I Am.

50. Nicodemus[743] says to them, the one that went close to him the first[744] time[745], the One that was one of them:

51. "Does our law judge man before hearing him and without knowing what he is doing?[746]"

52. They replied (*apokrinomai*) and they said (*eipon*): "Are you from Galilee[747] too? Investigate, and you will see (*idein*) that no prophet comes from Galilee."

53. And each one of them went back to their location[748].

---

743 In the Apocalypse we find the Nicolaiti, a word that comes from *nike+laos*, and they represent a group, without the individual I, that is being won by the mass (*laos*) of what is being agitated in the sub consciousness of man. In Nicodemus, (he is an individual, the individual I), the forces of freedom present in man win ego over. The greek language does not support the different interpretation that we find in the aspect group-individual.

744 At night.

745 In the subtle bodies, see John 3.

746 Nicodemus had the courage to testify that the Law cannot be applied passively and in a formal manner. It has to be applied with right judgment.

747 As a follower of Jesus.

748 Their own spiritual region.

THE IDOLATRESS (Lk 21,37 and 55)

1. And Jesus went to the mountain of Olives[749]
2. And at the making of the day[750] he was about to once again become in the temple (inner)[751] and the whole mass of people[752] came to him, and while sitting down, he was teaching them[753].

---

[749] It corresponds to the Seraphinic Gethsemane-Zodiac. Physically it is located east of Jerusalem where the Sun-Spirit rises. It is important to know that from Jerusalem you cannot see Bethany. Gethsemane means (from the spiritual composition of the word): the earth (physical location) where we expand to God; this location is within us, and the divine forces appear there and we can welcome them; here, the Mother Sophia gifts us the beginning for a new connection with God's mind, the Logos. From what we just said, it represents the aura of life that surrounds the pituitary gland, from which the word "halo" comes from, which means "crown", the highest one of the Sephirot (Keter). Therefore it represents the renewing, in the Christian sense of the higher dimension that we can access through the Crown. Esoterically it means "pressing of olives", and so the location (of consciousness) where olive is produces, and so where we work for the Christic Initiation. This is the consciousness "location" in which man can freely decide whether to accept the chalice of pain of the world to transform it in new Life. The halo corresponds to reaching the Seraphinic Zodiac, the dimension of love, that is achieved after the "exiting" of the chakra with 100 petals of the upper part of the head, which corresponds to Saturn (the last planet of the Zodiac), and after the elevation of consciousness beyond the physical body is the image of the Cherubinic Zodiac, through the 12 "tips" of the crown. A "spherical cap" forms that unites the 12 mountains in a 13th mountain; this is also represented in the form of the royal crowns.
With Jesus Christ taking the place of the fig initiation, the vine can come to life (to ascend to the heart) and the the olive tree to reach the Garden of the Olives, the highest part of the head. These three trees will find their synthesis, their "+1" in the Cross: the fourth tree of the initiation path which will bear fruit in eternity.

[750] Time in which the etherization of the blood happens: time in which all the present entities within man meet the Christ within themselves: it is also the hour of the Sun in Pisces. We are at the first day after the Feast of the Tabernacles; a new cycle begins.

[751] It's the temple of the I, between the temples.

[752] It's the Chosen People.

[753] He was at the Getsemani, which corresponds to the Cherubinic-spirits Zodiac of love, and so he was teaching the laws of Love.

3. Therefore the Scribes and the Pharisees[754] bring him a woman[755] that was completely (*katalamabano*) taken in idolatry[756]; and setting her standing straight in front of everyone[757]

4. They say (*lego*): "Teacher, this woman was completely (*katalambano*) taken in the act, idolizing[758].

5. Moses, in his Law, commanded us to stone (women) of this sort[759]: so what do you say (*lego*)?[760]

6. They said (*lego*) this to test him[761] so that they could accuse him. But Jesus, bending his head down, noted[762] with his finger towards the earth[763].

---

[754] They were part of a political and religious movement of great influence, and it was extremely connected to the Hebrew traditions. They believed in the resurrection of the dead and in angels; but they would hide their vices and their pride under the appearances of a hypocritical and formalist religion. The Pharisees were the "divided" ones since they would follow the Mosaic Law and they believed they were the best amongst the Jewish people. Their initiation would take place in the ether of heat that corresponded to the upper part of the brainstem.

[755] The nickname "Woman" corresponds to the step of Venus (the third one) and also to the one of the Sun (fourth). This nickname corresponds to the redemption of the fallen feminine part, the redemption of Eve within her. The woman represents thee higher aspect of the feminine within us, the soul that generates the Sprit.

[756] From "*moicheia*", which means idolatry and therefore, adultery of the spiritual feast.

[757] Usually translated with "in between".

[758] The woman, the soul, follows another spirit. This is the symbol of the entire misled humanity.

[759] The man, blinded by presumption and arrogance, "judges" without knowing that by doing so, he is judging himself because from this same judgment, he will be judged himself.

[760] They always try and test him, to put him in contradiction with Moses. If he would have forgiven her, he would have been against Moses; and if he would have judged her, then he would have been n contradiction with his law of Love.

[761] Also "to tempt him".

[762] The term "*katagrapho*" is usually translated as "he wrote". He is inscribing the error of Earth in Karma.

[763] He is writing on the Earth (that he already permeated with his spiritual Light and that is preparing itself to be a cosmos of love) the sin of the adulteress, to take the consequences on himself in regards to the karma of the earth. The sin and the sinner are written on Earth and it will the redemption will happen on Earth. The finger becomes a "living pen," and it imprints thee vital forces that emanate from the finger on the Earth.

7. Since they kept questioning him he raised his head[764], and he said (*eipen*) towards them: "Those of you that have no mistakes[765], throw a stone[766] towards her".

8. And once again, lowering his head, he described towards the earth[767]

9. But the ones that learned (*akouo*) this, One by One[768] left, starting from the eldest ones to the extremes; and only Jesus was left, and the woman (that once was) in front of everyone.

10. So Jesus, rose his head and said (*eipen*): "The Woman[769], were are (the ones that accused you)? No one convicted you?"

11. And she said (*eipen*): "No one, sir". So Jesus said (*eipen*) to her: "I do not convict[770] you either: walk and from now on do go wrong[771]!

---

[764] The physical Earth represents the head of the Being Earth, He gets ready to raise the Earth, to free her of the sin. The stoning ratifies the sin. The Law knew that this sin was going to be written on the Earth, and it was going to make her heavier in her evolution, and so, they would express the rebellion of the Earth through these sins. The circle of the elderly is like the circle of the Zodiac that administers karma. To get out of the circle of the Zodiac means to enter the Milky Way, the Divine Providence, and to entrust to Her the judgment.

[765] The term *amartia*, usually translated as "sin".

[766] In Hebrew, stone is *even*, which is a word formed by *av*, the Father, and *ben*, the Son. It is the symbol of the man whose consciousness has awakened. The awakened man becomes the Son of the Father. He tells us that every man is guilty of adultery because he left the celestial Father to unite with another father, the one that is a thief and a murderer from the beginning.

[767] Now he writes the sins of the ones that are present (starting from the eldest ones). Now their consciousness awakes and they are leaving.

[768] One is the Scribes and One is the Pharisees.

[769] Also "feminine" or "bride". Jesus gives back to her the title of bride, of soul united to her I. this corresponds to the redemption of her fallen part, the redemption of Eve within her.

[770] He did not come to convict, he came to free from the slavery of sins, for her to not keep feeling guilty.

[771] Do not make bigger sins, move your will towards redemption: it is the will that transgresses, the love towards evil that convicts man and prevents the Christ to help. It is an invite to go on the spiritual path again with no guilt; but instead, placing the will to do better in the center to arrive to inner completeness. It's a soul that "mistaken" the spirit; maybe it is Magdalen.

JESUS SPEAKS ABOUT HIS DIVINE MISSION (Is 49;6 Mt 5,14)

12. Jesus spoke to them again, and said: "**I am the light**[772] **of the world**; the ones who follow me will not travel[773] in darkness, instead they will have light of the spiritual life".

---

[772] At the Feast of the Tabernacles, it was characterized by the lighting of the big golden candle holders in the Temple, and their light could be seen from the city. This light had a ritual significance and the Temple, in those days, was called "Light of the world". Jesus' affirmation makes us understand that He is the true light that illuminates humanity and not the Temple or the religious authorities. Christ is the light of the whole cosmos, and here he specifies the task that he took on as a man: the one of being the Light that spreads spiritual Life to all humanity (*…Life was the light of men…*)… He came here to help us understand that the main purpose for human existence is to acquire the Light of true consciousness which is the full consciousness of the Truth and which is Life itself and we can achieve it by following Him. It's the *chakra* of Jupiter. This affirmation corresponds to the mastery of the sixth *chakra*, the one with 22 petals that is located on the forehead as the third eye. With the Christ, this *chakra* reaches its completion since now we can reach its true essence, which is the pituitary gland that leans on the Turkish chair (sella turcica): it is the true *chakra* and the third eye is its "door" for the Light. After this affirmation, He will be able to heal the man born blind.

[773] In the initiation path of inner transformation.

13. The Pharisees then said: “You are testifying about yourself, your testimony is not true[774]”.

14. Jesus[775] replied and said to them: “Even if I testify about myself, my testimony[776] is true, because I know where I come from, and where I am going[777]; but you do not know where I come from or were I am going[778].

15. You[779] judge according to the flesh[780], I judge no one[781].

16. And if I judge, my judgment is truthful, because I am not alone, but me, and the one who sent me, (who is a) Father[782].

17. And in your law it is said that the testimony of the men is true.

18. I am, testifying myself, and He who sent me[783], (who is a) Father, testifies about me.

19. And they said: “Where is your[784] Father?”

---

[774] Who is in the truth, does not need witnesses, and his truth is being recognized by everyone who is in the truth. Who is in the wrong, looks for other witnesses to support his position. By doing so, the Pharisees state that they have no Truth.

[775] As Son of man, the Higher I.

[776] Within him there is Jesus and the Christ (the Divine); there are already two testifying.

[777] This is the testimony of one who reached complete self-awareness and of the Divine presence within him.

[778] To be aware of where one comes from and where one is headed is the result of awareness of the self and the Divine presence within one's self.

[779] This “you” means the ones that are in the Fall and the ones that are immersed in the materialistic conception.

[780] You as the men that are in the falling state: in this case it is the lower aspect of the flesh to manifest itself. Jesus waits so that man can become a judge of himself and not of others, and this can only happen after a deep inner awareness…

[781] In front of the Christ, the human I judges itself.

[782] Jesus is the only witness and loyal Apostle to the Father and the only one who manifested and fulfilled His will.

[783] It's the Nathan Soul, sent by Adonai.

[784] Now they ask who His Father is.

Jesus[785] replied: "You do not know me, nor my Father; if you knew me, maybe you would also know my Father[786]"

20. He said these words in the treasury[787], teaching in the temple (internal)[788], and no one grabbed him, because his hour had yet to come[789].

21. So he said to them once again: "I will go and you will look for me, and within your sin you will die[790]. Where I go, you will not have the strength to come to".

22. So the Jewish people said: "Does he want to kill us, since he said: Where I go, you will not have the strength to come to?[791]"

23. And he said to them: "You are of the things of down here, I am of the ones up above. You are from this world, I am not from this world[792].

---

785 Always as Son of man.

786 He does not state a location, but a state of consciousness that belongs to the one that has a pure soul, which is a state in which the meeting between human and the Divine takes place.

787 The "room of the treasure". Jesus says these words in the room of the treasure to indicate which divinity took place of the Saint of the Saints. Close to the Treasure, there is the room of the Sanhedrin where Jesus will be convicted.

788 The forehead, which means in front of the "door" (third eye) of the pituitary gland.
There are various "temples". The main one, the Temple of Jerusalem, represents the forehead between the temples, and so the chakra with two petals, the so-called third eye. The second one is in Samaria-heart and the third one is in Galilee-perineum. In general, the temple is the place in which the spiritual forces manifest themselves.
The Greek language uses two terms for "temple". They are "*hiero*" and "*naos*". "*Hiero*" is the most sacred part of ourselves, the *sancta santorum*, where we are in our I Am and so in never-ending communion with the Christ. "*Naos*" is the external temple of which the first one was the one that, during the Exodus the Jewish people raised in the desert, and so it represents the Tent of the Alliance.

789 The hour in which he will win over death, and he will be able to say "everything was accomplished".

790 It's the original sin: to have welcomed Lucifer within oneself. Not even Jesus can forgive us if there is no regret, no strong will against falling again and coherence of one's intentions.

791 Unconsciously they sensed that to be spiritually reborn you have to be willing to accept the death of your own old man and to be reborn in the new with Jesus Christ.

792 As a "order of things", as *Logos*. The Christ is beyond the *Logos*. He comes from the Holiest Trinity, while the Logos is the Principle Son of the Holy Trinity. Also for His People, the Chosen People, he is in the world, but not "of" the world.

24. I told you that you would reach the depth of your death in your sins[793]: if you will not believe[794] that I am[795], you will reach the depth of your death in your sins".

25. And so they told him: "Who are you?" Jesus said: "The first cause, that also I speak to you[796]".

26. I have many things to say and judge about you[797]. But who sent me is truthful, and I say in the world[798] what I heard from Him".

27. And they did not understand why he was speaking about the Father.

28. Jesus said (*lego*): "When you will have raised the Son (*Hyios*) of man, then you will know that I am[799], and (that) I do not create (*poieo*) from myself but how my Father taught[800] me, that is how I speak.

29. And the One who sent me is with me, and He does not leave me alone, because I always create (*poieo*) for him the better things"

---

[793] Now the sins are plural because many more came from the first one.

[794] For the difference between "having faith" and "believing", see John 1,7.

[795] The goal is to reach the consciousness of the I Am, of each ones individuality freed from all the conditioning induced from the world; of the divine spark put within us by the Creator on the seventh day of creation when He rested within man and He sanctified him (Gen 2,2).

[796] It's the *Logos* in the Jesus with the Christ within him, the First of the Prologue. He is the first one of the creation of all visible and invisible things, the operating manifestation of the divine knowledge, the ultimate Holy Spirit that has within himself the full consciousness of the Father and the creating force of the Verb.

[797] To judge means to approve the paralysis, the evolutionary immobility, of the ones who are being judges. Therefore, Jesus does not judge because each creature is destined to salvation through a free process of perfection and improvement. Jesus makes us understand how the judgment moment has yet to come since now is the time of manifestation of Truth that will set us free from the slavery of our own mistakes.

[798] Jesus declares that he manifests the Truth that is within the Father and that He sent him, since Son and Father act together. To manifest Truth is not to judge; instead it is giving the forces of comprehension for the judgement of oneself.

[799] The Son of man, represented by Jesus, completely unites with the Christ and becomes "I Am" as Adonai (the secret name of God) which means "God is". Only John uses the expression "you will rise" both as Jesus "risen" on the cross, and as "risen" man to the higher levels of consciousness.
The 12 "I Am" of John's Gospel are: the Principle (8,25), the Life (11,25; 14,6; 14,19), the Light (8,12), the Truth (14,6), The Way/Path (14,6), the Son of the God (10, 36), the Good Shepherd (10,11; 10,14), the Door (10, 7;10,9), the Bread of Life (6,35.6,48), the true Vine (15, 1), the Resurrection (11,25), "I Am within my Father, and you are within me, and me within you" (14,20 and 17,20-23).

[800] There is a resonance between the Jesus Teacher (Zarathustra) and the Father: they both teach and this is the "Groom/Husband" aspect. The "Bride/Wife" aspect is found again in the sermon. The conscious thought which is the Father within man, permeated with will, gives completion to the impulse coming from the Spirit, and it "generates" what is translated in the word.

30. By talking this way, many had faith (*episteusa*) in him[801].

31. So Jesus said (*lego*) to the Jewish people that believed (*pepisteuka*) in him: "If you will stay in the logos[802], my own, you will truly be my disciples,

32. And you will get to know the truth and the truth[803] will set you free[804]".

JESUS RESISTS THE BOASTFULNESS OF THE JEWISH PEOPLE (Mt 3,9)

33. They replied (*apokrinomai*) (against him): " we are Abram's[805] seed and we never served anyone[806]; like you say: You will become (and you will remain) (*ghignomai*) free[807]?"

34. Jesus replied (*apokrinomai*) to them: "Amen, Amen[808], I say that whoever creates (*poieo*) the mistake[809], is slave of the mistake[810],

---

801 It is not said that they believe in the Truth that he teaches, but that they believed "in him", which means not through intellect but they recognized within Him, through the sense of Truth, the living model of the perfect man.

802 The evolutionary laws that He brings us and the reawaken our Spirit.

803 This truth is the one of the Prologue (John 1,14).

804 Let's remember that the Christ opens up the path of spiritualized Love to us, while redeemed Lucifer will give us the strength to reach the Truth that will set us free. It is the human I that needs to freely open to the impulse of the Christ. Lucifer gets redeemed when we open up to him with freedom of judgment and enthusiasm.
From the Earth-death we will reascend to the sphere of the Sun thanks to the impulse that the Christ gifted to us. From the Sun on he will take us to the redeemed Lucifer: the Paraclete. To all of this, the entering of Life will follow. For the complete vision of the "Paraclete" see John 14,16.

JESUS RESISTS THE BOASTFULNESS OF THE JEWISH PEOPLE

805 With this, they reinstate that they belong to a community that believed themselves to be free. But now it is about becoming individually free and not through blood.

806 They do not realize that they are under the control of their own mistakes.

807 In Latin "free" also means "son", and "son" corresponds to the seventh step of Initiation.

808 Universal Truth, he speaks as the Holiest Trinity.

809 Sins are the guilt caused by the physical body with its instincts and impulses. In Hebrew it is said *hata*, which means "to miss the target": the target is the recognition of the action of the Son that brings us to the Father. The mistakes are caused by following what comes up from the etheric body instead of the I.

810 Because it makes us slaves in our egotistical desires. It is better to be dominated by other people than by the demons of egoism.

35. But the slave does not stay in the house (*oicha*) for eternity[811]; (but the Son remains in eternity[812])[813].

36. Therefore, if the Son will set you free, you will be free in your essence[814].

37. I know you are Abraham's seed; but you are trying to kill me (*apokteino*), because the logos, my own, does not make space[815] for itself within you.

38. I mumble (*laleo*) to you what I saw (*horao*) near the Father; you also create (*poieo*) what you saw (*horao*) near your[816] father".

39. They replied (*apokrinomai*) and they said (*heipon*): "Your father is Abraham[817]".

40. Jesus replied (*apokrinomai*) to them: "If you are sons (*teknon*) of the Abraham[818], you would create (*poieo*) the achievements (*erga*) of the Abraham.

41. But now you are trying to kill (*apokteino*) me, man (*antropos*), who mumbled (*laleo*) the truth to you, who heard (*akouo*) near the God: this Abraham did not create[819] (*poieo*).

---

[811] He will be banished because he is a sinner.

[812] The Son of God remains in eternity. One who is not in harmony with God will lose the closeness to God.

[813] This phrase is only present in certain codices.

[814] Literally "essentially", in your essence, in your depths. Only the Christ won the world and so he is the only one that can gift us true freedom.

[815] Literally "he does not find a Light that creates him space". It's another reference to the sixth *chakra*, the one of the pituitary gland. Not listening to the impulse of the Christ is the same as "killing" him within us.

[816] Their "father" are Lucifer and Ahriman.

[817] They recognize the blood, and not the Spirit.

[818] There is a difference between the being a "seed" and the being "sons" of Abraham. The first is a biological aspect, the second is of the soul. Jesus invites them to be at least "imitators" of Abraham while they wait to become spiritual Sons of God.

[819] Abraham listened and honored the voice of God.

42. You create (*poieo*) the accomplishments of your[820] father". They said to him: "We were not born from the fornication[821], we have One only father: the God[822]".

43. Therefore Jesus told (*eipon*) them: "If the God was our father, you would spiritually love me as well: I came (*erchomai*) from the God and I am right (*heko*); I did not come from myself[823], but He sent me.

44. Why do you not know my[824] mumbling (*laleo*)? Because you do not have the strength to hear (*akouo*) my[825] logos.

45. You are from the father the devil[826], and you want to create (*poieo*) the desires of your father. He was homicidal[827] from the beginning[828], and he did not remain in the truth: because it is not truth within him: when he mumbles (*laleo*) the lie, he mumbles of his own things, because his[829] father is also a liar.

46. But I, since I say (*lego*) the truth, you do not believe[830] (*pisteno*) me.

---

820 See note on verse 38.

821 The physical procreative act, in comparison to the spiritual one, is to be considered a fornication. Man was destined to grow and multiply himself within consciousness.

822 They believe themselves to come from the Holiest Trinity, from God the Creator of Adonai.

823 With this he states that He has "His" own will, but he adjusted it to the one of the Father.

824 It's a plea to recognize him, to which they do not respond. Here we find the transition to the third transformation of the transubstantiation: from the "ferments/enzymes" to the "word".

825 Because they are not sons of the Trinity.

826 As a whole spiritual being, and so indicated with the article.

827 Satan is the one that acts against man by bringing him physical and spiritual death when we submit to him. His father is Lucifer. Satan is Lucifer's karma. Lucifer is a liar, because he knows the truth, but he does not say it. Satan, on the other hand, "did not stay", (he never was), in the truth, because he comes from another evolutionary system.

828 *Ap'arches*, which is from principle, from when he got closer to man. It's Satan. It's before the separation from Truth, consequentially to the action of the rebellion acted by Lucifer, who from helper of the creation wanted to become complete creator.

829 The term devil refers to the ones who distance man from the Truth: Lucifer and Satan.

830 The ones that are caught in the demonic tricks cannot believe him. For the difference between "having faith" and "believing" see John 1,7.

47. Who amongst you is accusing me of being wrong[831]? If I say truth, for what reason do you not believe me

48. Who is from God, listens (*akuou*) to the words (*rema*) of the God[832]. This is why you do not listen, because you are not from the God[833]".

49. The Jewish people replied and said (*eipon*) to him: "Aren't we right in saying (*lego*) that you are a Samaritan[834] and you have a demon?"

50. Jesus[835] replied and said (*eipon*): "I do not have a demon, but I do honor my[836] Father; and you are dishonoring me.

51. But I am not looking for my glory; there are the one that look for[837], and judge.

52. Amen, Amen[838], I say (*lego*) to you: if someone will guard my logos, he will not see (*theoreo*) for eternity[839]".

53. The Jewish people said (*eipon*) to him: "Now we know you have a demon. Abraham reached the depth of death (*apothnesko*), and the prophets; and you say (*lego*): if someone will guard my logos for eternity we will not try death for eternity[840].

---

[831] Within him, there is no trace of sin not even of the original one because he descended directly from the Man created before he could be influenced by the luciferic influence.

[832] The Holiest Trinity.

[833] All men, in their deepest essence, come from God drawing, origin from the Man create at His image and likeness, but that then wandered away from the divine order.

[834] The Samaritans were considered possessed by demons by the Jewish people.

[835] He was accused as man and as such he replies to their accusations.

[836]Making/Doing His will.

[837] It can be both looking for glory and so the judging as man and having power over humanity, and also the looking for truth and so becoming free and finding the Father, to then judge.

[838] Universal Truth, in the Holiest Trinity.

[839] He will not have death for eternity in that he will overcome it. The important thing is to "guard it", as Mariam did in her immaculate heart.

[840] The Jewish people do not understand and they repeat it wrongly: Jesus did not say "he will not experiment" but he said "he will not see" death of the soul and he will be saved for eternity. Additionally, the ones that will follow Jesus Christ's teaching, will experience death as a non-painful transition..

54. Are you better than our father Abraham, who reached the depth of death (*apothnesko*)? The prophets also reached the depth of death[841]. Who (you) creates (*poieo*) yourself?[842]"

55. Jesus replied: "If I glorify my own self, my glory is nothing; my Father, is the one that glorifies me, the one who you say (*lego*) is your God[843],

56. But you did not get to know him: I do know him[844]. And if I say (*eipon*) that I do not know him, I will be a liar, similar to you. But I know him and I guard[845] his logos.

57. Your father Abraham was pleased in seeing (*eido*) the day[846], my own: and he saw and he rejoiced[847]".

58. The Jewish people answered back (*eipon pros*): "You don't even have fifty years yet and you saw (*horao*) Abraham?"

59. Jesus said (*eipon*) to them: "Amen, Amen[848], I say to you: before Abraham became, I Am[849]".

---

[841] Jesus speaks of spiritual death, which nor Abraham nor the Prophets were ever subject to it.

[842] Who do you think you are?

[843] It's Jesus (with no article) that replies, and so the Nathan Soul that directly descended from Adonai (it is the Man in his image and likeness), and also the Jewish people recognize Adonai as their God.

[844] For the fact to have seen.

[845] Or "conserve", Jesus does so in relation to the Verb.

[846] Day as an experience of the I, that Abraham fulfilled when he understood the descending of Jesus on Earth; he rejoiced in front of his Holy Birth.

[847] From *chaire* which also means "safe" (see Lk 1,28).

[848] Jesus observes the verb, he can tell them a universal law (Amen, Amen) which refers to the Holiest Trinity.

[849] The principle of the I Am was brought to us by the Christ. Now the Christ highlights the difference between the being in time (in the existence-Abraham) and the being in the continuous present, in the now, in the I Am.

60. They chose some stones[850] to throw at him: But Jesus hid[851] himself and exited the temple (internal)[852].

THE HEALING OF THE BLIND (Mc 8,23)

1. And leading (in the path)[853] he saw (*eidon*) a blind[854] man from birth[855].
2. And his disciples questioned him by saying (*lego*): "Rhabbi[856], who did wrong, he or his parents[857], since he was born blind[858]?"

---

[850] These "stones" (from Greek *lithous*) are the dead thoughts that the Jewish people threw, as anathemas, on Jesus. Esoterically, the "stone" is the thought; these "stones" are the concepts of the Old Testament, from which the Jewish people are not able to distance themselves, and they try to use them against Jesus. In Hebrew, stone is said *even,* which is a word composed by *av*, the Father, and *ben*, the Son. Therefore, it is the symbol of the man in which the awakening of consciousness took place.
The awakened man becomes Son of the Father.
The Jewish people could not accept that God could reveal himself within a man.

[851] He entered in the dimension of "hidden".

[852] During his first visit to the temple, he drove all the negative forces that were present away, and now He is the one that needs to leave, since his teachings of Love and the invitation to the conversation are not being accepted.

[853] He is hiding from the Jewish people and he keeps being a guide for men. The destination is the chakra with two petals, where there is the "stone" of intellectual thought, and it needs to be renewed.

[854] Blind is the one who with an excess of egoism (of luciferic origin), can only see himself. In Hebrew, blind is said *iwer*, which pronounced *aor*, means "tunic of skin", which is the skin with which Adam was dressed after the Fall.

[855] As an archetype of humanity that, with the Fall, lost spiritual vision which causes the weakening of the Incorruptible Body.

[856] Sixth step; they grasp the Nathan Soul aspect.

[857] His hereditary lineage, the blood.

[858] This presumes that they knew the law of reincarnation.

3. Jesus replied (*apokrinomai*): "He did not do wrong, nor his parents, but because within him the works of God[859] could manifest.
4. It is necessary that we accomplish[860]the accomplishments of the one who sent us[861] while it is day-light; once night comes, no one has the strength to accomplish[862].
5. When I am in the world, I am the light of the world[863].

---

[859] From R. Steiner we learn that this "God" is the divine part present within ourselves. See the "*You are gods"* (John 10,34). He did not become blind because in a past existence he created the conditions so that he was going to be born blind, otherwise the Christ would have said that this illness was his fault. He was born blind as a free personal choice that was made before birth, probably to determine certain conditions of life that would bring him to develop specific qualities that would lead him to understand the action of the divine within him. In another interpretation, this blindness represents the loss of spiritual vision that all humanity has as a consequence after of the Fall. To spiritually see, many vital forces in the area of the eyes are necessary, and if they go missing the physical sight suffers as well. In either case, to heal, we need to connect to the profound I Am, to the divine part within us.
With this sixth miracle, Jesus' strength increases, and now He can act upon what goes from one existence to the other: upon the divine I within us. The Christ, bearer of the I Am of humanity, communicates His divinity to the present divinity within the man, and so he can acquire the capacity to heal himself through inner strength.
In any case: don't ever judge!

[860] It refers to the Jesus with the strength of the Christ within him and together they offer themselves as tools of the will of the Father.

[861]The Christ, the Cosmic I, descended to freely open the path of the Father to the human I Am.

[862] Jesus operated in unison with the zodiacal forces, precisely with the Bright Zodiac (or Mystic Lamb). The day represents wakefulness, and so when the consciousness (and the I) are present. On the contrary, at night, with the darkness, the I retreats, and the Christ cannot operate because He allows man to be free and at night, man is not free.

[863] See John 8,12. Now He can heal the man who was born blind, which is after he confirmed that His being is the Light of the world, and the blind man can recognize (see) within the Christ the ideal of humanity. His astral body is therefore experimenting a rebirth in Light.

6. After saying (*eipon*) this he spit[864] on the ground, and he created mud[865] from his spit, and he laid mud on his eyes[866] ,

864 Saliva has a strong purifying and healing power. It comes from the syllable "*sal*", but also "health", "salvation", Savior". In Hebrew, to spit is *yaroq* which is equal to *yereq*, the greenery, the green of life, of light, of eternity.
The forces of blood that are highly transformed live in the saliva; in the case of Jesus we can see the forces of His operating love within it and also His vitality.
On the opposite of the saliva-light we have the spitting on the face, and as a consequence of this gesture we will have a non-light that goes against the one that, through this gesture, has expressed his adversity. Spiritually, he is punished with leprosy. To spit on the ground is also an exorcism against the evil spirits.

865 In Italian, mud is also called "loto", the lotus flower with 2 petals. Clay recalls Capricorn, the force of Darkness. Jesus is the Light that defeats Darkness.
This "mud" reminds us of the man formed by clay; which is the man before the Fall. Clay substitutes the physical malformation of the eye; the saliva gives it life. It's important to notice how the word "mud" is repeated 5 times, and this is to remind us how "special" this mud is since it is created by Jesus with his own saliva, which represents the vital forces. With this mud, Jesus symbolically proposes once again the formation of man, and now of the new man, the man "that is going back up" and this can only happen on Saturday.

866 Spiritual and physical eyes.

7. And he said[867] (*eipon*) to him: "Go[868] below to purify yourself in the pool of Siloe[869], which meant Sent[870]. So he left and he purified himself, and he became seer and seeing[871].

[867] It is important to see how the blind man did not ask for anything. In fact, he couldn't ask for anything since he was in this condition from birth and so he had no other experience, or memory, of the Light. When he will be able to see, he will be able to recognize it and recognize the One who did him grace.

[868] The exhortation is to go through the Spiritual Path, and perfection oneself even more.

[869] *Siloam* in Greek is an acronym of *S* within the cave; *I* internal energy that flows from above to below; *L* the light of the Sun or the enlightened mind; *O* the forces that enter us; *A* the birth, the beginning; *M* the Mother, Nature with all that within her is incarnated; and *Siloah* in Aramaic means "emission, send" or "emit, send".
It was 16 meters long, 5 meters wide and 1 meter deep. It was probably located east of Jerusalem. It would get water from the river Gihon through a tunnel that ran for 530 meters.
During the Feast of the Tabernacles (or of the Tents), this water was brought to the Temple of Jerusalem among great fanfare and here it would get poured together with some wine in a tube that was positioned next to the altar and it would reach the valley of Kidron. It would be best to learn more about the pool of Siloe to which the blind man was sent to purify himself. Knowing that after he regained spiritual and physical sight, the blind man will say "I Am", we can connect this pool to a part of the head (we are in Jerusalem in Judea) where there is some spring water.
Since the higher I finds correspondence to the lower part of the cerebellum, we can see how in this area the central channel of the spinal cord (which carries the cerebrospinal liquid) goes up and it enlarges in the fourth ventricle. This enlargement, which corresponds to the entering of the lower cerebellum, is the headquarters of the Higher I, our pool of Siloe.
It is important to remember that there also was the Spring of Siloe that was found outside of the walls of Jerusalem, and the baptisms of the pagan proselytes would take place here as well. In this case, the Spring is the point of source in the central channel of the spinal cord and the Pool is where it enlarges. Compared to what Jesus gifts us, the Jewish person is placed on the same level as the pagan.
Let's remember that the "one with no strength" (John 5,1), finds himself in front of s pool, the one of Bethany which means "ditch, crevice, crack". It was located north of the temple (and so between Water and Earth, in the quality of "cold"), and it would separate a new neighborhood from the remaining city. Both with the pool "of the one with no strength" and the pool of the "Blind Man," the day in which the event takes place is Saturday, the seventh day, the day of going back up to God.

[870] The Sent (the person being sent) is a messenger, an Angel, and within the liquid element angels find the lowest level in which they can manifest. Let's remember that the Higher I corresponds to the dimension of the consciousness of the Angel.
In the case of the "one with no strength", it is the Angel that acts in his discretion, and in the case of the "Blind Man," it is him going to the pool and then calling out to the Angel: the "up-side down" ritual is beginning.

[871] The Greek verb is *blepo* (or *blepon*), which means both seer and seeing. The blind man has almost regained both visions. Now the Incorruptible Body sees.

8. And so the neighbors, and the ones who formerly spiritually (*theoreo*)[872] saw that he was (one) who asked beyond[873], said (*elegon*): "Isn't he the one who worked secretly and asked beyond?" Others said: "It is him!".

9. Others said: "No, it is not him, but he is similar[874]". He said (*lego*): "I am[875]".

10. And so the Jewish people said (*lego)* to him: "How were your eyes opened?"

11. He replied (*apokrinomai*): "The man[876], the said Jesus, created (*poieo)* mud, and he anointed[877] my eyes, and he said (*eipon*) to me: Go below Siloe and purify yourself[878]. I went and purified myself, and I lifted the tunic of skin that covered my eyes[879]".

12. And so they said (*eipon*) to him: "Where is he?"[880] He said (*lego*): "I do not know"[881].

13. They take the one that was blind to the Pharisees.

14. And it was Saturday,[882] the day Jesus created the mud and opened up his eyes.

---

872 Seen in the Spirit, with the spiritual vision. The spiritually "close" people are the ones that can see his aura, and they can see how its brightness changed and so they are indecisive in recognizing him.

873 Which means seeker of the spiritual Light. Normally translated as "beggar". Instead, it refers to a man that is searching within the Spirit.

874 We can hypothesize that with the eyes, the healing of the whole Incorruptible Body was achieved and so his "auric" aspect changed, thanks to the flowing of the forces of the I Am within him.

875 This is the only man in the Gospel that **pronounces the I am.** He found the Light of the Christ, the principle of the I Am within him and he confirms it. Through this, he arrived to the destination that he predetermined with the incarnation as the blind man.

876 Man as *antropos*: for now he does not say more about Jesus.

877 We have a particular unction. Usually it would happen with oil to prepare and protect the person when he or she was about to face a spiritual test, but not the unction of oil-light is happening with saliva-love.

878 He received the Grace of the action of the Christ, and he also needs to do his part so that the healing can happen.

879 From the term *anablepo*. In Greek, the term used for blind man means "tunic of skin that covers the eyes". Now the tunic that came after the Fall, can be lifted. The eyes are reopening to the spirit, man has regained sight and clairvoyance. Literally it would be "I regained sight".

880 They do not see and so they ask the blind man that came back clairvoyant where his healer is.

881 He spiritually sees but he does not know, he is not initiated. The first initiate from the Christ will be Lazarus-John.

882 Jesus, as Son of man, is Lord of Saturday, since Saturday is the day that was given to man to reconnect to the Creator. This miracle represents a step towards the Great Saturday: the Holy Saturday of Easter.

15. The Pharisees questioned him again about how he lifted the tunic of skin that covered his eyes. And he said (*eipon*) to them: "He put mud on my eyes, I purified myself, and I see[883] (*blepo*)".

16. Some Pharisees said (*lego*): "The man that does not respect the Saturday is not from God". Others said (*lego*): "How can a man that is in the wrong[884] have the strength to create such signs?" And it was schism within them.

17. Therefore, they said (*lego*) to the man that used to be blind: "What do you say (*lego*) about the one that opened up your eyes?" And so he said (*eipon*): "He is prophet[885]".

18. But the Jewish people didn't have faith (*epistensa*) about him, that he was blind, and he lifted the tunic of skin, until they called the parents of the one who lifted the tunic of kin from the eyes,

19. And they questioned[886] them (by saying): "If this is the son (*hyios*)[887], that you say[888] once was blind, how is it possible that he can now see (*blepo*)?"

20. His parents replied and said (*eipon*): "We know that he is our child (*hyios*), and he became blind;

21. How he can now see (*blepo*), we do not know; we do not know who opened his eyes: ask him; he has the age[889] to speak (*laleo*) for himself".

---

883 He repeats what was already said.

884 The Pharisees base themselves on the Mosaic Law, which they interpret in a rigid and dead way since they lost its meaning.
Sins are the faults caused by the physical body with its instincts and impulses. In Hebrew, it is said *hata* and it means to "miss the target": the "target" is the recognition of the action of the Son that takes us to the Father.

885 Prophet is the one that acts as an intermediary to the divine Word. He said it rightly by saying this since he grasped the fact that through Jesus, the Truth, the *Logos*, was able to manifest itself.

886 They refuse to accept the miracle that undermined all of their rigidity of thought.

887 It is important to see how they are talking about a spiritual son and not a carnal son.

888 The question makes us assume that they were lying, that they were being dishonest.

889The height, the I to reply. He is in the solar dimension and so he can talk "about" himself.

22. His parents said (*eipon*) these things, because they were afraid of the Jewish people: the Jewish people had already established that if someone approved[890] Christ, he would have become an outside Synagogue[891].

23. For this reason his parents said (*eipon*): "He has age, ask him".

24. For the second (time), they called the man that was blind, and they told (*eipon*) him: "Give glory to the God, we know that this man is doing wrong[892]".

25. And so he replied and said: "If he is wrong I do not know: I know only one thing, that having had the tunic of skin above my eyes, now (I see) (*blepo*)".

26. And so they said (*eipon*) to him: "What did he create to you? How[893] did he reopen your eyes?[894]"

27. He replied (*apokerinomai*) to them: "I have already told (*eipon*) you, and you didn't listen, what do you still want to hear? Do you maybe want to become his disciples[895] as well?"

28. And so they insulted him, and said (*eipon*): "You are his disciple; and we are disciples of Moses[896].

890From the Greek *omologo* which contains *omo* which means "take an oath" and *logo* which means word. The meaning of the word becomes "to say the Word of the oath".

891 Someone that is excluded from the Synagogue, the equivalent (in a worse way) to someone that is being excommunicated.

892 Which means "he glorifies the God and not the man Jesus" (who for them is a sinner). Not being able to reject the miracle, they try to discredit Jesus.

893 Not recognizing the action of Sacred Magic brought by the Christ, they try to reveal which magic art he used so that they could recognize the secret identity regarding its forms. "Magic" is a manifested action which is obtained through the use of invisible forces. It can be "personal magic" when the magician uses his secret individual force, or it can be "group magic" when the magician uses the forces of a group of people, which are being sucked in with a ritual (songs, meditations, prayers, sacrifices, etc.), and then they are utilized by the magician for his own purposes. Both these forms of magic fall into the category of black magic or ceremonial magic, and so the egotistical use of the spiritual forces that need to be "captured" through specific rituals. The only Christic type of magic is the Sacred Magic, which consists n making ourselves in instruments for the will of the Father: the spiritual world will manifest itself through us for His will. This type of magic foresees a minimal "ceremonial" part (think about the miracles of Jesus, in which only a simple hand gesture or phrase can move the magic act).

894 Now they try to attribute the miracle to a magic action operated by the Jesus.

895 The miraculous survivor, with this answer, indicates a great presence of spirit (and also courage): all these are manifestations of the I Am.

896 They do not even want to accept the idea that Jesus is a connection to the Divine just as Moses was.

29. We know that the God[897] spoke (*laleo*) to Moses; but we do not know where he is[898]."

30. The man (*antropos*) replied (*apokerinomai*) and said (*eipon*) to them: "In this he is admirable, that you do not know where he is, but he opened up my eyes[899].

31. But we know that the God does not listen to the ones that do wrong, but if someone is pious and he creates (*poieo*) his will, he listens[900] (*akuou*) to it.

32. From the temples[901] no one heard (*akuou*) that someone reopened the eyes of a blind[902] man.

33. If he was not from God, he would not have the strength to create (*poieo*) anything[903].

34. They replied and said (*eipon*): "You become whole in mistakes[904], and you are teaching us?" And so they kicked him out[905].

35. Jesus heard[906] (*akuou*) that they kicked him (the blind man) out; and, after finding him, he said (*eipon*) to him: "Do you believe (*pistevo*) in the Son of the man?[907]"

---

897 The Holiest Trinity.

898 Here is the contradiction: they admit to not know-understand-comprehend from where Jesus comes from, but they want to convict him.

899 The blind man proves to be present within the I Am.

900 The miraculous survivor specifies what "Ask and it will be given to you" means. In the force of faith, we need to honor him, and do His will: this is how Faith "works".

901 Here on Earth.

902 The miraculous survivor does not talk about himself, or the Grace that he received, but he looks at the greatness of the miracle itself: none of the "fallen" men had the gift of restoration of the spiritual vision.

903 The miraculous survivor always manifests his dignity and the fullness of the I Am.

904 The Jewish people were convinced that illnesses were a consequence of sins from the previous incarnation.

905 Not being able to reject the affirmation of the healed blind man who stated that Jesus came from God, they send him away from the Synagogue, from the community.

906 He spiritually heard. He is always connected to every creature.

907 Now Jesus asks this man, the one healed without asking for help, if he believes in Him, if he believes in the possibility that each and every man (bearer of the divine spark) has to return to the Father by following the example that Jesus, who is a true man, shows to him.

36. He replied, and said (*eipon*): "Who is[908]he, Sir, so that I can become a believer[909] in him?"

37. And Jesus said (*ephen*) to him: "And you saw (*horao*) him[910], and the one speaking to you, he is.

38. And so he said (*ephen*): "I believe, Sir!" and he bowed down to him[911]

39. And Jesus said (*eipon*) to him: "I came to this world for a judgment[912]: so that the ones who cannot see (*blepo*), can see[913] (*blepo*), and the ones who see (*blepo*), become with a tunic of skin above their eyes[914]".

40. And some of the Pharisees that were with him heard (*akuou*) him, and said : "Maybe we also have the tunic of skin above our eyes?"

41. Jesus said (*eipon*) to them[915]: "If you had a tunic of skin above your eyes, you wouldn't have gone wrong, but now you say: We see. Your mistake remains[916]."

---

[908] After receiving clairvoyance, he now asks for knowledge.

[909] To believe is more than having Faith. Faith is "towards" someone or something. "Believing" is "to put Faith" in someone or something, and so being "within it/inside of it".

[910] It is important to see how Jesus speaks in the past, since when he was blind, he spiritually saw him and that is where the spiritual healing came from, and now he sees him physically since the healing manifested on this level.

[911] Now he sees him and he is born again as The One that was "dominating" all of his nature: internal and external.

[912] It's an evolutionary necessity, a decision of the spiritual world, that what is about to happen needs to happen. It can also be translated as "to open/start a process".

[913] They regain spiritual sight.

[914] The ones who have an atavistic clairvoyance, like the Pharisees, will lose it.

[915] Jesus always invites everyone to a higher level of comprehension of the "above-ground" matters. The first level of comprehension should belong to the apostles, the second ones to the chief priests (or Pharisees), the third one to the Sadducees. Another level is added to these three, the "+1", which is given to the Pious Women. They are disciples (and so they also correspond to the apostles), they are priestly (since they are connected to the lineage of Abel and therefore of the priests), and they are romans (since amongst them there is Pilates' wife). For these reasons they will be the ones to grasp the importance and magnificence of the action of the Christ within Jesus and they will be the first ones to meet him after the crucifixion.

[916] If they would not see within the spirit, they would not be sinners because they would have already distance themselves from the old clairvoyance. By saying that they keep seeing, their sin (which is the relationship with the luciferic clairvoyance) remains.

THE PARABLE OF THE GOOD SHEPHERD (Is 40,11; Ez 34,11-23)

1. "Amen, Amen[917], I say (*lego*) to you: the one who does not enter the pen of the sheep[918] through the door, but instead enters from another side[919], he is a murdered[920] and thief.
2. But who enters through the door[921], is a shepherd of sheep[922].
3. The gatekeeper[923] opens the door form him, and the sheep hear (*akuou*) his voice, and he calls his own sheep by name[924], and he leads them out[925].
4. And when he takes his own[926] out,, he walks in front of them[927], and the sheep follow him, because they know his voice[928].

---

917 It's a truth that refers to the sphere of the Holiest Trinity. With this, Jesus establishes the exiting of the Jewish institution since it is not a bearer of the I Am, of Freedom and Love instead, it is anchored to the formal and hypocritical observance of the Law.

918 The sheep's corral, or pen, represents the house of Faith, the heart. Let's remember that the temple of Jerusalem had a door called "the door of sheep". This corral designates the corral, or atrium, where the Tent of the Meeting was located. By saying this, we can say how it refers to both the atrium of the Temple (spiritual dimension) and the corral of the sheep-Chosen People.
In a microcosmic sense, this corral- atrium is the dimension of the consciousness within us where the Higher I acts and where we can perceive the voice of the Lord and distinguish it from the voice of Lucifer or Ahriman, who also want to enter us.

919 The other initiation paths that are not connected to the impulse of the Christ.

920 Ahriman is a murderer. The thief is Lucifer. These forces want to take us to enter the spiritual world without the necessary inner work. We wither "ascend" through the chakras in a conscious matter (from in front, with the forces of Mariam) or we do it in an unconscious matter (from behind, through the re-awakening of the snake-Lucifer, Kundalini).

921 To go through the first door, the door of the Sun, we need the baptism of the Fire. The second door (zodiacal) is entered through the baptism of the Spirit.

922 Who goes through Jesus (the first door) becomes a shepherd as well.

923 Michael, who guards the door of the Sun-heart or Jesus who opens the door to the Christ.

924 Both as a name-numen (Holy Spirit) and as "secret" name, or spiritual name.

925 He helps us overcome obstacles, the corral, the old law, to leave and head towards higher dimensions, and to overcome the consequences of the Fall.

926 He freed them.

927 He is the Guide and not a teacher.

928 The voice of the Logos. This can be interpreted as He knows the Name of each Sheep, of each one of "His own". Let's remember that the throat, with the collarbones (small keys that close the entrance to the door on the east of the terrestrial Paradise, a door that is guarded by a Cherub with a flaming and rotating sword and the Jesus donated the keys to this door to Peter) which will continue with the arms (in hebrew *Sichem* which means "aim" "goal") and the hands, represents the force and the knowledge of the eagle within us. Let's remember how this cherub has a "Michael" nature, and just like Michael, he acts in the throat of man against the forces of the obstacle.

5. They will not follow a stranger, instead they will run away from him. Because they do not know the voice of strangers[929].
6. Jesus told (*eipon*) this parable. But they do not know what he was talking (*laleo*)[930] about.
7. So Jesus said: "Amen, Amen, I say to you that I Am the door of the sheep[931].
8. All the ones that came before me are murderers and thieves, and the sheep did not listen to them[932].
9. I am the door. If someone will enter for me, he will be safe, and he will enter, and exit, and he will find pasture[933].
10. The murderer only enters to steal, kill and destroy[934]. I came so that they could have spiritual life, and so that they would have it in overabundance[935].

---

[929] Because he recognize that within them there is no truth.

[930] Because they yet have to enter the new consciousness, the new "corral".

[931] He reinstates the exiting of the Jewish institution. It corresponds to the level of the cherubic Zodiac. He is the Door for us, and we are called to be like Him if we want to knock on this Door and open it. He is the Light that enlightens the way, which brings us to this inner Door.

[932] From this we understand that the sheep are the pure forces of the soul.

[933] He will be free in his actions. The pasture is the spiritual nourishment who will take him to be saved.

[934] To steal knowledge is the action of Lucifer against the Path, to kill is the action of Ahriman which brings us to lies against the Truth, to destroy is the asuric action which goes against the Path.

[935] The overabundance allows us to gift it to others, and this happens by irradiating our Incorruptible Body.

11. *I am the good*[936]*shepherd.* The good shepherd gives (*di domi*) his breath of life for the sheep[937].

12. The mercenary[938], on the other hand, and the ones who are not shepherds, and who do not have their own sheep, see[939] (*theorao*) the wolf[940] coming, and they abandon the sheep, and they run away, and the wolf steals and scatters the sheep[941].

13. Because he is a mercenary, he does not take care of the sheep.

14. I am the good shepherd: and I know mine and mine know me[942].

15. And I have other sheep[943], that are not from this sheep pen[944], and I need to lead those too, and they will hear my voice and it will become One only herd and One only shepherd[945].

---

936 Now he is not only the "door" but he also describes His activity of guidance and support towards the Chosen People. **This is the fifth I Am pronounced by Jesus and it corresponds to the level of the serafinic Zodiac.** Jesus is now confirming his being united with the Father. He went beyond being the Light of the world; he now turned down all the forces of the ego, and the Father can act within him and from him towards all the other men that are ready (Lazarus). After Lazarus' resuscitation, HE will descend to the physical body, and he will be ready for the Passion. Through the love for Lazarus, he descended to the underworld, and then, to Golgotha, and he will do this for the love all of humanity. "Good" is the one who reached the moral virtue of kindness/goodness, which is given to us from the conquering of the Loving Vital Spirit.

937 Usually translated as "he gives his life (or soul). The verb *psuche'* indicates the effusion of the vital breath. He pours (effuses) within us the forces of His pure soul which is Life for us. This soul, like in the Spiritual Communion, is the Holiest Mother of God.

938 Which means the one who acts with no true inner certainty; instead he acts for personal profit. It is important to know that the wolf can appear only when the mercenary is present: when the shepherd is there, he cannot act.

939 With spiritual clairvoyance he can see the spiritual events from far away (*theorei*)

940 He represents the solar demon that acts more in the night of a Full Moon (luciferic).

941 The mercenary is Lucifer, the ruler of false initiation; he is not the owner, he limits himself to "shear" the sheep and to steal their forces. The wolf is the solar demon, the 666; the sheep are the ones that belong to the Chosen People.

942 The Chosen People are connected to the uncorrupted Adam, to the Jesus; and within recognizing one another in the Truth, we can find the meeting with Jesus Christ.

943 Other religious currents.

944 From the Judaism.

945 After crossing the Door of the Sun, all religious form can reunite.

16. This is why the Father spiritually loves me, because I can (gift) my breath of life, and then take it up again[946].

17. No one takes it away from me[947], but I can impose it to myself, and I have the power to impose it and the power to take it up[948] again. I received this command from my Father.

18. Because of these logos, more division happened amongst the Jewish people.

19. Many said (*lego*) amongst themselves: "He has a demon and he is beside himself: why are you listening to him?"

20. Other said (*lego*): "These words (*rema*) are not the ones of someone who has a demon: does a demon have the strength to reopen the eyes and lift the tunic of skin that covers the eyes?[949]

THE CONSECRATION, THE LORD IN PEREA (1 Mac 4,59; 2 Mac 1,9)

21. Then came the festival of consecration[950] in Jerusalems, and it was winter[951].

---

[946] He announces his Resurrection and so His authority on Life. Since He has no sin, the forces of death have no power over Him.

[947] No one can take it away from the Christ; He is the one that donates it to us.

[948] To accept him within oneself after the terrestrial experience.

[949] This spiritual and physical healing shook the Pharisees up, since they realized that the regeneration of man had begun.

[950] The reoccurring event that celebrates the consecration (or Dedication) of the Temple of Solomon to God. Jesus probably goes there to indicate that the Son of God is by now incarnated in the man and so the man became the true temple.

[951] The festival happened in December and it lasted 8 days. For this occasion, big candleholder would be lit up just like in the Feast of the Huts (Tabernacles), and this is why it was named Festival of the Lights or of thee Huts (Tabernacles) in Winter.
As we just said, this event would always take place in the winter time. Maybe John wants to accentuate the death in which the law fell and so the festival took place.

22. And Jesus was[952] in the temple (inner)[953], in the porch of Solomon[954].

23. The Jewish people surrounded[955] him and they said (*lego*) to him: "For how long will you keep our devotion[956] high? If you are the Christ say (*eipon*) it openly."[957]

24. Jesus replied to them: "I said (*eipon*) to you and you do not believe[958](*pisteno*). The accomplishments that I create in the name of my Father, these are testimonies about[959] me.

25. But you do not believe because you are not my[960] sheep.

---

[952] Verb that indicates the esoteric "going around" the truth, to grasp it under all different points of view.

[953] For "Temple" see note on the verse 2,14.

[954] The mentioning of the porch brings us back to the 5 porches of the pool of Bethsaida, of the man with no strength (John 5,2). In a microcosmic sense we are in the area of the brainstem and the cerebellum. The temple is the location of the principles of the priests and the pool was the prosecution, the location where the Chosen People lied suffering.
The reference to Solomon brings us back to the first king who "dedicated" is own temple in the Feast of the Huts (Tabernacles). Solomon reminds us that his father, David, was the anointed, which means the Messiah, of the Lord: the title that will be given to Jesus.

[955] Now the Jewish people are "going around" Jesus; they surround him, probably in a hostile manner. Let's remember that they already suggested to kill him.

[956] From the Greek work *psyche'*, here it refers to the quality of the soul that opens up to the spiritual world. Let's remember that the Jewish people are the ones to talk this way.

[957] The tone is extremely harsh: they already decided to kill him. They want Him to declare himself, but He will never say it (except to the Samaritan: a woman).
The question reminds us of the one that was asked by the Baptist to the Pharisees: now they are afraid that He is going to declare himself king-Messiah, and that then he will ascend to the throne and causing their end.

[958] Here is the answer: it is up to them to recognize him basing themselves on the Words that he says. The same goes for the symbols and the institutions that he says that need to stop existing because His Work will replace them. For the difference between "having faith" and "believing", see John 1,7.

[959] He urges them to respond about His works: as long as they do not do so, He will not respond about being the Messiah. He does not offer "legal" credentials, instead they are objective.

[960] They do not belong to the Chose People even though they are Jewish; they do not respond to His calling.

26. My sheep hear (*akuou*) my voice[961] and I know them, and they follow me[962];

27. And I gift them eternal spiritual Life[963], and they will not be scattered for eternity, and no one will steal them from my hand[964].

28. What my Father gave me is greater than any other thing[965], and no one has the strength to steal it from the hand of the Father (mine).

29. The Father and I are One[966]."

---

[961] They spiritually hear His inner talking to men, to "his own".

[962] These are the characteristics of "his own".

[963] The gifts us spiritual life (Zoe) because when we take part in it and participate it, it becomes ours, and we are one with it (just like to John: "Here is your mother"). His soul, transformed in I Am, on the other hand, he gives it to us, and then he takes it again after His sacrifice so that he can keep giving it to humanity.

[964] It is something that cannot be stolen, but only be received as a gift. Therefore, thieves and murderers will never be able to enter Zoe, the Celestial Life, the springs, the spiritual Seeds, and Life. The hand, in Hebrew *yada* represents knowledge but it means "I love". This knowledge is a marriage; it is spiritual love.
At the end of our evolutionary path, we will be one with Christ, and with him we will be creators of a new evolutionary system in which we will act as an elite bearer of Love.
In the sense of the tri-articulation, the whole arm represents the Holy Spirit (while the forearm represents the Son and the arm represents the Father). In the tradition of the Psalms, the right hand represents the Holy Spirits that gives life and the left hand represents the Son who structures, molds, shapes. The hands put together represent the union of the force that structures with the knowledge that gives life.

[965] This thing is the new humanity that through Jesus Christ will manifest according to the will of the Father.
This represents a transition from the condition of "duty" to one of "Freedom". From this, the fourth aspect comes to life, the "+1", the "prize": to reach eternal spiritual Life.

[966] Jesus becomes the new sanctuary of the Father, and Grace and Truth (John 1,14) fill him up. The criticizing and opposition to Jesus become the criticizing of the Father. He brings us to the Father.

THE HOSTILITY OF THE JEWISH PEOPLE (Ps 81,6).

30. The Jewish people picked[967] up more stones[968] to stone[969] him.

31. The Jewish People then grabbed more stones to stone him.

32. Jesus replied to them: " I showed you many good[970] works of (my) Father, for which ones are you stoning me[971]?"

33. The Jewish people replied: "We are not stoning you for a good work, we are doing so for a curse[972]; and because you, man[973] as you are, claim to be God[974]".

34. Jesus replied: "Isn't it written in your[975] Law "*I*[976] *said: you are Gods?"*

35. If I said Gods[977] the ones to whom the verb of God manifested to them, and there is no strength to dissolve the Holy Writ,

---

[967] Literally "they lifted", just how the stone of Lazarus' sepulcher was lifted.

[968] They are the dead thoughts that arise from the formal and strict interpretation of the Law.

[969] Within this there is also the image of their "hard" consciousness, just like stone, and their refusal in listening the Word of Life.

[970] The adjective "good" and the reference to the Father, connect us to Creation when the Father "saw that what was made was good". Now the new Man is rising.

[971] Once again, since Jesus sees that His Word is not being accepted, he puts the attention towards His work since the works are "daughters" of the person and so they allow us to re-ascend to the qualities of the person. Once again, He reawakens the consciousness of the present people with a question.

[972] They do not reply about the works done to which they cannot object. The fact that they turned the temple into a house of thieves and the Chosen People became moribund, is not enough for them. They do not have the love of God and so they do not understand the plan of divine love.

[973] Not initiated.

[974]In reality, Jesus never said that he "was God" instead he used the words and he acted in ways to have people understand the fullness of His being and His union with the Father. With considering man becoming God a curse, the Jewish people deny the presence of the divine component in man and so they deny the possibility of the Fatehr returning.

[975] Jesus is no longer recognized in the Jewish Law.

[976] The reference is to the Psalm 81,6 which says: "You are gods, you are all sons of the Highest one". The Jewish people are shocked both by the fact that He said that His Father was God and that now man can become God.

[977]We understand that they are the spiritual Hierarchies of the Holy Trinity.

36. And to the one who the Father sanctified[978] and sent into the world you say: "you curse" because I said: "I am the son of God[979]?

37. If I do not do my Father's work, you do not believe me.

38. But if I do it, even if you do not believe in me, you believe in the works, so that you will know that within me there is the Father, and I within the Father".

39. They tried to grab him, and he got out of their power[980].

---

[978] Became Saint with the manifestation of the Dove at the Baptism of the Jordan.

[979] Son of the God of the Holiest Trinity: this Son is the Christ

[980] The word comes from the Hebrew *cheir* which means hand, strength, sphere of action, power of the crowd.
Jesus does not run away but he limits himself to not being grabbed since no human force or negative force can limit him in his action if He does not want it...

40. And he went to the other side of the Jordan[981] once again, towards the location where John was baptized[982] at the beginning (*protos*), and he stayed there[983].

41. And many came towards him, and they said (*lego*) that John did not create signs. But all that John said about these things, it was true[984].

42. And many believed in him there[985].

---

[981] The Jordan represents the force of the I that flows within man through the spinal cord. The Jordan connects the waters from below (amniotic fluid-womb) with the ones from above (Dead sea-head). Within man, the waters from below do not reflect the ones from above and so they flow towards death. As the divine seed reawakens within us, the wound from the fall (feet) can heal and close up and the flux gets inverted (hemorrhage), and we begin to take part in the cosmic Life. Jesus will also immerse himself into it (in the sphere of what is still not done) for then re-descend immediately. He goes through the path of Adam once again. He descends in the feminine-darkness side that he need to marry so it can be completed and done.
The expression "on this side of the Jordan" represents the whole man with his consciousness and so, by esoteric inversion, the Chosen People. From this we get that the expression "on the other side of the Jordan" represents the human condition of the ones that find themselves to be outside of the Chosen People. In this case, it also expresses the retreating in the spiritual world.
This "crossing" of the Jordan reminds us the transition of the Red Sea: from the freeing of the Egyptian slavery, to the freeing from the dead Law in the Love of the Father. This area is Perea.

[982] In Bethany of Transjordan. Bethany of Jerusalem represents the Loving Vital Spirit. Now He goes to the other Bethany, to get ready for the Resurrection of Lazarus which will happen in Bethany of Jerusalem. This is the Bethany of "preparation" (and here he baptized John, the "preparer" of the coming of the Christ), the second Bethany of "initiation". Bethany means "house of healing".
Let's remember that the Baptism of John was a baptism of water, and the disciple was kept under water for a certain amount of time so that he wouldn't spiritually experience his entire past life so that he could reconnect to the spiritual reality. When the disciple would come back out of the water, he would know of the reality of this higher dimension and so he would "know" that within him there is a part (the I Am) which can live without the support of the physical body. This transformed the dominating mentality in regards to the identification with the material physical body. With him he would feel "one" with the spiritual world and he would perceive that from the spiritual world the principle of the I Am was descending on Earth and thanks to His forces of spiritual love, all of the different egotistical "I" would be overcome and brought to unite (within the dimension of love).

[983] He goes back to the spiritual plane (beyond the Jordan). This is because He was not being accepted in the material plane.

[984] They go to Him because they accept him since they first listened to John, and they kept those words in their hearts.

[985] Being in the spiritual plane ("there") now, they believe in Him. This "there" represents the contrast between the terrestrial world and the reality of the spiritual world. It is important to see how the adjective "many" indicates a process of individualization.

LAZARUS RESUSCITATION[986]

1. He was someone with no strength (for the spiritual path)[987], Lazarus[988] from Bethany[989], from the village[990] of the Mary[991] and the Martha[992], her sister[993].

---

[986] This will be the seventh and last miracle that Jesus will perform. All the other one are "signs" or "prodigious healings". The miracle is an event that cannot happen according to the terrestrial laws. This is the main chapter of the gospel of John and it is said, three times, that "Jesus loved the disciple" and this is to accentuate the power of love.

[987] With the term "no strength", the evangelist is précising that Lazarus had no spiritual strength because of him "consuming himself" for the word of Jesus. "With no strength" indicates the process of decline in which the Incorruptible Body is in. Additionally, he was receiving the initiation from the Priests, who committed ceremonial mistakes and so Lazarus was dying.

[988] It is the first time that someone who is ill is being called by his name" this is to indicate that he is a disciple. Given the importance of this episode, we feel that it is necessary to talk about the spiritual meaning of the name Lazarus (in Greek *Lazaratos*). In ancient Greek, it means: "*L* the Light of the Sun that enlightens the mind; *A* begin; *Z* the cosmic Life which also is Gnostic consciousness; *A* begin; *R* the Father of the skies; *A* begin; *T* the Tau, the force that descends but that doesn't move, that is still; *O* descends, it stops, and it incorporates; *S* within ourselves, inside the inner cave". The word contains three beginnings (letter *A)*: of the Sun- Higher I, of the Mary Sophia-cosmic Life, and of the Father.
Since the Event of the Golgotha completely changed the action of the Verb, we can also find a meaning that is after the Golgotha from the same Greek alphabet. Read under this light, the name Lazaratos becomes: "*L* the confrontation of the thought with the world determines the domination of the forces of the Earth in the *A* etheric body; *Z* is the thought of Mary Sophia; *A* in the etheric, the existence within us; *R* the creating action of the Logos; *A* in the etheric; *T* resurrects; *O* brings in us; *S* as a logical thought". Therefore, we have John-Eagle coming to life: the intelligence of the heart.

[989] In the spiritual language, Bethany (literally "house of healing"), represents the "house" of the Vital Loving Spirit. The fact that this village is being mentioned as the location in which Jesus is retreating (John 10, 40), indicates that in that dimension, there is the Community established by Jesus. Bethany had already appeared at the verse 1,28. Now we are in Bethany of Judea.

[990] The village indicate the forces gravitating around a chakra.

[991] The level of Mary is not specified.

[992] According to the old Christian tradition, Martha was identified with the hemorrhage.

[993] Martha has the article because she is Mary's sister.

2. Mariam[994] was the one that anointed the Lord[995] with a scented oil and she dried his feet[996] with her hair[997]: and whose brother, Lazarus, was with no strength (for the spiritual path).

---

[994] This is Silent Mary, representing the conscious soul. We now have "three" sisters representing the three souls: the Mary Magdalen-the sentient soul; Martha-rational soul and Silent Mariam-conscious soul. Lazarus represents the I that comes to life and who unites with them.

[995] This episode will happen later on, chapter 12,1.

[996] The feet represent the kingdom of Earth, the *Malkut*, the terrestrial Kingdom and so the Mother, the Virgin Mother, the Black Madonna, the Mother of each and every terrestrial existence. For this reason, in the spiritual symbology, they are pictured as "wounded" and so they are in need of healing. Eve was also bitten by the snake on her foot. The wound is represented by the "false" (arch) of the foot and it is one "half" of the wound, the other one on the head represented by the fontanel. This is because the man created in God's image and likeness, who is the Zodiacal Man or First Adam, is represented by the zodiacal circle that was then "cut" between Aries-head and Pisces-feet and so it lost the "likeness" with the Creator.
We find a three plus one also in the feet:

- The Mary that throws herself at Jesus' feet at the Resuscitation of Lazarus (John 11,32);
- The anointment of the feet from Mary to prepare him for the test of victory upon the forces of death present on the feet (the oil would protect from the terrestrial forces- John 12,1);
- The Washing of the Feet with the Jesus which completely purifies the Apostles and heals the wound that came from the Fall (John 13,5);
- The Magdalen will try to grab him by the feet on Easter Sunday but the Risen Again will not allow that since after healing the feet and descending in the womb of Mother Earth, he will after ascend to the Father to complete the spiritual marriage between Mother Earth and Father Sky (and also heal the planetary sphere) (John 20,15).

[997] Hair represents the spiritual force that permeates the man. Let's remember that hair, being on the head, represents the "olive trees" of the Garden of the Olive Trees, and so the serafinic zodiacal dimension. From the Hebrew *sear* the trees are the "prince", the "principle planted on the spring of the being". The Hebrew term indicates the fear in front of the divine vision.

3. They sent the sisters towards him and they said (*lego*): "Sir, here (*idein*) the one that you brotherly love has no strength (for the spiritual path)[998]"

4. Hearing this, Jesus said (*eipon*): "This lacking of strength (for the spiritual path) is not towards death, but for the glory of the God[999], but so that the Son (*hyos*) of the God[1000] will be glorified through is".

5. Jesus spiritually[1001] loved the Martha, and her sister, and the[1002] Lazarus[1003].

6. Since he heard (*akouo*) he had no strength (for the spiritual path), he stayed days in the location[1004] in which he had been for two days.

---

[998] In Lazarus' case we are not referring to an old initiation caused by the Hierophant, instead, the process of separation of the etheric body from the physical body had happened in a "natural" way thanks to the sacrifices, fasting, and mystical ascensions that Lazarus would practice. This is why there will be the need of the Christ to help him "come back" to the body.
It is important to see how there is no petition, no request for help, but only information.

[999] The glory of the God indicates a manifestation of the operating Divinity: the complete clairvoyance and clairaudience of the Word of God in Light and in Voice.

[1000] Jesus would have given the new initiation to Lazarus, bringing him to the level of Son of God (Vital Loving Spirit). With this new initiation the Christ, which is the Son of the God, opens the new path to go back to the Father. R. Steiner translates this verse as: "*Illness is not death, but so that the God can manifest within him (*and he can get out of the arcane)".
This is the seventh and last miracle operated by Jesus ,mand we are present at an increase of His strength: now He can reawaken his impulse in another man so that he, permeated by it, can become another man: a great Initiated.

[1001] To the soul that asks (the sisters) the Jesus opens up spiritually loving. Before (verse 11.3) he loved "in a brotherly way", since they were cousins.

[1002] Let's remember that every time that a name has an article in front of it, it means that a reference to the higher spiritual entity present in that person is being made.

[1003] Now Lazarus is being mentioned last to indicate the unity of the group.

[1004] The location is Bethany of Transjordan, which is the location where the Baptist baptized, and there the Baptist declares that someone else will come after him to baptize in Spirit and Fire. It is odd that he stops for two extra days and that he does not just leave. The explanation is that he wanted to make it obvious that the Initiation of the priests failed (it would last 3 days and a half), and He was going to be the one bringing Lazarus back to life.
It is important to know that Lazarus was in Bethany of Judea: this is to indicate that there are two Bethanys, two Communities that follow Jesus: one is "widen" (the Transjordan) and so outside of Israel, outside of the Chosen People, and one is "restricted", formed by the family of Lazarus and it is located in Judea, within Israel. This last one mentioned though, still has some aspects attached to the past, to the Mosaic Law.

7. After this he says (*lego*) to the disciples: "Let's go to Judea"[1005]

8. The disciples tell (*lego*) him: "Rhabbi, the Jewish people are looking for you to stone[1006] you, and you want to go down[1007] there again?"

9. Jesus replied (*apokrinomai*): "Aren't the hours of the day twelve[1008]? If one travels[1009] during the day he does not stumble, because the light of his world[1010] sees (*blepo*),

10. But if someone travels during the night, he will stumble, because the light[1011] is not within him"

[1005] He is the one that decides the times. The return to Judea represents returning into the forces of Opposition of His acting, and this is why the disciples were worried.

[1006] Further on we will see how the stone that covers the hidden location (in the cranium) will be lifted.

[1007] From the Greek *hypago*, which means to come down a level (it also applies to the verse John 9,7 to replace "lead down").

[1008] Twelve is also the number of the dorsal vertebrae through which man can stand straight (after the "formation" with the 10 vertebrae sacro-lumbar that represent the Law). The Zodiac surrounds the rhythmic man through the 12 doors of the 12 vertebrae: we are entering the mysteries of Light.
These twelve hours represent the duration of the "sixth day", the one symbolically begun in Cana (see also 8.56) and that is not ending with the resuscitation of Lazarus. The seventh day will begin after this: "His time" where he will win "the hour of darkness". For the disciples, the 12 hours of light are the ones in which Jesus is with them.

[1009] The verb "travel" comes from "*peripatetico*", which means the one who walks around something and can capture all the different points of view and so can know it completely. In our case, we need to travel the "paths" of the Zodiac, which means to capture all 12 impulses that characterize the cosmic spiritual thinking: the 12 conceptions of the world (the 12 is the number of the "celestial" things). We are attached to one of these conceptions (the one corresponding to our astrological sign) and to capture all 12 of them allows us to reach the unity with God's Thought (1/12x12=1). With another mathematical equation, we can see how 1/12 (us) x (the others)1/12= 1/144 and 144 are the nerves (72x2) of the central nervous system (and it also corresponds to the Disciples). When all humanity will have reached this initiatic goal, then the 144 will become 144.000 of the Apocalypse (the number of the ones who will be saved). Let's remember that all numbers have a quantitative aspect and a qualitative aspect. It seems obvious to assume that John, the highest initiate, was mainly talking about the second aspect.

[1010] The expression "Light of the world" refers to the light of the passage 1.9. "He became light, the true one, which enlightens every man, who comes to the natural world". This Light is the Christ.

[1011] Of the Christ, true inner sun of truth and justice.

11. This is what he said (*eipon*), and after this he said (*lego*) to them: "Lazarus, our brotherly friend fell asleep[1012]; but I am heading out[1013] to reawaken him[1014].

12. The disciples said (*eipon*) to him: "Sir, if he fell asleep, he will be saved[1015]"

13. Jesus said (*eireka*) about his death[1016]; but they clearly thought that he said (*eireka*) about the one who fell asleep[1017].

14. Jesus then openly said (*eipon*) to them: "Lazarus is in the depths of death (*apothnesko*).

15. And I am happy[1018] for you[1019] that I wasn't there, so that you have faith (*episteno*)[1020]: but let's go towards him"[1021].

1012 It refers to the state of sleep that the initiate was put into by the Priests so that he could experiment the spiritual worlds, experiences that would then be brought to the awareness with the reawakening. The new path of initiation brought by the Christ presumes that man is completely conscious in all the phases of the initiatic process.

1013 From the Greek *porenomai*, which means to walk along the spiritual paths.

1014 In the Greek mythology, *Ipnosi* was the twin brother of death. This sleep is son of the night, of the three days of darkness that consciousness experiences during the old initiatic hypnosis and in which the separation of the etheric brain happens.

1015 They believe that Lazarus is still in the initiatic process, and they are afraid for Jesus' life since the Jewish people wanted to kill him.

1016 Lazarus, because of the wrong initiation given by the Priests (the planet Mercury was in a negative position compared to the Sun), went from a induced sleep (hypnosis) to death, and Jesus will be the one to bring him back to life.

1017 From the context, we can understand that if the disciples would have believed Him, or better, if they would have had Faith in Him, they also would have experimented what Lazarus was experimenting and going through: the Initiation of the Vital Loving Spirit and they would have become "John".

1018 From the Greek *chairo,* Like to Marian at the Annunciation.

1019 Take note of the contradiction amongst the announcement of Lazarus death and the invite to be happy: it's like saying that death is only a transition, and it is not a definitive condition like the Jewish people believed it to be.

1020 He does not put himself first. He is happy that the miracle that is about to happen will help them to have more Faith.

1021 He does not say to go and cheer up the sisters; He says to go and resuscitate him.

16. Thomas, the so-called Dydimus[1022], said (*eipen*) to his fellow disciples: "Let's go so that we can also be in the depths of death with him[1023]"

[1022] Dydimus means "twin", to indicate the importance that he had amongst the twelve.
The fact that the translation of this name is given, indicates its importance. Thomas is willing to die "with" Jesus, while Peter will be willing to die "for" Jesus (John 13,37).

[1023] Thomas, who is also called "Dydimus", which means Jesus' "twin" (because he is the bearer of the highest knowledge), recognizes the events that are about to happen, and he suggests that they also take part of the initiatic experience and follow Jesus in the kingdom of death. He believes that the 12 hours of "Light" are over and he wants to follow Jesus in the kingdom of the underworld. Let's also remember that amongst the 12 Apostles, Thomas represents the overcoming of doubt.

17. As Jesus arrived (*erchomai*), he found him being in the memories[1024] for four days.

[1024]In a materialistic sense, the word memory indicates the monument of the sepulcher in which the dead body is. In a spiritual sense, it is the condition of retrospective vision, thanks to which the initiate remembers his spiritual principle: the I Am, the being a part of God. The word "sepulcher" has an additional meaning. This word also indicates a consequence to the process of etherization of the blood. This process rhythmically modifies the blood current so that the etheric body can exit from that part within us that is the "sepulcher", that involucres us: from the head. The impulse comes to life from the heart-Sun after we welcomed the force of the Christ.

In Hebrew, the word "memory" corresponds to "male", and by this we are talking about the one who becomes "male" in the inner side, he "remembers" his inner skies: his divine origin. On the contrary of the "memory" where Jesus' body will be put, this memory is not "new". To "remember one's own divine origin" means to "know", with a new consciousness, that God exists and that we are part of Him, we belong to Him, we are called to go back to Him and so we need to do His will. To reject this is the sin of impiety.

At this point we might be asking ourselves why are first Lazarus, and then Jesus (on a higher level) being put in the sepulcher-memory? In the explanation that we are about to give, we can find a key to understand the path, the spiritual experience that they went through within those particular conditions.

From R. Steiner we comprehend that (second conference of the cycle" Inner Nature of man and life and death and new birth) to accomplish deep spiritual research, we need to get out of the physical body with our soul. To do so, there are two different ways: to simply go within space and begin to live within it and "looking" to the physical body from over there, or we can go deeper and deeper within ourselves. This way, we connect once again with the experiences of the soul that are more similar to the first spiritual experiences and we can try to reconnect through memory. For the fact that our soul holds on to thoughts and perceptions, we transform our inner life in something spiritual since within us something that is absolutely soul like-spiritual develops. The rising of imaginative clairvoyance consciousness is extremely similar to the soul content within us which is the heritage of memory. Therefore, we need to arise from spiritual regions to something that is behind memory. Amongst memories, spiritual images begin to rise of something that we did not used to know. The path consists on walking "backwards" the path of our own life (a retrospective vision) so that we can re-enter that spiritual world from which we descended to incarnate. This way, we exit space and are in time. Instead of "inside and out" we have "before and after", and this is a way higher path to enter the spiritual.

Along this path, we find the majestic and spiritual figure of the human ideal shaped in the image of God. This human ideal is like a temple and he is the religion of the gods. Here we perceive the actions of the helpers of humanity, of the divine beings that weaved within our being, within our soul, and they help us through the process of incarnation.

We reach a point in which we can go no further. The divine forces are within us and a tempting voice whispers to us to not reincarnate on Earth in a physical body, but instead, it suggests to follow with our being the actions of the gods that shaped us and to keep going deeper and deeper into the world of the Spirit. If we follow this luciferic temptation, we exit from the path that would take us to the great ideal of humanity. We can follow the temptation and enter the world of Spirit with our imperfections and there they would be corrected to perfection. In doing this, we would have to let go of the dispositions that we bring within us and that we yet have to develop in the direction that brings us to the great human ideal: we would have to give up to what we could become as men (complete freedom and love). By doing this, we would become irreligious in front of the world of the Spirit.

This is the moment in which Lucifer has the highest power upon man. He can make us forget what our great human ideal is. Therefore, a battle for the human souls comes to life amongst Lucifer and the gods. The result of this battle is that the primordial image of the man, the image that he was shaped thanks to his terrestrial existences, is being projected from time to space: it gets attracted (like a magnet) in the existence of space.

In this moment, we can also perceive the attraction towards the future parents: we improve with the sphere of space. This way, we overcome the luciferic temptation that would rather keep us in the spiritual spheres, and the protection consists in "covering ourselves" with corporeal matter. Helping us to descend in the world of sense, the helping spirits can support us in our evolutionary process.

To enter in the terrestrial existence, man needs to first elaborate his brain and his nervous system. This work is accomplished before he descends in collaboration with the spirits of Wisdom, and then, on Earth, the wisdom that he will express will be a reflection of this cosmic Reflection. On Earth, we are separated by the action of these spirits, and the Guardian of the Threshold makes sure that we do not reconnect before we are ready to do so, which means in a luciferic way, so that Lucifer cannot win in the temptation. These Wisdom Spirits give to us enough of their actions of wisdom to that we can begin our path of re-ascension. If we would speed the process up, we would find Lucifer tempting us so that we would stay in the spiritual world with all of our imperfections and without developing our dispositions (which are still imperfect). We would lose the goal of humanity: the great human ideal.

Here on Earth, surrounded by material things, we can receive new impulses from the divine spirits towards the far goals of humanity, and they can give us the strength so that, after we are dead, we can push ourselves a little more towards the great human ideal,

All of this has an Easter-like aspect of life, death and return with the victory upon Lucifer in the *post mortem* and we grasp how the divine spirits act within us for our own additional evolution. They lead the current of time, they allowed us to immerse ourselves in the space so that we could achieve enough consciousness that they thought we needed to have to re-ascend towards the great human ideal.

By going into space through the door of memory, we can be aware of how the divine beings act within us and how they dominate. We can allow this information to flow within us and we can grasp the right sense of the divine, which acts within us.

Therefore the soul, with all that it knows, perceives, thinks, feels and wants, becomes aware that is came from a deeper soul sphere, from a sphere within it that still resides within the divine, that flows in the current of time with the divine: we are born from God.

[1025]

18. It was the Bethany close to the Jerusalems within about 15 stadiums[1026].

19. And many Jewish people came towards the Martha, and Mary, to bring the evocative (*mhytos*) word about their brother.

20. The Martha, when she heard (*akuou*)[1027] that Jesus was coming, she went towards the lower side to reach him[1028]: while Mary was secretly working in the space of the inner temple (*oichos*)[1029].

21. The Martha then said (*eipen*) towards Jesus: "Sir, if you would have been here my brother would have not gone into the depths of death (*apothnesko*)[1030].

[1025]The Hebrew culture believed that the soul of the one that went to the other side would linger around the dead for three days, and then he would abandon him on the fourth day, when the lines on the face would start to go away. From this came the "security" of the truthfulness of the miracle that he was about to accomplish.

[1026] "Stadium" in greek means "space", and the Space is Son of the Light. Therefore, Bethany was fifteen "spaces" from the beginning of the spiritual path and then, after fifteen "steps", we arrive half way between the Higher I and the Loving Vital Spirit. Ten are the steps for the reawakening of the Higher I (the 10 steps are represented by the 10 Commandments), twenty for the reawakening of the Loving Vital Spirt and thirty for the reawakening of the Sprit Man (the thirty years of private life of Jesus). It is important to underline how the evangelist indicates "the" Bethany, and by doing this, he highlights its spiritual value. 15 stadiums correspond to a distance that goes from 185 to 197 meters.

[1027] Martha internally hears the coming of Jesus. Hearing is a sense connected to the ether of sound (or Chemical Ether) which connects to the sphere of Mars. From this we can see that the name Martha indicates this capability to connect to the sphere of Mars. In a spiritual sense, clairaudience, which is the capability to hear with "etheric ears" the Music of the Spheres, is a characteristic of the action of the Loving Vital Spirit in our astral body.
Martha is in the Loving Vital Spirit who acts in the astral body, and internally this refers to the connecting of the forces of the constellation of Libra (this is by basing ourselves at the specific connection present between the spiritual limb and the astral body in the period of the 12 Holy Christmas Nights): so that the Loving Vital Spirit can act in the I. (In Lazarus), the test of the Scorpio needs to be overcome, the test of death (from Libra to Scorpio).

[1028] She also descends.

[1029] Mary (with no article) remains in the subtle bodies where she secretly works to gather the forces (she is sitting down) to get ready to become "the" Mary. "The" Martha got out of the subtle bodies to meet the Jesus.

[1030] According to some old Christian traditions, the woman hemorrhaging was Martha and so she knew very well which strong forces of life were acting within the Jesus. And so in her phrase we can see a subtle scolding. The initiation would take the initiate to the border of death. Lazarus, because of the mistakes of the priests, went into the depths of death and so he is dead.

22. But I know[1031] that anything you ask to the God, the God[1032] will give it to you".

23. Jesus replied: "Your brother will resuscitate[1033]".

24. The Martha told him: "I know that he will resuscitate in the resurrection of the last day[1034]".

25. Jesus said to her: "I am[1035] the resurrection and the spiritual life[1036]; who believes[1037] in me, even if he was in the depths of death, he would spiritually live[1038].

26. And whoever spiritually lives and believes in me, will not be in the depths of death for eternity[1039]. Do you believe in this?[1040]".

1031 In reality, she believes to know, but she does not have a full understanding of what is about to happen. She says "I know" to indicate the certainty that is within her, and thanks to this, Jesus will tell her that Lazarus will resuscitate. She sees within Jesus a mediator close to God. She hopes in a miraculous intervention.

1032 The Divine of the Holiest Trinity.

1033 He does not tell her how, when, and thank to whom this will happen.

1034 The last day corresponds to the seventh day of creation. With this she exposes the similar Hebrew belief on death. Her "I know" entails that she already knows the Jewish doctrine on death. But for Jesus, the last day is the one of His death when will have completely transformed (in the "likeness" of the Father) the body of Jesus.

1035 Now the cosmic dimension and cosmic consciousness of Jesus Christ is speaking. This I Am also lives in the depths of man.

1036 It is not about healing or mediating close to the Father: the Christ is Life himself and so he can gift it to the ones who have Faith in Him and he can resuscitate them immediately!

1037 For the difference between "having faith" and "believing", see John 1,7.

1038 Jesus replies that it can happen now and this is thanks to His action. Additionally, every man will be able to do so, thanks to the presence of the Christ within him.
This calling to the I Am, corresponds to the awakening of the *chakra* with 8 petals that is located on the top of the head. This spiritual center is the door to the connection with the sphere of Saturn. It is the center of the revelation of the gnosis, and it is the door towards the Crown, towards the Father. From this *chakra* we can grasp the Glory, the Light (clairvoyance) and the Voice (clairaudience).

1039 From this the vacuity of the human conception of death.

1040 He knows Martha's faith really well, but he wants her to openly testify to herself and the ones who are present.

27. She said: “Yes Lord, I believed that you are the Christ, the Son of the living God, I believed that you came into the world[1041]”.

28. This being said (*eipon*), she went (*aperchomai*) to secretly call Mary, her sister[1042], saying (*eipon*): “The Teacher is near and he is calling you[1043]”.

29. As she heard (*akouo*) this, she quickly[1044] and swiftly rose, and she went (*erchomai*) towards him:

30. Jesus had yet to get (*erchomai*) to the village, but he was always in the location[1045], where Martha went below (*hypantao*).

31. The Jewish people[1046], the ones who were in the house (*oikia*) with her and brought her the evocative word, seeing that the Mary swiftly rose (*anistemi*) and left, followed her presuming that Jesus would come down to the memory[1047] to then cry[1048] there”.

[1041] Martha says something (authentication), and Jesus replies with a question and with “Do you believe in this?” But Martha responds something else, she declares her faith in Jesus Christ, but she does not confirm what Jesus is asking her as a test of Faith. The same thing she said will then be said my Mary Magdalen, who Martha goes to call right away since she was not able to adequately reply to the question. Mary Magdalen will cry and Jesus will accomplish the miracle. Martha replied with the knowledge; Mary Magdalen, on the other hand moved the forces of the heart. Martha speaks of the resurrection of the last day and she does not understand that Lazarus can resuscitate immediately. Mary Magdalen, on the other hand, will believe that it can happen.

[1042] Take note of the “occult/hidden” action, which means in the spiritual plane and the article in front of the word “sister” is there to indicate the spiritual level of the action that is taking place.

[1043] Jesus did not call the Magdalen; he spoke to Martha and Martha, inadequate, she feels that the answer is for the Mary Magdalen, and she spiritually calls her.

[1044] She recalls the Spirit within him. She heard the voice of the Shepherd and she replies.

[1045] In an area of the spiritual plane connected to the auric dimension of Martha.

[1046] The Jewish people are Martha’s people, and they are within her. The people express themselves with the language (they were consoling her) and they are etherically united. Mary gathers (pick up) her etheric forces connected to the people and she takes them to the I (she rises), who transforms them in Loving Vital Spirit.
Lets remember that with the term “house”, they are referring to the auric spiritual dimension that surrounds the physical body.

[1047] See note on verse 17.

[1048] They do not understand. They follow her and they see her cry, which means she is calling the Spirit. Mary Magdalen will also cry on the cross. We cry when the astral is far away from the I (to cry from pain) or when we are united with the Higher I (to cry for joy).

32. The Mary[1049], arriving where the Jesus[1050] was, fell to his feet[1051] as she saw (*idein*) him and she said (*lego*): "Lord, if you would have been here, my brother would have not deeply died".

33. So Jesus, seeing (*eidon*) her crying, and the crying Jewish people who came with her, trembled in the spirit and he activated the crowd within him[1052].

34. And he said (*eipen*): "Where did you put him?"

They said (*lego*) to him: "Lord, come, and see (*idein*)[1053]".

35. And Jesus experimented the spiritual coldness of the Earth.[1054]

36. So the Jewish people said (*lego*): "This is how we fraternally loved him".

37. But some of them said (*eipon*): "Did he not have the strength to open the eyes[1055] of the blind (born)[1056], to create so that even this one would not go into the depths of death?"

1049 Now Silent Mary is manifesting in her higher being

1050 Jesus and the I Am, the Higher I to which Mary reaches, and she "sees" it, while Martha "heard" it. Mary represents venus, which is the inner light who sees, and who know sees the I Am, the Sun, Jesus. From the etheric point of view, Mars and Venus are two celestial sphere who talk to each other, and Martha calls Mary.
Mary Magdalen also represents the Work in Black of the Alchemists. The purification of the inner planets is completes with the reaching of Venus and looking at the Sun.

1051 For "feet" see verse 11,2. Mary understood that something great was about to descend and so she puts herself at the "feet" to welcome it.

1052The crowd is the unison of the spiritual entities that act from the higher worlds to determine the descending of a certain spiritual force within man. In this case, Jesus activated the crowd that was within him, which is the unison of the spiritual forces that help and collaborate to His mission. It is the crowd of the Baptist.

1053 They put themselves in his hands.

1054 In greek it is *dakruo* and it usually is translated with "he cried". *"Da"* indicates both the Earth an what descends like a resin (like a "tear") from a tree towards the ground and *"kruo"* (and "*crio*" indicate cold). The cold of the Earth indicate the experience that He goes through when he descends in the Ade, in the underworld, to free Lazarus from death.

1055 The eye indicates the necessary death for the process of resurrection. After the tests of the Work in Black (wedding with the Mother), the eyes of the ones that overcame the tests are ready for the divine vision.

1056 To give again sight to the man born blind represented the stronger penetration of the forces of the Christ in Jesus, to the point that He was able to act as Lord of Karma. Let's remember that blind is the one who can only see himself because of an excess of egoism (luciferic matrix). With the reawakening of Lazarus, the Jesus reawakens the forces of the I Am in Lazarus, and he gifts him the initiation of the Father.

38. So Jesus, once again shivering within himself[1057], came (*erchomai*) to the memory: (which) was a hidden part[1058] and a stone was put on it.

39. The Jesus said (*lego*): "Lift up the stone[1059]"

Martha, the sister of the one who was (completely) dead (*teleutao*), says (*lego*) to him: "Lord, he already smells, it has already been four days[1060]".

40. The Jesus tells (*lego*) her: "Did I not tell you (*eipon*) that if you believe(*pisteuso*), you will see (*opsomai*) the glory of the God[1061]".

41. They lifted up the stone[1062] and the Jesus lifted his eyes[1063] and said (*eipon*): "Father, I give thanks to you[1064] because you heard me (*akouo*)[1065]".

42. I know that you always hear me (*akouo*)[1066], but I said (*eipon*) it through the crowd that surrounds us[1067], so that they are believers (*pisteuso*) that you sent me".

1057 The battle was won shortly earlier on the Spirit plane: now, with the second shiver, it needs to happen on the material plane. Jesus activates the crowd thanks to his connection, through the Nathan Soul, with the Baptist.

1058 After the shiver in the Spirit, which means in the sphere of the heart-Sun. the Jesus experiments the spiritual coldness of the Earth, and so in a microcosmic spiritual sense, it ascends to the cranium, in the hidden cave, and precisely in the Turkish Saddle, and the pituitary is right above it, which is a gland with a triangular pyramid shape (etheric). In the esoteric geographical sense, let's remember that Bethany represents the Loving Vital Spirit.
Within us, the memory of our divine origin has a stone (in front or above) that stops us from seeing it, knowing it, and the forces of the obstacle, Lucifer and Ahriman, put this stone there.

1059 To lift up the stone that is within us. The weight of the consequences after the Fall.

1060 Here is Martha's rationality manifesting.

1061 It refers to what was said in verse 25. He scolds her about her lack of belief: His love had already created the miracle. The Glory is the clairvoyance and clairaudience of the God.

1062 We can hypothesize that the stone was lifted from the crowd.

1063 For "eye" see note on verse 37. High/above indicates the dimension of the Father.

1064 Jesus gives thanks, which means he goes back to the received Grace. By doing so, the Grace is completed. It is important to see how he did not "pray" to the Father.

1065 It is from the event of the Transfiguration that the Jesus receives the authority to be "heard" from the Father. We now have the "certainty within the request". He gives thanks before it comes to life in the material plane. We do not have the "ask and it will be given to you" anymore, now we have "ask (with certainty) and it is given to you". This can happen when our will corresponds to the one of the Father.

1066 When we do His will.

1067 The one he activated within himself (v.33).

43. This being said, with a great voice[1068] he said (with strength): "Lazarus, ,here, outside.[1069]"

[1068] As the Word that manifest itself and acts.

[1069] Jesus descended in the coldness of the Earth and he frees Lazarus, while the crowd had lifted the stone. It is now Lazarus (who has been renovated by the forces of Life coming from the Christ) turn to act and follow the Jesus who calls him to come "here" and he shows him the way "out". It is important to see how "out/outside" also indicates the fact that from that moment on, the new initiation will be directly given by the Christ, and it will be in the light of the Sun and it will no longer be a secret in the mysteries. Through death, Lazarus came know the reality of the spiritual world and then the reality of the return to life, and now he needs to testify it to the people. We now have the composition of a new triad: Martha/ Mary, Mary Magdalen/Venus and Lazarus/Sun.

44. And the one who once was dead (*thesko*)[1070] came out[1071], with his feet[1072] and hands[1073] blocked[1074] with (hidden) restrictions, and his sight was blocked all around by a veil. The Jesus said (*lego*) to them: "Untie him[1075], and allow his to come down here[1076]".

[1070] Here is the result of the "prayer of certainty".

[1071] Pay attention to the contradiction: he was dead and he descended on his own. He displays the attributes of death, but he is alive!

[1072] He was hindered because of the spells (the bands, the "restrictions") made by the priests, which created in him hidden restrictions. The spiritual sight (the face) was also hindered, veiled because of the shroud, which is the veil that had been placed upon him.

[1073] The hindering of the feet comes back. The feet represent the kingdom of the Earth, the *Malkut*, the terrestrial Kingdom and so the Mother, the Virgin Mother, the Black Mother, the Mother of all terrestrial existence. This is why, in spiritual symbology, they are represented as "wounded" and needing healing. Eve was also bitten by the snake on the foot. The wound is represented by the "false" (arch) of the foot and it is "half" of the other wound, the one on the head represented by the fontanel. This is because man is created in likeness and image of God. The Zodiacal Man or First Adam, is represented by the zodiacal circle which was then "cut" between Aries-head and Pisces-feet and so he lost the "likeness" with the Creator.

[1074] The order is being given by the crowd, and it indicates how Lazarus is now free from the ties with the world and the veil of unconsciousness: he can now testify the truth of the Spirit that the Christ brings to humanity. Jesus does not tell him where to go: the Community saw, and now he is free to go.

[1075] The miracle happened because seven necessary conditions were present:

- To have an active Faith (Martha)
- To have a contemplative Faith (Martha)
- To have put all of his own forces into the fulfillment of the ideals of the Spirit (v.1)
- To have reached the condition of being "loved" by the I Am (v.3)
- To have died to the world (v.14)
- To respond to the divine command (v.43)
- To be free from all ties (v.44)

[1076] In the Secret Gospel of Mark, it is said: "*and they arrived to Bethany where a certain woman was, and whose brother was dead. And she came, she bowed down to Jesus and she said "son of David, have mercy on me". But the disciples scolded her. And Jesus, angered, went with her on the step where the grave was, and immediately they heard a great scream coming from the grave. And by getting closer, Jesus moved the stone that was keeping the sepulcher shut. And immediately, going towards where the young man laid, he extended his hand and helped him get up by taking his hand. But the young man, as he saw him, immediately loved him and he asked if he could stay with him. As they left the grave, they entered the house of the young man, since he was rich. And after six days, Jesus told him what he needed to do, and that evening the young man went to him wearing a cloth of linen over his nakedness. And that night, he stayed with him, because Jesus taught him the mystery of the kingdom of God. And once he left that location, he went back to the other side of the Jordan*".
This episode is the one of the Resurrection of Lazarus and the "great scream" is the one that would happen in the initiation when the initiate would finish the process. This scream is "all is completed" (see John 20,30)..

THE SANHEDRIN OF THE POPES (Lc 16,31)

45. Many of the Jewish people, who came (*erchomai*) close to the Mary[1077], and saw (*theaomai*) what Jesus created (*poieo*), had faith (*episteusa*) in him.

46. But some of them went amongst the Pharisees[1078], and they said (*eipon*) to them what Jesus[1079] created (*poieo*).

47. They then gathered the High Priests (*arche'*) and the Pharisees (the) Sanhedrin and they said (*lego*): "What are we creating (*poieo*)? This man (*antropos*)[1080] creates many signs".

48. If we leave him like this, everyone believes (*pisteuo*) in him, and the Romans will come and deprive us of authority, and the location[1081] and the ethnicity[1082].

49. But One, a certain one of them, of the name of Caifa (*Kaiafas*)[1083], since he was the high priest of that period, said (*eipon*) to them: "You know nothing,

50. Neither do you think[1084] that it is convenient that only One man (*antropos*) goes in the depths of death (*apothnesko*)[1085] for the people and all ethnicity does not become lost".

THE SANHEDRIN OF THE POPES

[1077] Silent Mary, representing the consciousness soul. The Magdalen "ascended" to the level of Mariam, from the sentient soul to the conscious soul "going through" the development of the affectionate soul (crying for her brother Lazarus).

[1078] They were part of a religious and political movement of great influence, extremely connected to the Hebrew traditions. They believed in the resurrection of the death and in angels; but they would hide their vices and their pride under the appearances of a hypocritical and formalist religion. The Pharisees were the "divided" ones since they would strictly follow the Mosaic Law, and they believed to be the best amongst the Jewish people. They had an initiation that would take place in the ether of heat which corresponds to the brainstem.

[1079] No article; they do not grasp the Christ within him.

[1080] Not initiated. They always grasp the human aspect of Jesus.

[1081] The temple as a sacred place (and also of power). The priests are worried about the destruction of the past, of the traditions and their symbols.

[1082] The Hebrew ancestry, the Chosen People, the marriages "prepared" in the Temples.

[1083] It is a variable of the name Cain.

[1084] The verb is *logizomai*, which contains "logos". The exact translation would be "logicizzate".

[1085] The human sacrifice, in which he is being offered to save the ancestry, the hereditary current.

51. And this did not come from him: since he was the high priest of that period of time, he said that Jesus would have reached the depth of death for the ethnicity[1086],

52. And not only for the ethnicity, but to pick up in One the sons (*tekna*) of the God, the ones that were lost[1087].

53. From that day they decided to kill him (*apokhteino*).

JESUS RETIRES FROM JERUSALEM (Par 30,17; A 21,24)

54. The Jesus did not walk openly walk around in the presence of the Jewish peoples, instead he went towards the region[1088] close to the desert, in a city called Ephraim[1089], and there he stayed with the disciples.

55. But the Easter[1090] of the Jewish people was getting close and many went towards Jerusalems[1091] before the Easter to purify[1092] themselves in the fire[1093].

[1086] To save the ethnicity (the Hebrew "cream"), it is needed that Jesus dies in the *laos*, in the people.

[1087] Caifa mentions the return to the Father, but he wants to kill the one who is the Way to do so.

[1088] This "region" is still in the Kingdom, in the Cherub Zodiac; it is a part of it..

[1089] The fact that the city is "called" means that it is a spiritual name. "E" is the expansion in the new "*phren*", which means in the new breast. The "city" is the etheric oval organ from which the Children in us are born.

[1090] In the Gospel of John, three Easters are mentioned: the *first one* (John 2,13) at the purification of the temple, the *second one* a little bit before the multiplication of the bred and the fish for the 5000 (John 6,4), and finally the *third one* a little bit after the resuscitation of Lazarus (John 11,55). This shows us "three normal" Easters, followed by a fourth "special" one: the one of the Resurrection. The action of the Christ within Jesus keeps going for three years and four months (3,3, in the decimal system) just like Lazarus stayed beyond for three days before being resuscitated and just how Jesus resuscitated after three days and a third (80 hours). In a broader sense, the Christ also remained in the grave represented by the physical body of Jesus for three years and four months.

[1091] From the Cherub Zodiac to the Serafinic Zodiac..

[1092] The verb "to purify" is *hagnizo*, which means to purify with the fire: they received the Baptism of Fire..

[1093] See note John 22.23. With the special ritual.

56. They were looking for the Jesus: and they would say amongst each other[1094], remaining in the temple (internal)[1095]: "Why do you think he did not come to the feast?[1096]"

57. And the high priests and the Pharisees gave order that if someone knew where he was, they would have to get him[1097].

JESUS' ANOINTING IN BETHANY (Mt 26,6-13; Mt 21,1-11; Mc 14,3-9; Mc 11,1-11; Lc 19,26-40)

1. The Jesus went to Bethany[1098] six days before Easter[1099], where Lazarus was, who Jesus' raised from the dead[1100].

1094 It is the beginning of the Christian Community.

1095 For "Temple" see note on verse 2,14.

1096 To the Easter. They are preparing the new Easter: the one of Resurrection.

1097 They look for him in the spiritual regions but they do not have the capability to see him.

1098 Bethany means "House of Healing" of man, which is the House for the Vital Loving Spirit, the principle Son.

1099 This is the fourth Easter of the Jesus: the "+1". In the Gospel of John, three Easters are mentioned: the *first one* (John 2,13) at the purification of the temple; the *second one* a little bit before the multiplication of the bred and the fish for the 5000 (John 6,4); and finally the *third one* a little bit after the resuscitation of Lazarus (John 11,55). This shows us "three normal" Easters, followed by a fourth "special" one: the one of the resurrection. The action of the Christ within Jesus keeps going for three years and four months (3,3, in the decimal system) just like Lazarus stayed beyond for three days before being resuscitated and just how Jesus resuscitated after three days and a third (80 hours). In a broader sense, the Christ also remained in the grave represented by the physical body of Jesus for three years and four months. Now a new path is getting prepared for the transition from the "sixth day" to the "seventh day". He goes to Lazarus because he is the first one to experience this path of resurrection that now Jesus is getting ready to complete.

1100 This expression will be repeated three times in this chapter (John 12,1; 122,9 and 12,17) to indicate the greatness of the event and the completion that relates to all three of the human components (body, soul and spirit).

2. And there they created (*poieo*) a communion[1101], and the Martha ministered[1102], and the Lazarus was One[1103] of the ones who were standing straight with him[1104].

[1101] From the greek *deipnon*, which means "main lunch" and "feast", which is communion, convocation of the spirits (I) promoted by an ideal message. This Dinner kind of represents a polarity with the Last Supper. In this Dinner, the love of the disciples for him is being expresses, and in the second one His love for all humanity is being manifested. In both Dinners, the "traitor" will be manifested: in Bethany the luciferic foundation of his betrayal is being explained (*he was a thief*-12,6), and in the Last Supper his last decision and his union with Satan will take place.

[1102] Third step of Initiation. Now Martha is in the affectionate soul (she takes care).

[1103] It represented the "unison" of the forces that were ready at the last resurrection.

[1104] We can grasp the overall picture: Martha ministered (Venus' step), Lazarus-John is in an exclusive relationship with Jesus. The banquet, The Dinner, becomes the metamorphosis of the funeral banquet: as Lazarus was resuscitated, the sadness of death transforms into joy of life, of victory (even though is it yet to be completed because it is not yet a resurrection, which means the body of flesh was not completely transformed yet) upon death.

3. The Mary[1105], took a pound of precious ointment[1106] of beaten nard[1107] and she spread[1108]

[1105] It is not clear who this "Mary" is. We can hypothesize that Mary Magdalen ascended to the step of Silent Mary and so this "Mary" is already the "being Mariam which is manifesting itself in Magdalen.

[1106] The "Mariam" indicates her initiation aspect, the Alchemist. The pound corresponded to approximately 330 grams.

[1107] This action is important because the vase of alabaster represents a calcareous astral cavity, and therefore the inner part of the soul that needs to be purified. Alabaster is a calcareous stone that can be worked in such a way that it almost becomes transparent in the light. Limestone represents the force of Ahriman within us, the hate, the fall into darkness; and so the alabaster represents the transformation of darkness into light, the victory upon Ahriman.
The oil was of nard, a plant that grows in the Himalaya and so it represents the forces of Light and Heat. The oil is formed on the plants, thanks to the alchemy operated by the forces of Fire onto the liquid-lymphatic element: to be more precise, they are the spiritual forces coming from the constellation of Pisces that operate this transformation. Pisces are the constellation that represents the impulse of the Christ. From the Apocrypha we learn that within the oil part of the umbilical chord was kept), and also part of the foreskin of the Baby Jesus. We now have the whole image; the conservation of a symbol of the reproductive element of the Jesus that then is gifted to he Jesus himself by the one who transformed within herself the luciferic forces connected to reproduction. By what we just said, we can grasp the preciousness of everything. Mariam was donating to Jesus the most precious part of herself, the part that had her Loving Vital Spirit in it, son of the transformation of her etheric body.
Lazarus (as Spirit) received this transformation at his resuscitation thanks to the Jesus. Mariam, on the other hand, gifted hers since she achieved it through the evolutionary process of the soul. This makes us think that they were "soul mates" and what is achieved by one, will be achieved by the other one as well. The vase of alabaster corresponds to the coccyx in the human body, to the "sacred" bone: the limestone-alabaster. The nard together with the alabaster is effused around Jesus' head. We now have the completion of the Path within us: starting from the chakra with four petals (coccyx), we purify ourselves all the way up to the head (coronal chakra of eight- or a thousand- petals). This unction is a memory of the old ceremony of unction with which the initiate would be purified before ascending to the macrocosms so that he would become "invulnerable" to what could have happened in the physical plane. The new Christic unction will take place at the Last Supper when he will say to feel "one" with what manifests on Earth as a solid (*I Am the bread of life*). Mariam represents the humanity that goes back to her true Groom: from eternity, the divine Groom is waiting for humanity his Bride to crown her.

[1108] With this unction-purification the Jesus will be ready to deal with death, and he will give the Twelve the strength to follow him through the Washing of the Feet that he will gift to them.

it on Jesus' feet[1109] and she dried his feet with her own hair[1110], and the house[1111] was filled with the scent of the ointment.

4. One of his disciples, Judas the Iscariot, who was about to hand him over, says (*lego*):
5. "Why wasn't this ointment[1112] sold for three-hundred coins[1113] and was given to the poor people[1114]?"

[1109] The feet represent the kingdom of Earth, the *Malkut*, the terrestrial kingdom and therefore the Mother, the Virgin Mother, the Black Mary, the Mother of all terrestrial existence. For this reason, in the spiritual symbology, they are represented as "wounded" and they need to be healed. Eve was also bitten by the snake on her foot. The wound is represented by the "false" (arch) of the foot and it is the other "half" of the wound, the one on the head represented by the fontanel. This is because man is created in the likeness and image of God. The Zodiacal Man, or First Adam, is represented by the zodiacal circle that was "cut" between Aries-head and Pisces-feet, and so he lost the likeness with the Creator. From this, we have the episode of the unction of the feet by Mariam to prepare him for the test of the victory upon the forces of death present on the feet (the oil would protect from the terrestrial forces). At the Washing of the Feet, Jesus completely purifies the Apostles, and he heals the wound that came from the Fall for humanity. The Mariam represents the humanity that goes back to her true Groom: from the eternity, the divine Groom waits for the humanity, His Bride, to crown her.
Magdalen-Mariam will also try to grab him by his feet on Easter Sunday, but the Risen One will stop her from doing so because after the healing of the feet and after descending on Mother's Earth womb, he needs to ascend to the Father to complete the spiritual marriage between Mother earth and Father sky.

[1110] Hair represent the spiritual force that invade man. Let's remember that since they are on the head, they represent the "olive trees" of the Garden of Olive trees, which is the zodiacal serafinic dimension. From the Hebrew *sear*, they are the "principal", the "principle planted in the spring of the being". The Hebrew term also indicates the fear in front of the divine vision.
In this case, the action reminds us of the Hebrew initiation process intended to connect the sphere of thought with the one of will (from which the strictness of the Law to shape the will). The act accomplished by Mariam represents the ending of the Hebrew initiation process and the preparation of the Christic one.
The alchemy is now completed: the waters from below (sacrum) go up along the Jordan (spinal chord) to the waters from above (head).

[1111] All spiritual dimension.

[1112] From the greek *piprasko* which also means to betray, to secretly sell, outside of the laws (moral).

[1113] It corresponds to a significant sum for that time period. A coin was one day's pay for a man. 300 coins represent almost a whole year worth of work.
In Hebrew, the 21st letter is the 300 and it is *s'in*, which means "tooth" and it indicates "movement", dynamism on the cosmic plane. As a bone, it corresponds to Saturn as a doorway for spiritual nourishment.
For the Cabala, the paths of knowledge are 32: like the teeth. With this, we can understand what everything is being completed: all the transformations of man, all the paths of initiation.

[1114] Poor of Spirit: the ones who are "searching" for the Way.

6. He said (*eipen*) this not because he cared about the poor people but because he was a thief[1115] and, having a proud[1116] tongue, he would grab (*ebastazen*) what was thrown[1117].
7. Jesus then said (*eipen*): "Leave it alone, so that I can guard it until the day of my burial[1118].
8. The poor people are always with you: but you do not always have me[1119]".
9. So the crowd of the Jewish people[1120] understood that he was there, and they came, not only for the Jesus, but also to see (*idein*) Lazarus, who rose from the dead.
10. So the high priests said to also kill (*apokteino*) Lazarus,
11. Because many people because of him were removing[1121] themselves from the Jewish people and believed[1122] in the Jesus.

[1115] This is the luciferic aspect of Scorpio; Satan will follow to this.

[1116] The term being used is *rkomon*, formed by the words that mean "tongue", "language" and "flowing head of hair", "to make proud", "dragging". The unison of these two terms can turn into "proud tongue". With this, Judas luciferic aspect is characterized. He was already possessed by the luciferic spirit of the Hebrew people since he was part of the party of the Zealots. Normally, this is translated as "purse" since Lucifer acts in the hollow organs, concave, just like purses.

[1117] The stone of emerald of the crown of Lucifer was thrown in the sacrum of man (Auric Legend). The luciferic forces acted in him, and they would put whatever they wanted in it.

[1118] Literally "preparation for the burial". The day of preparation that is being spoken about is the same of the passage, which is seven days before Easter (and so the completion of Man), the Saturday before the hour 18, before the Palms. This also brings us back to the anointment that the Pious Women wanted to do before the morning of Easter Sunday, but they were not able to do so since he was Risen Again. The ointment of nard represents the Loving Vital Spirit, and it's the preparation to enter the Kingdom.

[1119] He does not say that they will "no longer have him"; instead he says that they won't "always" have him. After the resurrection he will say: And here, I am with you all days until the completion of eternity (Mt 28,20).

[1120] The Jewish people represent the old Hebrew current.

[1121] Because he testifies the ending of the old initiation and the transition to the one operated by the Christ. Additionally, he frees us from dogmas, prejudices, and fears and he opens us up to the Path of Freedom in Love.

[1122] For the difference between "having faith" and "believing", see note on the verse 1,7.

TRIUMPHAL ENTRANCE IN JERUSALEM (Ps 117,25 ss; Is 40,9; Zch 9,9)

12. But the day after[1123], the crowd that came (*erchomai*) to the feast, having heard the Jesus, came to Jerusalems,

13. They grabbed the branches of the palm trees[1124] (ceremonial) and they went towards him yelling "*Hosanna*[1125], *blessed is the one who comes in the name of the Lord*[1126] and the King of Israel[1127]".

1123 Sunday corresponds to the first day of Creation when God said: "*Let there be Light*!" *And Light came. God saw that light was good; and he separated light from darkness. God called the light "day" and the darkness "night". Night came, and then morning: first day (*Gen 1,3-5).

1124 Only John talks about the presence of palm trees.
The rabbinic interpretation indicates the branch formed by palm, willow, and myrtle. The palm, in ancient symbology, referred to the symbol of martyrdom. Its meaning is of victory, ascension, rebirth and immortality. It connects to the Phoenix, and it has the function of tree of life. It also anticipates the Resurrection after death. The palm has the same symbolic value of the resurrection of the martyrs (Ap 7,9).
The willow represents the sacred tree of life symbolizing cyclical renewal and fertility. In classical symbology, the one who destroys her own fruit is the Great Mother or Mother Earth who, in a perennial cycle of life and death, generates her sons and daughters, and then she reabsorbs them in her womb. From the Hebrew tradition, in the Feast of the "Huts" (Tabernacles), the feast of gratitude for the harvesting of the fruit of earth.
The myrtle was considered a representation of the greatest love, both sacred and profane. The bride would wear a crown of myrtle on the wedding' day, symbol of conjugal union. In the Medieval tradition, "Water of Angels" was the distilled liquid of myrtle flowers from which ablutions would be made to conserve beauty and love. These branches were used for the Feat of the Huts and at the Dedication. They would be shaken as they would sing the Psalm 118 (*Give thanks to the Lord*...).
The mentioning of the "palms" creates a recap between the three feasts (Easter, Huts, and Dedication of Winter Huts) and it summarizes the great occasions of Jesus' activity.

1125 The esoteric composition of the word is the following: "(H) the spiritual entity that descend and becomes accessible to us; (O) through a vortex that he brings to the Earth to unite with it; (S) in our dark inner being. (A) this is the beginning; (N) of the logos within us; (N) now the action of the logos; (A) begins; (N) the logos within us. The original composition of the word might have been "*hosanna*"...

1126 The third Lord, corresponds to the Father of the Holy Trinity (sphere of Saturn).

1127 It is the human aspect of Jesus, connected to the royal current of David. The article on Israel reminds us of the Chosen People. David means "of a strong hand". Let's remember that with the expression "Son of David", the Hebrew people were referring to the Messiah.

14. Jesus having found a little donkey[1128], he sat[1129] on it, just how it is written:

[1128] The female donkey represents the physical body that has yet to be set free. The little donkey is her "little son", and therefore the seed of the Spirit Man within us. The donkey also represent the ancient initiatic culture of the Asii, people from which the Hebrew people came from. The female donkey that is tied up (see Mt 21,2) represents the impossibility, for the old initiation, to reach the Son of God. In Mc 11,4 the female donkey is tied to a threshold, which is the doorway to the spiritual world. It is important to say that in the old initiations, the image of the female donkey with her baby donkey represented the Constellation of Cancer, the zodiacal constellation passing in front of which the un reaches the highest point in the sky and then it begins to go back down. This is like saying that Cancer represents the descending of the spiritual zenith to get ahold of the forces and then bring them on Earth for a new beginning (baby donkey). Let's also remember that Cancer in Greek also means "cave" (rib cage), and in the cave, the Nathanic Jesus was born, amongst the ox and the donkey (see Lc 2,7). This finds a celestial correspondence in the constellation of the Ox and in the cluster called "of the Donkeys", celestial bodies that are found in the constellation of Cancer around the "Crib" star (which means "nativity scene"). Let's remember that this "baby donkey" is "the (masculine) little Girl" of the Spirit Man, which no initiate had ever contacted or reawaken within themselves.
The Greek word *polos* means "foal", "virgin", "little girl", "little boy". This Little Girl/Boy is understood in an animal form (foal), since in that time period the seers would still "see" spiritual realities in the forms of animals (for example, the Mystical Lamb, Fish, Doves, the Ox and the Donkey, etc…). Thi little Girl/ Boy is the most elevated Girl/Boy that man could ever develop and o it corresponds to the Christ within us, on which no man has yet meditated (worked internally) on. It is necessary that humanity consciously and freely recognizes and collaborates to the arrival of the Principle Christ within us; for this reason, the two disciples are sent to release him and bring him to the Light to Jesus so that, with the Baptism of Blood that is about to happen, this Girl/Boy achievable by all humanity. This will correspond to the victory upon death, to the freeing of the Incorruptible Body from the material physical body and to the strength to descend into darkness and free Adam…

[1129] He meditated upon this so that this higher reality would become accessible to all initiates and to all men.

15. *"Do not fear, daughter of Sion*[1130]*, your King*[1131] *is coming, sitting on a little male/female donkey*[1132]*"*.

16. At first the disciples did not understand these things, but when Jesus was glorified, they remembered that such things were written of him, and they created (*poieo*) this to him[1133].

17. So the crowd was testifying, the one that was with him, when he called the Lazarus from the memory and he raised him from the dead[1134].

18. And because of this a big part of the crowd came towards him, because they heard (*akouo*) that he made this sign.

19. The Pharisees said (*eipon*) amongst themselves: "See (*theoreo*) that you will not profit from anything? Here, the world is going[1135] behind him".

[1130] This term refers to the Chosen People. Precisely the Daughter, the Virgin of the Chosen People, and therefore the purified soul in Mariam level.

[1131] The Groom.

[1132] The Girl-Boy of the Spirit Man. The Chosen People became the People "of the" Chosen Ones, since now they are such because of their freedom of choice and not because of their origin.

[1133] Only after the enlightenment of the Paraclete Spirit (Pentecost) they will be able to understand the event that they are living. For the complete vision of Paraclete see John 14,16.

[1134] We now have two crowds: the one that goes towards him from Jerusalem and the one that was with him after the resuscitation of Lazarus. We can see how in the first one, there is a current that is highly ahrimanic (materialistic interpretation of the Law), and the second one if highly luciferic because it was still connected to the old initiation to which Lazarus had to go through.

[1135]Because His words are Words of Truth and Love on the contrary of the cold and strict Law that they were bringing.

20. But there were some Greeks[1136], the ones that ascended (spiritually) to bow at the feast.

21. These ones got closer to Philip[1137], the one from Bethsaida[1138] of Galilee, and they asked him: "Sir, we want to see (*idein*)[1139] the Jesus".

22. Philip came and said (*lego*) to Andrew[1140]: and then again Andrew and Philip came and said to the Jesus[1141].

23. The Jesus replied (*apokrinomai*) by saying: "The time has come for the Son (*hyios*) of man (*Anthropos*)[1142] to be glorified.

1136 Pagans, or better Greeks, that follow Hebraism. Jesus' followers are not only Hebrews, now He acts universally.

1137 The greek *Philippos* means "lover of thought". The spiritual attribute that this Apostles incarnates is decision. Greeks go to an apostle by the greek name to show how they connect to him through the forces of the old greek initiation.

1138 Corresponding to the constellation of Virgo, it means "House of the Fish", which is where the christic force finds a spiritual home. It also means "mercy" since from the axis Virgo-Pisces the therapeutic process descends, and therefore the Graces, the Mercy.

1139 They ask to spiritually "see" the Logos in Jesus.

1140 From the greek *andreia*, courage, the virtue in the *aner*, the Enlightened man. The spiritual attribute that incarnates prayer. For what we just said, in Philip we can see the one representing (in this passage) the current of the wise, of the Magi; and in Andrew the current of the ones pure of heart, of the Shepherds. Let's remember that Jesus, the one to whom they get close to, represent the summary of these two spiritual currents.

1141 In two, united, they turn to the Principle Christ present in the Jesus, this because the two currents (Magi and Shepherds) united, and therefore they determine an inner marriage. Philip goes to Andrew (and the two "get close") to unite with him, and then together they have access to the Christ.

1142 The moment of the Passion and Resurrection has arrived. "The time has come", (just like he will say in his priestly Prayer (John 17,1), was the phrase that would be pronounced in the culminating point of initiatic ceremonies: the time has come in which the Son of man can manifest himself. He does not say that "he will manifest"; instead he says that "he will be glorified" in each and every man. Therefore the divine seed present in every man from the moment of creation can now manifest itself so that we can welcome the christic impulse within ourselves.
Silent Mariam prepared for this. The Soul can now be in the Spirit; now that the Gentili have "asked". This is the "Little Girl" of the Christ.

24. Amen, Amen[1143], I say to you: if the grain of wheat does not reach the depth of death by falling, it will remain alone; but if it reaches the depths of death, it will bring many fruit[1144].

25. The one who loves with the soul[1145] his own soul (*psyche*)[1146] body, will send it to perdition, and the one who do not gets pleasure[1147] from his soul (*psyche*) body in this world he will protect it, for the eternal spiritual life.

26. If someone ministers for me[1148], follow me, and where I am, my[1149] minister will also be there. If someone ministers for me, the Father[1150] will honor him.

1143 The two "Amen" indicate that a universal truth is about to be exposed. He announces the imminence of his sacrifice. At 2,4 and 6,7 he announced that His time had yet to come.
The short example of the grain reminds us of the myth of Demetra's school in Eleusi (let's remember that the Greeks are the ones that talk to Him), where they talk about the fall of the soul in the world of darkness and its regeneration, thanks to the hero that descended to the underworld where the forces of the afterlife gift his the necessary forces escape and bring the soul that fell back to life; just like a seed receives the forces to reemerge as a plant from the Earth. He speaks to the Greeks through images of their spiritual culture. These Greeks were converted to Hebraism, and therefore they were part of the Chosen People, People for whom He arrived.

1144 In the Christic path, if we do not go through the death of the Darkness within us, we remain alone, like a stone on the ground. If we go through the life-giving death, then we will bear fruit.

1145 This soul love indicates an attachment (desires, passions) that needs to be overcome.

1146 The soul body, tied to the sentient soul. It is the life of the soul.

1147 Also "to dread" "to despise" "to be detached".

1148 The one who becomes His helper, and follows his steps with veneration. This is the one who understood the centrality of the I Am.

1149 The one who is ready to follow the Christ along the path of death and resurrection will be recognized by the Christ. He will be "his" minister. This represents the third step, the one of Venus.

1150 This Father is not "His" Father. The level of "minister" corresponds to the religiosity and devotion connected to Venus, cosmic headquarters of the Principality, the Principle Father of the Third Hierarchy. The fact that we are still talking about the sphere of Venus allows us to comprehend that we are yet to be in the full development of the test of Death and Resurrection, and its completion will take us to the Glorious Body, the stellar Light of the Serafinic Zodiac, the House of the Father. The ones who are open to "minister" this event, which mean to support with his inner light the sacrifice of the Christ, are still ministers. He participates in the test, but he is not the main character. The step of "minister" is at the level of the Principality, the Principle Father of the Holy Sprit and the Holy Trinity.
We can now see how the test of Death and Resurrection is tri-articulated: *first* we are available for the initiatic death ("ministers"), and we resonate with the Father of the Holy Spirit; *then* we acquire the forces to actually complete this passage (like Jesus did to the Gethsemane) and to transform the Evil to Good and therefore resonate with the therapeutic principle (the Son) according to the will of the Father, and therefore with the Father aspect of the Son (see John 17). *Lastly*, the sacrifice can take place, we enter the sphere of will, and therefore fully enter in the Father of the Father, and arrive to His spiritual House. After these three steps, we reach the *fourth* one: we remain united with humanity and we descend as helpers.

27. Now my soul (*psyche*) body is agitated[1151]. And what should I say (*eipon*) Father, save me from this hour? But this is why I came, towards this hour[1152].

28. Father, glorify your name[1153]". And a voice came from the sky: "I glorified it, and I will glorify it again[1154]".

29. The crowd, who was there and heard this, said[1155] that thunder[1156] came. Others said: "An angel mumbled (*laleo*)[1157] to him".

30. Jesus replied (*apokrinomai*): "This voice came not because of me, but because of you.

[1151] This agitation comes from the soul body of the Jesus, in which the instinct of life lives, of survival. In front of the death prophecy of the Jesus, this part of his body gets agitates, since He also is a man. For a deeper study of all the other agitations, see note on verse 11,33.

[1152] The hour is the one in which the Jesus, and therefore the principle of the I Am, can manifest himself to the whole world. The I of the Jesus answers back to the voices of the soul body, and he consciously accepts the sacrifice, and he overcomes the temptation of the lower body, and he transforms them.

[1153] It is the Holy Spirit in all his aspects, including the Holy Spirit within us.
R. Steiner states that with this expression, it is referring to the ending of the process through which the etheric body of Jesus, in which the Christ resides, became a perfect life-giver of the human physical body, thanks to whom the etheric body of Jesus looked alive. See note on verse 31.

[1154] The *first* glorification happened at the Baptism on the Jordan, the *second* one at the Transfiguration; the *third* one is the one that is now manifesting; and the +1 will follow it: at the Cross.
The first time, the Father spoke at the Baptism at the Jordan (this is my Son the one spiritually loved); the second time at the Transfiguration (listen to him!); the third time at the announcement of "His hour" (John 12,28). Lastly, there will be a fourth "dialogue" between Jesus and the Father: at the Cross when Jesus will be the one "talking" to the Father (*Eli, Eli, lamna sabactani*).

[1155] This crowd is manifesting in Jesus.

[1156] The thunder, esoterically, represents the Voice of God that gifts spiritual forces to man.

[1157] Based on their own knowledge, everyone would perceive in a different way: from the Father to an Angel.

31. Now[1158] it is the judgment if this world[1159]: now the prince of this world will be thrown out[1160].

32. And I, if I will rise from the ground[1161], I will pull everything towards me[1162]".

33. He said this to specify for which death he was about to enter the depths of death.

34. The crowd then replied (*apokrinomai*): "We did not hear from the law that the Christ would stay in eternity, and how can you say: it is necessary that the Son of man rises[1163]? Who is this Son of man[1164]?"

35. Jesus then said (*eipon*) to them: "For a little bit of time the light is still within you[1165]. Go while you have the light, so that the darkness will not completely (*katalambano*) take over you, and the ones who go through darkness do not know where they will descend (*hypago*).

[1158] Here, His hour has begun: that hour that was not yet there at the Wedding at Cana.

[1159] The world will go towards the consequences of its own decisions. Now it is in front of the truth and it can decide which path to take. Let's remember that the term "judgment" (in Greek *Krisis*) is connected to the etymology of chaos and Christ, and it indicates the chaotic moment in which, with the right discernment, we can meet the Christ. The alternative is always the path of pain.

[1160] The Prince is Satan, Ahriman, who will go back to his evolutionary system. With this event, with the complete transformation of the etheric body of Jesus, thanks to the Christ, and the new action in the physical body that comes from it, Lucifer and Ahriman have no more power on the physical body and therefore they are thrown out of the world. In reality, we know that Evil is basically Good "out of place", and therefore Ahriman can finally go back to his "place", now that he finished the task that he was called to do by the father: to make Light hard so that it would have a material consistency.

[1161] The Son of man, represented by Jesus, completely unites with the Christ and he becomes "I Am" like Adonai (the secret name of God) which means "God is". Only John uses the expression "will be risen" in the sense of "obtaining victory". By winning death over, Jesus Christ gets rid of the last veil that stops us from reconnecting with the Father: death is the door to the Father. The Christ accomplishes his mission: to substitute the old image of death (as an "ending") with the new image: death is the Father that always lives. Thanks to the Christ entering the etheric body of Jesus (and through this also in the physical body), there is no difference between "etheric" life of Jesus Christ before and after the Golgotha. This death does not extinguish; instead, it is life itself.

[1162] It is like saying that when will be in the era of the consciousness soul, then he will attract the human being in his wholeness to him. This will happen when man will not identify himself with the lower I but with the I Am within him.

[1163] In reality, having united himself with the Earth, Jesus Christ will remain "in eternity" united with us.

[1164] Son of Man is the one who manifest the true man, the one formed in the image and likeness of the Creator. This man is Jesus himself (Nathan Soul).

[1165] He says that the Light is "in" you and not "with" you. With this, He is saying that His life-giving action is within us. Then we will have to experience the darkness to transform it.

36. While you have light, believe (*pisteuo*)[1166] in light, to be generated as sons (*hyuos*) of light[1167]. Jesus mumbled (*laleo*) these things, and he left hiding from them.

INCREDULITY OF THE JEWISH PEOPLE (Is 53,1; Rom 10,16; Is 6,9; Mt 13,14 ss.; Mt 10,40)

37. (Even though) he accomplished many signs in front of him, they did not believe in him[1168],

38. so that the verb of Isaiah the prophet would achieve fullness, he said: "Lord, who had faith (*episteusa*) in what they heard from us[1169]? And the arm[1170] of the Lord was revealed (*apokalypto*) to whom?"

39. this is why they did not have the strength (*dynamai*) to believe, because Isaiah also said (*eipon*):

40. "He accepted the eyes[1171], and made their heart hard, because they did not see (*eiden*) with their eyes and they do not understand with the heart and they change and you heal them[1172]".

[1166] For the difference between "having faith" and "believing", see John 1,7.

[1167] And not sons of the serpent-Kundalini. To the question on who is the Son of Man, Jesus does not respond in a direct manner, instead he gifts us an image of the goal of humanity: to be born in the Light following the Truth that He bring us, making us Free.

THE INCREDULITY OF THE JEWISH PEOPLE

[1168] The Jewish people did not capture the action of the Christ, but John testifies it.

[1169] The prophet Isaiah identifies himself in the one that was sent by the Father, and he needs to verify that no one grasped the truth of what the Christ is bringing to humanity.

[1170] In Hebrew esotericism, the arm represents the Divine in its wholeness. In the esoteric point of view, the arm is the image of Divine Providence, and therefore of the Milky Way. In the trinity point of view, the arm is articulated in arm/Father, forearm/Son and hand/Holy Spirit.

[1171] The eye indicates the necessary death for the resurrection process. This takes us back to the healing of the man born blind-Bartimeo, with the miracle of the renewal of the grasping of the Light in the Incorruptible Body.

[1172] After the Fall, blindness comes and the hardening of the heart. The Christ will be the one who will heal us.

41. Isaiah said (*eipon*) these things, when he saw (*eidon*) His glory[1173] and he spoke (*laleo*) about Him.

42. However, many also amongst the principles of the priests had faith (*episteusa)* towards him; but because of the Pharisees they did not approve (*homologheo*), to not become excluded from the Synagogue[1174].

43. They spiritually loved the glory of men (*Anthropos*), more than the glory of God.

44. So Jesus said (*krazo*) and said (*eipon*): "Who believes in me, does not believe in me, but in the one who sent[1175] me.

45. And who spiritually (*theoreo*)[1176] sees me, spiritually (*theoreo*) sees the one who sent me[1177].

46. I came as light to the world[1178]: so that everyone who believes[1179] me does not remain in the darkness[1180].

[1173] To see the glory of God means to have full clairvoyance and clairaudience with Him. This gift was made to Isaiah as an anticipation of the new conscious Initiation and so that he could testify. In the old Initiation, since the strength of full consciousness was missing, it was not possible to see the glory of God.

[1174] This exclusion corresponds to being excommunicated, which means to be completely excluded from the religious and social life.

[1175] Jesus is "sent" from the Father Adonai, the Father of the Holy Trinity. "The" Jesus is sent from the Father of the Holiest Trinity. Jesus here distinguish himself from the Father, Father from which he makes the will.

[1176] Which means he meditates in Him, and through Him he goes back to God.

[1177] The Lord God, Adonai. The verb being used is *theoreo* which means to spiritually see from a distance. The path of the prayer of the heart takes us to the *theo-oria.*

[1178] It is the purest Light of the Nathan Soul, and it corresponds to the sixth *chakra*, the third eye. This is the second I Am pronounced by the Jesus, and we find it in John 8,12 at the Feast of the Tabernacles.

[1179] To believe is the next step to "having Faith". The one who believes puts all of his Faith in the being to whom he is turning to. Faith is still "towards" someone or something: it is still external.

[1180] Here is the explanation of the effect that comes from having Faith in Him: by believing in Him, the darkness of spiritual ignorance goes away and also the darkness of sin, since we become directly enlightened in the path that takes us to the Father.

47. And if someone had heard my words (*rhema*) and did not protect them, I do not judge him[1181]; I did not come here to judge the world, I came here to save the world[1182].

48. The one who rejects me and does not welcome my words (*rhema*) has the one who judges him. The verb (*logos*) that I mumbled (*laleo*), that one he will judge on the greatest (*eschatos*) day[1183].

49. Because I did not mumbled (*laleo*) from myself, but from the One who sent me. Father, He gave me order (*entole*) on what to say (*eipon*) and what to mumble (*laleo*).

50. And I know that His order (*entole*) is eternal spiritual Life. The things that I mumble (*laleo*), just like the Father said them to me, I mumble (*laleo*) them[1184].

[1181] He does not want a Kingdom based on laws and punishments for the ones who does not respect them, instead, He wants a Kingdom of Love in which we all will enter.

[1182]In Jesus, the Nathan soul lives, which will sacrifice itself for the redemption of the world.

[1183] The last day corresponds to the seventh day of Creation, day in which we "ascend" to God. This means that at death, when we will "ascend" to God, we will see the reality of our Spiritual Image (the Christ, the "stone that was discarded which became the cornerstone"), and we can judge our own selves.

[1184] Now the pronouncing of the Jesus resounds up to the Father of the Holiest Trinity because the Father gave everything to the Son. When he does something, or says something, he is in "direct link" with the will of the Father of the Holiest Trinity, and for this reason, He can be conscious tool of the Christ.

1185

COMMONALITY, WASHING OF THE FEET[1186] (Mt 26,27; Mc 14,25; Lc 22,23; Ps 40, 10)

1. Before the feast of the Easter[1187], Jesus, knowing that his time[1188] had come to cross over from this world towards the Father[1189], having spiritually loved his Jewish people[1190] the ones (that were) in the world, he spiritually loved them for the accomplishment (*telos*)[1191].

COMMONALITY, WASHING OF THE FEET

[1185] Here, the second part of John's Gospel begin and it is divided in three parts: the first "foundation of the new community n the force of love" (chapter 13-14) ends with the invite of Jesus to the disciples to leave with Him and go towards the Father. The second "the new community in the midst of the world" (chapter 15-16) includes the instructions that he gifts to the disciples to go through the world, that they find to be hostile, with Jesus. Lastly, the third (chapter 17) contains the prayer of Jesus for the community that is present and for the one of the future.

[1186] Overview of the multiplications:

- The *first* is for the 5.000 and 12 baskets come forward (the 12 is the number of the "celestial" things). After this, Jesus will walk on the waters and Peter will descend in the water but he will drown. Philip will say that 200 coins are not enough to feed the people: to the Gift of the multiplication, the 12 will respond with a lack in Faith.
- The *second* is for the 4.000 (and 7 baskets come forward (number of the planetary things). The disciples will forget to take the loaves of bread: to the Gift they do not respond with an adequate Consciousness.
- The *third* is the Last Supper (the Commonality) and it is for the 12. After this, at the Gethsemane, they do not pray (lack of faith) and they do not keep vigil (lack of consciousness).
- The *fourth* (the "+1") is the miraculous Fishing (John 21,1) and it is for 7 disciples. The 7 are on a boat, and they throw the fishing net on the right side on command of the Risen One (faith). Peter wraps his hips and he throws himself in the sea ("descending"), and then he ascends ("going back up"), and he drags the nets on earth (to descend and then ascend means to expand to the various consciousness, to bring them here on earth, from which the boat was far, from about 200 cubits: man) with 153 big fish. Then Peter will not manifest spiritual love (*agapeo*) for Jesus (he already lost consciousness).

It is important to see how in the Last Supper reported by John, there is no mentioning of the institution of the Eucharist. This can be interpreted with the fact that the Eucharist "of word" is typical of the third type of connection between man and the divine and it is connected to the astral body. The fourth path, typical of the conscious soul, is connected to the consciousness of the I Am, and the Gospel of John takes us to this consciousness (let's remember that the 12+1 I Am cited in the text).

Here we start the path of Christian Initiation, path that is formed by seven stages which are: 1) the washing of the feet; 2) the flagellation; 3) crowning of the thorns; 4) the crucifixion; 5) the death; 6) the sepulcher and resurrection; 7) ascension.

[1187] We are now two days before Easter, in this case of the fourth Easter, the "+1" of the three. The day begins Wednesday at 18.00 (6pm) and will end Thursday at 18.00 (6pm). This day corresponds to the fifth day of the Creation, in which animals were created.

[1188] Now he can announce that His time has come. This time was announced on verse 12,23.

[1189] Of the Holiest Trinity since he finished His work.

[1190] Here is the seed of love for the new Community, the New Jerusalem.

[1191] Therefore, he also loved us in the moment of death on the cross by forgiving us.

2. And so it becomes the commonality (*deipnos*)[1192], having already the devil[1193] rejected, (*ballo*) to the heart[1194] of Judah (son) of Simon Iscariot[1195], of delivering it[1196],

3. knowing that the Father gave him everything in his hands[1197] and that he came from God and he was headed (*hypago*)[1198] towards the God.

4. He rises from the commonality[1199] and he leaves (*titehmi*) the clothes[1200] and, taking (*lambano*) a linen cloth, he wrapped himself[1201].

1192 See the note on verse 12,2. The Commonality of love.
This Commonality-Supper represents a polarity with the Commonality-Supper of Bethany. In this last one, the love of the disciples for him is being expressed, in the first one His love for humanity is being manifested. In both of them, the "traitor" is being manifested: in Bethany the luciferic foundation of his betrayal is being explained (*he was thief-12,6*), in the Last Commonality-Supper was his final decision and his union with Satan.

1193 Literally "spirit of dispersion".

1194 Judah was characterized as "thief" (John 2,6), which means as an entity that steals, and Lucifer is the one who "stole" the Cosmic images of true Light from Mary Sophia.

1195 Let's remember that Judah was the reincarnation of Oedipus, and also that he repeated the destiny to kill his father and unite with his mother. The name "Iscariot" reminds us of the place of Initiation in which Judah and his father received the Mysteries, the Island of Keriot. Judah appears as the polar opposite of Jesus: the Jesus glorifies the Father and "ascends" to a higher Father (the Holiest Trinity), whereas Judah kills him.

1196 From the Latin word *"tradere"* which is usually translated as "to betray".

1197 So that humanity could go back to the Father and interrupt the process of the Fall that would have been irreversible if it kept going on.

1198 The Holiest Trinity gave all the power to the Jesus, who is now getting ready to leave his dimension of origin (the Father of the Holy Trinity, since Jesus brings the Nathanic Soul) to then arrive to the Holiest Trinity. Jesus is preparing himself to open the Way for all humanity on how to operate to win over the Fall connected to Lucifer and Ahriman.

1199 He is elevating himself above the level of consciousness of the group.

1200 They represent the unrefined etheric body and therefore the body of form/shape. In this case, they represent the forms in which He gave His teachings. But now is the time for a higher and more elevated teaching which will make the Apostles capable of freeing themselves from external interests.

1201 Jesus wraps his hips (which correspond to the zodiacal impulse of Libra, the border between the Bright Zodiac and the Dark Zodiac, between consciousness and unconsciousness of man) with linen, which with its starry seeds incarnates, in an eminent manner, the forces of Light. With this gesture, Jesus is indicating the process of awareness of the unconscious, of the darkness within us. Peter will bring up this gesture again in the miraculous fishing (see John 21). The kidneys are symbol of both strength and fragility. What was conquered in the lower human sphere, now becomes the seed for the higher sphere since they control the genital sphere, and at the same time, they open the higher path to the Verb. They are the organ of intuitive listening. They lead the transition from water to blood (which then becomes Spirit) and the transition from salt to fire that then becomes Light.

5. Then he threw water in the basin[1202] and began to wash the feet[1203] of the disciples and to clean[1204] with the linen, with which he wrapped himself.

6. He then gets close to Simon Peter. And Peter[1205] says (*lego*): "Lord, will you wash my feet?"

1202 As image of the purifying Grace that descend on souls (the basin).

1203 It is important to see how only John talks about this event but he does not report on the event of the institution of the Eucharist. With this passage, John, the disciple of spiritual love, receives the 10th Gift, the one of the Order of Melchisedek, while the other Apostles receive the 7th Gift.
The feet correspond to the constellation of Pisces, the last part that we need to purify within ourselves: the purification of the will, the will that acts by protecting and not by abusing the power.
The feet represent the kingdom of Earth, the *Malkut*, the terrestrial Kingdom and therefore the Mother, the Virgin Mother, the Black Virgin, the Mother of all terrestrial existence. This is why in spiritual symbology, they are represented as "wounded," and therefore they need to be healed. Eve was also bitten by the snake on her foot. The wound represents the "false" of the foot and it is one "half" of the other wound, the one on the head represented by the fontanel. This is because the man created in the image and likeness of God, which is the Zodiacal Man or First Adam, represented by the zodiacal circle, which was "cut" between Aries-head and Pisces-feet, and therefore we lost the "likeness" with the Creator.
If we take a deeper look at it, the feet are never still, and we cannot control them in the little movements: this is to indicate that "others" act through them. In the heel, we can see the will (in an Ahrimanic way), in the false the feeling (in a luciferic way) and in the front part the thinking (where we should be the masters).
The feet represent the contact between divine will and humanity and they indicate the descending of a higher level of consciousness in man to which man needs to ascend even through all the difficulties of the terrestrial acting.
We also have a three +one in the feet:

- The Mariam who throws herself at Jesus' feet at the resurrection of Lazarus (John 11,32);
- The unction of the feet from Mariam to prepare him to the test of the victory over the forces of death present on the feet (the oil protected him from the terrestrial forces- John 12,1);
- The Washing of the Feet in which Jesus completely purifies the Apostles and he heals the wound that came from the Fall (John 13,5);
- The Magdalen will try to grab him by the feet on Easter Sunday but the Risen One will stop her from doing so since after he healed the feet and descended on Mother Earth's womb, he needs to ascend to the Father to complete the spiritual marriage between Mother earth and Father sky (John 20,15).

1204 With the water he purifies himself from the inner filth (luciferic), and with the linen that brings new light he can get rid of the deep filth (sediment, Ahriman), a new form for the inferior man. The filth, the darkness, remains in the linen, and the linen gifts his plasmatic Light. He is the one who directly cleans us; he directly intervenes with His hands to purify us from the residual impurities. The Washing of the Feet happened with a cosmic resonance in the sphere of the Holy Trinity; "now" she resounds with the sphere of the Everything of the Everything, which is the first un-manifested sphere.

1205 Here, Peter represents the man.

7. Jesus[1206] replied (*apokrinomai*), and said (*eipon*) to him: "What I create (*poieo*), you now do not know, but you will understand (*ginosko*) it afterwards"[1207].

8. Peter tells (*lego*) him: "You will not wash my feet in eternity[1208]". The Jesus replied (*apokrinomai*) to him: "If I do not wash you, you will not have part[1209] with me".

9. Simon Peter tells (*lego*) him: "Lord, not only my feet, but also my hands and head[1210]".

10. The Jesus tells (*lego*) him: "Who has been baptized[1211] does not have the need to wash himself except the feet[1212], but he is entirely pure[1213]. And you are pure[1214], but not all of you".

1206 The Nathan Soul, the archetype of the Man before the Fall. To Peter (no article), Jesus replies (no article).

1207 We often spend most of our live without understanding, with no "comprehension". Here it is being told to us that we need to work within ourselves to develop this understanding, and we also need to allow Him to work within us to help us purify ourselves from the material world. Therefore, we always need to be grateful and thankful.

1208 Peter worries about himself, that the "afterwards" will become for eternity. This gesture can be read as a rejection dictated by the non-understanding of the act of humility connected to the Washing of the Feet. He thought that this possibility was for something in the future and not from now on. He sees in the gesture of Jesus an excessive humiliation for him who is impure. With this he declares the rejection of the Love of the Christ. From this comes the comparison (repeated 5 times in the Gospel) with John.

1209 Also "destiny", "fate". If Jesus does not open the way to Christian Initiation, to which the first step is the Washing of the Feet, Peter certainly cannot do it on his own.

1210 Peter now understands his mistake in rejecting Grace's help which was being offered to him, and he asks for complete initiatic Purification, since he is now aware that the whole human being needs this kind of help.

1211 In water, and therefore the baptism of John the Baptist.

1212 To walk in the spiritual world.

1213 Every man, with the support of Grace and acting according to the Father's will, can purify himself "almost" completely. But the final freedom from earth, with its laws and necessities, can only be done by the Christ who is now opening the Path to humanity.

1214 They received the Baptism of Water, the inner purification that reawakens within us the memory of the divine origin. The fact of "remembering one's own divine origin", means to "know" that God exists and we are part of Him, we belong to Him, we are called to go back to Him, and therefore we need to make His will. To reject this is the sin of impiety.

11. He knew the one who delivers[1215] him, and this is why he said (*eipon*): "Not all of you are pure".

12. (After he) washed the feet, he took (*lambano)* his clothes and sat down (*anapipto*)[1216], and he said (*eipen*) to them: "Do you understand what I created (*poeio*)[1217] for you?"

13. You call me Teacher[1218] and Lord[1219], and you say well, because I am.

14. If therefore I, the Lord and Teacher, washed your feet, you also need to wash each other's[1220] feet.

15. I gave you the example[1221], so that as I created (*poieo*) to you, you also create.

[1215] The verb is conjugated in the imperfect tense, and so the action is already happening since Judas had distanced himself from the real comprehension of the teaching of Jesus for a long time now. Jesus did not want to create an independent Hebrew state; instead he came to bring back the Chosen People, the Eternal Israel, to the House of the Father.

[1216] He puts his clothes back on and he goes back to sitting at the table, and therefore he takes on a form of teaching to which the Apostles could easily access.

[1217] He gifted us the law of "free" sacrifice, and who will put it into practice will be blessed (verse 17).

[1218] The Teacher Jesus, the I of Zarathustra present in the Jesus. This is how they used to call him.

[1219] The sphere of Saturn. He is both Zarathustra and the Nathanic Soul, but then again he is even more; he is the bearer of Christ. But for their consciousness, he allows them to refer to him this way.

[1220] He speaks adapting to their level of consciousness. Let's remember that the initiatic step of the Washing of the Feet is the first one of the Christian Initiation. It consists of becoming aware (from the ones who are spiritually superior) of being in debt for the gifts that they received from those inferior to them, and their state of being dependent on who is inferior to them. Who "stays behind" in the spiritual path allows others to receive the strength of the ones that have given up. R. Steiner reminded us that the ones who are more evolved and advanced, contracted more debts. An example of this passage is the relationship between man and plant: man is superior than plant, but without it he cannot live and breathe. In his humbly "bowing down" in front of a being who is spiritually inferior, man experiments humility and the fraternity with the Cosmos.

[1221]Also the "model" or "sign". The Light that he gave us shapes us: it's up to us to repeat the gesture bringing our own Light to our brothers (linen), the foundation of the New Jerusalem.

16. Amen, Amen[1222] I say to you, there is no servant[1223] higher than his lord, nor apostle higher than the one who sent him.

17. If you know these things, you are blessed[1224] if you create them.

18. I do not say (*lego*) about you all; I know the ones that I elected[1225]; but in order that the Scripture comes to completion: *Who eats the bread with me, put his heel[1226] on me.*

19. I tell you know, before the becoming, because when I will become you will be believers that "I am[1227]".

20. Amen, Amen[1228] I say to you: who welcomes the one that I will send[1229], welcomes me, and who welcomes me, welcomes the one who sent me".

1222 A universal truth is being announced.

1223 The being blessed corresponds to the entering in the solar sphere. Lucifer, on the other hand, rebelled and he did not want to serve God, and he was "enmeshed" in the sphere of Venus. His home remained on the Sun as a disturber/heckler of the inner Sun, the Higher I.

1224 It's about putting into practice what is being said and what is not being said: the institution of the "external" Eucharist substituted from the "inner" one of John in Love with the Jesus. It is apparent that John, in his report of the Last Supper does not mention the institution of the Eucharist in the two types of bread and in the wine.
The Christ, being the Lord of the Earth since he united with her. The bread, which comes from the grain and therefore from the Earth, represents His body. All that is in a solid form represents Hi body, all that is in liquid form represents His blood, Hi soul. The symbols of the Eucharist become two realities. As man permeates more and more in the Christic impulse coming from the Golgotha, then he is able to reunite with the Christ (also with no external tools), with the spiritual Communion. It will evolve from the physical plane to the spiritual one. John is already putting himself in this dimension: his is the Gospel of the Gospels.

1225 Judas was accepted by the Jesus but he was not chosen from Him.

1226 It is the will being activated, and also the part that is extremely ahrimanic within us. Earlier, the Jesus washed the feet of the disciples, and now the temptation of pride and to stand against the Jesus and to give him the cold shoulder is presenting itself. This way, the unity of the Twelve is broken, and the forces of opposition can enter. Judas, maker of this gesture, becomes the "*mercur*" (negative) between Jesus and Evil. The heel represents the tail of the Scorpion.

1227 With no additional objectification, it is the Principle of the I Am. This is the 13th I Am, the synthesis of the 12. He will repeat it at the soldiery at the Gethsemane. Being in the I am is the foundation for spiritual love, for the New Jerusalem. Let's remember that in the New Jerusalem there will no longer be temples (churches, universities, banks, etc). (Ap 21,22).

1228 Another universal truth.

1229 Jesus will send us the Paraclete, which is the redeemed aspect of Lucifer (after the Golgotha). For the complete vision of the "paracletes" see John 14,16.

JUDAS UNVEILED (Mt 26,21-25; Mc 14,18-21; Lc 22,21 ss.; Lc 12,27)

21. Having said (*eipon*) these things, Jesus was disturbed[1230] in the spirit and he testified and said (*eipon*): " Amen, Amen I tell you that one amongst you[1231] will hand me over.

22. The Jewish people[1232] looked (*blepo*) amongst each other (towards) the disciples, not having (*aporeo*) the means (to understand) about who he was speaking of[1233].

23. And One of his disciples, the one that Jesus spiritually loved[1234], was resting[1235] on the breasts[1236] of Jesus[1237].

JUDAS UNVEILED

[1230] The spiritual turmoil was internal, and it's needed to activate the Incorruptible Body with the I.

[1231] It is the separated part, Judas, that will hand him over. Within the soul of the Twelve, he represents what was operating amongst them that was not transformed. This is a universal truth, since there will always be someone who does not recognize him.

[1232] Other people that were present in the Commonality; maybe the servants? The Jewish people from the previous passage (12,37)? They observe the scene and they question one another.

[1233] They do not look within their soul; instead they search through the disciples the reason that Jesus spoke that way. This is the "stopped" moment from Leonardo in his Last Supper.

[1234] This is John the Evangelist, "spiritually loved" (which is, in the esoteric use of time, "Initiated") from Jesus united with the Principle Christ. This expression has already been used to indicate Lazarus (John 11.3): we understand that John the Evangelist is Lazarus resuscitated.
The verb being used is Greek is *agapeo* (spiritual love) and in Latin it's *diligere* which means "to choose": this means the disciple "chosen" amongst the other ones to bring the highest message. This is because he freely "had chosen" to follow and love Jesus.

[1235] The verb portrays this "leaning on" while "pointing up/directing oneself towards the above".

[1236] Where the etheric organ is, which as a supersensible "etheric egg", the gestation of the Children takes place.
In the womb, the conception and birth of the Child happens; in the breast He will feed himself and therefore He will grow, and at the cross he will be an adult and therefore active and capable of following Jesus.

[1237] This image symbolizes the transformation that took place within John: he is the only one that gets to the point of being able to listen to what lives in the heart of Jesus.
The fact that John leaned his head on the breast of Jesus indicates a condition of deep Communion, and this supports the reason for which the Gospel of John does not speak about the institution of the Eucharist: he is always in Communion with the Jesus.
It important to see how in verse 1,18 it is Jesus that is on the breast of the Father: the Only-Begotten Son, who is in the breast of the father.

24. Therefore Simon Peter[1238] hints on asking who he was talking (*lego*)[1239] about. And he says that he said who he was talking about.

25. Leaning on (*anapipto*) the Jesus' chest[1240], he says (*lego*) to him: "Lord, who is he?"

[1238] In his Gospel, John narrates about five comparisons, contrasts of position, between Peter and John (the disciple that Jesus loved) as an anticipation of the two churches that were rising (of Peter and of John).
The first is at the Last Supper (John 13,24) when Peter shows that he is not in the Spiritual Love; the second one is at the capturing of Jesus when John enters the atrium, and he is willing to take the same fate while Peter stays outside (John 18,35); the third one when they run together to the sepulcher and John will believe in the resurrection (John 20,2); the fourth one is at the fishing when he will be the one to recognize the Risen One (John 21.7); the fifth one is at the famous "feed my lambs" when Peter declares that he does not spiritually love Jesus (John 21,20).

[1239] Peter knows to be impure (like the other ones) and therefore he goes to John, who is the one that is recognized by everyone for being the closest to Jesus.

[1240]First, he was in the womb (cove in which we spiritually come to life); now he is in the breast, the headquarters of feelings, of the heart, and he is being welcomed. He is "born" in the spirit and he begins to speak. Let's remember that in the moment of resurrection in Bethany, within Lazarus-John, the Child was already born in the Vital Loving Spirit; now this one, leaning in the center of love, is experimenting the third birth within himself, the one of the Spirit Man. After this birth, the John moves his head above the breast, and therefore he begins to feed himself of the forces of the Father, and he can make His will: he will be at the Cross, where he will receive Mariam as Mother.
John leans his head on the breast, which is a gesture that reminds us of the posture of the head in the moment of death; this could be the moment of initiatic "death" for the birth of the new Child in the Spirit Man. He will become active when, at the Cross, John receives a new Mother.
We can therefore understand why in John's Gospel, he does not speak about the institution of the Eucharist; it is the "way" to reach the Christ and through Him also to reach the Father, but John is already on His breast, in communion with Him. The Eucharist is given to us "in memory" of the love of the Christ, but John is already in His love (the Jesus spiritually loved him). Therefore, if we are in His Love, the external Eucharist is not necessary because the true Eucharist is Love.
As we will see further on, John the evangelist is never mentioned by name but only through a periphrasis of his gesture at the Last Supper. Within this, we can capture the fact that John leaned his spiritual ear on the heart of Jesus, and he grasped the "divine secret" of the cosmic love. Only one who has completed the inner work can achieve this hearing. John hears his "Spiritual Name," he is ready to be reborn, he becomes Verb.

26. The Jesus replies (*apokrinomai*) and says (*lego*): "He is the one for whom as I baptized[1241] the bite (of bread[1242]), (I will) give[1243] it to him.[1244] Therefore baptizing the bite, he will give it to Judas of Simone Iscariot[1245].

1241 The verb used (*bapto*) corresponds to baptizing, and it is usually translated as "to dip". The Jesus began the path of initiation with the Washing of the Feet ,and now the baptism of love for Judas is taking place: will he be able to welcome him and win over the temptation of Lucifer-Ahriman? This "baptism of love" can be grasped within accepting and loving one's own destiny, forgiving, loving others, always giving people a possibility, etc.

1242 This bite is of bread, even though it is deduced from the term used for "bite".

1243 The Jesus, by operating in this particular way, offers Judas a new force to win over the temptation to which he is subjected. Judas will not accept this Gift, and therefore Satan will be able to enter him. It is important to underline that not even John, who knew who the traitor was, exposes him, and this is because he also entered the sphere of Christic Love. He incarnated the figure of Jesus' "friend".
This bite, which is secretly and lovingly being offered, is not mentioned by other Evangelists. We can now grasp a polarity amongst the three Evangelists and John. The three do not speak of the bite, but they talk about the institution of the Eucharist, while John does not speak of it, but he speaks of this bite of love with which the Jesus is ready to offer parts of His loving forces to help Judas: this is the Eucharist in John, the spiritual Eucharist.

1244 Here is the meaning of the Last Supper by R. Steiner. The Christ indicates the bread and the wine by saying: "This is my body, this is my blood.... With this he wanted to create the transition from an animal nutrition to the vegetable one, which is something that is more elevated. In that period of time, there were two different classes of men: the ones that fed themselves with meat and blood, which are the pre-Christians, of which Jesus did not consider. Secondly, there were men that would only kill plants, they would "extract" their juice-blood; they would drink wine and eat bread. He does consider these last ones, they are the pioneers of the future humanity. The meaning of the Last Supper is one of a transition in nutrition from one based on dead animals to one based on dead plants. When our fifth sub-race will end, we will have a sixth one, and then we will understand the meaning of the Last Supper, and animals will not be eaten anymore. In the future, we will have an evolution that foresees an additional rise from a vegetable alimentation to a mineral one. Bread and wine will need to be once again sacrificed, abandoned".

1245 All of Judas "names" of being mentioned, and this is to express his terrestrial and spiritual wholeness. This gets him closer to Simon Peter (so called) at the announcement that he will reject him (John 13,36). We now have the contrast between the old lunar Initiation represented by Judas and the new Christian one represented by John.

27. And after the bite, Satan[1246] entered him. Jesus says (*lego*) to him: "What you create (*poieo*), create it quickly[1247].

28. But none of the dining companions[1248] were clear (*ghinosko)* on for what reason he said (*eipon*) this.

29. Since Judas had a prideful[1249] tongue, some believed that Jesus said (*lego*) to him: "Ransom the things that we need for the feast[1250], or to give something to the poor[1251]".

[1246] In that moment, Judas I was not completely present (even though Jesus called him out), and this opened the door to Satan, which is the impulse of the materialistic conception, to accomplish the kingdom on Earth, just what Judas wanted Jesus to do to free Palestine by the Romans. The fact that Judas did not accept the offer of help that Jesus gave him, made it so that Satan would use the forces donated by Jesus that he did not accept.
In Mt 26,14 (when he goes to the priests and begins the betrayal), Judas is mentioned as "the one called the Judas", and this indicates his I being "on vacation", his Spiritual Name, and the incapability of Judas to "be named", to refer to himself. Thanks to this mobilization of the I, the bite was able to open the path for Satan. Let's remember that S. Paul says: "Who gets the Bread and Wine without discerning the Body and the Blood of th Lord, he will eat and drink his own conviction" (I Cor 11, 27).

[1247] Jesus speaks to Satan and he gives him permission to act. "The" Satan is present, which is the supreme being of the satanic Hierarchies. By passing the bite, we can see how Jesus himself chose the one who would hand him over, and he chose Judas because the luciferic forces were already present within him (see note on verse 29), and therefore, in a karmic way, it was possible that Satan-Ahriman could enter him.

[1248] None of the ones that were sitting at the table. Only John, who leaned his head on Jesus' chest, had the necessary forces of Love to understand. From this, we can assume that Jesus did not speak externally; instead everything was done in a silent way for the world. Only the ones who had ears to listen, heard.

[1249] The term used is *glossokomon*, formed by the words that mean "tongue" or "language" and "flowing hair", "to make proud", "dragging". By putting these two terms together, we have "prideful tongue". Within this, the luciferic aspect of Judas comes to life, who was already possessed by the luciferic spirit of the Hebrew people since it belonged to the party of the Zealots. Normally, it is translated as "purse", since Lucifer acts in the hollow organs, concave, like purses.

[1250] The Easter. For Easter they needed lamb, unleavened bread and wine. Now they are in Holy Thursday, while Easter was going to start after Friday night. We now are at the pre-Easter dinner. The Lamb symbolizes humility and sacrifice, the victory over pride in which Judas was the prey.
Part of the disciples believed that this virtue could be redeemed, which means to acquire it in a initiatic sense (since Judas was only mentioned with initiatic titles). Something that is already ours is being "redeemed", but after the Fall it was taken away from us.

[1251] One who already possesses these redeemed forces, can donate to the ones poor of spirit, to the ones who search for the Spirit with a truthful heart. This is the precept that was also given to the young rich man: sell the old spiritual forces and give the proceeds, which is their transformation, to the ones poor of spirit.
The apostles were still caught in their conditionings and mental forms, and therefore they understand only what they understand.

30. Since he grabbed (*lambano*) the bite[1252], he immediately exited[1253]. And it was night[1254].

NEW PRECEPT

31. When he left, Jesus says (*lego*): "Now[1255] the Son of Man is glorified and the God[1256] was glorified[1257] within him[1258]"[1259].

[1252] This bite represents the Life that Jesus gifts to the disciples, Judas grabs it to betray it, to take possession of it, to suppress it. In the Prologue it is said: "*Within the same he was (since always) Spiritual Life and Spiritual Life was (since always) the Light of men; and the Light manifests itself in darkness, and darkness did not take possession of it* (John 4,5).

[1253] Judas understood the "secret" words of Jesus and he know has two possibilities: to win over the satanic temptation, or to reject the bite of Christian initiation in Love that is being offered to him with so much love. In this last case, he would have had to explain to the ones that were present why he would do so. Therefore, he rather interpret Jesus phrase for himself, and he leaves.

[1254] As a state of consciousness, the time of Darkness, the darkness in which Judas fell in. he rejected the Light, the one that manifests the Life, the divine Love (see the Prologue).

NEW PRECEPT
With this passage, Jesus will give the precept of love to the disciples, the love that only John reached.

[1255] Here, His time has begun: the time that at the Wedding at Cana was not yet there. This "time", the time of darkness, is inserted in the rhythm of the "time frame" that lasts 18 hours, from 21 (9 pm) on Thursday to 15 (3 pm) on Holy Friday.
Now that John (a man) has reached and has manifested spiritual love, it is not important that Jesus is "good and loving", the important thing is that a "normal" man is that way. If the normal-man is John, which is Lazarus, which is Cain, then the transformation of man has happened.

[1256] Of the Holiest Trinity.

[1257] It is clear. Outside it is night time, but inside it's light. Now that Judas wants to betray him, He is getting ready for the sacrifice. He accepts it, and therefore of making the Father's will manifesting His glory-love.

[1258] Through Judas. With Judas exiting, Jesus declares the accomplishment of His work: He reached the likeness with God and he is ready to multiply as Son of Man and become Son of God. With the exiting of Judas, the Passion begins and therefore Jesus' final path. On verse 31, He expresses His Love and the one of God for man (up to Judas), on verse 322 he shows the love of God communicated to man through Jesus. On verse 31, the Glory is manifesting, on verse 32 it is God that manifests it through Jesus. The theme that has already been expresseD in the Prologue comes back: and from his plenitude we all received grace for grace (John 1,16). The continuous exchange between love and love, between shown love (from Jesus through gifting His life) and the communicated one (the gift of the Holy Spirit from God), are represented with the blood and the water that will flow from Jesus rib-cage.

[1259] Some codex say: "If the God was glorified within him".

32. The God will also glorify him within himself: and soon he will glorify him[1260].

33. Dear sons (*teknion*)[1261], I will be with you just for "a little" more time[1262]. You will look for me, and like I said (*eipon*) to the Jewish people: where I go, you do not have the strength to come to[1263], and now I tell you as well.

34. I am giving you a new "order": so that you spiritually love one another just like I spiritually loved you, (so that) you would also spiritually love one another[1264].

35. Within this, everyone will understand that you are my disciples, if you will have spiritual love[1265] with one another. [1266]

1260 Through Jesus. The God is glorified within Jesus who offers himself to make his will and therefore, simultaneously, the God will bring him within himself, in His Glorious Light.
We can finally say that the big conflict between Light and Darkness, which tempted him multiple times, is ending. If Jesus wouldn't have let Judas leave, he would have fallen in Satan's last temptation: to impose His will on Judas or to not forgive him.

1261 He says this because now he is united with the Father. "Dear Sons" corresponds to the sixth step of initiation. They no longer are "brothers". The ones who follow the teachings will become Sons of the same Father.

1262 Even if they did not realize it, the betrayal is over. This "little" will be completed at 16 o'clock, 16.00 with another "little" when the disciples will come back to see Jesus.

1263 In the Holiest Trinity, to which man will have ascended developing Perfection. They are not ready yet for this big step of immensurable love.

1264 He loved us to gift us love, and therefore we also can love each other spiritually. John is the only one to report this new precept: this means that he knew how to listen to Him. This is the precept to become "Dear Sons" of the Father. This passage is extremely important because it is the foundation of the new Cristian Community, and it replaces the Mosaic Law and therefore the old Alliance. The first commandment was about loving God; now it is God that loves us and we are called to multiply this love. He does not ask us once more to love him or to reciprocate the love. To love God now means to accept Him within ourselves, to recognize Him as a presence and force of love. By loving others, we make God always present and active within ourselves. Within this, He receives His Glory.
This love is given to everyone (Washing of the Feet). Then he forgives the enemy (Judas) up to the price of life since love wins over hate.

1265 This type of love needs to be visible: testified.
This verse represents the "+1" of the previous one which represented the "3" of love.

1266 This exhortation, the new precept, is found in between the betrayal of Judas and the prophecy of denial of Peter, which is the same place where Matthew puts the institution of the Eucharist. John, with his commandment, explains to us the true meaning of this last one. As he already said in verse 6,56 "Who eats my flesh, and drinks my blood, remains in me, and I within him". The Eucharist becomes the identification with Jesus through the assimilation of His Life and death. It is the constant memory of His love for us until we also reach this dimension of love.

PROPHECY OF PETER'S DENIAL (Mt 26,33; Mc 14,29; Lc 22,31.34; Lc 21,18)

36. Simon Peter says *(lego)* to him: "Lord, where are you going?" The Jesus replies (*apokrinomai*): "Where I go, you do not have the strength[1267] to follow me: but you will follow me later on[1268]".

37. The Peter says (*lego*): "(Lord), why do I not have the strength to follow you now[1269]? I will leave (*tithemi*) my lower part *(psyche)* for you[1270]".

38. Jesus replies (*apokrinomai*): "You will leave your soul for me? Amen, Amen I say to you: the rooster[1271] will not crow, that you will deny[1272] me three times".

PROPHECY OF PETER'S DENIAL

[1267] The Marian force that transformed the soul. Peter is caught up in the enthusiasm but he does not have the strength or the consciousness to follow Jesus up to the Holiest Trinity. John will have it at the Cross.

[1268] When he will have received the Spirit, he will also be able to go don the path that takes to unconditional love.

[1269] Peter did not grasp what Jesus said about the disciples, Peter does not accept the answer and he persists with his attitude of wanting to know where HE is going, and as a consequence, there is the prophecy of his denial.

[1270] Peter declares himself to be open to offer his soul to be available in serving Jesus - soul and not spirit, *fileo* and not *agapeo!* He does not understand that it is not about giving his own soul (or own life) for the Christ, instead it is for man, for the love towards others. By offering his life to the Lord, he shows his dedication to Him and not to men. Once again, he has a hierarchal and strict view of his relationship with the Jesus, and he considers it right for a subordinate to give his live for the higher one.
Peter needs to spiritually ascend to the point of offering to Jesus his soul which has been transformed in a Marian sense.

[1271] Symbol of Fire, of the higher I, of a recall of the I within him.

[1272] Also "you will reject". Jesus reminds us that Satan is always ready to take advantage of every situation that shows any kind of inner weakness. Peter is not called to give his life for Jesus for the reason that no one can substitute himself to Him as a Savior; instead Peter needs to give his life like Jesus did, for man. Peter, seeing his false idea of the Messiah crumble, will end up denying him.

VERB OF INTERCESSION (Mc 11,22; Mc 16,19)

1. Don't let your heart be troubled[1273]. Believe[1274] in the God, and also believe in me[1275].
2. In my Father's house there are many tasks[1276], if it wasn't so, would I have told you that I was going to prepare a place for you[1277]?
3. And when I will be gone and I will have prepared a place for you[1278], I will come[1279] again, and I will take you on near me, so that where I am you will be.
4. And where I go[1280], you know the way[1281].
5. Thomas said: " Lord, we do not know where you are going, and how do we have the strength to know the way[1282]?"

VERB OF INTERCESSION

[1273] Also "do not disturb". Do not allow Lucifer to activate his troubles within you.
This exhortation was necessary because of what was happening at the Supper (Washing of the Feet, betrayal, announcement of His departure) which had shaken up the disciples.

[1274] For the difference between "having faith" and "believing" see John 1,7.

[1275] He encourages them to stay strong within Faith so that the denial does not happen, so that they do not fall into fear: this is the key to not fall.

[1276] There is a place and job for every "kind" of way and man who ascends to His Father.

[1277] The promise of the Prologue is now fulfilled: "*But to all the ones that welcomed him, he gave them the power to become sons of God, to the ones who believe in his name*" (John 1,12). With the fruit of his death, this will happen.

[1278] This place is for His disciples and not for the Jewish people who are oppressed by the Law and the ones who oppress other men.

[1279] It might seem odd that this verb is in the present form, but this is explained by saying that it is referring to His Second Coming (John 6,39), on the plane of etheric Life, with which He opens the way for His Father. He is in the present, outside of time. He is there for all of humanity, and he can be met in every moment in time, as soon as man (immersed in the earthly becoming) is ready for this meeting.

[1280] The phrase in Greek has an ultimate aspect: the conquering of a dimension that will be so forever.

[1281] Because he is the Way, the dimension of the highest cosmic consciousness. The Way is therefore the one of love.

[1282] Jesus speaks according to spiritual reasoning, but the man (Thomas) is moving in terrestrial reasoning. Thomas is also present at the resuscitation of Lazarus "*We also go to be in the depths of death with him*: (John 11,16) and he was ready to descend in the kingdom of death with Jesus. He understood that Jesus will die but he does not understand how he can enter a new life. For him, death is an ending with no return and therefore he does not understand where Jesus is going. Even after the resurrection, he will find it hard to believe in the Risen One.

6. Jesus said to him: "**I am the way, and the truth and the spiritual life[1283];** no one comes to the Father, if not through me[1284].
7. If you have known me, you will also know my Father, and from now on you know Him and you have seen Him[1285].
8. Philip says (*lego*) to him: "Lord, point out the Father and that is enough[1286] for us".
9. The Jesus says (*lego*) to him: "I have been with you for a long time and you haven't had me in clarity (*ginosko*) Philip? Who saw (*horao*) me also saw *(horao)* the Father. Why do you say: Point out the Father?[1287]
10. Do you not believe that I am within the Father and the Father is within me? The words (*rema*) that I say (*laleo*) to you, I do not say them from me. But the Father, the one that stays within me, creates (*poieo*) his fulfillments[1288].
11. Believe in me[1289]: I am in the Father and the Father is in me[1290]. If anything, believe because of these achievements.

1283 With this affirmation, He immensely expands what was said in the first verse (about believing in Him). It can also be seen as our I Am is the Way, the Truth and the Life.

1284 Because He comes from the Father, and the Father within us is the complete consciousness and knowledge of our spiritual I Am.

1285 Now the Christ has expressed Himself with such clarity that the Apostles can recognize that He is present and operating within the Jesus. The goal is the likeness with the Father through the Son.

1286 Philip has yet to understand that the Christ and the Father are One. He was invited by the Jesus to follow him (John 1,43-45) and Philip identified him through the writings (Law and Prophets) and he has yet to grasp that Jesus brought us the completion, the transformation of the Law into operating Grace and Truth.

1287 Jesus had already promised this to Philip and Nathanial with the phrase: "*Amen, Amen I say to you, you will see the open sky and the Angels of God will ascend and descend above the Son of man*" (John 1,51). Philip does not understand that within Jesus, God is present.

1288 The Father fulfills His works by manifesting as the Son, as Logos, so when the Son speaks, he is expressing the Logos (even though he needs to use forms that are suitable for man).

1289 The theme of believing comes back.

1290 Jesus insists on the complete harmony between Him and the Father.

12. Amen, Amen I say[1291] to you who believe in me, the fulfillments that I create (*poieo*), he will also create (*poieo*) them and he will create[1292] bigger things then this as well; because I am heading (*poreuomai*) towards the Father[1293].

13. And anything you will ask in my name[1294], this I will create (*poieo*)[1295], so that the Father will be glorified within the Son.

14. If you will ask me something in my name[1296], I will create (*poieo*).

15. If you spiritually love me, you will guard (*tereo*) the commandments (*entole'*)[1297], mine,

---

[1291] From this verse, he will mainly speak in the future tense:

- The works higher than this one (v.12);
- He will send the Spirit of Truth (v. 16-17);
- He will come back (v.18);
- The Son and the Father will live within the ones who practice His Word (v.23).

[1292] The work of Jesus is only the beginning. He does not suggest himself as the goal, as the highest expression of love: each one of us can do more.

[1293] The Christ, going to the Father of the Holiest Trinity after experimenting being human, will bring us with Him, and therefore we will also make the work of the Father. Everything is reunited.

[1294]The name is the Holy Spirit. Now He underlines that within Him the Holy Spirit is present. In this verse, the Trinity is recomposed.

[1295] This is why we will do higher work: because He supports us.

[1296] The Community with Him.

[1297]Also "precepts", "orders", "commands". Given the identification with Him, the commandments forgive every character it is imposing. Who does not love Jesus, cannot love others; who does not love others, does not love Jesus. The fact that he says: the commandments, "mine", indicate the polarity of love to the ones of Moses (otherwise he would have said "my commandments").

16. And I will guard (*tereo*) the Father, and another Paraclete[1298] will be given to you, so that it will be with you for eternity,

17. The spirit of truth[1299], that the world[1300] does not have the strength[1301] to receive because he does not see it spiritually (*theoreo*), nor does he have it in clarity[1302]. You have it in clarity (*ginosko*), because it stays near you and it will be within you.

18. I will not leave you orphans[1303], I come[1304] near you.

[1298] Paraclete comes from *parakleo* which means "person who is called to be near, so assist, to help, to intercede; like the lawyer in the judgment. The Jesus says "another" Paraclete because this is the third Paraclete, the Spirit of Truth of the following verse, while redeemed Lucifer after the Golgotha will be the fourth Paraclete, the "plus one", the "inner" Paraclete who will descend with the Pentecost. Lucifer was the one who "veiled" the Truth, and now, returning at the Father's service, he gives it back to man.
Let's remember that the **first Paraclete** (which is "intercessor" or "lawyer") is Mary the Helper, which assist the soul through the path of redemption.
The **second Paraclete** is Jesus himself, the "external" Consoling: "*Come to me, all of you who are tired and oppressed, and I will restore you*" (Mt 11,28).
The **third Paraclete** is the Spirit of Truth who on Easter's evening, Jesus breathed upon his disciples and said: "*Receive the Holy Spirit*" almost begging them to accept his gift (John 14,16). This is the Incorruptible Body completely personalized from Christ within Jesus.
The **fourth Paraclete**, **the "plus one",** is the redeemed Lucifer who will descend at the Pentecost upon Mariam (**the first Paraclete**), upon the Apostles who ascended to the step of Jesus (**the second Paraclete**), upon which the Risen One had already breathed His Spirit (**third Paraclete**).
To be more precise, the third Paraclete is the Incorruptible Body Risen Again and it is articulated in three aspects: the Holy Spirit (John 14,26) who is the Path; the Spirit of Truth (John 14,17) who is the Truth; and the Saint of the God (John 6,69) who is the Life. One of his aspects (if it can be called such) is the **Paraclete Angel** who is gifted to us as a helper through our evolutionary path.

[1299] The sense of the word "truth" in John means both the divine reality and the knowledge of the divine reality. The traditional interpretation, especially the Catholic one, intended the "truth" especially in the second meaning, in the dogmatic meaning. The Spirit leads the church.

[1300] The fallen part.

[1301] If there is no Marian force (the presence of the first Paraclete), the third Paraclete, the Spirit of Truth, cannot be received. For the complete vision of the "paraclete" see John 14,16.

[1302] The discerning that needs to be applied is the spiritual one.

[1303] It also means "blind", and therefore orphans in the sense of being disconnected with the Father but also blind towards the Paraclete Spirit. The Christ speaks in a "triune" way: as Father, Son and Holy Spirit.

[1304] Also "accept", and therefore another Trinitarian aspect. The Holy Spirit comes and, through the Son, we are accepted within the Father.

19. A little bit more and the world will not have me in the consciousness. But you have me in the consciousness[1305]: I spiritually live and you also spiritually live.

20. In that day[1306], you will discern **that I am in my Father and you are in me and I am in you.**

21. The ones who have[1307] my commandments[1308] and they abide by them[1309], those are the ones who spiritually[1310] love me. But who spiritually loves me, will be loved by my Father[1311] and I will spiritually love him and I will manifest myself to him.

22. Judas, not the Iscariot[1312] one, tells (*lego*) him: "Lord, what happened that you are about to manifest yourself to us and not the world?[1313]"

23. Jesus replied (*apokrinomai)* and said (*eipon*): "If someone spiritually loves me, he will guard (*tereo*) my verb and my Father will spiritually love him, and we will come close to him, and we will create (*poieo*) an adobe[1314] close to him.

24. Who does not spiritually love me, does not guard (*tereo*) my verbs. And the verb that you hear is not my own, but of the one who sent me, (of the) Father[1315].

1305 It's referring to the Passion on the etheric plane of the Second Coming, an event within which the Etheric Christ sacrificed himself by being "killed", which means within His true essence was erased, in the consciousness of men, who turned to the materialistic conception of the world.

1306 When the Paraclete will arrive.

1307 Like "he welcomes within himself".

1308 Also "commands". Only the activity in favor of man concretely expresses the love for Him.

1309 Ob-*serve*, to serve, minister to the Sun.

1310 One who welcomes the commands of the Christ internally, and serves them with devotion in freedom, is in the *a-more* (love), in the overcoming of the Law, because he chose for love to follow the Christ. He does not obey to the external precepts, instead he has them within his heart.

1311 The action of love for Jesus entails an answer of love from the Father, which will translate into a personal answer.

1312 He is Judas Taddeo, who incarnates the virtue of patience.

1313 He hoped in a glorious return of the Jesus and not in a personal manifestation. The coming of Jesus on the physical plane was "for everyone". The second coming, on the etheric plane, will be for the "ones who are ready for it".

1314 It is the same as verse 2. After the Paraclete will be given to us (v.16), now also the Father and the Son are coming.

1315 Jesus identifies himself with the Father.

25. I said (*laleo*) the things, while staying near you.

26. And the Paraclete, the Spirit the Holy[1316] that the Father will send in my name, that one will teach you one thing, and he will remind[1317] you of all that I said (*eipon*).

27. I leave you peace[1318], I give you my peace; not like the world gives[1319], I give to you. Don't let your heart be troubled, nor afraid[1320].

28. You heard that I said (*eipon*): I go (*hypago*) and stay (*erkomai*) near you[1321]. If you spiritually love me, with no doubt you will rejoice (*chairo*) because I head towards (*poreuomai*) the Father, because my Father is higher than me.

29. And now I told you, before I become, so that once I became, you will be believers.

30. I will not say (*laleo*) much more to you; the Prince of the world is coming and within in me I have nothing[1322] .

[1316] Holy means "separated". In our case, it indicates both the action of sanctification, and personalization (separation) of our spiritual principle.
To be more exact, the third Paraclete is the Incorruptible Body Risen Again and it is articulated in three aspects: the Spirit the Holy (John 14,26) which is the Path; the Spirit of Truth (John 14,17) which is the Truth; and the Spirit of God (John 6,69) which is Life.

[1317] Also "will suggest"; it's the helper. This is the third Paraclete, which comes from Jesus' transformation itself. For the complete vision of the "paraclete" see John 4,16.

[1318] Peace indicates the condition in which the Christ acts within us, up to the physical body. The feet are joined at the head and the unity is reestablished. This bear fruit; this fruit is the condition of peace. This fruit-word contains the new seeds which will be sowed and they will multiply according to the indication given from God to Adam. Let's remember that in Hebrew, peace is *shalom* which means "accomplishment".

[1319] The peace "left" is the one of who respects the Law; peace follows wars, which are the spiritual tests. But he "gives" us His Peace, which is Love. He gives to us for love, while the world gives for egoism, to have something in return. The Gifts of the Christ are given to us for the world, not for ourselves nor for Him. The fact that he underlines that this peace is "his own", indicates that it is the daughter of the full fulfillment of the whole human being. This is given to us in the sense of "to give to someone with care" (Greek *didomi*).

[1320] The turmoil is the action of Lucifer (against the Holy Spirit), and fear is of Ahriman (against the Father).

[1321] He does not use the future tense but the present tense. He will give to us on Easter Sunday the Saint of God, which is His Incorruptible Body completely transformed from the I am, which will follow the descend of the Paraclete Spirit.

[1322] Within Jesus, nothing is connected with Evil, Lucifer and Ahriman, which was the consequence, and therefore they have no power over Him.

31. But in order for the Father to have the world that I spiritually love clear, and like the Father commanded me (*entellomai*[1323]), that is how I create (*poieo*): Rise up, we are leaving from here[1324]".

THE GRAPEVINE AND THE BRANCHES (Ger 2,21; Ps 79, 9-16; Sir 24,23; Mt 3,10; Mt 5,16; Mt 13,40; Mt 15,13; Mc 11,24)

1. I am the vine[1325] the truthful one[1326]: and my Father is the farmer[1327].
2. Every branch within me that does not bear fruit, he takes it away and every (branch) that bears fruit, he purifies it, so that it bears more fruit[1328].

[1323] As *entole* "commandment".

[1324] This is the final exhortation towards which the whole passage is heading: to rise in the I to leave the world (experimented through death) and enter the Kingdom with Him.

THE GRAPEVINE AND THE BRANCHES

[1325] It corresponds to the spiritual *chakra* of the moon that is being activated; the grapevine substitutes the fig tree in the path of Initiation. With the Jesus Christ, instead of the fig, the grapevine will come to life (to reach the heart) and then the olive tree to reach the Garden of the Olive Trees, the peak of the head. These three trees will find their synthesis, their "+1", on the Cross: the fourth tree of the path of Initiation. The grapevine was also a symbol of the Chosen People: the True Vine is being declared in contraposition to the vision of the Old Testament.

[1326] The one who affirms a part of truth, because in this moment, because of the consciousness of the ones who are listening, he cannot reveal it entirely.

[1327] Jesus Christ is the only spring of spiritual life since he operates according to the will of the Father. The vine, with the red juice of the grape, it represents the blood. Therefore Jesus is the "juice of life, the spiritual heat that transforms the water in wine and in blood". Just as life is the manifestation of the work of the farmer, He is the manifestation of the will of the Father.
The making of the Father's will is articulated in three aspects or phases:

- To respect the Commands that He gave to us ("Father" aspect);
- To do what He tells us inwardly with the inner Word ("Son" aspect)
- To be completely available to Him, at His service ("Holy Spirit" aspect).

This also represents a transition from a condition of "duty" to one of "Freedom".
From this, the fourth aspect comes to life, the "plus one", the "prize": to reach the eternal spiritual Life.

[1328] This "more" in Greek has more of a quantitative sense than a qualitative sense - the fruit connected to Initiation. This is the advice to the new Christian Community: every branch needs to be alive to bear fruit, and therefore each member has a growth to go through and a mission to accomplish. The Father defoliates the ones who do not bear fruit since they could bring death to the Community by infecting the good branches. This means to turn down one's own interest and disaffection to one's own terrestrial existence (John 12,25).

3. You are already purified[1329] for the Verb that I said to you.

4. Stay within me[1330], and I will stay within you. Just like the branch does not have the strength to bear fruit from its own if it does not stay on the vine, you wouldn't be able to either if you do not stay with me[1331].

5. I am the vine, you are the branches; who stays within me, and I stay within him, he will bear many fruit, because without me you do not have the strength to do anything[1332].

6. If someone does not stay within me, he will be thrown out, like the branch and it will dry up, and then they gather them and throw them in the fire[1333] and they burn[1334].

[1329] Only for the fact of having heard the Word are they are purified. The word acts on the I by reawakening it, by making us "reawakened", "enlightened". If we will be able to practice the Word, we will enter the Kingdom. There is an initial purity and one of growth. The first one by defoliating the branch-man on the true vine-Christ, and the second one by practicing His teaching of love.
The theme of purity comes back multiple times with John: At the Wedding at Cana with the half empty jars of water while waiting for the new purification through the new spirit-wine (John 2,6); in the disciples of the Baptist, which was to break the old ritual of the baptism and therefore it prepares us for a new baptism (John 3,25); the washing of the feet no longer as a purifying ritual but an the beginning of the path of initiation (John 3,10). Now we are talking about the purity of the message-Logos received and accepted.

[1330] In intimacy and communion.

[1331] Just like the branch gets sap from the vine, we cannot bear fruit without the connection to the spiritual world. The first connection is the Word, which unites the head with the heart. Then the connection needs to stabilize in the Feeling and the Wanting with putting it all into practice. It no longer is the Law, with its strict and empty forms, that is keeping us alive in the spiritual life. He can only gifts us a part of the Truth because our consciousness is reduced; but if we stay within Him, then we will be able to bear more fruit.

[1332] Here we are hinting at the Eucharist where the flesh and the blood correspond to His life and His death to then resurrection. Earlier (John 15,2), we were talking about "fruit"; now we are talking about "many fruit".

[1333] The ones who gets further and further away from him loose the vital sap, and therefore they become dry and they will lack the force of love. The fire is the element that creates within the physical body the inner fire which then finds expression in blood circulation. The Christ brought into the world a new impulse which can flow in blood circulation, and therefore, by staying "within Him" no physical support is needed (like the Baptism of water) to connect to the world of the Spirit, and it is enough to grasp the soul in His impulse so that the experiences of the astral body transfer to the etheric body and we become clairvoyant. A new category of initiates is coming to life. The first one amongst them was Lazarus-John. From what we just stated, we understand that this Child "falls" amongst the new and old spiritual forces.

[1334] The verb uses both the singular and plural form. The singular form represents the individual judgement, while the plural form represents the universal judgement, the collective one. With fire, we enter the definite death instead of the eternal one.

7. If you will stay within me, and my words (*rhema*) will stay in you, what you will want, ask for it, and it will be put into being (it will become)[1335] for you.

8. My Father was glorified within this, so that you will bear many fruit and you will become[1336] disciples for me.

9. Just like the Father spiritually loved me, I also spiritually loved you[1337]. Stay in the spiritual love, my own[1338].

10. Just like I guarded the orders (*entole*) of my Father and I remain in his spiritual love.

11. I said (*laleo*) this to you so that the joy[1339], mine, stays with you so that your joy is full.

12. This is the commandment (*entole')[1340],* mine, that you spiritually love each other, just like I spiritually loved you.

13. No one has a higher spiritual love than this, that someone places his lower part (*psyche*) for the one who he brotherly[1341] loves.

1335 From *ghinomai*, the verb of Life. The requirement is to stay within Him with the unison of the strength of thought and feeling so that a new will can come to life which will be in compliance with the will of the Father.

1336 Also "you will be made". This is the son of the request of verse 7. The union needs to be complete and not only made of thoughts which are mostly abstract.

1337 This is because the Father generated the Son, and Jesus Christ will always love the humanity that He created. He loves it from the very beginning (that is why the verb is in the past tense).

1338 It is man's job to stay in His love since He will never stop loving us.
We have three meanings of "like":

1. Relationship between Father and Son: like the Father spiritually loved me, I also spiritually loved you. Stay in the spiritual love, mine (v.9);
2. Relationship between Son and man: if you will observe my precepts you will remain in my spiritual love, like I respected the commands of my Father and I remain in his spiritual love (v. 10);
3. Relationship between man and man: that you will spiritually love one another, just like I spiritually loved you (v.12).

1339 From the Greek *chara'. Chairo* means to rejoice and also joy. It is what comes to life within us when the soul adapts to the Spirit. We therefore have the subjective joy that comes from practicing love, and the objective one for the fruit that comes to life. The archangel Gabriel, at the Annunciation of Mariam, also uses this term.

1340 In John, we always only find the command of the spiritual Love.

1341 Or "friends". Only spiritual love reaches this point. It is about dedicating oneself to testifying towards the ones that are in the "world". Let's remember that the Greek term from which the word "soul" comes from is *psyche*, which does not only indicate the soul, but also all of the supersensible part of man.

14. You are my brotherly friends, if you will create (*poieo*) what I am commanding you[1342].

15. I do not say to you servants, because the servant[1343] does not know what his Lord creates (*poieo*); but I told (*eireka[lego])* you friends[1344], because all the things I heard from the my Father, I had you have them in clarity[1345].

16. You did not elect me, I elected you[1346], and I appointed you so that you would go (*hypago*) and bear fruit, and your fruit will last; because whatever you will ask to the Father, he will give to you[1347] in my name..

17. This I command[1348] to you, that you will love each other[1349] spiritually.

[1342] If we reach spiritual love with each other, for the Christ, we are brotherly friends. Lazarus was already mentioned as "friend" (John 11,11). The spiritual relationship with Him is even higher, and it is reached "after" the "brotherly". We go from a "general" relationship (to be grafted within Him), to a "subjective" one: to be His friends.
Let's remember that this "command" is not an imposition, but an ascending of consciousness which goes to the same level as the Father. From this we understand that we operate freely according to the will of the Father. Like the level of "minister" corresponds to the sphere of Venus, the one of "servant" to the Sun-Higher I-Beatitude, so that the "friend" takes us to the level of the Zodiac (the House of the Father, the Sanctity).

[1343] Step of the Sun. Mutual love makes us become Sons of God and it puts us to the level of Jesus. Then (John 20,17) we will become "brothers". Between the servant and the friend there is, as a difference, the complete familiarity.

[1344] Step of Mars.

[1345] This verb indicates the inner education.

[1346] Also one who becomes "friend" does not become so thanks to himself, since "earlier" he followed the world. It is the mercy of the Christ that elevates us to this level. First, we are "called", and when we answer back we are "elected/chosen" and we enter the Kingdom. Therefore, the becoming "friends" is not thanks to us but because of His grace. Let's also remember that Judas was not called by Jesus, but was instead brought to Him from his wife-mother.

[1347] And therefore He makes us apt to the liberating mission. We just need to be united with Him.

[1348] The verb *entellomai* also means "to give a task". So He does not give us orders; instead he suggests that we follow Him.

[1349] In Greek, "each other" is *allelus*, which has an assonance with *alleluia*, which is the word that indicates the process of purification of all of man's bodies.
The passage of love here ends, and Jesus repeats the commandment of love, the condition to be united with Him and bear fruit. Jesus now encloses within him the living love of the Father, the operating love of the Son and thee absolute love of the Holy Spirit.

THE HATRED OF THE WORLD, THE PARACLETE, THE TESTIMONY (Ps 34,19; Ps 68,5)

18. If the world[1350] hates you, be clear (*ginosko*) that it hated[1351] me first (*proton*)[1352].

19. If you were from the world, the world loves brotherly love what belongs to it, since you are not from the world[1353], but I elected[1354] you from the world, this is why the world hates you.

20. Remember the verb, that I said (*laleo*): a servant is not higher than his Lord[1355]. If they will persecute me, they will also persecute you; if they guarded (*tereo*) my verb, they will guard yours[1356] too.

21. But they will create (*poieo*) all of these things towards you because of my name, because they do not know the One who sent me[1357].

[1350] The terrestrial world in which Lucifer is the Prince. In this context, it will be represented by Jerusalem.

[1351] Hatred is of the ones who oppose themselves to the Light. The world hates Good and the ones who want to follow it. The word *misos* (hate), in Greek, means "abomination", which means inhuman/ merciless (*abhomine*). It also is the opposite of *dirigere*, the Latin verb which is equivalent to the Greek verb *agapao*, "spiritually love", the spiritual love that gives everything.

[1352] Because He is our Guide, First in the Light

[1353] The Christ took us away "from" the world. When we enter His People, we are "in the" world, but the world does not own us any longer. We cannot be with Jesus and the world.

[1354] This is the confirmation that he is speaking to the Chosen People, to the souls that the Father has chosen at the beginning of time to be the bearers of His evolutionary work, the souls that the Christ came to call to bring them back to the Father.

[1355] He said this at the Washing of the Feet (John 13,16). Back then, he said it to indicate the path of reciprocal service; now he is saying it to show the inevitable consequences of acting this way: the persecutions.

[1356] The verb will be "ours" in the sense that, once we enter the Chosen People, we will be able to be bearers. This is why we will be constantly suspected, mocked, and we will feel pressured to give up on following the path, up to feeling hatred. But it is our job to bear fruit (John 15,16).

[1357] In the Light of love, the oppressors, the ones who created false images of God, and who created a punitive God, they counterpose hatred.

22. If I would have not come and (I would not have) spoken (*laleo*)[1358] to them, they would have no mistake[1359], but now they have no excuse[1360] for their mistake.

23. Who hates[1361] me, also hates my Father[1362].

24. If I would not have created (*poieo*) within them the accomplishments that no one else created (*poieo*)[1363], they would have done wrong; but now and they have etherically (*horao*) seen, and they hated me and my Father[1364].

25. But in order that the Logos would reach its fullness, which is written in their world[1365]: they hated me undeservedly[1366].

1358 From Greek *laleo* which means "to release a judgment or a sentence". Given the assonance with *alleluia*, the word that is "pronounced/expressed" purifies all the bodies.

1359 Generally translated as "sin". In Greek, it is *hamartian* which is the intensifier of *Mathranita*. In the Essene initiation, the creating forces of Nature (the Angels) would also include two "mortal" male creatures (which means incarnated): Elxai and Yesseus (the Jewish people Jacob and Esau'), which symbolically represent the principles of Good and Evil. Elxai comes from El-Hai (Living God) and Yesseus from Yesod, the negative principle of the Kabbalah. These two incarnated entities had two female equivalents: Marta and Martana (or *Mathranita*).

1360 Also "apparent reason".

1361 The word *misos* (hatred) in Greek, also means "abomination", which is inhumane/merciless (*abhomine*). This hatred represents thee egoism taken to the extreme. The initial "O" can represent the luciferic snake who bites his own tail, creating a closed circle that excludes everything.
It is interesting to notice how the Italian word "*odio*" (hate) has no etymology in Greek. It is as saying that it has no connection with the Verb Greek is one of the last "spiritual" languages, connected to the original Truth).

1362 Because He manifests the real God: the Father.

1363 There were different people who were operating various miracles.

1364 They have the error (in Greek it is *hamartian*) because they did not recognize the work of the Christ, and therefore they hated Him and the Father.

1365 The fact that they did not correctly interpret the divine Law but instead made it dead and an instrument of oppression, this is why he doesn't recognize it and he defines it as "theirs".

1366 The words being mentioned belong to Psalms 35,19 and 69,5. By saying this, Jesus gets further away from the Scriptures not because of their origin, but because they haven't been understood and actually, they have been betrayed.

26. When the Paraclete will have arrived, that I will send you to the Father, the spirit of truth that comes[1367] from the Father, that he will testify about[1368] me.

27. You will also testify, because you were with me from the beginning[1369].

THE PERSECUTIONS

1. I said (*laleo*) to you these things so you won't be shocked[1370] (scandalized).

2. They will create (*poieo*) you "outside-synagogues"[1371] [1372], but a time will come in which anyone[1373] who will kill (*apokteino*)[1374] you will think that they are working in God's[1375] service.

[1367] The "coming from" is a "proceeding solemnly for" someone. Therefore, this Paraclete (the Spirit of Truth that he will blow upon his disciples on Easter Sunday) acts in favor of the progress of Creation and the spiritual evolution. He continues the evolutionary impulse from the Father. This Paraclete is the Spirit of Truth, and it is the third Paraclete. For the complete vision of the "paracletes" see John 14,16.

[1368] From the Greek *peri*, which literally means "around", "from all different point of view". It evokes the image of the Christ-Sun of which the Twelve Spiritual Apostles testify about from all the different point of view.

[1369] Beginning as *archei*, and therefore as "First" (John 1,1). We have been with Him from the Old Sun when the cosmos was illuminated, and also when the darkness started and part of humanity preferred the Darkness, while the Chosen People stayed within Light.

[1370] "Scandal" literally means "hidden danger", "stumbling block" of the foot. The word "sin" also comes from "foot". The scandal is therefore the hidden danger that makes us sin.
He had already used this expression in verse 6,61, and it was referring to the desertion of the disciples. Now he warns them to avoid other desertions connected to the fact that they will be confronted, battled, by the religious institutions. Another element of obstacle comes from certain thoughts in which we are immersed, and they do not allow us to open up to new thoughts.

[1371] Also, they will consider you outside of the ecclesiastic context. Basically, you will be "excommunicated".

[1372] The Priest could declare the expulsion of a Jewish person from the rituals of the synagogue, and this would happen through an excommunication.

[1373] Now the persecutors are more: not only the Jewish people but also everyone who believes in a God of death. He brings us Life, the resurrection of flesh, the eternal life.

[1374] Let's remember that there also is the spiritual killing which comes from the fact of not recognizing a Truth.

[1375] Of the Holiest Trinity.

3. And they will create (*poieo*) thee things to you, because they had no clarity[1376] in the Father, nor in me[1377].

4. But I said (*laleo*) these things to you because, when their time will come, you will remember the things that I said (*eipon*)[1378] to you: I did not tell (*eipon*) you these thing from the beginning because I was with you[1379].

THE WORK OF THE SPIRIT OF TRUTH

5. Now I head (*hypago*) towards the one who sent me[1380], and none of you is asking me: where are you going (*hypago*)?[1381]

6. But because I told (*laleo*) you these things, the labour[1382] filled your heart.

[1376] The teaching was needed to change the mind, but they have not discerned between Good and Evil.

[1377] Jesus explains to them why they will operate in this manner because by doing so, he will free them from the reverence towards the religious institutions.

[1378] Therefore the world and the religious institutions will hate them because of His message of Life and Love. "Their" time begins with the moment in which Judas takes the bite and Satan enters him.

[1379] Up until now he spoke about "his" persecution, but now he is speaking of the persecutions of the disciples.

THE WORK OF THE SPIRIT OF TRUTH

[1380] Now he can internally turn to the Father in a definitive manner, since he made his will.

[1381] They are still caught in themselves, and they believe death to be the end of everything. They do not understand that through death they can reach the Father. They feel hurt because they feel as if His help is missing, and they do not ask for explanations because they believe them to be unnecessary since they believed death to be the end of everything. They were all worried about themselves.

[1382] From the greek *lype* which means "pain of birthing/ labour pain", and here it refers to the labour for the birthing of the inner Child. His words work internally even though the conscious still cannot comprehend that.

7. But I say the truth to you: it is better[1383] for you that I go (*aperchomai*); if I wouldn't go, the Paraclete[1384] will not come near you; but if I start walking (*poreuomai*), I will send him near you[1385].

8. And by coming, that one[1386] will make the world conscious about the mistake[1387], and about justness and about discernment[1388].

9. As far as the mistake/error, it's about that they do not believe in me[1389].

10. And about justness[1390], is that I go (*hypago*) towards the Father, and (you) will no longer spiritually (*theoreo)*[1391] see me.

1383 Literally "to melt", "to take out", "to come together". In italian we also have "*con-viene*" (convenient), which is "*viene-con*" (comes with).

1384 The third Paraclete: the Spirit of Truth that He will blow upon the disciples on Easter Sunday. For the complete vision of the "paracletes" see note on verse 14,16.

1385 From this, we understand that the coming of this Paraclete will be a major help to them in regards of His presence. This Spirit will be the one to give the force of the Truth to the disciples, from which also Freedom and Love and therefore loving Him like He loved us. Jesus is now for them an external model; afterwards he will act within them.

1386 The Paraclete.

1387 The mistakes in which we fall…

1388 Therefore, the ones who judged him will be judged, and the judge (Him) will be absolved. The discernment is of the Spirit.

1389 To get out of the error/mistake, we first need to have Faith and then believe in Christ. It is the aspect of Jesus the Teacher that expresses himself this way, and the judges did not have it in Him. To be aware of the mistakes, we need to recognize that our own egotistical will needs to be subordinated to a more elevated concept of justice and love towards all the creatures, and we need to elevate ourselves to the Creator of everything.

1390 The Greek term is *dikaisune* which expresses justice in the sense of the right behaviors that each one of us, from within, should develop. It is the principle of the Buddha that expresses itself through justness (the eightfold path). It is the virtue of the Righteous. The proof that Jesus was in the right will be in the acceptance of the Father.

1391 From the Greek *theorao*, "I spiritually see, indicates the inner condition thanks to which we contemplate God. In this case, He goes to the Father and the Apostles do not follow him (on the right path) and therefore they loose the vision of the Father.
We can see how within this phrase there is a reference to the Ascension, the moment in which any residue of the old clairvoyance is being taken away from the Apostles, and therefore "they lost" the direct vision of Jesus. This external vision was renovated in the inner perception of the Being of the Christ, who reawakened within them the Pentecost. See R. Steiner *The Destiny of Man*.
In every spiritual test, we are always alone because we are called to overcome it without any direct external help: otherwise our I Am wouldn't be able to completely manifest.

11. And about discernment, that the prince of this world[1392] has been discerned[1393].

12. I still have many things to say to you: but now you do not have the strength to grasp them (on the spiritual plane) (*bastazo*)[1394].

13. And when that will come, the Spirit of Truth[1395] will lead you to the truth; it will not speak (*laleo*) from its own[1396], but what he heard he will say and he will declare[1397] the things that will come[1398].

14. That will glorify[1399] me, because he will get it (*lambano*) from mine and he will declare it to you[1400].

[1392] Satan, the Spirit of Darkness who inspires them.

[1393] Unmasked, or declared for what it is. It means "taken away from the filth" and therefore the world becomes "clean-world". This actions comes from the Spirit of Truth that the Risen One will send to us. There are three steps of error/mistake: the mistake of the world (the lacking of Faith), the lacking of justness of the Jewish People (which makes it so that they lose His vision since the Father will now return), and the discernment that the tricks of Satan are being unmasked, and therefore they bring him the Light.

[1394] Also "of pondering". They still do not know how death will come and how all of the set of rules will change.

[1395] In the vision of the Work, this **Spirit of Truth** is the Spirit of the Spirit of God, which is the Spirit created from man in his process of complete spiritualization of his own humanity. **It is not the Paraclete Spirit (redeemed Lucifer), and it is not the Son of man,** since this is Jesus himself as a true man, the Spirit that He will blow upon the disciples on Easter Sunday.
This created Spirit is the combination of all the faculties and qualities that he attracted to himself as a man, while also drawing at his divine side, the Father within him, and that he made his own by developing them and practicing them. This Spirit is also Holy Spirit: the Holy Spirit within us. For the complete vision of the "paracletes" see verse 14,16.

[1396] Not in a subjective way. He makes us become aware of the objective laws of the spiritual reality by manifesting them to man through the development of higher consciousness.

[1397] It is more than an announcement, it is something for certain and real.

[1398] In the work of Jesus, there is still a lot that hasn't been explored yet which will ascend to the consciousness only in time, thanks to the action of the Paraclete Spirit. What needs to come is the Kingdom.

[1399] The Paraclete Spirit will allow us to see His Face (John 1,14).

[1400] The Paraclete will get the message from Jesus, and also the verbs that he gets from the Father and the glory of the love which He will irradiate with His death, and he will declare it to the disciples so that they will understand why the Paraclete is the Spirit of Truth. For the complete vision of the "paracletes" see John 14,16.

15. All that the Father has, it is mine[1401]. This is why I said that he will get it from mine and declare it to you[1402].

REASONS OF JOY

16. A time ("little")[1403] and you will no longer spiritually see me, and then again a little bit of time and you will see me (*opsomai*)[1404].

17. Therefore the disciples[1405] said (*eipon*) about him to one another: "What is this that he is saying to us: a little bit and you will see me?[1406] And: "That I head towards (*hypago*) the Father?[1407]"

18. They then said: "What is this "little" ("small")? We do not know[1408] what he is saying (*laleo*)".

1401 First of all, what he has in common with the Father is the Glory (John 1,14).

1402 This verse was added.

REASONS OF JOY

1403 In Greek *micron*, which is "the first element". It represents a step of growth for the I, our "first" (in importance) fundamental element. It is the "13th" I am which is not ready to come to life within them. See note at verse 18. This "little" reconnects to the "little" of the 13,33. The disciples will see him again only after His resurrection because He will have to ascend to the Father, since he is a completely spiritualized man, to receive the fullness of his own Glory for the fact that he gifted all of himself for the evolution of humanity. After this, He will only be visible for the spiritual gaze.
Jesus picks the phrase back up of the verse 14,19 "*A little bit more time and the world will no longer have me in the consciousness. But you do have me in the consciousness: since I spiritually live and you also spiritually love*", and he indicates the assistance of the Paraclete Spirit. Now he says: "*and again a little bit and you will see me, because I am going to the Father*". Now he is developing the theme of His assistance to them.

1404 This is a terrestrial "you will see" and it will take place after His resurrection.

1405 These are the 72 disciples. From the text we can hypothesize that the "spiritual" disciples are inspiring the "terrestrial" disciples to ask the question.

1406 In the new etheric.

1407 Therefore, they have not comprehended what His absence means, His ascending to the Father. This is highlighted by the fact that this phrase is repeated four times (John 16,16-17-18-19).

1408 Literally, "we do not see". It refers to the fact of "knowing" a word, "the little" (with the article). This "little" also means "one by one". This can refer to the human I (the first element, "I Am the Lord, Your God"). "One by one" the disciples will lose spiritual vision, for then reconquering it, they are renewed "one by one". This "little" is therefore the I, the Child that comes to life within them. It is the Initiation in the I brought by the Christ to man, and the disciples are getting ready for it, even though they are not conscious of it yet.

19. Jesus had clarity (*ginosko*)[1409] on the fact that they were about to ask it to him, and he said (*eipon*) to them: "About this look are you it asking one another why I said (*eipon*): "a little and you will no longer spiritually see me and then a little bit more and you will see me?"[1410]

20. Amen, Amen[1411] I say[1412] that you will call the spirit[1413] and you will suffer[1414] and the (spiritual)[1415] world will rejoice (*chairo*); but you will grieve[1416], but your pain will become your joy (*chara*)[1417].

[1409] It is the individual force of the Jesus that operates the discernment.

[1410] Jesus repeats the phrase to ingrain it up to the etheric body of the disciples because the first time they did not understand the I.

[1411] A universal truth is being announced: this promised joy will never be less.

[1412] **Jesus announces the Spirit of Truth (the Spirit of the Spirit of God).**

[1413] Wrongly translated, usually as "you will cry".

[1414] Also "you will cry", which is of you, for the pain that comes with the path towards the birthing of the I.

[1415] As "the order of things". It is the world of the spirit that is joyful for our inner changes.

[1416] The pain of giving birth comes back (see note on verse 6).

[1417] When you will have passed the test.

21. When the woman[1418] gives birth she has pain[1419], because her time[1420] has come; but if[1421] she generated the little child (*paidion*)[1422], she does not remember the oppression[1423] for the joy that a man (*Anthropos*) was generated to the world[1424].

22. And now you have pain[1425], but I will see (*opsomai*) you again[1426] and your heart will rejoice and no one can take your joy away[1427].

23. And in that day you will pray (*erotao*)[1428] nothing to me. Amen, Amen I say to you: what you will ask (*aiteo*) the Father in my name He will give to you[1429].

1418 Also "female" or "bride". Jesus gives her back the title of bride, of soul united with her I. This nickname represents the higher aspect of the feminine within us, the soul that generates the Spirit.

1419 From *thlipsis*, the pain of giving birth, the labour for the Higher I.

1420 The time to generate the Child, the time for which she was born.

1421 This "if" indicates that she also might not be able to do so.

1422 With this term, it refers to the fruit that comes to life within us from the union between the right-rational-empirical-masculine part and the left intuitive-creative-feminine part. To the right-left union, the union above-head-sky and below-metabolism-earth is added. From these unions, "the (masculine) child (feminine)" comes to life to indicate that it is masculine nor feminine. We have three children: the Spiritual Self (the principle of the Holy Spirit within us that comes to life from the transformation of the astral body), the Vital Loving Man (the Son within us that comes to life from the transformation of the etheric body) and the Spirit Man (the Father in us that comes to life from the transformation of the physical body).

1423 The force of weight-gravity that is opposing the etheric force of order.

1424 With this, we allude to the process that will show us a new humanity. He is the Groom, the humanity is the Bride, and now the new man is coming to life. John looks at this new humanity as a goal and gift from Jesus to us. From this, we understand why he hasn't reported any genealogy of Jesus nor the conditions of His birth: for him the man is completed only when he has reached and manifested the fullness of love.

1425 Again "labour pain".

1426 We are born when the Christ turns His yes upon us. This moment in which he will see us corresponds to His return in the plane of Life (etheric).

1427 Also "he will tear".

1428 "You will ask by praying". We will have direct communication, and therefore it will no longer be necessary to "ask" the Spirit.

1429 Jesus assures us the complete union with the Father. He is not an intercessor, instead he takes us in His dimension of Son. The Father will gift to us because the Son has the richness of the Father (John 3,35)

24. Up until now you asked (*aiteo*) in my name: you will ask (*aiteo*) and you will receive (*lambano*)[1430], so that your joy will be full[1431].

THE FAREWELL

25. I said (*laleo*) these things to you in proverbs[1432]. There will come a time in which I will no longer tell you proverbs, instead I will declare[1433] you openly to the Father.

26. In that day you will ask (*aiteo*) in my name and I will not tell you that I will pray (*erotao*) to the Father about you[1434].

27. The Father loves you in a brotherly way, because you loved me in a brotherly way[1435], and you believed that I came[1436] from God[1437].

[1430] We will reach the birthing of the Child, the "little", within us. This way of asking presumes the descending of the Spirit, and this is why he said : "*it is better for you if I leave*" (John 16,7 and 14,16).

[1431] Which is "in fullness", from the Greek word *pleroma*.

THE FAREWELL

[1432] Images or similes or words that prepare us for the Path.

[1433] He gets closer to His coming back, and therefore he will be able to openly speak to his disciples about the Father through the Spirit of Truth (the Spirit of the Spirit of God who He will blow upon the disciples on Easter Sunday- see note on verse John 16,13).

[1434] He is reiterating that He is not an intercessor; the intercessor is the Spirit of Truth (the Spirit of the Spirit of God-see note 16,13).

[1435] Jesus declares our ascending to the union in love. This way we will be in direct contact with the Father.

[1436] Also "I extended myself", "I went beyond the limits" (in a positive way), "I am flowing", "I became known", "I progressed" not from the lying form (our own) of the Father, but from the true form (His): the one that takes us to the eternal Life.

[1437] Of the Holiest Trinity. The Christ "went beyond the limits" of the Holiest Trinity, which is the Divine who supports the whole Cosmos, and he entered in the ones of the Holy Trinity, which is the one of the evolutionary system.

28. I came from the Father and I came to the world[1438]; and once again I release[1439] the world and I begin to walk (*poreuomai*) towards the Father[1440]".

29. His disciples say to him: "Here, now you are talking (*laleo*) openly[1441] and you are not saying any proverb[1442].

30. Now we know that you know everything[1443], and you do not need someone to pray (*erotao*)[1444] to you; in this we believe[1445] that you came from God[1446]".

31. Jesus[1447] replied (*apokrinomai*) to them: "Now you believe?

1438 We are in front of the "trinitarian" talk of John. Within him the Christ is manifesting as One and Trine. First, we have the God (the One), then the "are" (Christ), the Father, and then the "effused" (the Holy Spirit).

1439 He effused in the world, and the world becomes released, freed, to go back to the Father.

1440 Now the disciples understand and they realize that the world, the one that is around them, the *maya*, is the external expression of the Father and the death is the name of the Father, and with Jesus they will go back to the Father.

1441 From the Greek *rema* (particular aspect of the Verb-Logos). Now the disciples understand that the Jesus is talking in the trinitarian aspect of the Christ.

1442 Openly talking with no similes being used. Now they know that he came from the Father and that he knows everything. They know that he will unite with death to win it over and to take us to the Father. Lucky them who know have everything clear!

1443 They grasp the knowledge aspect of the Jesus, the aspect connected to the Holy Spirit.

1444 "More" could be added to this. There is no need to ask more to understand.

1445 For the difference between "having faith" and "believing", see note on verse 1,7.

1446 They grasp the Jesus that is within the Holy Trinity, and not in the Holiest one.

1447 With no article. The disciples recognized Jesus in the Holy Trinity (precisely in his Holy Spirit aspect), therefore Jesus replies to them, and not the Jesus.

32. Here comes the time[1448], and it came[1449], the time in which you will be scattered[1450], each one of you towards your own things[1451], and you leave me alone[1452], and not only because the Father is with me.

33. I told you (*laleo*) these things so that you will have peace[1453] in me. In the world you have oppression, but have courage, I overcame[1454] the world![1455]".

1448 It is the time of the division, of Scorpio; in a daily meaning it is between 8 pm and 10 pm.

1449 The disciples did not understand the divine aspect of the Jesus, and therefore they have already been obscured.

1450 From the Greek *skorpizo*, a word that contains the Scorpio, which is the force that brings death in the Zodiac, in the 12 constellations that the Apostles represent. The constellation of Scorpio, in the circle of the 12, is represented by Judas.

1451 One's own aspect, egotistical.

1452 Peter will be the one who will represent the maximum of the desertion amongst the Apostles.

1453 Let's remember that peace indicates the condition in which the Christ acts within us, up to the physical body. The feet conjoined to the head, and the unity has been re-established. This gives fruit, and this fruit is the condition of peace. These fruits-Word contain the new seeds which will be sewed and they will multiply according to the indication given from God to Adam. Let' remember that in Hebrew, peace is *salom* which means "accomplishment".

1454 Also "lorded". The Jesus overcame the active forces of the obstacle in the world through death.

1455 With this passage, the theme of the persecution from the world end: He has won it over for us! He does not leave us. We are the ones that through tests and temptations get further away from Him.

THE PRIESTLY PRAYER OF JESUS[1456]

1. Jesus[1457] said (*laleo*) these things: and by lifting up his eyes[1458] towards the sky, he said (*eipon*): "Father[1459], the time[1460] has come, glorify your Son (*hyios*)[1461], so that the Son[1462] glorifies you[1463];

[1456] This dialogue finds its roots in the day of Reconciliation, day in which the High Priest would enter in the Saint of the Saints (Holy of Holies) and he would pray the Lord for the whole community of Israel. No one had to participate in the ceremony, and only the High priest could do this once a year. The ceremony would foresee the sacrifice of a lamb (whose blood would be sprinkled on the altar) and the burning of the incense "*so that the cloud would veil the throne of God and the priest would die*". This anticipates the Last Supper, when Jesus himself will be the Priest and the Lamb for the whole humanity. Since He is within the Father, the cloud of the incense will not be needed. With this prayer, Jesus shows us how to pray the Father in the sanctuary of our own heart.

[1457] Now Jesus is speaking in his human aspect. He will speak in the third person for the first three verses: therefore it is Jesus-God who became man, the emanation of the Father, to who He talks to by referring to his human part, which is the Jesus-Man who knew how to reach the complete union with the divine part within him, and therefore he was able to become a perfect Man.
After the first three verses he is Jesus-Man-Son who, permeated by the Christ, addresses His prayer to the Father interceding for the whole humanity.

[1458] The eye indicates the necessary death for the process of resurrection. After the tests of the Work in Black (in the Black Opera the marriage with the Mother), the eyes of the ones who overcome them are ready for the divine vision. To lift one's eyes means to turn to the Father.

[1459] Of the Holy Trinity.

[1460] The time of the seventh day, the time announced at Cana, and this period started six days before Easter.

[1461] The Logos

[1462] The Son of man, Jesus within us.

[1463] The glory of the Father consists in the work itself that the Son is capable of accomplishing.

2. Just how You gave[1464] him[1465] power of every flesh[1466], so that everything You gave him, he gives it Eternal Spiritual Life[1467].

3. This is the Eternal Spiritual Life: that they have You in clarity (*ghinosko*)[1468], the only truthful God[1469], and the one who you sent[1470], Jesus Christ[1471].

[1464] From this moment on, the verb "to give" (*di domi*) appears in this chapter 17 times.

[1465] To the Solar Logos. From the Sun, the Authorities act.

[1466] It refers to the authority that the Father gave to the Son upon the still incomplete man, upon every force of evil, and it is also the power the He gave to man so that he can become the lord of his own human nature by transforming it up to the likeness in the divine one.
For a deeper study of the word "flesh", see note in chapter 1.13.

[1467] The Logos brings back the Life to the beings that fell in the terrestrial existence, but not all of them: only the ones who have been entrusted from the Father to the Son, and therefore the ones who began to head towards the Father.

[1468] This verb will be repeated for 7 times and it does not refer to an abstract knowledge, instead it refers to the direct experience of the Truth and the Divinity towards the Freedom and Love.

[1469] A part of the truth of God: the one relative to the Holy Trinity, and not the Holiest one. This is because the disciples, just a little bit earlier than this, did not comprehend it.

[1470] Now he speaks to the God of the Holiest Trinity.

[1471] Now it is referring to the Christ, and therefore the aspect Son of the Holiest Trinity. We are in front of a dialogue that is outside of space and time; the passage began with Jesus speaking to the Father (sphere of the Holy Trinity), and it ends with Christ turning to the Father of the Holiest Trinity.
This is the aim of the terrestrial mission of Jesus Christ: to make men conscious of their own individuality and of their divine origin so that they come back to being One with the Father. The fact of "remembering one's own divine origin" means to "know" that God exists and that we are part of Him, we belong to Him, we are called to return to Him, and therefore we need to make His will. To reject this is the sin of impiety.
It is important to see how the expression "Jesus Christ" is used only twice: here and in the Prologue (1,17). With the term "Jesus" we refer to the human being who hosted the Logos and the incarnation of the Christ, with "Christ", we refer to the divine entity itself. With "Jesus Christ" we refer to the one sent by the Father in his wholeness and perfection, bearer of Life, Grace and Truth through which He will regenerate us completely into the body, soul and spirit.

4. I glorified you on earth, I accomplished the work you gave me so that I would create (*poieo*)[1472];

5. And now glorify me Father, close to you, with the glory that I had, from before the time the world was close to you[1473].

6. I manifested your name[1474] to men, that you gave me from the world. They were yours[1475] and you gave them to me: and they will guard (*tereo*)[1476] your verb (*logos*)[1477].

7. They had clarity (*ghinosko*)[1478] that everything you gave me, is from you[1479],

8. Because the words (*rhema*)[1480] that you gave to me, I gave to them[1481]; and they themselves welcomed them with truthful clarity that I came[1482] from you, and they had faith (*episteusa)* that you sent me.

1472 The Nathan Soul, which incarnated itself in the Jesus, which is the man who remained in the original condition of created man (therefore without receiving the luciferic influx) and who "was" in the evolutionary-logos law, and who was in the Father's breast; the Nathan Soul asked the Father, which is the favorite Son, if he could be able to help the fallen humanity (last Adam), his helpless brothers. And the Father entrusted the work of redemption through which Jesus, the Man became Son, will manifest the glory of the Father.

1473 The world "initially", which means at the beginning of Creation, before the manifestation, was in the Glory.

1474 The essence of Father God, who is the Love at the highest level.

1475 It is the People of God, the Chosen People, the Eternal Israel. It is composed of 144.000 men whose name is written in the Book of Life from "before" the world. The Christ came for them, for the "lost sheep of the House of Israel".

1476 Also "conserve", or "safe-guard" (the original divine spark). This Verb was sewed from Jesus Christ in the human souls, and after being reawakened, it gives us the strength to "believe" even though there is an abuse of power in the world upon the human consciousness.

1477 Now they recognized the Christ, the force that wins Evil and the Death and he becomes their Guide for going back to the House of the Father. Christ also says, "*You are with me from the beginning"*.

1478 Also "discernment", like verse 8.

1479 From the Greek *para*, also "near".

1480 Like *rema*, particular aspect of the Verb.

1481 This is the glory of the Jesus Christ: to have made known to the world the true Word of the Father, which is Life itself.

1482 Also "exited". See John 16,27.

9. I pray (*erotao*) around them; I do not pray (*erotao*)[1483] around the world, but around the[1484] ones you gave me, because they are yours[1485].

10. And you gave them to me, and I was glorifies within them[1486].

11. And already I am not in the world[1487], and they are in the world, and I am coming close to you. Holy Father[1488], safeguard (*tereo*) them in your name, the ones you gave[1489] to me: so that they are One[1490], like us.

[1483] For the material order of the world.

[1484] Also "around". The Christ prays for the Chosen People. The Christ created the world, and within it there is the Chosen People (which comes from the Father). The Christ descend in the world to help the Chosen People to go back to the Father. Now the members of the Chosen People are fruit of the world, since they conquered the freedom and love in the confrontation with the world.

[1485] He reiterates that he is talking about the People "of the" Chosen Ones. "His" are the ones who believe that the Christ acted within the Jesus.

[1486] The Christ is glorified in the world. Only by entering a body of flesh (of the Jesus) He entered the world.

[1487] The Christ is already out of the world. He already overcame the world. His disciples are still connected to the world. With the Passion, he will have to do so in a public manner, so that all of humanity can see it and follow Him.

[1488] Now the Jesus turns to the Father and to the Holy Spirit for what he will request that he will formulate in verse 17 to sanctify them with the Truth.

[1489] This "name" is the Christ in Jesus. On Jesus, the Holy Spirit descended from the Father, and he manifested the Christ. Additionally, Jesus' name is "Father": He is our Father like a New Adam, a new archetype of the man.

[1490] This is the goal of man: to be One, to reach the unity between man and creation to rebuild the cosmic man, the Man created in the image and likeness of the Divine, from the man who is fragmented in infinite personalities and who needs to come back to the original unity by bringing his own individual peculiarity.

12. When I was with them, I safeguarded (*tereo*) them in your name[1491], the ones (that you gave to me), and I protected[1492] them and none of them went in perdition[1493], if not the son (*hyios*) of the perdition[1494], so that the Writing would fulfill itself.

13. And now I came close to you, and these things I say (*laleo*) to the world, so that they can have the joy, mine, accomplished[1495] within themselves.

14. I gave them your verb, and the world hated them, because they are not from[1496] the world, like I am not from the world.

15. I do not pray (*erotao*) that you take them away from the world, but that you protect them from the evil[1497].

16. From the world they are not[1498], just like I am not from the world.

17. Sanctify[1499] them in the truth.

18. Just like you sent me into the world, I also sent them into the world[1500].

[1491] The Name contains the whole spiritual essence of a being. It contains the entirety of the characteristic capabilities. In this case, it is Love.

[1492] From the Greek *phylasso*: to watch over, to be vigilant, to defend, to protect.

[1493] Or "lost". The seed that He put amongst us will make it so that each one of us, even through the infinite ups and downs, will go back to Him.

[1494] Men are the ones who do not recognize the Christ. They are the sons of the Darkness, the sons of the Anti-Christ, of Satan-Ahriman, the ones who follow the principle of the anti-solar principle: the Solar Demon. They do not descend from Our Father; instead they belong to another evolutionary system.

[1495] Also "brought to its fullness". The liver is the organ which accumulates the heaviness and gravity of the world, and also the innate Light of the inner work that has been done. It carries the richness that will then become resurrection: the transition through the door of the gods.

[1496] First (v.11), he said that the disciples were "still" in the world, and now that they are not "from" the world anymore. This means that they can still have material ties but these ties will no longer develop a power (ambition, richness, power, greed, etc.) over them.

[1497] The Chosen People need to stay in the world to perfect themselves and transform the Evil into Good. The "evil" is the Anti-Christ.

[1498] The Chosen People.

[1499] Bring them into the Holiest Trinity ("in the" truth). This is the request of the "Holy Father" of verse 11.

[1500]Now the Christ is the one who is sending the Chosen People to testify. They do not need to shut down, isolate themselves, instead they need to testify the divine Love.

19. And for them I sanctify myself[1501]: so that they also can be sanctified in the truth[1502].

20. I do not only pray for them[1503], but also for the ones[1504] who will believe thanks to their verb[1505] in me:

21. So that everyone will be One, just like You, Father, (are) in me, and I am within You, so that they will also be One within us[1506]; so that the world believes that you sent me.

22. And the glory[1507] that you gave me, I gave to them, so that they will be One, like we (are) One.

23. I within them and you within me[1508], so that they will be accomplished *(feleioo)*[1509] to One, and that the world has clarity (*ghinosko*) that you sent me, and you loved them spiritually, like you spiritually loved me[1510].

[1501] Jesus is the one sanctifying-sacrificing for the Chosen People.

[1502] To Ascend to the Kingdom of the Holy Trinity.

[1503] The Chosen People.

[1504] The other part of humanity, which in virtue of Faith can enter (through Grace) in the Chosen People even though they do not belong to it originally.

[1505] That truth that is given to them of living internally. These become His "sent", which are His witnesses.

[1506] Not only united like a complete communion between men to recreate the broken up unity of the Fall, but One in the Father and Son united, to complete in complete perfection the path of growth and multiplication for which man was created.

[1507] See John 1,14. This aspect of Glory is the path of love for the Perfection, which is the entering in the Holiest Trinity.

[1508] **Jesus repeats the eleventh I Am: the announcement of the Baptism of Fire (see also 14,20).**

[1509] Now the path is clear: from the reawakening of the Jesus within us (the Higher I, the Holy Spirit in us) thanks to Faith, to the entrance in the Chosen People, to the ascending through the Christ up to the Father of the Holiest Trinity.

[1510] The Father loved the Son-Christ since he generated Him equal to him and he loves men, in spite of the Fall, so much that he send His Son to save us.

24. Father, I desire[1511] what[1512] you gave me so that where I am they also will be there with me[1513], so that they spiritually see *(theoreo)* the glory, mine, that you gave to me[1514] because you spiritually loved me before the establishment[1515] of theworld.

25. Fair[1516] Father, even the world did not have You in clarity (*ghinosko*)[1517], but I had You in clarity, and they had clarity that You sent me.

26. And I made Your name known to them, and I will make it known[1518] so that the spiritual love with which You spiritually love them will be within them, and I within them[1519].

1511 This represents the acceptance of the karma, and also the "bringing back" of the Chosen People to the Father.

1512 In some codex it is translated as "I desire what you gave to me", referring primarily to the Chosen People.

1513 In the same state of consciousness. Temporally, this becomes the Gethsemane, the "being vigilant" with Him while confronting the forces of the Obstacle.

1514 It is the Divine Mission, His task as the one sent by the Father.

1515 Literally the "throwing below", maybe referring to the Fall or the manifestation of God's project. In Genesis, when God created the sky and the Earth, it is not meant to be intended in the material manner; instead it needs to be seen as the soul-like elements and the spiritual elements that needed to serve to help man grow and multiply according to the divine plan.

1516 It is the request of Jesus to the Father so that he remembers the loyalty of his disciples in contrast with the incredulity of the world. The request is that He is "fair" with his disciples by allowing them to be in the level of "Sons".

1517 It also can refer to "biblical" knowledge, which refers to the union of husband (spirit) and wife (soul), from which the son comes to life (the Child).

1518 The action of the Christ continues throughout time.

1519 The Father is referred to as "fair" (v.25) for the ones who will not want to recognize Him and towards whom He will have to manifest Himself under this aspect, and it is the time of Love, love with which He helps and supports everyone who want to ascend to Him.

AT THE GETHSEMANE (Mt26,36-56; Mc 14,32-49; Lc 22,40-53)

1. Jesus having said these things[1520], he exited with his own disciples on the other side of the creek of the Kidron[1521], where there was a garden[1522], in which he entered and also his disciples[1523].
2. But also Judas, the one who delivered[1524] him, knew the place[1525] because Jesus often gathered there with his disciples.

[1520] This phrase gives a determining character to what will follow.

[1521] The name "Kidron" reminds us of the cedar, the evergreen tree connected to the forces of Saturn, which is a planet that hosts the forces of sacrifice operated with warmth and love. The article underlines the spiritual aspect of the cedar. Literally "Kidron" means "darkness". Let's remember that the metal of Saturn, lead, in German is "the blue". The forces of Saturn act within us in the upper part of the head. Therefore, the Jesus is path of time towards the Calvary (cranium), which corresponds to the "fontanelle" and also the seventh *chakra*, which connects us to the spiritual worlds.
The Kidron Creek indicates the passage from the terrestrial "world" to the one of the Spirit, towards the Father. It indicated the border of the city, and David, by crossing it, ran away from a conspiracy (2Sam15,14-23). Jesus also leaves Jerusalem, "this world" which wanted to kill him, and he heads towards the Father.

[1522] From the Greek *kepos*, which indicates "the garden", the "sky", the "garden" hairstyle (with a shaved head in the middle to welcome the spiritual impulses, typical of the religious people). In a microcosmic sense, the Jesus is entering the zodiacal sphere, going through the threshold of Saturn-Cedar. This is His House, the world of the Father. It is important to see that in the Gospels, His terrestrial house is never mentioned.
It is the first time that the term "garden" appears to remind us of the Garden of Eden. This "garden" will reappear in the Passion and in the Resurrection to indicate that it is a garden of Life.

[1523] If we read closely, Jesus does not enter the garden with the disciples; instead he enters it before them. They will enter the garden at verse 19,41 where it is said that in the garden there was a new sepulcher in which no one ever entered. To enter this garden of Life, it will be necessary to deliver one's own life to the Christ for the love of man.

[1524] Usually translated as "he betrayed", from a wrong translation from the Latin word *trader* (deliver). The greek text gives us no doubts: in reality, Judas did not "betray"; instead he wanted to push the Jesus to take a political stand, as King of the Jewish people. Therefore, he wanted to esoterically "deliver" the aspect "Rhabbi" of the Jesus, the soul of the Buddha directed to compassion. We can also say that by calling the Jesus "Rhabbi" (and not "Lord" like the other Apostles did, see Mt 26,25), he wants to deliver "this" aspect of the Jesus, the part of infinite sweetness that was gifted to him by the Buddha. In other words, Judas does not mean to deliver "all" of Jesus; instead he is trying to hinder the action of the "Rhabbi". This term, in the whole Gospel of Matthew, is being said referring to Jesus, and only on the cited verse and the moment of the kiss (Mt 16,49). The text indicates him as "delivery agent", and only the wrong translation made him become a "traitor". This would also explain his regret towards the consequences of his gesture: he became aware that his betrayal (to deliver the Rhabbi) was used by the priests beyond his intentions, and this allowed the capturing of the Jesus.

[1525] Therefore, he also knew the spiritual truths that take us to the place of Life since he is Jesus' disciple.

3. Therefore the Judas[1526], having taken (*lambano*) the coil[1527] and some helpers[1528] from the leading ones amongst the priests and the Pharisees[1529], he comes there with lanterns[1530] and torches[1531] and weapons[1532].
4. Therefore Jesus, knowing about all the things that were happening above him[1533], by getting out[1534] he said to them: "Who are you looking for[1535]?"

1526 He does not enter the garden with Jesus. The spiritual knowledge is not enough to enter the Kingdom if the heart is not pure.

1527 The term "coil" indicates the turmoil of darkness, which is activated by the one who has the initiatic luciferic title of "King Snake". This title was probably attributable to the roman initiation and to Pontius Pilate (see note Mt 27,27). In an exterior sense, it represents the current of soldiers or courtiers.

1528 The ones who ministered with the priests, and therefore not soldiers but the religious people (which nowadays correspond to deacons); we can see how to capture the Jesus, the initiatic forces are active, and not soldiers or man of "law enforcement".

1529 They were part of a religious and political movement of great influence, extremely connected to the Hebrew customs and traditions. They believed in the resurrection of the dead and in angels; but they would hide their vices and their pride under the appearances of a hypocritical and formalist religion. The Pharisees were the "divided" ones since they strictly followed the Mosaic Law, and they believed themselves to be the best ones amongst the Jewish people. They had an initiation that would take place in the ether of heat which corresponds to the upper part of the brainstem.

1530 Representing the astral (as a turned off lantern).

1531 Also lantern of the sky, and therefore the Sun here in its luciferic aspect which indicates the Ego, the luciferic spirit. The lanterns (soul) and the torches (in this case the I-ego) produce exterior light for the ones who do not have inner Light. Judas represent the man who desires to achieve the Christian truths according to his own point of view, in the light of his limited comprehension. He needs soldiers and weapons to push Jesus to declare the theocratic kingdom on Earth.

1532 Also "tools for the battle", it mostly refers to the shield, and it represents their occult protection from the forces of Good. They also represent the physical plane. In the other evangelists, it is specified that they are referring to swords and canes (clubs), and in Hebrew occultism the swords represent the "daring" (to dare) and the clubs/canes represent the "wanting" (to want).

1533 It is the turmoil of evil which is getting closer to Jesus and that He knows really well. It is important to underline the fact that in John, there is no mention of the "sweating blood" of the Jesus. Let's remember that He had the power to offer His life from himself and then to reclaim it.

1534 He is the one that gets out of the garden (from the world of the Spirit) towards the terrestrial sphere from where the crowd was coming and Saturn-Cedron goes through, which is the sacrificial love; and he offers himself to the light of Jupiter which was corrupted by Lucifer (lanterns and torches).

1535 Also "who are you asking?", which means "of which I are you looking for?" This question reminds us of the one said by the two disciples after the Baptism at the Jordan (John 1,38); the difference consists on the fact that the first time, the question had as a purpose the entering in His life, and now He is the one who enters death and therefore ascends to the Father. This is to indicate that the will of search needs to be precise because it comes from a new consciousness.

5. They replied (*apokrinomai)*: "Jesus the Nazarene[1536]". Jesus said (*lego*) to them: " I am[1537]". But there was (unmovable, standing) (*histemi*)[1538] with them also the Judas, the one who delivered him.

6. As he said (*eipon*) to them: "I am[1539]", they all drew back[1540] and fell to the ground[1541].

7. Once again he asked them (to their higher being)[1542]: "Who are you looking for?[1543]" And they said (*eipon*): "Jesus the Nazarene".

8. Jesus replied (*apokrinomai*): "I said (*eipon*) that I am; if you therefore are looking for me[1544], let them[1545] go (*hypago*)".

9. To fulfill his own verb he said (*eipon*)[1546]: "I did not send to perdition anyone amongst the ones that you gave me".

[1536] They are looking for the man Jesus, initiated in Nazareth. Philip also identified him as "the one from Nazareth": the parallel continues.

[1537] **This is the 13th I Am. With this, Jesus indicate that within Him, the Divine Cosmic I is completely incarnated in Him and he is a true man and that man is the new bearer if the I Am (see 13,19). The Divine I and the Human I are One.**

[1538] This "staying" is the staying of an object, with no verticality and presence of the I. He is amongst his new companions: with the "black" crowd.

[1539] This is the 13th I am, with no other clarifications. Now the Man reached the fullness of this step. He is the 13th constellation: the spiritual Sun, the headquarters of the I Am.

[1540] Literally "they got further away from the things behind". The crowd falls back, in the direction of the Earth. Let's remember that Jesus is located between the Zodiac (Gethsemane) and the planetary sphere.

[1541] When Jesus manifests His authority over everything through his Word, the ones who are in the power of darkness are annihilated, they are annulled.

[1542] From the Greek *eperotao: epi+erotto.*

[1543] It is odd that Jesus, the one they are looking for, is the one to ask them who they are looking for. By doing so, He wants call within them a flicker of consciousness regarding they were about to do.

[1544] If you are looking for "me", which means if you are not looking for the cosmic I Am which incarnated within him, but are looking for the "terrestrial" man then you can get him since he will allow them to take him. Now the soldiers are not falling back anymore because they can hold up the "me", which is the lower human I. it is important to see how only John tells us about this particular capturing of Jesus. This is the 13th I am cited in the Gospel, now the Man is the new bearer of the I Am. The true I Am, the Cosmic I Am will get further and further away under the appearance of a young man (Mc 14,50-52).

[1545] This "them" is referring to the disciples that He wants to save.

[1546] He said to them; see note 17,12.

10. Therefore Simon Peter[1547], who had a knife[1548], pulled it out and hit the servant of the prince of the priests, and he cut[1549] the little ear[1550], the right[1551] one. The servant had the name Malcho[1552].

[1547] Let's remember that Simon is his old name before he was initiated to "Peter". Therefore, he is the terrestrial and impetuous man who throws himself at the servant of the priest.

[1548] It is the knife that was used for sacrifices; once again, it is a religious object, not a military one (the "sword", as it is usually translated). In an esoteric way, it represents the tongue and, connected to it the human thought, which can refer to the terrestrial things or the celestial things (like the two wires of the sword: one looks at the sky and one looks at the Earth). The Greek term is *machaira,* which reminds us of the Sanskrit *Makara*, which means "sea monster"; and it is also is the name of the Capricorn sign, which is the sign of the "door" of the Darkness and Evil, and it represented as a being with a fish tail. Since the sign of Capricorn falls on winter solstice, we can see within it the "hour if darkness" (John 16,32 and 17,1).

[1549] More precisely "divided".

[1550] The ears are the third organ to perceive, to listen. The feet are the organs for the Earth; the kidneys for the inner voice; the ear for the voice of God. Thanks to them, man can maintain a vertical position and ascend from the animalistic horizontal position which belongs to the "incomplete" man. Thanks to the human ear, the man learns to talk, which means that he acquires the competence of the Word. The inner ear (cochlea) corresponds to the head, and it has the function of equilibrium and verticalization, and within these functions, there is wisdom and intelligence. The middle ear (cavity and eardrum) is connected to the central part of the body, the area of inner transformation. The external ear (ear canal and auricle) welcome the external transformation in the complete immobility.

[1551] All of this reminds us of the consecration of Aaron and his children. To consecrate them, they used to anoint them with blood (of a sacrificed animal) on various parts of the body, included the right ear. Peter's gesture, which conceived a reformatory Messiah of the Hebrew institutions, symbolizes the destitution of the High Priest.

[1552] From the text we understand that it is a initiatic name, probably connected to Capricorn. "Malco" is a variable of "Moloc", one of the names of Baal-Ahriman; the modern version is "Malcolm". Moloc was a divinity of Syria (the earth of the forces of Evil) where the firstborn would be sacrificed. His appearances remind us of the "buck" of the Christian tradition. It was the dark god of the Sun, and therefore he represents the Solar Demon.
Remembering the little cut off ear, we can see how through it, which means through the inner part of the ear that look like a vortex, the negative turmoil could enter the man. Peter, with a mantram, "cuts" the connection between the negative turmoil and Malco, who is the servant (the minister of the prince of the priests); which is a term that indicates the ones who reached the solar spiritual level.
Additionally, let's remember the meaning of Malco in Aramaic which is "king," and he represented the High Priest (he was "the" servant of him). He represents the political power at service of the religious power (just like the Papal State).
From this, we can deduce that the crowd had an anti-solar character, which is the opposite of the action of the Christ-Sun and therefore connected to the solar anti-Christic demon, Sorat. Let's remember that in that moment, Sorat was acting so that the Passion would fail; only the missing entrance in the terrestrial evolution of the forces of Love brought with the sacrifice of the Golgotha, would have allowed him to find a place in the evolution of the Earth.
See the "Apocalypse" regarding this fact of R.Steiner.

11. Therefore the Jesus said (*eipon*) to the Peter: "Put the knife in the scabbard[1553]. The chalice[1554] that the Father gave me, will I not drink it?[1555]"

[1553] From the Greek *theke*, which means "sepulcher". It is no longer time to act with mantric formulas which recall the remote faculties connected to magical actions. This sentence of the Jesus is the "shrine", the "sepulcher" for them. In the rituals of Mitra (in the third era of culture, the era Egyptian-Chaldean) they would use the sacred knife for the divinatory sacrifices and to connect to the spiritual world. This was overcome by the Jesus with the sacrifice (bloodless) of the Bread and the Wine. (See note Mc 8,2).

[1554] Containing the so-called Evil of the world connected to the lower I. He is called to drink it to transform it in the harmony of the higher I.

[1555] That is not the way to find the new path to the Father, but He will be the one to deal with the High Priest by showing him the glory of the Father.

JESUS IN FRONT OF THE SANHEDRIN, NEGATION OF PETER (Mt 26,57-75; Mc 14,53-722; Lc 22,54-71)

12. The coil[1556] and the commander[1557] and the helpers of the Jewish people[1558] blocked[1559] the Jesus[1560] and they tied him up[1561].

13. And (they) first lead him towards Hanan[1562]; he was the father-in-law[1563] of the Caiaphas, who was prince of the priest of that time[1564].

1556 All of the spiritual "black" forces together evoked by the priests.

1557 Literally "*chiliarco*", which means "commander of the thousand warriors". In an esoteric sense, the "warrior" is the third step of the Persian luciferic initiation, and it indicates the ones who know how to read the occult writings. Therefore, he is a military "commander" that knows how to act with the "coil".

1558 The complicity between political-military power (the commander) and the religious power (the coil) is completed: both see within Jesus a danger for their interests. Let's remember that the collaboration of these two powers is the most direct manifestation of the Anti-Christ.

1559 From the Greek *syllambano*: also "they understood", they perceived that the Christ was the one who acted in that moment through Jesus, and that is who was in front of them.

1560 They want to get "the" Jesus, which is the Christ within Him. In Markus, we find that the Christ gets away from them in the form of a child.

1561 Also "they connected", which means they connected the links of the occult writings by understanding the events: the quality of the esoteric level of "warrior".
This reminds us of the passage of Isaiah 3,9: "We connect the right, because it is to us unbearable! But they will eat the fruit of his work".

1562 Hanan was the High Priest from 6 to 15 A.C., but he was actually drawing the strings of the Sanhedrin.
Hanan or Anna, is both a masculine and feminine name, and it means "graceful", therefore "the one who has Grace", which is the operating Love of God. This word can be read in two different directions (from the beginning to the end and viceversa) without changing, and this represents the two different loves between which man can choose: the love towards terrestrial things and the one towards spiritual things. Let's remember that Anna (feminine) was also the mother of Mary. "An" also means "breath", "hypothesis", "decision". "Na" means "negation". All together "Anna" can mean "the possibility of choice". Anna of Mary chose the love for the Spirit; this Hanan chose the Law.

1563 Between the two there is a "father-son" connection. In this way, there is a pact that goes beyond the juridical title: the axel of Evil between Hanan-religious and political power and Caiaphas-the power of the orthodoxy is being established, the one of the dead Law. John reports the religious-political institution as the highest enemy of man and therefore of God. To this, the "commander" of the roman troops is added (18.12).

1564 In reality, Caiaphas is the Vice-President (vice-prince) of the Sanhedrin, and he was the head of the court who judged the orthodoxy according to the Law. The High Priest is a different figure from the prince of the priests. But sometimes these two figures would match up.

14. And it was Caiaphas[1565] the one who suggested to the Jewish people that it would be better if only One (numeral) man (*Anthropos*) would go in the depths of death for the people (*laos*)[1566].

15. Simon Peter[1567] and another disciple[1568] were following the Jesus. And that disciple was known to the prince of the priests, and he entered with the Jesus in the atrium of the prince of the priests[1569].

1565 In Greek *Kaiafas*, or also *Kainan*, is a variable of the name Cain.

1566 It should be the Chosen People. Therefore Caiaphas, inspired by the spirit of the Hebrew people, loses the connecting with the Spirit of the Chosen People, and this Spirit was Michael; and now it is the Christ himself (from when Jesus-man ascended to Jesus-Christ). Therefore, we are in front of the "falling" of major events:

- Anna has Mary as a daughter, from whom Jesus is born; this Hanan has a daughter (focused on the terrestrial things) who will marry Caiaphas-Cain (in his aspect of man who separates himself from the spiritual worlds).
- The Chosen People (formed by the spiritual ties) "fall" in the Hebrew people (formed by blood ties).
- An additional passage will be the one going to the judgment of the Sanhedrin (composed of 72 members) instead of being praised by the 72 disciples.
- This will culminate in the fake "Son of God" (Barabba, in Hebrew "Son of the Father"), who is freed instead of the true Son of God.

Caiaphas predicted that Jesus would have put an end to the religious power of the priests and also the strong blood tie that was present in the Hebrew people, since Jesus was the one bringing more consciousness which would have freed them in their relationship with God and other men.

1567 It's the third time that Peter is being called "Simon", which is his "terrestrial" name, maybe to predict his three denials: denial of the body, soul and spirit since they were still not perfect.

1568 In his Gospel, John talks about five comparisons, contrasts in position, between Peter and John (the disciple that Jesus loved).
The first one is at the Last Supper (John 13,24) when Peter shows that he is not within the spiritual Love; the second one is at the capturing of Jesus when John enters the atrium of the priest and is willing to go through the same thing as Jesus while Peter remains outside caught up in his own fears (John 18,15); the third one is when they will run together to the sepulcher and John "will believe" in the resurrection (John 20,2); the fourth one will be while fishing when John will be the one to recognize the Risen One (John 21,7); the fifth one is at the famous "feed my lambs" when Peter will declare that he does not spiritually love Jesus (John 21,20).

1569 The fact that John can enter and the fact that he is not mentioned, can also mean that whoever gives up his will (with no "name") can follow the Jesus in any circumstance of life.

16. And the Peter was (unmovable/standing: *histemi*) near the door[1570], outside. The disciple then exited, the other one, who was known to the prince of the priests, and he said (*eipon*) to the doorwoman[1571] and he let Peter in.

17. The little girl, the doorwoman, then says (*lego*) to Peter: "Aren't you also from the disciples of that man (*Anthropos*)?" That one says (*lego*): "I am not[1572]".

[1570] The Doorway to the spiritual world. This reminds us of the parable of the Good Shepard, who give life for the sheep (John 10,11). John enters. Peter, fearful for his life, cannot enter.

[1571] In Greek *thuroros* , masculine gender but with feminine adjective. This "androgynous (masculine and feminine)" indicates a spiritual entity. In Latin, the doorwoman is *ostiaria*, from which the meaning of the host as a door to the sacrifice comes from. *Ostia* means "scapegoat victim". Peter does not internally go through this doorway because he is not willing to sacrifice; and the doorwoman, the host that is accepted to access the Passion, does not enter him because he will not respond adequately. John is the one that offers this to Peter.
We now have the parallelism again with the "doorman" of the passage of the Good Shepard.

[1572] It is the negative version of the I Am pronounced by the Jesus at the Gethsemane to the guards. Now the inner world of "Simon" Peter and his values will be the ones falling to the ground, ripped apart by the fear of losing his life.

18. The servants and the assistants[1573] were[1574] (*histemi*) making a charcoal fire[1575], because it was cold[1576] and they were warming up[1577], but Peter was also with them, who was standing (*histemi*)[1578] and he was warming up.

19. Then the prince of the priest questioned (*erotao*) the Jesus about[1579] his disciples and about his doctrine[1580].

[1573] Having denied the fact of being a disciple brings him immediately back to the external world, enemy of Life, amongst the ones who serve the Enemy: now he is the one who falls, so to speak, "backwards".

[1574]Unmovable, standing.

[1575] Also "making a fire". In an alchemical way, the fire to purify the charcoal-carbon in the physical body of the Jesus is being lit, and also to free the Incorruptible Body (or Glorious Body). In an alchemical sense, we are in front of the ignition of the Athanor.
Fire is the element that ignites, within the physical body, the inner fire which can then find its expression in the blood circulation. The Christ brought into the world a new impulse that can flow within blood circulation and therefore, staying "within Him" we do not need any physical support (like the Baptism of Water) to connect to the Spirit world; all that is needed is to grasp within our soul His impulse so that the experiences of the astral body can pour into the etheric body, and we become clairvoyant. Therefore, a new category of initiates comes to life. The first one amongst them was Lazarus-John.

[1576] Literally a "wind that cools down and dries out", therefore a cold wind with an ahrimanic nature. In Greek, it's *psycos*, similar to *psyche*, the soul or vital breath. We therefore are in front of the breath that brings life. This reminds us of the image of the breath of the dragon.

[1577] The Greek term indicates also a soul-like warmth that they recall to themselves, and it is as if it comforting to them.

[1578] Now he is in the I, now "Simon" is not there. Peter is found again in the I. He rejected the spiritual warmth coming from the Jesus (John, on the other hand, followed it) and therefore he is forced to warm up "outside" in the physical warmth, since within himself he is experiencing the soul-like coldness that comes from fear. With Jesus, there are no compromises: whether with His warmth that distributes Spiritual Good or the cold of the darkness of lies.
It is important to see the parallelism with Judas at the Gethsemane: "But Judas was also with them, the one who delivered him".

[1579] For more point of view (see the "going" of the Jesus). It also applies to the continuation of the verse.

[1580] The interrogation begins in order to know how many are following the Jesus (fear of the loss of the religious and priestly power) and also to know who the entity is that acts within the Jesus. It is an attempt of discernment of the Spirits.

20. Jesus[1581] replied (*apokrinomai*) to him: "I openly[1582] talked (*laleo*) to the world; I always taught in the synagogue[1583], and in the temple (inner)[1584], where all the Jewish people[1585] gather[1586], and I never spoke in secret[1587].

21. Why are you begging (erotao) me? Beg the ones who heard[1588] what I said (*laleo*) to them; these ones know the things I[1589] said (*eipon*)".

22. Having said these things, One of the assistants[1590] who is next to (*paristemi*) him gave a slap[1591]to the Jesus, while saying : "This is how you reply (*apokrinomai)* to the prince of the priests?"

1581 Without the article, since it is the test of Jesus and not of the Christ to confront the Sanhedrin.

1582 Also "in the fullness of the Word"; (See John 16,29).

1583 Where the gathering of the followers would take place.

1584 In the heart of men. For a deeper study of the "temple" see note in verse 2,14.

1585 The Jewish people are the advocates of the religious-political system. The Jesus people would have had to represent the "pure" people of Israel; the Galileans were the "hybrids", the people is Israel "mixed with the world"; the Samaritans, placed at the two extremes, represent the possibility of a new union between the "pure" current and the "hybrid" one of Hebraism. The Jesus gifts something to all three people: in Galilea, the Bread of Life (with the multiplication); in Samaria, the Water of Life (the Samaritan woman at the well); in Judea the Blood of Life (the Passion).

1586 Also "they agree". It is in the therapeutic zone of the rhythm that everything "gathers"; therefore it is the synagogue of which Jesus speaks about, and its inner temple is the heart.

1587 Probably Hannan asked him which ones were the mysteries that He communicated to the disciples. This question has a double purpose: to know which spiritual truths were being spread and also to put Jesus to death since the betrayal of the teaching of the Mysteries in ancient times was punished with death.

1588 Jesus invited the prince of the priests to speak to the ones who heard, therefore the ones who "felt". Jesus invites them to not interpret his words with the intellect/head, but instead with the forces of the heart, where the men come and gather (v.20). He invites them to look at the action accomplished by the Verb in the hearts of men, not the external words with which it manifested.

1589 After all, the priest should worry mostly about what the disciples understood of the teaching of the Jesus more than the teaching itself.

1590 It represents the ones who are subordinates to the political-religious authorities and that cannot accept that their "boss" is being contradicted since they identify themselves with him.

1591 As an action directed to the cheek, which corresponds to the I. in a positive way, it was the sign of liberation given from the owner to the slave (from which the slap of the Confirmation comes). In a negative way, it is a gesture of challenge to the I of the other person (like in a duel). The slave (One) automatically acts as a confirmation of his condition as a non-free man.

23. The Jesus said (*eipon*): " If I said (*eipon*) evil, testify about evil; if instead it is good, why are you hitting me?[1592]"

24. And the Hanna sent him tied up[1593] to Caiaphas, the prince of the priests.

25. And Simon Peter was standing[1594] and he was warming up. And so they said (*eipon*) to him: "Aren't you also from his disciples?" He denied[1595] and said (*eipon*): "I am not".

26. One from the servants of the prince of the priest said (*lego*) that he was brother-in-law[1596] of the one to whom Peter cut[1597] the little ear off: "Did I not see (*eidon*) you in the garden with him?"

27. Therefore the Peter denied again: and immediately a rooster[1598] sang[1599].

[1592] As always, Jesus tries to help everyone in growing and raising their own consciousness, even the ones who are his enemies.

[1593] They are the secret binds present so that the Jesus cannot act. Hanan could not manipulate and "win" over Jesus, and therefore he forces him.

[1594] Peter remained spiritually "still", he did not participate in the events, and he is still in the disposition in which we left him while Jesus keeps going through his path to reach the Father. Up above, the interrogation of Jesus took place, while the one for Peter took place below.

[1595] Now it is the public apostasy.

[1596] Malcolm's sister, the solar demon, is Lucifer. Therefore, this servant, who "married" the luciferic soul, is an ahrimanic entity.

[1597] Also "strip", "separate the head from the heart". (See verse 10).

[1598] Symbol of Fire, of the Higher I, of the calling of the I in him.
Peter, on this occasion, is showing all of his weaknesses and impetuousness. He was busy putting his soul at Jesus' service (13,37), but he did not have the necessary forces to actually do so. In Luke (Lc 22,61), it is said that Jesus stared at him in the eyes, and therefore Peter came back to the consciousness of the I, and he understood the denial that he made.

[1599] From the Greek *phoneo* which means to call by name. Peter remains in the darkness.
We have three denial of Peter: to the doorwoman (the threshold of the positive spiritual world); to the People (Chosen); to the servants of the priests (negative spiritual world).

THE JESUS BEFORE THE PILATE

28. They took the Jesus from the Caiaphas to the headquarters of the Roman governor[1600]. It was morning[1601]; and they[1602] do not enter the headquarters because they did not want to be defiled, but to (be able to) eat the Easter[1603].

29. The Pilate[1604] came out amongst them, and said (*phemi*): "What accusation do you have against this Man (*Anthropos*)[1605]?"

[1600] The headquarters of the Roman governor was the official residence of the one representing Roma, where the Jewish people could not enter because they would get contaminated upon contact with the pagans. The word "*pretorio*" (headquarters in Italian) resounds with Bull (*Toro* in Italian), symbol of the roman cult of Mitra. We can hypothesize that the praetor (magistrate), which in this case is Pilate, would become so since he was initiated into the cult of Mitra (the pre-Christian form of Michael), and he would grasp who Jesus truly was.

[1601] The morning of Friday, 3rd of April of 34 A.C. This is "the day" for which He came: the seventh day, the day of the return to the Father.

[1602] The High Priests who, united with the Pharisees, are also called "Jewish people": all the political-religious power.

[1603] See note John 2,23. The evening of the Thursday having gone by for the Jewish people, the Friday began already, and therefore they cannot enter a pagan house because they do not want to be contaminated. It is important to take note of the hypocrisy of the ones who decided to kill an innocent man, but they are careful to not enter a pagan house.

[1604] Pilate "comes out" and therefore he bow to the religious customs.
Pilate means "armed with a javelin", and it corresponds to the initiation of Mars. It also means "hairy", and it indicated the connection with the astral forces of the Earth which bring atavistic clairvoyance. The hair connects us to these forces, and this is why in old initiations they would have long beards and long hair. Now, this "look" helps us unite with the forces of the old clairvoyance, but it does not help with the conscious relationship with the Spirit. We can see how Pilate combines different initiations upon himself, as it was typical of Romans: the magistrate's court-Bull, the initiation of the javelin-Mars (he is a soldier), and the connection with the terrestrial forces (the hairy).

[1605] Pilate does not use polite expressions, he knows who Jesus is, and he know is he is called the one from Nazareth, which means the descendent of David, of the royal lineage. In the Greek text, "man" has the article in front, and therefore it recalls the spiritual element present in man.
We can see the process of Jesus together, and it develops in four phases (or three plus one):

- A first gathering, which is the instruction of the process accomplished by Hanan and another official gathering after this in the Sanhedrin near the palace of the Caiaphas (John 18, 1-12);
- The examination of the cause by Pilate (John 18,28-38); who does not find him guilty;
- The request of an opinion by Erode (Lc 23,8-12, an episode that has been omitted by John) with the pretext that Jesus was Galilean and therefore he would have to be under the jurisdiction of Erode;
- The conviction near Pilate (John 18,39-19,16).

30. They replied (*apokrinomai*), and they said (*eipon*): "If he wasn't someone who created (*poieo*) evil[1606], we wouldn't have delivered him[1607].

31. The Pilate said (*eipon*): "You get (*lambano*) him, and have him in clarity[1608] according to your law[1609]". The Jewish people said (*eipon*) to him: "We do not have the right to kill (*apokteino*) anyone"[1610].

32. So that Jesus' verb would fulfill, meaning with which death he was getting ready to go in the depths of death (*apothnesko*)[1611].

33. Therefore the Pilate re-entered the headquarters and he called the Jesus[1612], and he said (*eipon*): "Are you the king[1613] of the Jewish people[1614]?"

1606 This first coming out of Pilate, with the reply of the Jewish people, corresponds to the first phase of the alchemical Work in Black (which started with lighting up the coals v 18, 18). The Work in Black corresponds to the initiatic Purification, which the Christian tradition calls Purgatory, and which corresponds to the planetary spheres of Moon, Mercury and Venus. Here we are at the Moon's threshold, recalled by the terrestrial-lunar Initiation of Pilato and of the Jewish people (which act here as people, pushed by the luciferic lunar current of the blood) and the operating of "evil".

1607 Pilate asks for the accusation to have a just process, and the priest do not reply to him in a relevant manner since they have already decided to kill Jesus. They want Pilate to approve of their decision and not that he formulates a judgment.

1608 From the Greek *krino*, from *krisis*, which means discernment, choice through which we can reach the Christ (*Christos*). Pilate does not accept to approve of their decision and therefore the battle between the two powers begins.

1609 He understands that he is in front of a "quarrel" of the belligerent priests and he does not want to enter.

1610 With this, they make us understand that they decided Jesus' faith. Pilate then makes their contradiction and guilt towards the Law apparent (to not kill…).

1611 This manner is the crucifixion, an extremely humiliating manner that no Roman citizen could be convicted of, and it represented the exclusion both from the Hebrew and Roman society: but His Kingdom is not of this world (which means it is not connected to the religious-political power which is anti-Christic).

1612 He want to question him privately without the pressure and influence of the priests.

1613 John focuses a lot on this accusation of Jesus to indicate that His Kingdom is not of this world. This declaration, if demonstrated, would have also hit the interests of Rome (the emperor would be the one to elect him king), and therefore Pilate is investigating about this.

1614 He should have said king of Israel (theological denomination) and not of the Jewish people (religious and racial denomination). With this he remarks the racial and religious division with the Romans.

34. And Jesus[1615] replied (*apokrinomai*) to him: "Are you saying (*eipon*) this for yourself or did others[1616] say (*eipon*) this about me?"

35. The Pilate replied (*apokrinomai*): "Am I maybe a Jewish person[1617]? The ethnicity (*ethnos*), your own, and the prince of the priests delivered you to me[1618]; what did you create (*poieo*)?[1619]

36. Jesus[1620] replied (*apokrinomai*): "The Kingdom[1621], my own, is not from this world[1622]; if the kingdom, my own, were to be from this world, also the assistants[1623], my own, would

---

1615 As a man, without manifesting the Christ Principle.

1616 The astral beings to which Pilate was connected through the atavistic clairvoyance. Jesus wants Pilate to find the answer within himself. The dialogue is taking place inside the headquarters and therefore in private and Jesus allows Pilate to understand and grasp His true essence, so much so that Pilate declares him innocent.

1617 Pilate declares to not be the Hebrew authority's tool and he does not belong to the Chosen People, and therefore it is clear that he is replying to the Jesus that the forces of the Earth upon him "instructed" him in a clairvoyant way.

1618 We are at Mercury's threshold at the Work in Black, recalled by the relationship between the king and his people, amongst which Pilate acts as a bridge, as an alchemical "Mercur". We can see how "Pontius" means "bridge", and *pyle* (in Greek) means "door". Therefore, Pilate is the bridge to the door of the Passion.

1619 He does not want to reply to what he sensed: that Jesus truly is the King od the Jewish people, the spiritual king.

1620 Still a man.

1621 Let's remember that the Kingdom is the dimension of the Loving Vital Spirit and it resounds with the sphere of the Cherub Zodiac. Only thanks to the conscious I, from the increasing consciousness that it can develop, that man can enter it. In the sense of the Sefirot *Malkut* is the Kingdom, and by this we mean the terrestrial sensible world in which the human I acts consciously. To enter the celestial kingdom before the Christ, the initiate needed to dim his I. With the Christ the human I will be the one to enter, in its fullness, in the celestial *Malkut.*

1622 God's Kingdom is not connected to Earth, but it is connected to the Skies. He came to show humanity the way to go back to the Kingdom of the Skies.

1623 They are the Hierarchies of the Christ. The term is the same as the "assistants" of the prince of the priests that we met at the Gethsemane, of which we know find the positive correspondent in the Christic Hierarchies.
Jesus, by seeing an opening of thought within Pilate, educates him on the true nature of His Kingdom which is Truth and Love. It is important to see how Jesus is not concerned with how the process if going since he already knows the outcome. The outcome will allow Him to be Savior of humanity, but he interested in reawaken the consciousness of each and every man to whom he is dealing with.

have acted[1624] so that I wouldn't be delivered to the Jewish people; therefore the kingdom, my own, is not from here[1625].

37. The Pilate[1626] then said (*eipon*) to him: "Therefore you are no king[1627]?" The Jesus[1628] replied (*apokrinomai*): "You say I am king"[1629]. This is why I became[1630]; and to this I came into the world, to testify about the truth: whoever is from the truth, hears my voice[1631]".

[1624] Meaning a Christic "battle", which does not use violence. Instead, it uses the loving force of the Verb. "His" assistants, since they are not from "the world" and they do not follow the logics of abuse and battle, act with the free action of man. The Jesus makes us see how if his people would follow the logic of the world, they would act upon their own initiative, but they do not act because they are working towards the conquering of human freedom, even if the price is the cross. The Christ respects our freedom and he waits to intervene for the moment in which we openly "ask" for his actions.

[1625] Jesus does not reply to the second part of the question "what did you operate?" since he is rejects the hypothesis of a regality based on force, on the "what did you operate?"

[1626] The initiate, Pilate, is always the one speaking to Jesus.

[1627] With the term "king," it also refers to the initiatic title that is relative to the fifth step of the old Initiation, the one through which one would become bearer of the name of his own people, in this case the Jewish people. Pilate probably had the level of "Lion", the fourth step (he was the head of many "warriors", the term which indicates the third step). By grasping that Jesus was at a higher level of his hypothesis that he was at the fifth step, since he could not understand how his spiritual position was even more elevated.

[1628] Now the Christ responds to Jesus Christ, revealing his origin and goal, way more elevated than the hypothetical step of Pilate.

[1629] He does not add "of the Jewish people", since He operates for all humanity.

[1630] Also "entered the Life" (from *ghignomai*).

[1631] These words remind us of the parable of the Good Shepard, whose sheep recognize His voice. Let's remember that the throat, with the clavicles (little keys that close the path at the entrance of the eastern door of the terrestrial Paradise, which is a door guarded by the Cherub with the flaming and rotating sword whose keys, Jesus gifted to Peter) will continue with the arms (in Hebrew *Sichem* which means "term", "goal") and up to the hands, which represent the strength and the knowledge of the eagle within us.

38. The Pilate says to him: "Who is truth?[1632]" And having said this, he went out again near the Jewish people and said (*lego*) to them: "No fault[1633] is within him[1634]".

39. There is amongst you[1635] a tradition that I set free[1636] One at the Easter[1637]; do you therefore want me to free the king of the Jewish people?"

[1632] "The" Pilate" does not grasp the virtue brought by the Christ, which is the Truth that sets us free (John 8,32), that is why he immediately goes out without waiting for an answer, since he did not recognize that in front of him was the Son of God. For a second, he ascended in consciousness at the Zodiacal level, but he descended right away to the level of Mercury. He reasons in terms of law, and therefore he finds himself "chocked" between the Hebrew and the Roman law. From this limit of consciousness, his indecisions come up which culminate in "washing the hands" of Jesus. Pilate understood correctly how, from the point of view of the Law, Jesus' situation has no way out, there is no certain solution (he does not find faults according to the Roman Law but he also cannot declare him innocent because the Jewish people are accusing him. They went to him because they cannot kill: it is a standoff situation, which is created because no Law can "contain" the Jesus Christ, since He is the representative of the free overcoming of the Law itself. Pilate was not able to grasp the positive message hidden in this situation, which is the necessity to overcome the Law with a free act of love, which transforms the Law in Truth, which is a space of freedom that opens the doors to Grace (John 1,17). The freedom, in fact, is the inner space that allows divine love to operate within us as Grace. The freer we are, the better and more can Love act within us. To unite Grace and Truth means to unite Love and Freedom, to reach man's goal: this is the possibility that Jesus Christ brings to us. It is a possibility of which Pilate is in front of its doors, but he cannot see it. He remains imprisoned in the Law, in the old pre-Christian spiritual paths.
Pilate will repeat three times "in Him I find no fault" (John 18,38; 19,4; 19,6) to indicate the absolution in the physical plane, in the soul plane and the spiritual plane.

[1633] Also "cause".

[1634] He does not say that he "does not find him guilty"; instead, he says "In Him there is no fault". Him, the I Am, never did any "wrong". With this, he understood that Jesus is the Man with no sin who descended on Earth for our salvation.

[1635] Pilate is talking to the black crowd and not the Jewish people. There is no historic trace of the tradition that is being mentioned, and therefore it refers to a spiritual tradition and not an external one.

[1636] Also "to let them go" or "put in the light".

[1637] See note John 2,23.

40. They yelled[1638] once again saying: "Not him, but the Barabbas[1639]". And it was the thief[1640] Barabbas.

[1638] The black crowd is always the one acting.

[1639] Pilate did not make the name of Barabbas, he did not put concrete alternatives out there. The Jewish people are the ones who protest. The fact that Barabbas is not being "presented" indicates that the priests knew him extremely well.
In Hebrew, "Barabbas" means "Son of the Father". According to the Hebrew tradition, his complete name was "Jesus Barabbas". He, therefore, is the false Son, the Son of the Father killer of the Jewish people (John 8,44), that now is being freed. The crowd was not able to use the discernment to which the initiate Pilate called them to do more than once (see note in the Glossary).

[1640] The Greek term *lestes* means "thief" and "killer", and it contain both the luciferic aspect (the thief) and the ahrimanic aspect (killer) of this false Christ.

HERE IS THE MAN (Mt 27,226-30; Mc 15,15; Lc 23,16-22)

1. And then since the Pilate grabbed (*lambano*) the Jesus, he scourged him[1641].
2. And the soldiers, having braided a crown of thorns[1642], put (it) on his head[1643] and they wrapped him with a purple[1644] cloth.
3. And they would get close to him, and they would say: "Rejoice[1645] (*chairo*), king of the Jewish people"; and they would whip[1646] him.
4. The Pilate came out again, and he said (*lego*) to them: "Here, I will bring him out[1647], so that you will be clear (*ghinosko*) that I find no fault within him[1648]

[1641] Pilate heads back into the headquarters, and we question whether it is the Pilate that "scourges" Jesus with his spiritual whips.
In the roman legions, the Mysteries of Mitra were spread, and they were formed by seven stages of soul development which were represented by the washing of the feet, the flagellation, the crowning of thorns, the crucifixion, the mystic death, the burial and resurrection, and the ascension. The ones sentenced to death would be additionally mocked by having them go through the stages that would take them to this metaphorical death before they would undergo the true torture. This also happened to the Jesus and he transformed in His process of auto-initiation: in the Christian path to the Father for all of us.

[1642] The crown of thorns is the first one of the 5 wounds that will be infliction to the Jesus. In a deeper sense, we understand from R. Steiner that in ancient times, the human I could live within men only if they had a bodily wound or they presented a certain wound: this was to manifest the power that damages the body (Achille's tendon, back of Sigfried, wounds of Oedipus). Only a wounded body could adapt to the greatness of the I (which then was an anticipation of time), since the human I penetrated for the first time in its entirety in a human body. With the Jesus, 5 wounds were necessary to "match" the I brought by the Christ.

[1643] The headquarters of the I; it represents an asuric attack to the human I (let's remember how in the Parable of the Sower, the thorns represent the asuric forces).

[1644] It represents the luciferic astral. The whole thing is a caricature of the royal signs.

[1645] Exhortation that the Archangel Gabriel directed to Mariam.

[1646] Jesus allows them to do so since they were the grotesque symbols of the kingdom of the world. This is the flagellation on the physical plane, which in its violence it represents an ahrimanic attack upon the Jesus. Therefore, we have the cloth-Lucifer, the whips-Ahriman, and the thorns-Asuras.

[1647] He takes him outside the headquarters towards the Jewish people. But Jesus will exit on his own. We are at Venus' threshold in the alchemical Work in Black. Just like Venus welcomes, elaborates and gifts, Pilate has (negatively) welcomed Jesus, "elaborated" him with whips and thorns, and now he is presenting him (he "gifts" him) to the people. With this, the negative image of the three steps of the Purgatory is completed, and the Jesus will have to redeem during the Passion.

[1648] Pilate is speaking to the Jewish people, and therefore the people, hoping he can pull Jesus away from the priests, and he is showing Jesus in miserable and humiliating conditions. But the crowd is subject of the Sanhedrin, and it doesn't have its own consciousness.

5. Therefore the Jesus came out with a crown of thorns and a *purpurea* cloth. And says (Pilate)[1649] to them: "Here[1650] is the man (*Anthropos*)".

6. When the princes of the priests and the assistants say (*eidon*) him they yelled: "Crucify, Crucify him[1651]!" And the Pilate said to them: "You grab (*lambano*) him and crucify him; I do not find within him a fault[1652]".

7. The Jewish people replied (*apokrinomai*): "We do not have a law, and according to the law he is obligated to go in the depths of death because he created (*poieo*) himself son of God[1653]".

[1649] Pilate shows him to the Jewish people in those conditions. The actions of the soldiers had other motives as well. United with the demonic coil, they wanted to extract all of the subtle bodies from Jesus: the "physical" bruises for the Man spirit, the horn for the kingdom-Loving Vital Spirit, the red luciferic cape for the spiritual Self, and therefore Pilate presents to the Jewish people the man with the triad of Evil within, instead of the divine Trinity.
Obviously, this whole process was tried to be put on Jesus but it did not come through.

[1650] It also means "you see". Jesus now "appears" to be seen. In reality, Pilate does not show to the Jewish people Jesus as "Jesus", in his enlightened being. Instead, he presents him after being whipped (incomprehensible since he couldn't find a fault within him: why then punish him?), wrapped in the purple cloth and crowned with thorns. This archetypal image is being offered to the Jewish people by Pilate saying : "Here is the man (the spiritual image of the man)". The Pilate wants to spread the image of the attacked man and also the man who is being obstructed by three forces of Evil: this had to be the man that the Jewish people, in the intentions of Pilate, needed to see as the highest archetype of humanity. The Jesus is the man redeemed, but the Pilate wants them to see him as the fallen man, to which we do not know there is a chance of redemption. On the other hand, if the Pilate acted that way, it is because he recognized whom Jesus truly is: with this, the recognition of the Jesus, on behalf of the Romans, takes place.

[1651] It means "stop him", like taking away the ability to move, and therefore his freedom. And therefore the Man (the I Am) is the true enemy of the Jewish people and Jesus brings the I Am to them. They, the oppressors, cannot stand the One who frees the Man. They first invite Pilate to wanting to kill (by instigating him in an ahrimanic way), and only in a secondary way, they indicate to kill. The crucifixion was the most terrible execution and the meanest of torture reserved to the worse wrongdoers, since it would cause an extremely slow and painful death.

[1652] It is the second time that Pilate wants to free Jesus. In Jesus, not only is there no fault, but not even the "cause" of fault, which means that which could generate a fault. The Jesus has nothing "fallen" onto him.

[1653] With this title, in the old Mysteries, it indicated the initiate in whom a divine principle would directly live. This title was also given to the roman emperors after conquering (through force) the initiations. With this, the accusation takes on two aspects: for the Jewish people He is profane since (for them) no one could be the same as God (whose name was unpronounceable), and for the romans since by doing so, the Mysteries would be public and the emperor was the only one who could aspire to them.

8. When the Pilate heard this verb, he highly[1654] feared.

9. And he re entered the headquarters[1655] and he said (*lego*) to the Jesus[1656]: "Where are you[1657]?" But the Jesus did not give him an answer[1658].

10. The Pilate says (*lego*) to him: "You do not speak (*laleo*) to me? Do you not know that I have the power[1659] (to release you), and I have the power to crucify you?"

11. The Jesus[1660] replied (*apokrinomai*): "You have no power over me if it wasn't given to you from above[1661]. This is why the one who delivered me to you has made a greater[1662] mistake".

1654 He already recognized him as just, and now he fears even more because he is afraid that he is going to have to kill the Son of God. Additionally, the accusation has an implication towards the emperor, and he is afraid to compromise himself in front of the emperor himself without defending the initiatic rank.

1655 A new private dialogue begins.

1656 The Initiate Pilate ("the" Pilate" has the ability to talk to the Christ who was acting (from above) within the Jesus. "The" Pilate knew how to direct his words both to the human and the divine - another sign of his elevated initiation and of his discernment towards the events.

1657 He asks him is spiritual origin (or descendants), to understand if he truly is the Son of God. He also asks him his level on initiation. For the Roman religion, the gods could descend on Earth and look like humans.

1658 Also "he did not defend himself", "he did not make a choice", therefore he did not enter into the division. See how "the" Jesus does not defend himself from terrestrial insults. Jesus only tries to reawaken the consciousness.

1659 The power corresponds to a solar initiatic step. This power is only terrestrial.

1660 Jesus replies (not "the" Jesus) as a man who needs to overcome his test. The Christ in him, on the other hand, limits himself to experiment the Passion, since he is greater than this human provocation.

1661 Now Jesus speaks and he testifies His absolute devotion to the Father. Every power comes from Above, both if man had to fight to have it, or it is just "happened" to him. In either case, it always implies a heavy karmic condition.

1662 With this, Jesus "absolves" the Pilate who will try another time to set him free. Pilate is an initiate with a luciferic stamp with some ahrimanic "intrusion". The one who delivered Jesus, therefore Judas, went through an even deeper fall, because within him, Satan-Ahriman completely entered in.

12. From this (moment) the Pilate tried to release him[1663]. But the Jewish people said: "If you free (release) this one, you are not Caesar's friend; whoever creates (*poieo*) himself to be king, contradicts[1664] the Caesar".

13. Therefore the Pilate, having heard these verbs, took the Jesus outside, and he sat[1665] in the podium, towards a place called Litostroto[1666], and in Hebrew, Golgotha.

14. And it was Parasceve[1667] of the Easter, almost the sixth hour[1668], and he said (*lego*) to the Jewish people: "Here is your King[1669]".

[1663] Also "set-free", "to put him in the light". Now Pilate understood that there is another authority above him, and he does not want to go against it.

[1664] From the Greek *antilego*, opposite of Logos. Therefore it is a Logos (the one of the Christ) that is opposite to the one of the Caesar. Now the religious accusation becomes political. Pilate is afraid of the repercussions that these words could have on him, and so he decides to abandon Jesus to his destiny.

[1665] The phrase is ambivalent: it could be Jesus sitting on the bench, on the throne of King of Israel in which the God's magnificence shines and not the human magnificence.

[1666] It means "location with a tiled floor or a floor with a mosaic"; the "mosaic" recalls Moses, bearer of law and order. It is a place with strict rules.

[1667] Which means "preparation". Between Friday and Saturday.

[1668] It corresponds to 12 noon, the time in which the luciferic forces act the most (they manifest in the bright Sun that blinds and dulls the consciousness). Between this time and the death on the cross (15.15), 200 minutes will go by which represent the terrestrial things (the 100) which have been attacked by the principle of division (the 2). Now the forces of the obstacle try the "everything for everything" before Jesus wins over Death.
At 12 noon, the preparation of the lambs for the Easter sacrifice would begin.

[1669] Spiritual King. First Pilate declared him the "Innocent" (John 18,38), then the "Man" (John 19,5). Now, after sitting on the podium, he fulfills the last attempt to save Jesus and he declares him "King" (John 19,14), even though he knew what danger this statement would imply. Pilate, more or less unconsciously, captured the deep truths of the Jesus: He is Innocent, Man, and King.
But the uncertainty of the subject keeps going on: Jesus could also be the one declaring himself to be such. This is because this scene is exposed with both narrative value and theological value.

15. And those ones would say: "Take him out, take him out[1670], crucify him!" The Pilate said (*lego*) to them: " I will crucify your King?" The princes of the priests replied (*apokrinomai*): "We no do not have a king, if not Caesar[1671]".

16. Therefore he delivered him to them so that he would be crucified. And after grabbing (*lambano*) the Jesus,[1672] they took him away.

[1670] Also "sublimate him" (as an alchemical transition from solid to gas, without going through water, through the "dry path", the alchemical path of the consciousness). This sublimation, this transition from solid to gas, will be accomplished by Him but on another level, at the Sepulcher when His body will etherically disintegrate (and imprint on the Shroud).
Also "get him out of the way", from above, below, right, left, forward and behind. These are the 6 directions from which Evil acts against us. The Jesus comes from Good, from the middle.

[1671] The prince of the priests, representing the luciferic forces. They deliver themselves to Ahriman (represented by the materialistic Roman Empire) by saying these words and denying all religious beliefs and the same Hebrew unity just to convict Jesus. The two forces of Evil come together against the Christ. In reality, the priests had "Caesar" as king for awhile now (which is the absolutism), since they connected to the religious-political power.

[1672] This is what mattered to the forces of Evil: to take Jesus away, to take him the farthest way from human consciousness so that Light does not enlighten the darkness, and so that the human consciousness does not get transformed.

JESUS AT THE CALVARY SCENE (Mt 27,32-56; Mc 15,21-41; Lc 23,26-49; Ps 21,19)

17. Holding in his hands (*bastazo*)[1673] his own cross[1674], he went out towards the so called Place of Skull, which is said in Hebrew, Golgotha[1675],

18. Where they crucified him, and with him two others, on one side and the other, and in the middle the Jesus[1676].

19. The Pilate also wrote a title[1677], and he put (it) on the cross. And it was written: Jesus, the one from Nazareth, the King of the Jewish people[1678].

1673 Because he welcomed it from the spiritual plane.

1674 The cross, with its four arms, represents the four natural Kingdoms, the Nature that He came to redeem and bring back to the Father. On the path of Christian initiation, this corresponds to bringing materiality, the imprisonment of the material body, and the consequences that it entails (instincts, desires, etc.). this reminds us of what was said in Mt 16,24: "*Who wants to come behind me, deny yourself, take your cross and follow me..*"
The Egyptians also used a cross (*l'ank*) with the upper part empty: now, that empty space is filled by the Jesus and the cross, the key to the spiritual world which becomes a tool for eternal salvation.

1675 From the Hebrew *Gulgolet* means "place of the skull", more precisely is means "freedom from exile" and in man, it corresponds to the head having the chakra with 1000 petals on top, which is the spiritual center that connects us to the Zodiacal sphere, to the Father. Inside of it, we have the thalamus (or "optical chambers") as the expression of the last inner marriage between the right part (Father-wisdom) and the left part (Mother-intelligence) of the brain. Below there is the pituitary gland (the fruit of the union) which leans on the Turkish saddle (sella turcica): the Grail cup within us.
The skull is connected to the thoughts of the man fallen in matter and hardened within the terrestrial desires.
The love of the Christ breaks the material forms of thought and it gifts to man the chance to free himself from Satan's slavery.
The word Golgotha also refers to the city of Golgi, which is located in Cipro in front of Syria. This last one represents Sirius' star, the double star macrocosmic location of Lucifer's and Ahriman's forces. In the square of the elements, Cipro is at Crete's level, and therefore it corresponds to the median axis between the above (element Earth and Water), and the below (element Air and Fire), and so it represents the mercurial element. Cipro represents the "east" aspect of clay and therefore the door of Michael, what the alchemists called the "dry path", the path that brings us directly to the Spirit by going through death and resurrection. This is, therefore, an antagonist (in the good) to Syria-Sirius-Evil, and it represents the forced transition for the Macrocosmic Initiation.

1676 The Jesus is the center of human consciousness and on the sides there are the thieves, the wrong tendencies of the human soul. Let's remember that the Christ, even if "from above", is always connected to the experiences that the Jesus is fulfilling.

1677 Also "inscription". The word "title" indicates the value, the worth (the title) of a person: in this the level of Jesus that Pilate captured.

1678 The title is exact, since Jesus is the King of the Chosen People. The Pilate recognizes the value as initiate when he writes "from Nazareth", "the" King of the Jewish people. By doing so, he contradict the Jewish people who said that Caesar was their king.

20. So they said to the Pilate, the princes of the priests that Jesus himself said (*eipon*): "I am King of the Jewish people[1679]".

21. The Pilate replied (*apokrinomai*): "What I wrote, I wrote[1680]".

22. So the soldiers, the ones that crucified the Jesus, grabbed (*lambano*) his cloths[1681] and created (*poieo*) four parts[1682]: one part for each soldier. And the tunic[1683] had no stitching, weaved together through the above.

23. They answered back amongst each other (*eipon pros*): "Let's not divide it, but we receive in fate[1684], around it, to who it belongs"; so that the Writing[1685] would fulfill itself, (which says): "*They divided the cloths amongst each other, and on my vesture[1686] they cast lots[1687]*". Therefore the soldiers created (*poieo*) these things.

[1679] They eliminate the articles, therefore the spiritual consequences of the title, so that they can make him appear as only a man.

[1680] This sounds like a conviction of the workings of the Jewish people.

[1681] The cape has various symbols. In Hebrew, it represents royalty, the kingdom. The old kingdom of the Jewish people now goes to the pagans, since the Jewish people did not recognize Jesus. Additionally, He came for all humanity. The salvation comes from the Jewish people and it extends over the whole Earth.
The cape means also the transmission of the prophetic spirit (episode of Elijah with Elisha).

[1682] It was custom amongst the soldiers to split the goods of the one convicted to death. The clothes represent both the forms inwhich He needed to cover himself with to speak to men, which the men split amongst each other to continue to use them according to their own point of view, and they also represent the Earth, divided and violated by men. In a spiritual evolutionary sense, the Earth is formed by four triangular parts "stitched" up between each other. These lines of suture are the lines of the volcanos. The soldiers represent the ahrimanic beings that want to break and wound the Earth. Let's remember that the third step of Persian Initiation was the one of soldier-warrior: now we are in front of the disciples who are Ahriman initiates.

[1683] The tunic represents the etheric body, which is undividable. The tradition tells us that it was woven by Mariam, which is like saying that the etheric is "woven" by Mariam-Zoe. She contains and protects the Earth. This tunic also represents the deep spiritual teaching that He gifted to us, and it cannot be wounded. The tunic, in one whole piece, was part of the clothing of the High Priest, and no one else could wear such thing.
The tunic represents also the unity that remains within His teachings, the unity of the Spirit that receives from above.

[1684] It was a divinatory act, and their specific intention was to receive from the spiritual world specific information they wanted to us as some sort of talisman. The spiritual world decides who to give it to.

[1685] This is Psalm 22 of David that foresees with precision all of the Passion and Death of Jesus. This Psalm, at verse 22,2 contains the famous *"My God, why did you abandon me?"* (Mt 27,46) with which the Jesus ends all of the Writings, and he helps us understand who He truly was.

[1686] It represents the internal vest (the slip, the undervest).

[1687] They were throwing pieces of wood or something else as a magic action to send the Pious Women away (the capes/the souls) who were protecting the Jesus. That is why we cannot understand the plural usage of the capes or cloths.

24. Near the cross[1688] of the Jesus there were[1689] his mother[1690] and the sister of the mother[1691], Mariam, the one of the Cleophas[1692], and Mariam the Magdalen[1693].

[1688] They do not say "under" the Cross, but "near". Let's remember that in the mountain, "under the Cross", there was Adam's skull. Which was placed there by Noah after the Great Flood.

[1689] In the firmness of the I. this presence is the one that acts so that the tunic will not get torn.

[1690] They were in Spirit, as a presence and force. The Salomonic Mary that generated him in the physical plane (who Matthew and Mark call "Mary Salome") represents the old "bride".

[1691] The Nathanic Mary present in her from the moment of the Baptism of Jesus in the Jordan.

[1692] Cousin of the Salomonic Mary, mother of James and John of Zebedeo. Now she represents the moment in which the Being of Mariam reaches (or manifests) His Glory. For the term "glory" see note 1,14.

[1693] The Magdalen represents the Bride of the new community, the sentient soul that arrived to the level of the consciousness soul, of Silent Mariam. Note the articles, they are present everywhere. Magdalen (Magdala) in Hebrew is said *migedal* which means tower, but it also contains the root *meged* which means "the best". It is a city on the Sea of Galilea, and it represents the constellation Taurus- throat.

25. (The Jesus) then, seeing the mother[1694], and the disciple that he spiritually loved[1695] that was standing there, says (*lego*) [1696] to the mother: "Woman[1697], here (*idein*) is your son (*hyios*)".

[1694] Now he "sees" the Mariam Being that is "close" to the cross. It no longer is "his" Mother, but the Mother par excellence. All the mentioned Women are enclosed in the term "mother", the Being Mariam. The soul reaches its glory-Cleophas and the Spirit-John presents itself. Now we are in front of another mystery. Now the characters are changed, John "appears" and Magdalen "disappears": now there is the Being Mariam, the Cosmic Mother. John had the task (since he is Lazarus reawakened) to have the wisdom of the Christianity reach humanity, to have the principle Christ flow in the astral body. To have this happen, it was necessary that the Christ principle would unite with the etheric principle represented by the Mother. With the phrase: *"Woman, see your son",* Then to the disciple: *"See your mother,"* His active principle (brought by John) is united with the maternal principle brought by the Mother.

[1695] It is John, the resurrected Lazarus, who had already secretly "ascended"; he is "already standing up".

[1696] The first time, the Father spoke at the Baptism at the Jordan (this is my spiritually loved Son); the second time, at the Transfiguration (listen to Him!); the third time at the announcement of "His hour" (John 12,28). Lastly, there will be a fourth "conversation" between Jesus and the Father: at the Cross when Jesus will be the one to "speak" to the Father (*Eli, Eli, lamna sabactani o Lama schabachtani, or Lama asaphtani).* He expresses four expressions. Luke will cite three more: *"Father, set them free, they do not know that they operate"* (Lk 23,24); and to this follows *"Amen I say to you, today you will be with me in the Heaven,"* talking to the "good" thief (Lk 24,43); and lastly, *"Father, I deliver my spirit to your hands"* (Lk 23,46). In John, the three final expressions are: *"Woman, see your son".* Then he said to the disciple, *"See your mother"* (John 19,26)… and then he said: *"I am thirsty"* (John 19,28), and then: *"It is fulfilled"*, which means that the whole initiations is completed (John 19,30). The words *Eli, Eli..* are at the beginning of Psalm 22 which illustrates, in the most profound way, the entering of the Messiah in the setting of human pain. It is also called the Psalm of David (and the Messiah is also called Son of David). It goes like this: *The Lord is my shepherd: I lack nothing; on grass pasture he lets rest and he leads me on calm waters. He encourages me, he leads me on the right path, for love of his name. If I had to walk in a dark valley, I wouldn't fear evil, because you are with me. Your cane and your crook give me comfort. In front of me, you prepare a meal under the eyes of my enemies; you put oil on my head. My chalice overflows. Happiness and grace will be with me for the rest of the days of my life, and I will live in the house of the Father for many days.*

[1697] The nickname "Woman" corresponds both to the step of Venus (the third) and the one of the Sun (Fourth). Let's remember that this nickname corresponds to the redemption of the fallen feminine part, the redemption of Eve within her. The woman represents the higher aspect of the feminine within us, the soul that generates the Spirit. In Mariam this happened from the moment of the Annunciation when she offered herself to make the will of the Father.
The making of the Father's will develops in three aspects or phases:

- Respecting the Commands that he gave us (aspect "Father");
- To do what He tells us internally with the inner Word (aspect "Son");
- To be completely at His disposition, at His service (aspect "Holy Spirit").

This also represents a transition from the condition of "obligation" to the one of "Freedom". From this, the fourth aspect comes to life, the "+1", the "prize": to reach the eternal spiritual Life.

26. Then he says (*lego*) to the disciple: "Here (*idein*) is your mother[1698]". And from that time the disciple took (*lambano*) her with him[1699].

AGONY AND DEATH OF JESUS (Is 21,16; Is 68,22; Ex 12,46; Nm 9,12; Ps 33,21; Zch 12,10; Ap 1,7)

27. After this, since the Jesus knew everything was fulfilled (*teleioo*)[1700], so that the Writings would get fulfilled, he says (*lego*): "I am thirsty"[1701]

1698 Mariam represents the soul-spiritual part within man which is the path between thought and its manifestation. She, therefore, gave the Child Her purest form of Heat so that He could rise from Her breast, and Joseph brought him to Light so that he could then be covered by the "thick" shell brought by the shepherds. Therefore Mariam, in Her highest meaning, is also the Cosmic Virgin Sophia, since she is the forces through which the thoughts of the Creator Father come to life. The divine thoughts become the Thinking Gods (luciferic before the Fall) that are like a Son, and they contrast to the cosmic Mother by "robbing" her of the cosmic images of the formation of the world.

1699 Intimately, in what makes him an individual. From that moment, the Being Marian becomes the Mother of all humanity who "searched" and overcame all of the ties with the political-religious institutions.

1700 He arrived to his end, he was consumed, completed. The Incorruptible Body of Jesus is now completely characterized by the Christ. But he only "knew" the death that now becomes, from being door of Hades to the door of the Father. Now the Writings would need to be fulfilled, which means that the Jesus needed to give a sign to the ones that were waiting for the event. His inner experience is already enough and completed.

1701 It reminds us of the water asked to the Samaritan woman, and therefore the thirst of spiritual Life. Thirst is connected to the liver, the organ of depuration. The Jesus accomplishes the last act of depuration of the human body. He is the "thirsty one", the one that goes to the Holiest Trinity (of who is "thirsty") first. Every time we go from one spiritual level to the other, we are "thirsty".

28. A vase[1702] full of vinegar was laying down[1703]. Then, putting around an hyssop[1704] a sponge full of vinegar[1705], they put it close[1706] to his mouth.

[1702] The vase reminds us of the six jars of water laying down at Cana which contained the Laws. The fact that is transformed itself into vinegar indicates the degeneration of its content: the love into hate, the condition that sentenced the Messiah to death.

The vase, in ancient times, was symbol of the human heart. To the thirst of human salvation, it responds by offering what lives in its heart: not the blood-wine but the putrefaction-vinegar, which is wine turned sour, which did not become Love. The human soul is drenched in this: like a sponge. Therefore he is the "thirsty one" par excellence, the intermediary condition connected to the transition from the Zodiac to the Milky Way.

It is important to remember that He refused the wine mixed with myrrh (Mc 15,23) which had the goal to distort sensitivity and therefore the consciousness.

[1703] From the Greek *Keimai:* " to lay, to be laying down". It was at the feet of the cross.

[1704] The hyssop is a plant connected to the forces of Fire, and it supports the I and its organization. The hyssop also supports the rhythmic system of man. It is the plant that is used to spread the freeing blood of the Easter lamb in the moment of exiting Egypt. The theme of the Transition to the Kingdom of the Father comes back.

[1705] "Vinegar", in Greek, is said *oxos*. The esoteric meaning of this word is: "it is what penetrates in the deepest depths of darkness". The Jesus is able to completely incarnate the Christ principle within Him. In the sense of the esotericism post-Golgotha, oxos means "the decision to descend to the underworld to free Adam and to go back to the Father to transform all of this into a spiritual logic that is comprehensible to all humanity". This is the comprehension of the Event of the Golgotha.

It is the ninth hour when the veil of the Temple is rent, and the transition from the 6 (the sixth day of creation, the creation of man) to 9 (the number of transformation) began in Cana, where the Christ, by becoming the seventh jar, transformed the water into wine for the consciousness of the ones who were present. Now the wine has also become sour for a part of humanity: the soldiers give to the Jesus, who is thirsty of Spirit, the sponge soaked in vinegar. Now everything has been fulfilled: the wine within Him became blood and the blood has been poured, the Spirit comes and Jesus gives his Spirit to the Spirit of God.

[1706] From the Greek *prosphero*: to take towards.

29. As he received (*lambano*) the vinegar[1707], the Jesus said (*eipon*): "It is fulfilled[1708]". And,

[1707] Which is after accepting death brought by hate. Here, it is being specified that he does not drink it but instead, he rejects it. To reject it, he had to recognize it, and therefore had to smell it. From this, it had the action of regeneration within Him, like the breath of life that God blew into the nostrils of Adam to gift him life.

[1708] From the Greek *teleo*, "carry out, to finish a task". The work that was given to him from the Father is now done. From this verb *eis telos* comes, which indicates the achievement of perfection. In this verse the verb "to fulfill" is being said three times, and the expression "everything is fulfilled" used to be used by the Greeks in the culminating moment of the initiation, when the union with the Spirit would happen. Jesus therefore experimented death on the cross as a Perfect Man, and we will also "die" with Him when we will put our ego on the cross.

once he bowed his head[1709], he delivered the spirit

[1709] The verb has an active form, like saying that the intention of the gesture is His saying "yes" unconditionally to the Father.

[1710].

[1710] Jesus delivers the Spirit of the Christ, which he was able to keep within himself in a complete way only for a minute. The Spirit of Jesus is still present in him, and his consciousness continues: now he will descend to the darkness to free Adam.
Now the Incorruptible Body is completely characterized, and the whole being of Jesus is being kept together by His I, He completely transformed the material physical body; now the matter is completely spiritualized, now on the cross there is only the Incorruptible Body of Jesus, which is His non-material physical Body that He "thickened" to not disappear from the cross and to complete his mission to descend into the underworld. Now the unity between Jesus and the Christ is forming: the Being Jesus-Christ is being established. This non-material physical Body can be can be assimilated by the primordial Earth just like it was formed by God, and in the sepulcher this non material physical Body will sublimate, atomize, and it will descend into the Earth uniting with the material, blending with it. And with it, as a divine inoculate, it can active the process that will bring it to the spiritual Earth, to the primordial essence (*"And then I saw a new sky and a new earth, since the first sky and the first earth disappeared*…Ap 21,1).
This is also the reason why Joseph of Arimathea will go ask the Pilate the *soma* (living physical body) and he will give him the *toma* (dead body).
The other evangelists, use different expressions (Mc: *"breathed his last breath"*, Mt *"he released the spirit"*). Therefore, Jesus gifts the new Spirit, son of the victory over Evil, to the New Community (in Love) that is near Him: the Being Mariam and the Being John. At the same time, the veil of the temple is rent (Mt 27,51) and the Saint of the Saints appears with the Ark of the Alliance with the two cherubs (the ones who, in the Old Sun gifted, the Incorruptible Body to man), who had the body of a lion, wings of an eagle and the head of an angel (like the sphinx). This represents the man in his path of initiation: now the path is open to everyone.
By winning death over this way, Jesus Christ took off the last veil that prevented us to reconnect to the Father: death is the door to the Father. The Christ accomplishes his mission: to substitute the old image of death (seen as the "end") with the new one: death is the forever-living Father. Thanks to the permeation of the Christ in the etheric body of the Jesus (and from this body to the physical body) there is no difference between the "etheric" life of the Jesus Christ before and after the Golgotha. This death does not turn life off, instead, it if life itself.
If the blood of Jesus wouldn't have been spilled on the Golgotha, man would have become spiritually hard within egoism, and the etheric body after death couldn't have brought with it any of the wisdom of the physical body and with time, it would have withered. Man would have lost all the fruit of the physical life, of the experience on Earth. Earth would have also failed in its evolutionary process. With the blood coming from the wounds of the Jesus, the etheric body of man that comes out upon death from the physical body comes back to life, it acquires new wisdom and therefore it can give life to the physical body as strength and life. So the physical body will shape as the Incorruptible Body (Body of Resurrection), the body that became everlasting. Therefore man's resurrection, with the conquering in the physical body, is saved. The germ of the decomposition brought by Lucifer and Ahriman is won over. The first germ of this new life will be in the brain, in the thought that came to life. When Jesus's blood poured into the Earth, the Earth began to shine, to become a new Sun; and its aura, which was slowly dying, began to shine new colors. The event of the Golgotha permeated the Earth with astral Light which then became etheric Light, and at the end it will be physical Light. Men's etheric bodies that are permeated with the impulse of the Golgotha are permeated with this Light of the Christ that flows in their etheric bodies and in the Glorious Bodies (or Bodies of Resurrection). This Christic Light is then re-irradiated from the Earth and it forms an Etheric Ring around it (which the Christ calls "Holy Spirit") from which the Christ is now manifesting Himself. This Ring will become a new planet: the new Sun, a new evolutionary cosmic "center".

30. The Jewish people, since it was Parasceve[1711], so that the bodies (*soma*) would not remain on the cross on Saturday, since that Saturday was a great day[1712], therefore (*erotao*) asked the Pilate that their legs[1713] would get broken and that they would be taken away[1714].

31. The soldiers came, and they broke the legs of the first one, and of the other one, who was crucified with him.

32. Once they got to the Jesus[1715], they found him already dead[1716], and they did not break his legs[1717].

[1711] The day of preparation for Easter, Friday. The priests are afraid to contaminate Easter's "formalities" and so they "nicely" ask to Pilate that he sends someone to break the legs of the ones that are crucified.

[1712] The Easter. From now on, it will be the day of the redemption of Adam.

[1713] The text literally talks about "shins", and therefore the bone structure of the double bones shin bone-calf bone, and therefore the image of the luciferic division. The legs represent the forces of the libido within us, and only the man that dominates them becomes apt to completely travel the path of inner transformation.

[1714] Literally "lifted" or "taken away".

[1715] The fact that Jesus has the article reveals to us, without a doubt, that he was alive in the Incorruptible Body.

[1716] He appeared as such in their consciousness.

[1717] It needs to be remembered that in the history of humanity, no initiate was ever able to penetrate with the consciousness within the physical and chemical mysteries that are part of the formation of bones. With the Jesus, for the first time, this happens, and therefore his body became able to incorporate the forms of the bone structure in the evolution of the Earth. This is because the "bone" taken away from Adam could have been transformed only by one God: the Christ. For the evolution of man, it is necessary that he can take to the *post mortem* the forces (that he elaborated) of the forms of the bone system: forces that are able to win over death (represented by a skeleton). If they would have broken the bones, a human force of a lower character would have been inserted in the forces that the Christ was exercising on the bones of the Jesus: that form needed to stay completely under the control of the Christ.

33. But One[1718] of the soldiers[1719] pierced with the point of a spear his side[1720], and water[1721] and blood poured out immediately.

34. And the one who saw (*horao),* testified that his testimony[1722] was true. And he knows that he says truthful things, so that you also will believe.

35. These things became so that the Writing[1723] could be fulfilled: *No bone will be broken by him*[1724].

[1718] This "one" is not an indefinite pronoun but the number one. This indicates the presence of the soldier as a spiritual individual.

[1719] According to the tradition, this is Caio Cassio Longino, who at the contact with the blood on the eyes, healed the physical sight and he acquired the spiritual sight.

[1720] To be precise, he hit him between the third and fourth right rib, where the rib that was taken out from Adam to form Eve (this is why on the right there is one less rib because the whole system is "scaled" towards the above to cover the space of the missing rib). Adam was "put to sleep" and Jesus "bows his head". Adam will become the Resurrected and Eve will become the Mariam Magdalen. The blood that comes out purifies this first division that happened between man and woman.

[1721] From this opening, the forces of spiritual Life come out (water) for the whole of humanity, and the forces of the individualized Spirit come out as well (blood). The diagonal gesture of the spear determines the diagonal crossing of the little room-heart, and therefore it breaks the six actions of Evil that try to reduce the space of our inner Freedom.
Adam called "uoma" (woman: in Italian man is *uomo* and woman is *donna.* By putting an "a" at the end of *uomo*, it becomes feminine), the one that was extracted from him and later on he will call her "mother of all living beings" (Gn 3,20). Mariam is called "Woman" and "Mother" and to Her Jesus entrust the community of believers.

[1722] Therefore, John declares to be the "disciple that Jesus loved" and he testifies his testimony: John the Baptist offers the first one, to the Law; John-Lazarus offers the second one, to Love. The first one "prepares" us for the coming of the Christ (and esoterically it corresponds to the so-called current of "Arthur"); the second one preserves the gift (and it corresponds to the current of the Grail). This testimony of John is an aspect of the Grail, the Grail under the cross. What was expressed in John 1,6-9 is now being completed. The initiate "John" is united with "the being John", for everyone that reached this step, just like Jesus united with the Being Christ.

[1723] Everything was already fulfilled at verse 19,28. This was only a sign for men. The external Grail is a path towards the Christ, a sign of how to reach him, but not the experience of the Christ. Let's remember the indication of R. Steiner according to which the Grail (from one point of view) is formed by the image of the cross, in which the man (vertical axis), the animal (horizontal axis), the plant (again the vertical axis, but upside down compared to man) and Earth (in which the cross is being planted in) are being woven. This indicates the action of renewal in all the Kingdoms brought with the Golgotha.

[1724] The terrestrial forces of the crushing do not enter within the Jesus. See verse 19,33. No bone needed to be broken on the lamb of the Exodus either (Num 9,12).

36. And again another Writing says: *We will look (opsomai) towards the One that they pierced*[1725].

THE JESUS PLACED IN THE MEMORY (Mt 27,57-61; Mc 15,422-47; Lc 23,50-55)

37. And, after these things, Joseph, the one from Arimathea[1726], being a disciple of the Jesus, but a secret one[1727], for the fear of the Jewish people, he prayed (*erotao*) to the Pilate to bring up above[1728] (*airo*) the living[1729] body of the Jesus[1730]. And the Pilate approved. So they came and brought him up.

[1725] The passage is Zc 13,1 and it goes like this: *"In that day there will be a gushing spring to wash away sin and impurities"*.
Jesus' persecutors, for their own salvation, sooner or later will have to look (internally) towards the One that they pierced (see Apocalypse 1,7).

[1726] Let's remember that Joseph is a name given to the ones who "grow in God". He was an initiate in Arimathea, which means "*rama*" (city located on a hill) and *"theos"* (God), and therefore *city* or location *of the inspirational consciousness.* Joseph was also Jesus' uncle and therefore he could practice a blood rite to have the body back. Joseph of Arimathea and the Pilate meet on the etheric plane, which is a plane determined by the crowd-coil with which the Pilate surrounded Jesus. Joseph is therefore asking that the crowd- coil is released so that it would let go of the physical body of Jesus.
Let's also remember that Joseph of Arimathea is represented with a turban on his head: the turban that he was always connected to which connects him to the union between Bride and Groom in the dimension of the Infinite One…

[1727] Joseph of Arimathea was a member of the Sanhedrin and the term "secret" indicates that maybe it was the second step of the Persian Initiation, the "Hidden" or "Secret".

[1728] To bring into glory, in the Father. Just like Joseph raised the Little Child so that the Logos could descend on him, now Joseph of Arimathea raises the Incorruptible Body of the Jesus so that it can be seen by the Father and it can be prepared for Resurrection.

[1729] This "body" is the *soma*, which is the body permeated with life in contrast with the *toma*, the dead body.

[1730] With the article. The Christ is always within him, they are one.

38. And Nicodemus[1731] also came, which at the first he came near the Jews at night[1732], and he had with him a mixture of myrrh and aloe[1733] which weighed about one hundred pounds[1734].

[1731] He was one of the head Pharisees and he sympathized with Jesus, in whom he hoped for a religious renewal. He judges opposite of the Law the sentence given to Jesus, and he wants to honor the body. The Nicolaiti of the Apocalypse (*nike*) (they are a group, without the individual I) are won by the mass (*laos*) of what is being agitated in the human subconscious. In Nicodemus (he is an individual, an individual I), the forces of freedom present in the man are the ones that win ego over.
The Greek language does not support the different interpretation that we find in the aspect group-individual.

[1732] Nicodemus had already met with Jesus in the "astral" (John 3,9). Nicodemus had asked for the "birth from Above", now he is no longer doubtful instead he is able to make his Faith in Jesus public. To him and Joseph of Arimathea, Jesus gifts His body that will resurrect in just a little bit. Nicodemus will then be able to testify that the "birth from Above" is possible. He will write one of his Gospel in which he will describe the descent of the Jesus into the Underworld for the liberation of everyone. This described descending also corresponds to the descending that happens in him and in humanity.

[1733] This mixture was not being used for embalming but instead it would be used to perfume the alcove (Prv 7,17) and the clothes of the king-groom (Sal 45,9): without knowing it, they get Him ready for the sepulcher bed, to lay on the Grail Cup.

[1734] Almost 17 kg. One pound formed by 12 ounces, therefore 100x12 ounces, and therefore the continuity of existence (represented by the 12, the divine Light, the number of the celestial things) is being brought to the number of the mysteries of matter (the 100). The myrrh is a vegetable exudate that is esotherically defined as "fire that drips", it is the therapeutic action in Michael's path, which is the therapy through the spiritual work of consciousness, that brings the Spirit to directly act within us; the aloe is a vegetable of Light. It is"liquid light" and it supports the therapeutic action in Raphael's path, the old way of the remedies and the pharmaceuticals. Their synthesis brings the renewal and the union of all therapy, and it manifests with the Resurrection.
It does not refer to a physical anointment (like the one of the Pious Women on Sunday morning). They are spiritual anointments. By talking about oils and aromas, we refer to what is transformed in the sacrum (in the physical-liquid seminal plane), offered and brought by the Memory, which is as spiritual nourishment to the pituitary gland so that it can irradiate its Light in the whole Incorruptible Body. Therefore there is a male contribution on Friday evening from Joseph of Arimathea and Nicodemus (John 19,38-39; in John nothing is said about what the women bring). In Matthew (27-61), on Friday evening, the Mary Magdalen and the Mary Salomonic secretly worked in front of the grave (therefore they were elaborating forces: this represents the female contribution). In Mark (15,47), the Mary Magdalen and the Mary Salomonic spiritually saw where he was being put (Friday night). On Sunday morning, the same women (16,1) brought the aromas, which represent the air-astral element, while the oil represents Fire… In Luke, on Friday night, the pious women "prepared" the aromas and the anointments (23,56); on Sunday morning (24,1) the Pious Women brought the prepared aromas to the Memory…
A medical note: when we rub in a substance, it enters up to the central part (bone-darkness-hate) of the organism through the current of the nerve, which represents the Head-Golgotha and the Tree of the Knowledge of Good and Evil…

39. Therefore they grabbed (*lambano*) the living[1735] body of the Jesus and they wrapped it in linen with the aromas[1736], as it was a Jewish tradition to embalm[1737] this way.

[1735] This "body" is the *soma*, which is the body permeated with life in contrast with the *toma*, which is the dead body.

[1736] The linen represents the forces of Light (the seed of linen has the shape of a star), and the aromas support the development of the Upper Limbs. This fabric of linen is the Holy Shroud. The shroud (which represents the material "veil" put on the Incorruptible Body) was "paid" by Pilate, so that it could be put on Jesus' body to "veil" the body and therefore the whole event (this was the condition that he had to give the body to Joseph of Arimathea). Let's remember that the Jesus was already free of the shroud-veil from when he was captured at the Gethsemane (Mc 14,52)..
If we read a little deeper into this, Jesus is not being "anointed", but the aromas are being put together with the linen. From this we understand that the only anointment that He received was the one from the Silent Mariam (John 12,3).

[1737] In reality, the Jewish people wouldn't embalm the dead instead they would surround them with aromas to purify the environment. They believed that by doing so, the path post mortem would be easier. Embalming represents the fall of the mysteries of Death, operated by Baal in Egypt, and the Jewish people believed in this. In the embalming, the one who is dead is being "held back" by secret bonds from going through his path of getting out of the body, so that he cannot ask spiritual questions to the worlds. But the Jesus, is not being subjected to this satanic practice.

40. And in the location where he was crucified there was a garden, and within the garden[1738]

[1738] This garden reminds us of the one of Eden, in which Adam was yet to be corrupted.

a new memory[1739], in which no one had yet been put

[1739] The word "sepulcher" also has a deeper meaning. In Hebrew, the word "memory" is equal to "male", and with this last word, we mean the one who internally becomes "male", which means that he "remembers" his inner skies: his divine origin: with the deposition of the Jesus, a "new" memory comes for humanity, the one of resurrection. The fact of "remembering one's divine origin" means to "know" that God exists and that we are part of Him, we belong to Him, we are called to go back to Him and therefore we need to make His will. To reject this is the sin of impiety.

So know we have another question come up: why are Lazarus (first) and then Jesus (at a higher level) put in the sepulcher-memory. The "first memory" (connected to the experience of Lazarus-John) is the one of the divine origin in man, and therefore it is a memory of "descending". The second memory is the one that is happening now: the resurrection of Jesus. Therefore this is a memory in "ascension". In what is about to happen, we can find the key to understand the whole path, the spiritual experience that they went through with those particular conditions.

From R.Steiner we understand (second lecture of the cycle: Inner Nature of Man and Life Between Death and New Birth) that to fulfill spiritual investigations that are particularly deep, it is necessary to leave the physical body with the soul. To do so, there are two ways: to simply get out in space and begin to live within it by "looking" at the physical body from there (the so-called "astral travel"), or we can do so by going deeper within our selves (and this is the "ability to be in one body but in two different places" that is brought to us by the Etheric Christ). This way we reconnect to the experiences of the soul that are more similar to the ones of the spiritual experience, and we can try to reconnect to them through memory.

By the fact that our soul preserves thoughts and perceptions, we transform our inner life into something that is spiritual since within us, something that is absolutely soul like-spiritual develops. The rising of the clairvoyant imaginative consciousness is similar to the soul content that is the patrimony of memory within us. Therefore, it is about rising, from spiritual regions, something that is behind our memory. In between memories, spiritual images begin to rise of something that we used to not know. Another path consists in going backwards through our life's path up to re-entering that spiritual world from which we descended to incarnate. In this way, we exit space and we find ourselves just within time. Instead of "in and out", we have "before and after" and this path is a much higher path to the spiritual entrance.

Along this path, we find the spiritual and great figure of the **ideal man** who is formed in the image of God. This ideal man is like a temple and it is the religion of the Gods. Here we can perceive the actions of the helpers of humanity, of the divine beings that wove within our being, within our soul, and that help us through the process of incarnation. So now we are at a place where we cannot go forward, the divine forces are within us and one voice is tempting us by telling us to not reincarnate once again on earth in another flesh body. Instead, it tells us to follow, with our being, the action of the gods that formed us and penetrate more and more the worlds of the spirit. If we follow this luciferic temptation, then we exit the path that will take us to the great ideal of humanity. We can follow the temptation and enter the world of the spirit with our imperfections and there they would be corrected into perfection. But by doing this, we need to give up the dispositions that we carry within us and that we still haven't developed into the direction that takes us to the great human ideal: we would have to give up to what we could become as men (the complete freedom and love). By doing so, we would become non-religious in front of the world of the spirit.

This is the moment in which Lucifer has the maximum power over man, he can make us forget what our great human ideal is. Therefore a battle between Lucifer and the gods for the human soul begins that gently pushes us to the great human ideal. The result of this battle is that the primordial image of man, the image that he formed thanks to his terrestrial existences, is being projected from time into space: it is attracted (like a magnet) in the spatial existence.

In this moment we also perceive the attraction to the future parents: we become in tuned with the spatial sphere. This way, we overcome the luciferic temptation that wants to keep us in the spiritual spheres and the protection consists in covering ourselves with matter (body). Helping us to descend to the world of sense, the helping spirits can support us in the evolutionary process.

To penetrate the terrestrial existence, man needs to elaborate his brain and his nervous system first. He accomplishes this work before descending in collaboration with the spirits of Wisdom, and then, on earth, the wisdom that he will minister will be like the reflection of this cosmic Wisdom. Here on earth, we are separated by the action of the spirits and the Guardian of the Threshold that they provide for us so that we do not reconnect to them before we are ready, which means to protect us so that Lucifer cannot win us over with temptation. These spirits of Wisdom give to us enough of their action of wisdom that we can begin our path or re ascension.

If we would speed the process up, we would find Lucifer tempts us so that we remain in the spiritual world with our imperfections and without developing our dispositions (which are still imperfect). We would loose humanity's goal: the great human ideal. Here on earth, surrounded by material things, we can receive new impulses towards the future goals of humanity from the divine spirits that can instill within us the forces so that, after we are dead, we can push ourselves a little bit more towards the great human ideal.

By going into space through the **door of memory,** we can be aware of how the divine beings act and dominate within us, we can permeate ourselves with the divine and acquire the right sense of the divine that operates within us.

Now the soul, with all of this, knows, perceives, feels, thinks, wants and is aware that it arose from a soul-like sphere that is deeper, from the sphere within her that resides in the divine, that flows in the current of time but it rises with the divine: we are born with God.

[1740].

41. So because of the Parasceve[1741] of the Jewish people, since the memory was close, (was) where they put the Jesus[1742].

[1740] This means that others, after Him, will descend.
So we have these parallels:

- Bethlehem is of a calcareous nature (Ahrimanic Fall); the Golgotha is of calcareous nature (victory over the ahrimanic death).
- Jesus is born from Mariam and Joseph; Jesus dies between Mariam and John (which is the Joseph- the one who grows in God- and reached the step of John),
- Jesus descended from the Father through the door of the constellation of Cancer (rib cage); now he descends to the Father who is in the depths of the Underworld and he dies going through the door of the wound of the rib cage,
- Jesus is born by crossing the stars called ox and little donkey; he dies between the two thieves spirits: Lucifer and Ahriman,
- Joseph grabs him from Mariam and "*he gave birth to the son of her the firstborn; he wrapped him spiraling cloths and he turned him to the sky*" (Lk 2,7); Mariam Magdalen and Joseph of Arimathea will anoint him in light by the oil.
- Mother is the "virgin" breast of Mariam; new "mother" is the "new" sepulcher,
- His birth is announced by the Angels (Lk 2,11); His resurrections is announced by the Angels to the Magdalen,
- Jesus descended from the terrestrial Heaven, which is the Garden of Eden in which he lived (as a Nathanic Soul) without being subjected to the Fall; Jesus is being put in a garden and the Magdalen will confuse him for a "gardener".

[1741] Third reference to the Easter (the "old" Easter). Now we are at the new Easter, the fourth, the one of the resurrection.

[1742] For them Jesus belongs to the past.
It is important to see how in John there is no mention of the horrible suffering that Jesus needed to go through. It is like if the things that are happening to his are being contemplated from up above, with the detachment of one who sees them with the eyes of the Spirit and who understands the cosmic importance. Let's remember that the Gospel of John is "written" for the Angels.

THE MAGDALEN, PETER AND THE OTHER DISCIPLE AT THE MEMORY (Mt 28,1-10. Mc 1-11, Lc 24,1-12)

1. In the (day) One of the Saturdays[1743], Mariam the Magdalen[1744] came in the morning, while it was still dark[1745], to the memory[1746]: and she saw (*blepo*)[1747] the stone lifted[1748] from the door, from the memory.

[1743]It corresponds to Sunday morning. Saturdays are the combination of the days (holidays) dedicated by the people of Israel to the connection with the Creating Spirit. The "one" is being determined, which is the spiritual value of the One, of the new path opened by the Jesus for a new Unity with God. In Genesis (Gn 1,5) they talk about the "First day" to indicate the beginning of the process, of the creation that comes from God. Now we are in front of a new One, a new process thanks to which we go back to God.
The "sixth day" ends, the formation of the new Man (chapter 2,1-19,46) and the "seventh day" begins, the re-ascension to the Father.

[1744] Just like the first period of the sixth day begins with the nuptial scene (the wedding at Cana), now we have a new nuptial: between the Risen One and Mariam Magdalen (His Community) in the reconquered garden of Eden.
Magdalen in Hebrew is *Migedal* which means "tower" but it also contains the root *meged* which means "the best". It is a city on the Sea of Galilee and it represents the constellation of Taurus-throat. According to the tradition, she is the Silent Mariam that washed Jesus' feet: she is searching for the Light that went missing once Jesus descended to the Underworld.
The Magdalen in the new Community of the Messiah represents the "Bride".

[1745] We are at the dawn of a new era, but the forces of darkness are not yet completely defeated. This is another reason why the Risen One will encourage the Magdalen to not touch him: the new Easter is not completed yet.

[1746] Usually translated as "sepulcher", in reality the term *mnemeion* indicates the monument (funeral) that "reminds" of the past perfect. The word "monument" indicates to recreate unity (the "*mono*" with the "mind"). The "memory" is the state of consciousness of the Spiritual Self, in which the Time is reunited (past, present, future) in the Light. The stone is "lifted", the chakra with 2 petals of the forehead is open in a spiritual level.

[1747] This looking is *blepo*, which means to see with the soul.

[1748] Also "taken away". If it would have been in its place, it would have meant Jesus' definite death.
This stone is the chakra with 2 petals (the chakra of the intellectual initiation, or of thought) that is being reactivated: now the door is open. In Hebrew, stone is *even*, which is a word formed by *av,* the Father, and *ben*, the Son. Therefore it is the symbol of the man in which the reawakening of the consciousness happened. The reawakened man become Son of the Father.
The stone is lifted by the redeemed Lucifer, the new Paraclete represented by the "good" thief.

2. Therefore she ran and she got to Simon Peter[1749], and the other disciple, which the Jesus loved in a brotherly way[1750]m and she says (*lego*) to them: "They raised the Lord from the memory[1751], and we do not know[1752] where they out him!"

3. The Peter and the other disciple exited[1753] and they went to the memory.

4. The two ran together, and the other disciple ran faster than the Peter[1754], and he reached the memory first.

1749 The Magdalen is talking to the man "Simon" that is about to become "the" Peter. Within this, Peter represents the humanity at the threshold of the spiritual world. In verse 18,15, it is also Peter that enter the garden (the Threshold) of the palace of the High Priest. But there he failed his test.

1750 The problem of which disciple "who is spiritually loved" and who is not "spiritually loved" comes up. He is John, whom Jesus said would have (with the others) to become his "friend" is he was going to do what he order them to do (John 15,14).
The two represent the active Faith (Peter) and the contemplative Faith (John).
Peter will be called to this step in the passage 21,15 when the Risen One will ask him: *"Simon, of John, do you "spiritually" love me more than them?"*. As we know, Peter will respond that he loves him in "brotherly way". At the third reply, the Risen One will ask him to follow him, which means to walk to reach the goal of the spiritual Christic Love…
In his Gospel, John narrates about five contrasts, contrasts of position, between Peter and John (the disciple that Jesus loved). The first one is at the Last Supper (John 13,24) when Peter shows that he is not in the spiritual Love; the second one is at the capturing of Jesus when John enters the atrium willing to go down the same road as Jesus while Peter waits outside (John 18, 15), the third one is when they will run together to the sepulcher and John will believe in the resurrection (John 20,2), the fourth one is at the fishing when he will be the one to recognize the Risen One (John 21,7), the fifth one is the famous "feed my lambs" when Peter will declare to not spiritually love Jesus (John 21,20).

1751 Not the Lord (the Jesus) is "lifted", which means that he is free of everything that happened - formality, blood, people: a new "memory" has been born.

1752 The plural "we" indicates that the Magdalen is not talking about herself and her spiritual forces and higher developed components, with which she was not able to grasp the new dimension reached by the Jesus Christ.

1753 Now it is the "Peter" that is acting, and not the "Simon". He "exited" from the body to fulfill a spiritual research. The Magdalen had already fulfilled her research, and now the two disciples are investigating Jesus' new dimension.

1754 The article underlines the spiritual value of the action of the Peter.

5. And overlooking[1755], he saw (*blepo*) the linen laying down, (*keimai*), but he did not enter[1756].

6. Simon Peter also arrived, following[1757] him, and he entered the memory[1758], and he spiritually[1759] saw (*theorao*) the linens[1760] laying[1761] on the ground,

7. And the shroud[1762], that was on his head, was not laying (*keimai*) with the linens, but independently[1763] wrapped in one place[1764].

1755 He becomes aware of the signs of life (with the face, the location of consciousness), of the new dimension towards which Jesus directs himself; but he still cannot comprehend how he won death over. To do so, he needs to bow, since the access to the sepulchers are always of lower dimension (so that they can close it with a stone that isn't too big). This represents the "tight path", the path of the consciousness of the I, the "eye of the needle" to go through to enter the new Christic Initiation.

1756 Probably to have a moment of reflection to prepare himself to what he was about to see.

1757 Simon Peter is "behind", therefore he feel safer since he can follow a guide: in this case it's the disciple that is loved by the Jesus.

1758 Peter shows himself to be a precursor (the impulsive) amongst the Twelve, and the Jesus will gift him the keys to the Kingdom. Let's remember that in Hebrew, Peter is said *Petros'* which means "the one who opens": even now he is "opening the path for the others".

1759 He sees as a clairvoyant or prophet (from the Greek *theorao).*

1760 Let's remember that linen is a fiber that is strongly weaved with forces of light.

1761The cloths were in the location where the Body was put but the Body is no longer there, it dissolved and left the cloths empty.

1762 The shroud was a type of big handkerchief that would wrap the head so that it would support the jaw and it would be tied above the head. It was a sign of death; whereas the linen (sheets) were a spousal sign. This determined the image of the petals of the chakra with 8 petals (also said 100 petals) opened (the edges of the bow) at the top pf the head. After the opening of the chakra with 2 petals (the stone, connected to the forces of Jupiter), now the one with 8 petals is opening up, connected to Saturn. The path to the Zodiac is open, for the celestial headquarters of the forces that support the Body of Resurrection, for the House of the Father.

1763 Also "with a different quality" and "differently". Also in the man, after death, the body (remembered with the linens) and the head (shroud) fulfill different paths. The folded linens represent the nuptials and the descending to the underworld (in the Earth) that the Jesus is fulfilling.

1764 Or "position". The shroud enters in the unity, in the One. It seems like the shroud wraps the head of Jesus and this needs to be explained. The shroud, put in a particular position, indicates that Jesus is completely united with the Father, which is the Creating Thought, the One par excellence.

8. So the other disciple who arrived to the memory first also entered, and he saw (*eidon*)[1765], and he had faith (*episteusa)*[1766];

9. He did not know the Writing: "*He needs to rise again from the dead*[1767]".

10. Therefore the disciple came back again amongst each other[1768].

APPEARANCE OF THE MAGDALEN

11. But Mariam was standing outside of the memory, calling the spirit[1769]. While she was calling the spirit, she overlooked[1770] the memory.

[1765] From the Greek *eidein* which means the "physical" vision after the death of the etheric one: this is because it is the past of *horao,* which is the etheric vision. From this comes the "believing" (in contrast to Peter).

[1766] Now John "believes". He is in tuned with the Love and the Life of Jesus and therefore he understands and believes in the resurrection. For the difference between "having faith" and "believing", see John 2,11.

[1767] The passage in Isaiah 26,19-21. Everything was already fulfilled on the cross. The Jesus fulfilled the next events as signs for humanity, to confirm the Writing. With the term "from dead", it is referring to the process of Initiation through which we rise again "from" being dead, which means after having experienced the death in life.

[1768] They bring to their consciousness what they spiritually grasped. Mary Magdalen remains near the memory.

THE APPEARANCE OF THE MAGDALEN

[1769] Mary, as a soul, needs the Spirit to show her the way. Her faith is still connected to the external forms, and that is why she was crying because she was believing in an irreparable loss.

[1770] She also becomes aware. Apparently, her looking in the sepulcher-memory makes no sense since she was the one that informed the disciples. Probably now she is trying to "see" in a higher dimension, she is trying to "spiritually" see and she will "see" the two angels.

12. And she spiritually[1771] sees (*theorao*) two angels, that were sitting in shining[1772] (clothes), One near the head and One near the feet[1773], where the body[1774] of the Jesus had lain.

13. And they say (*lego*)[1775] to her: "Woman[1776], Why are you calling the spirit?" She says (*lego*) to them: "They lifted my Lord and I do not know where they put him".

14. These things being said (*eipon)*, she looked towards the things behind[1777] and she spiritually sees (*theoreo*) the Jesus who was standing[1778] and she did not know it was Jesus[1779].

[1771] The same seeing of Peter, it is *theorao*, the spiritual vision through the third eye. The passage reminds us of the Canticle of the Canticles in which the bride looks for the groom (Ct 3,2).

[1772] The color of the purification of the soul from the luciferic forces; the victory over death.

[1773] From R. Steiner we learn that in Matthew and Mark, a young man appears who is the same one who ran away in the moment of the capturing of the Jesus at the Gethsemane (Mk 14,51-52),therefore it is the entity of the Christ itself that is manifesting to the Pious Women. Always R. Steiner shows us how, in the moment of death, the clairvoyant grasps these two figures at the head and at the feet of the terrestrial body of the dead, which represent the detachment from the subtle bodies.
Magdalen will grasp this last aspect.

[1774] This "body" is the *soma*, which is the body permeated with life, in contrast with the *toma*, the dead body.

[1775] The Risen One appears first to the women and then to the men, this is because women's brains are usually less hardened than men's; they are more open than men's brains.

[1776] Let's remember that this nickname corresponds to the redemption of the feminine fallen part, the redemption of Eve.

[1777] It is an "internal" turning, a change in consciousness. Behind us, behind the head, there is the presence of the world of the Spirit.

[1778] Which means standing up to indicate that the Resurrection happened.

[1779] She sees "the" Jesus and she does not understand that it is "Jesus". She sees the Risen One, the Incorruptible Body ascended to Body of Resurrection, and she does not recognize his identity with the man Jesus that she knew. Now she is in front of Jesus united with the freed Adam with the Being Mariam and John within him.

15. Jesus says *(lego)*: "Woman[1780], why are you calling the spirit[1781]? Who are you looking for[1782]?" Believing he was the gardener[1783], she says (*lego*) to him: "Sir, if you were the one who held him in your hands (*bastazo*)[1784], tell me where you put[1785] him: and I will bring him above (*airo*)[1786].

[1780] Here is the fourth "Woman".

[1781] The Risen One again repeats the question of the angels to indicate that there is no reason to cry. Also the Gethsemane, the Jesus asked the same question to the soldiers that came to get him.

[1782] With these two questions, He tries to reawaken the consciousness within the Magdalen to the new dimension to which Jesus ascended.

[1783] Also as the Risen One, Jesus is dressed in a simple way, in a humble way and he is not covered in lavish cloths.
The gardener, who is the one who takes care of the Garden of Eden, and therefore the uncorrupted Adam. He is the New Adam. Another translation of the term *kepuros* is "orchardist". This term resounds with the Latin word "*orior*", which means "to be born". The orchardist is the one who takes care of the plants that are born into life. In Greek, "new plant" is said *neo-phiton*, which is the one who goes down the spiritual path. The Magdalen sees the orchardist, the one who takes care of the birthing of the Children. Let's remember the connection between this garden, the one of the Gethsemane and the Garden of Eden.

[1784] She feared the living *soma*, the lifted one and the one supported by the above. The Son of the man, represented by Jesus, is completely united with the Christ and he becomes "I Am".

[1785] At the Fall, God asks Adam "Where are you?" (Gn 3,9), and now Magdalen asks, "Where did you put him?". It is the same phrase, only now it is the man (the Magdalen) that does not find, does not recognize, the Risen One.

[1786] For the work that Joseph of Arimathea had already done.

16. The Jesus says (*lego*) to her: " Mariam[1787]!" Turning around[1788] she says (*lego*) to him in Hebrew: "Rabbouni" (who is said Teacher[1789]).

[1787] The strength in his voice makes it so that the Magdalen recognizes him; it is like saying that the voice, the Logos, remained the same between the terrestrial Jesus and the Risen One, it is like saying that the same Logos lives within them.
From this moment on, Mary Magdalen is being called this way by the Risen One and the Evangelist. This indicates a new spiritual level of the Magdalen: Mary becomes "Mariam". This is not just a simple difference of pronunciation (from the Greek to Hebrew). The adding of the ending M esotherically recalls the balance between Thinking, Feeling and Wanting, and it also resounds with the constellation of Aquarius, which is the constellation that brings us the forces of the Angel and of the Initiation within the Higher I.
The level of Mariam indicates the presence of all of the spiritual Love within the soul-woman, up to the Love of the Father. It is the seventh step of the soul's Initiation. The Magdalen needs to be penetrated by the sacred force of the Word to recognize Risen One, the Risen One that was manifesting himself in the Incorruptible Body of Resurrection.

[1788] She no longer looks at the sepulcher, the memory, now she is in the present, in the Meeting with the Risen One.

[1789] *Didaskalos*, which is the aspect Zarathustra in the Jesus, but this "being said" is meaning that in reality, it is not like this. The Rabbouni is connected to the aspect of Buddha within the Jesus. Now Adam, Zarathustra, Buddha, Christ: all is One in the "Jesus", the Risen One. The Rabbi is the Judaic teacher, the Rabbouni is the new Teacher: the Risen One.
It is important to say that the Magdalen still does not comprehend the deep nature of the Jesus. Thomas also will have the same problem, but he will understand when he will say "My Lord and My God" (John 20,28).

17. The Jesus says (*lego*) to her: "Do not touch[1790] me, I have yet to ascend to the Father[1791]. Start walking (*poreuomai*) towards my brothers[1792] and tell them: here, I ascend towards my Father and your Father[1793], and my God and your God[1794]".

18. Mary the Magdalen arrives to the disciples and she announces[1795]: "I saw (*horao*) the Lord and he told (*eipon*) me these things".

[1790] In the sense of "grabbing", "taking". In Matthew he talks about "not grabbing the feet", and a more physical vision is being captured within this moment, since the Risen One was inclined to "flutter" on Earth. The spiritual aspect is to be seen in the fact that the Risen Again is reborn. He is born from the Spirit, and therefore he is "generated by the One". If a feminine element (which is of the soul) would have touched him, it would have taken away his spiritual forces, and therefore He would have lost his spiritual wholeness born from the One… Additionally, He still did not complete the process of resurrection (which lasts three days and three nights) and so He still needs to purify the cosmos from the luciferic Fall, which is an action that He is about to fulfill by "ascending to the Father".
The Baptist was "born from a woman" and therefore he was the bearer of the masculine spiritual element and the feminine soul element. The task of the "born from the Two" is to announce the coming of the "born from the One" (and John announced Jesus, just like the Magdalen announces the Risen One"..
Through this we are witnessing a metamorphosis of the Nathanic Soul: Jesus, freeing the fallen Adam, completes his mission, and he will become the bearer of the Christ for humanity in eternity. The Being Mariam, from nurturing the things of the heart (Announcement), becomes the announcer: now Mariam-Sophia can announce the Salvation. The Being of John Baptist participates to the Resurrection of Lazarus, by allowing part of his solar-Abel nature to flow through him (the remaining will act as a Crowd with the Jesus). The Lazarus was Cain and therefore bearer of the lunar current of thought. The union of these two currents, of the two sons of Adam, determines the reforming of the One. And this One has the name of John…
We now have the new Adam, The Risen One, the new Eve, Mariam, and the new Son ("see your mother", John 19,27). With John: the new humanity begins, which overcame the enmeshment of the world.

[1791] He needs to ascend to the Father to receive, as a man completely spiritualized, the fullness of his own Glory since he donated all of himself for the spiritual evolution of humanity. After that, He will only be visible for the spiritual vision.

[1792] Let's remember that in verse 20,2 the "disciple who was brotherly loved" had already appeared and then, by believing, he ascends to the level of "John". Wwe can hypothesize that his brothers were all ready to go from "caring" for the spiritual world (in Greek *fileo*) to the loving of the spiritual world (in Greek *agapeo*): the believing.
The Father of Jesus is now the Father of the disciples.

[1793] For the ones who are brothers of the Risen One, the Father is unique, while for the "normal" humanity, the Father is a "murderer and fake from the very beginning" (John 8,44).

[1794] Here is the new pact between the Divine and humanity. Now with His Sacrifice, He brought all of humanity to his same rank: the one of Sons of God, of "My God and Your God".

[1795] From the Greek *angellusa*, Mariam becomes a messenger, like an Angel.

THE JESUS APPEARS TO THE DISCIPLES[1796] (Lc 24, 36-49; Mc 16, 14-18)

19. Being the evening of the day[1797], that one, the One of the Saturdays[1798], and since the doors[1799] were closed, where the disciples[1800] were for fear of the Jewish people, the Jesus came and he stood straight in the middle[1801] and he said (*lego*) to them: "Peace[1802] to you!"

[1796] It is important to see how John does not mention the apparition of the Risen One to the two disciples of Emmaus, maybe because John had already grasped the Glory of the Risen One in the moment in which he was looking at the sepulcher and he "believed", which means he reached the security of Faith (John 20,8).

[1797] The darkness falls on them, and fear and doubt are still present within them.

[1798] Which is Sunday. It is the beginning of the new spiritual era: now the creation has been completed and the New Alliance has started.

[1799] We are probably still in the famous "chamber on the upper level", of the cenacle, and so it indicates the higher spiritual dimension. The doors are closed because only the ones who received the Washing of the Feet can be in there. The Risen One enters it with His Body of Resurrection, which is the non-material physical Body that He was able to rarefy and condensate as he wanted to and this shows the power that He reached on matter.

[1800] They regained the article: the New Alliance in the Love has begun.

[1801] He places himself in the center of the new Community: this one is founded on Love, and it dissolves all of their fears by giving them Peace.

[1802] Peace follows war, therefore the test is done. The Risen One, giving them peace, gifts them the forces to overcome the inner difficulties and sufferings that come with not being in a state of Grace with Him. The peace indicates a condition in which the Christ acts within us, up to the physical body. The unity has been re-established and it bears fruit; these fruits are the condition of peace. This fruit-Word contains the new seeds that will be sowed, and they will multiply according to the indication given by God and Adam. Let's remember that in Hebrew, peace is *salom* which means "accomplishment/fulfillment".

20. And, having said (*eipon*) this, he showed his hands[1803] and his side[1804]. The disciples rejoiced (*chairo*)[1805], and welcomed (*idein*)[1806] the Lord[1807].

21. So he said (*eipon*) to them once again[1808]: "Peace to you[1809]! Like the Father sent[1810] me, I will also send[1811] you".

22. And having said (*eipon*) this, he blew within (them)[1812] and he said (*lego*) to them: "Take (in the spiritual plane; *lambano*) the Holy Spirit[1813]".

[1803] They represent the Holy Spirit and the Son that He will gift them. Since the Incorruptible Body completely united with the physical body, the wounds inflicted to the Jesus are also engraved on the Risen Incorruptible Body.

[1804]Where the spear entered, between the third and fourth rib of his right side, the rib taken out from Adam to form Eve. In the rib-cage wound, the Apostles can "see" the New Adam, the re-establishment of the original unity. The side and the hands represent the birth of the New Adam in the Holy Spirit and in the Son within us.

[1805] The Joy comes to life in the soul, when it conforms to the Spirit. Before, the Risen One acted directly in the soul (appearance to the Magdalen), and now it acts in the soul of men.

[1806] This to see is *idontes,* which is *idein* which means to grasp the laws and the forces of the *Logos.*

[1807] The Spiritual Self that the Risen One brought to them.

[1808] By repeating this sentence, the Risen One imprinted it on their etheric body.

[1809] When he left them he promised: "*I will leave you Peace, I gift you my peace" (*John 14,27).

[1810] " The One who's been sent" is plenipotentiary for his task. "The one sent" by the Father is the Son.

[1811] The "mandate" has a limited power for a determinate task. It is the Holy Spirit aspect of the manifestation of the divine task.

[1812] He blows within them, inside of them, which means that the action of the "blow" acts within us. The verb that is being used (insufflate) is the same one used in Genesis when God "blew" in Adam's nostrils the blow of love (in Hebrew *hahav*) which gave him life (Gn 2,7). It is important to see how the blow takes place in the nostrils since they are directly connected to the brain (freedom), and it gives this through the heart (love)… With this blow, the Light that was weaved within him also moves, and this Light is the one of the Incorruptible Body that the Risen One is now gifting to the Apostles so that it can act as an "inoculum" on the Incorruptible Body of the Apostles…
Let's remember that this is the Spirit of verse 6,69: the "Holy Spirit of the God". Already back then, the Apostles were able to perceive the presence of a new Spirit, created by Jesus as a man-God and that could be defined as "the Holy Spirit of Jesus" (or the Spirit of the Spirit of God). This Spirit is not being left to humanity by Jesus: this is the physical body permeated by the Incorruptible Body and then again individualized from the I Am. Now this process has been completed.

[1813] The disciples receive what they grasped of the Risen One: the aspect Holy Spirit, "His" Holy Spirit": the Spirit of the Spirit of God… it is without article, and therefore it is the Holy Spirit of the Holy Trinity.

23. The mistakes (*amartia*)[1814] of some, that you will put in the light, will be put in the light[1815] for them; and (the ones) of some, that you will dominate[1816], will be dominated[1817] (by them)".

THOMAS CONVINCED

24. And Thomas, One of the Twelve[1818], the so-called Dydimus[1819], was not with them when Jesus came.

25. Therefore, the other disciples said (*lego*) to him: "We saw (*horao*) the Lord". And he said (*eipon*) to them: "Unless I will grasp (*idein*)[1820] in my hands the sign of the nails, and I will put my finger[1821] in his hand, and I will put my hand on his side, I will not believe (*pisteusete*)[1822].

1814 They are the mistakes, the faults, that came from the Fall of man.

1815 The mistakes is being put in the light by the disciples with their own presence (like the "almost" whip of Jesus when the merchants at the Temple ran away on their own). Therefore, the person that has within himself the mistake can become aware of it, make it conscious and therefore correct himself.

1816 That you will have overcome within yourselves, and so you are testifying this overcoming.

1817 With these words the Risen One entrusts to the disciples the task to act as bearers of inner peace, and having the capability (thanks to the Holy Spirit that they received) to testify and help men.

THOMAS CONVINCED

1818 Now the spiritual representative of the Apostles arrives, while in the previous verses we were speaking of the disciples. The fact that Thomas is the One (number) of the twelve, testifies that in this moment the Apostles are a community and he was about to get lost because he was not there for the first appearance of the Risen One.

1819 It means "Twin". It is the title that Jesus Christ gives to him and, by doing so, he entrusts him the "secrets of the sky and the earth". His Gospel will be the Gospel of discernment.

1820 This seeing is *idein* which means to grasp the laws and the forces of the Logos.

1821 Fingers have a precise meaning: thumb-Venus-head; index finger Jupiter-gallbladder; middle finger-Saturn-spleen/pancreas; ring finger-Sun-liver; little finger-Mercury-heart.

1822 The fact that hands and finger have an article makes us think that he is asking for a spiritual proof. Thomas does not say this because he is lacking faith in the Jesus (he declared to be ready to follow him in the death- John 11,16), but he was afraid that the disciples had fallen in a collective suggestion. For his rank, He believed himself to be able to recognize the reality of an appearance from a suggestion. For the difference between "having faith" and "believe" (see John 1.7).

26. And after eight[1823] days, the disciples were inside[1824] once again and Thomas was with them. The Jesus came, while the doors were closed[1825], and he stood straight in the middle[1826] and he said (*eipon*): "Peace to you![1827]".

27. Therefore he says to the Thomas[1828]: "Bring your finger here and hold (the Logos; *idein*) my hands, and bring your hand, and put it on my side[1829] and do not become incredulous, but become a believer[1830].

28. The Thomas[1831] replies (*apokrinomai*) to him and he says (*eipon*): "The Lord of me and the God of me![1832]".

29. The Jesus says to him: "Because you saw me[1833], you also believed: blessed are the one who do not grasp (*idein*)[1834] me and they have faith (*pisteuo*)[1835].

1823 The number of Mary, the soul of the disciples is completed in her transformation in Spiritual Self. We are in the fullness of the seven days of the new creation: the one operated by the Jesus Christ. The Body of Resurrection insufflated by the Risen One into the disciples, acted.

1824 Which means within the self, united with the Risen One.

1825 The *chakras* are still, and the new Initiation is being prepared, and through it the *chakras* will begin to spin in the opposite direction.

1826 As a new center of them and also as a center of the new rotation of the *chakras.*

1827 This is His greeting.

1828 Now the Risen One is speaking to the spirit present in Thomas.

1829It was prohibited to the Magdalen to touch the Risen One, while Thomas was being invited to do so. This is because the Risen One completed the formation of the new Body of Resurrection. It is important to know that Thomas will not touch him.

1830 It is like saying that Thomas is yet to be one or the other: now he is invited to become a believer (*ginomai*). It means to go from having Faith to believing.

1831 The man replies and as a man he grasps the Christ. Since he is the "One" of the Twelve, now they welcome the Christ.

1832 This expression can also be seen as: "Lord of my I and God of my I", which means "Lord and God who communicates to me the consciousness and the force of being an I according to my true spiritual original nature". Therefore, he was looking for the deep truth of the Jesus.

1833 It is *horao*, the etheric vision.

1834 This seeing is *idein* in the present participle form, and so they are the ones who see and understand the laws and forces of the logos.

1835 During the Supper he said: "Blessed be the one who, without seeing, believes" (John 113,17). Once again we have the topic of believing.

30. And so the Jesus created (*poieo*) many more signs in front of his disciples, which are not written in this book[1836].

31. And these things have been written so that you will believe that Jesus is the Christ, the Son of the God, and so that by believing you will have eternal spiritualLife in his name.[1837]

[1838]

APPEARANCE OF THE JESUS AT THE SEA OF TIBERIAS[1839]

1. After these things, the Jesus manifested himself again[1840] to the disciples on the Sea of Tiberias[1841]. And (he) manifested himself like this:

1836 Esoterically, the "book" is the story of the incarnations of the entelechia of the man. Therefore, John tells us that there is still something more.

1837 This is the only way to pursue the eternal spiritual Life. This is basically an epilogue of the Gospel. What will follow is an opening to other future dimension, a preview of the future.

1838 It might appear odd that there is another chapter after the epilogue that we just read. We can understand from reading the verses how the Gospel of John ended with chapter 20, but now with chapter 21, a new "cycle" begins in the Father since the event happens in Galilee-Father… The mission of the new Community and of the Risen Jesus begins.

APPEARANCE OF THE JESUS AT THE SEA OF TIBERIAS

1839 For a full vision of the multiplications see note at chapter 6.

1840 This indicates that this is a "special" manifestation of the Body of the Risen One. It will not be at closed doors, amongst the community of the disciples. It will be in the open, and therefore this Body has developed stronger forces. Additionally, it is not being precised when this happens: it is a little bit like saying that it can always happen.

1841 We are in the area of Capernaum, which is 3km west of the village in an area which its original name in Greek was *Heptapegon*, which means seven springs. We are in Galilee, the Galilee where Jesus' mission to achieve the level of Risen One started, and now he is coming back to manifest amongst his people, like the One who united the experiences of the Heavens, of the earth and of the Underworlds to gift the forces to begin "their" mission.
We are "on" the lake and therefore in the dimension of the Spirit (the water represents the soul). Only John, amongst the four Evangelists, gives a testimony about this event. This passage represents the transition from the sphere of the Holy Trinity to the sphere of the Holiest Trinity, which is the transition that John made by becoming "Eagle".
The fact that the lake was called "Tiberias", which is the "political" name connected to the Emperor Tiberio, and not of "Galilee", indicates the breaking away from the Judaic world.

2. Simon Peter and Thomas, the so-called Twin, and Nathanial the one from Cana of Galilee, the sons (*hyios*) of Zebedeo and two others from his disciples[1842] were together[1843].

3. Simon Peter tells (*lego*) them: "I am going (*hypago*) to make the helmsman[1844]". They tell (*lego*) him: "We are coming with you". They exited and went up to the little boat[1845], and in the night, that one, they didn't finish anything[1846].

[1842] The disciples are seven, like the seven springs of Capernaum, and the seven is the number that completes the manifestation of an event on Earth.
Peter is still called with his "laic" name. Thomas, with his title, given to him by Jesus, is being called Twin. Nathanial, of whom we remember being "teacher of Israel", and is therefore faithful to the mission of the Chosen People (the fact that his origin in Cana is being mentione, which has never been specified before, connects him to the Mother of Jesus, the Israel, present at the Wedding of Cana and then at the cross and therefore "integrated" in the new community, in the new Israel). Then there are the sons of Zebedeo: John and Jacob whose names are not being given here. From the context, we understand that one of the "nameless" is John the Evangelist, while the spiritual research indicates the Manu, which is the highest entity that prepares the sixth era of culture, the era of the civilization of love, the seventh disciple.

[1843] In the commonality of the hearts.

[1844] Maybe from the difficulty because of the absence of the Jesus, he goes back to practicing his old spiritual responsibility.

[1845] This is the "little boat" of Peter, and then there will be the really little boat of the other ones (verse 8). With the term boat (or little boat), they are referring to the Hebrew *Merkaba,* which is the transformed part of us (or the part of the conquered upper limbs) with which we move in astral world (the sea). It corresponds to what was individually developed by the Son of God. "Boat" is also "ship", which in Italian is *Nave* which contains the *Ave*. it is also (in Italian boat is barca) *Bar-arche'*, the Principle Son. In Greek, it comes from the *Pleiadi* (Michaelian Force). Therefore it is the Principle Son that stays in the soul, from which he have the seed of the Vital Loving Spirit. "*Navis*" in Latin, contains "*avis*" which in latin it means "bird", which is an animal connected to the Old Saturn and therefore to the future Volcano, the conquering of the Man Spirit. There also is "Vis", which is the force of Mary. Therefore "Boat" is the Principle of the Son of God. The "little boat" is individualized. It also corresponds to the "navigating" within the inner waters: from the "water of below" through the spinal fluid up to navigating the cerebrospinal fluid.

[1846] Also in the previous fishing (Lk 5,1), during the night they didn't catch anything. This is because they are still moving in the sphere of the darkness and they do not have enough inner force, the force of the I Am. The night means the absence of Jesus, the Light of the world.

4. And by morning[1847] Jesus[1848] stood on the shore, but the disciples didn't have the clarity (*ghinosko*) that it was Jesus.
5. Therefore the Jesus tells (*lego*) them: "Children[1849], do you not have fish?[1850]". They replied (*apokrinomai*): "No"[1851].

[1847] In the hour of the Sun in Aries… A new era begins, a new phase of consciousness. Now there is the Light of the Risen One.

[1848] The Risen One is standing in the vertical of the I am. He is on the lake shore, just like when he called the first apostles. But now he does not get in the lake, in the soul sphere; he will always stay on the shore. In the whole passage, he manifests himself as Jesus. He speaks like the Jesus (Christ) and he is being recognized like the Lord (the Risen One). This is because men are the ones who need to recognize him, he is always present, but it is fundamental to not act "during the night", without the light of the I Am: He is present, but he is not manifesting himself.

[1849] It is the first time that the Jesus calls the apostles this way. It indicates that having received the Holy Spirit (insufflated by Him), the transformation that will bring them to a new inner birth is taking place within them: the one of the I Am, Sons of the man. When this will happen, then they will become "Sons". This term refers to the fruit that comes to like within us from the union of the right-rational-empirical-masculine part and the left-intuitive-creative-feminine part. To the union right-left, there is another union that is taking place which is above-head-sky and below-metabolism-earth. From these unions, "the little girl" ("the" is masculine in this case and "little girl" is feminine) comes to life to indicate that it is neither masculine or feminine. Mainly, we have three children: the Spiritual Self (the principle of the Holy Spirit in us that comes to life from the transformation of the astral body), the Loving Vital Spirit (the Son within us that comes to life from the transformation of the etheric body) and the Spirit Man (the Father within us who comes to life from the transformation of the physical body).

[1850] They events of the beginning of the Gospel where Jesus calls his first apostles on the Sea of Tiberias are being repeated.
He is the Bread, and the fish is the experience that the I brings. He is asking if they have spiritual nourishment for their souls, if they found anything in their inner search. Please note the sensitivity with which the Risen One speaks to the ones who had abandoned him.

[1851] Since they are in the soul (there are seven of them in the lake), they do not have the spiritual forces, and the question of the Risen One disorients them.

6. He says (*lego*) to them: "Throw the net[1852] towards the right[1853] parts of the little boat[1854] and you will find". And so they threw the net and they didn't have the strength to pull up the majority[1855] of the fish[1856].

[1852] As a combination of the spiritual connections and links, the discernment of the Spirit to grasp the Truth. The net also represents the new woven etheric that united the disciples that developed the new Community of love: now they are called to be active and move together.

[1853] The right part (also of the spinal cord) represents the active spiritual component (also of the man). He invites them to move in the Spirit. The Risen One invites them to be active and to passively wait for the Grace. By moving at night, they were lacking the indication that comes from the Spirit.

[1854] The Hebrew *Merkaba.*

[1855] The ones that precede the multitude (and then the crowd will come); the multitude of the Aries, and then the Zodiac of the Father will follow.

[1856] The fish are also the symbol for what lives in our subconscious and that needs to be brought into our consciousness, from which we have the various miraculous fishing events. The fish scales represent the ahrimanic aspect, and his fowl-smelling inner parts represent the luciferic aspect. Being with no "neck" represents the lacking of words, of the Logos. Let's remember that they were created by God on the fifth day (and therefore they are less evolved) while the other animals were created on the sixth day.

7. The disciple, the one that Jesus spiritually loved, then says (*lego*) to the Peter[1857]: "It is the Lord[1858]". So Simon Peter, having heard[1859] that he is the Lord, wrapped[1860] the band[1861], and he was naked[1862], and he threw himself in the sea[1863].

8. And the other disciples came with the other little boat[1864]. They were not far from the land[1865] but about two hundred[1866] cubits, and they dragged the fish nets.

1857 Let's remember that in his Gospel, John talks about five contrapositions, contrasts of position, between Peter and John (the disciple who was loved by Jesus).

1858 Now John recognizes the Christ within the Risen One. In front of the same signs, John recognizes the Teacher, but Peter does not. Only one who has the experience of spiritual love knows how to recognize the signs of the Spirit.

1859 The Peter understands from John that he is the Risen One.

1860 From the Greek word *diazonnumi*, which is a term connected to *diazosis* which is the Zodiacal belt, and also connected to the term *diazoster*, which is the twelfth vertebrae (where they are "nocchierando????), at the height of the *diazoma*, the diaphragm. Peter is naked because he did not take on his own role as a disciple by not accepting the death of the Jesus as a supreme expression of Love. He is the only one to makes such a gesture, since the other ones did not resist as he did, the Love of the Jesus and they did not reject it.
The kidneys are symbols of strength and fragility. What has been conquered in the lower human sphere now becomes the seed for the upper sphere, since the kidneys control the genital sphere and at the same time they open the higher path to the Verb. They are the organs of the intuitive hearing. They are the head of the transition between water and blood (that then turns into Spirit) and also the head of the transition from the salt into fire that then becomes Light.

1861 From the Greek *epienduma*, which literally means "what is above near what is incarnating", which is the I. He ties his clothes just like Jesus wrapped his hips at the Washing of the Feet, and he throws himself in the sea which represents the Zodiac ad a new baptism of purification.

1862 "Naked" means without the body of form: of the form-thoughts with which he has been living, with and that limited him in welcoming the teachings of the Christ. Lastly, naked means "without the clothes-cape" of the love of verse 19,23.

1863 Not only in the Sea of Tiberia, but in the whole "see" of the Cherubic Zodiac. Once again, the Peter proves to be a forerunner amongst the Twelve.

1864 It is smaller than the little boat, and it includes the Spiritual Self and the Loving Vital Spirit.

1865 This space that separates them from the Mainland is extremely interesting. As well will see further on, it corresponds to the man, the planetary man, the Egyptian Zed. If we remember that they are close to Capernaum, and since Capernaum is north of the Sea of Tiberias, we understand that they were coming from the south, which is the direction along which Bios flows, the biologic life in the Earth. So they are coming from Bios, the terrestrial existence, and they are headed towards Zoe, the eternal spiritual Life. What is left now to be done is the transformation of the planetary man: the 200 cubits....

1866 It is the number of the bones of the human body, and therefore it represents the First Zodiacal Adam... they need to overcome these "bones", which is where the limestone hosts the forces of hate and the ahrimanic hardening.

9. As they descended to the land[1867], they see (*blepo*)[1868] anthracite[1869] laying down[1870] (*keimai*) and the little fish[1871] laying on top, and bread[1872].

10. The Jesus tells (*lego*) them: Bring some of the little fish[1873] that you caught[1874] now[1875]".

[1867] They descend on the land from the higher dimensions that they were in.

[1868] It's a supersensitive vision, they have a precognition.

[1869] Anthracite has the same root as *antropos*, the Man fallen in carbon-coal. This is the body of coal; so the body diamond-carbon is set free. This indicates how the "naked" Peter thanks to the work he has done, receives the complete purification of the body and he connects with the uncorrupted First Adam… They do not see the Risen One, but the coal, the fire that purifies him.
This anthracite-antropos can be seen in an alchemical sense as the carbon that, as it burns, purifies itself and therefore frees from within the light, the diamond-Adam, of which it is formed by: the antropos, who is the "soul" man that looks at the Spirit, goes back as Adam: spiritual man in the image and likeness of God.

[1870] Like the linens laying in the sepulcher. They are the forces of the material physical body that are being "laid" down.

[1871] It is the I Am that takes us and that begins to be available for humanity.

[1872] This is the spiritual nourishment.

[1873] It is important to highlight how these fish (and we are hypothesizing that it is fish) are "small", while in the next verse they will speak of "big" fish. Therefore we are in front of two different things.

[1874] From the Greek *piazo*: it is to catch, or keep close with the spiritual forces.

[1875] The ones that they received, from their I Am: the rest is given by Him.

11. So Simon Peter descended[1876] and he pulled the net to the land which was full of one hundred fifty three[1877] big fish. And even though they were so many, the net did not break[1878].

12. The Jesus says (*lego*) to them: "Come, eat[1879]". And none of the disciples dared to spiritually (*exetazo*) investigate. "Who are you?", knowing that he was the Lord[1880].

13. The Jesus is there and he receives (*lambano*) the bread, and he gives[1881] it to them and similarly the little fish.

[1876] He ascended to the higher dimensions. It is important to see how the Risen One was talking to the group and once again, Peter takes the initiative. The Risen One doesn't even reply to this gesture.

[1877] This is the number of the stars of the Dark Zodiac that goes from Virgo to Pisces, which is the part within us that we still have to penetrate with our consciousness. It is important to say that the "Program of the Kingdom" given by Matthew (Mt 3,1-7,29) is written in 153 verses, like the 153 big fish of the miraculous fishing. Also the Great Gallery of the Pyramid of Cheope measures to the ceiling 153 feet. At the 351 degree (reard backwards, according to the Hebrew tradition, of 153), which is the absolute degree of the zodiac, the constellation of Pisces begins: sea Pisces and celestial Pisces, like in the Creation. The 153 is also found in the Book of the Maccabees in the chapter 9 verse 54, and this is the only part of the Old Testament in which this number comes out. The number 152 corresponds to specific Hebrew letters, which are "*Bny h'Ihym*" which means "Sons of God". The promise made by Jesus to Peter comes to a completion: "*You will become a fisherman of men*" (Lc 5,10). Soon after he will send him "*to feed my lambs*" so that they will become Sons of God.

[1878] The Zodiac was a closed circle and Lucifer penetrated up to it and "cut" it between Aries and Pisces. So the man opened up (separated) between Aries-head and Pisces-feet. Now Peter "closes back up" the Cherubic Zodiac. He has the strength to bring to the awareness the inner experiences and what he is living in his depth: he meet the Guardian of the Threshold.

[1879] From the Greek *aristeuo*, it means to nourish oneself of the best things with Him, which means to enter in communion with Him.
Now everything needs to go back to One, the seven springs, which correspond to the seven Rishi Saints of ancient India that need to go back to the original spring, the cosmic One.

[1880] The Risen One.

[1881] All the verbs are in the present tense to indicate the continuous presence of the Risen Jesus (he arrived…) when within the continuous presence the love flows. This gift is His Grace. The gesture repeats both the one of the multiplication of the bread and the one of the fish (grabbing it, dividing it) and the one of the Last Supper (Mt 26,26-29). On that occasion, He declared that the bread represented His spiritual Body (Incorruptible Body), His Word of Eternal Life, and the wine His Blood, which is the new Spirit that he was bringing. Now he does not say anything: he lets the disciples understand on their own the meaning of those substances. Additionally, he does not bless and he does not thank the Father: He is within the Father: they are One and He gifts the forces to the Spirit Man..

14. This is already (the) third (time) (that) the Jesus manifested himself to the disciples, risen from the dead[1882].

THIRD CONFESSION OF THE PETER

1882 The first appearance of the Risen One was on Easter Sunday, as the Son of the Man bearer of a new Spirit that insufflates within them. The second Sunday after that one (with Thomas), he shows up as the Son of God bearer of the Christ and eternal spiritual Life. The third appearance was at the miraculous fishing on Tiberias Lake, as Father God, Lord of all planes (up to the Zodiac and beyond). This will be the definitive one.
This reminds us of the three falls of man (in his three constituent parts), the three denials of Peter, and then the three manifestations of the Risen One.
To this one, a fourth manifestation follows: the dialogue with Peter about the *fileo and agapeo.*

15. As they ate (*aristao*), the Jesus says (*lego*) to the Simon Peter[1883]: "Simon, of John[1884], do you spiritually love me more than these ones[1885]?" He says (*lego*): "Yes Lord[1886], you

---

THIRD CONFESSION OF THE PETER

[1883] Now the Peter has grown up, and has reached the condition of "John", and he has entered in the freedom and now the Risen One speaks to him.

[1884] With the previous passage, Peter ascended to the Cherubic Zodiac (son of the "Saints"); now the Jesus changes his name once again..

[1885] The other disciples, who were in the "little little boat". Since Peter always took the initiative and declared to be ready to die for Jesus, now the Risen One asks him about the true aspect that qualifies a man: the love.

[1886] Without the article, he does not see the Risen One anymore. He stops at Mars.

know[1887] that I love you in a brotherly way." He says: "Feed my little lambs[1888]".

16. The Jesus tells (*lego*) him once again: "Simon of John, do you spiritually love me?" He says: "Yes, Lord, You know that I love you in a brotherly way". He says to him: "Feed[1889] my sheep[1890]".

[1887] We are in front of a first modification of Peter: at the Supper (John 13,37) he claimed to know himself better than Jesus did (*" Lord, why do you not give me the force to follow you now? I will lay down my soul for you".*)

[1888] In the Gospel, John speaks of the Lamb indicating the Child up to the Holy Trinity, the fullness of the Logos, the Principle Son of the Holy Trinity.
In the Apocalypse, John speaks about little Lambs, which are the Children of the Perfection (the Milky Way, the Divine Providence), and therefore he describes the actual era: the one of the Etheric Christ.
We can also capture the complete vision between the Gospels and the Apocalypse:
With the miraculous fishing of the 153 "big" fish, Peter captures the reality of the Dark Zodiac, which is the Lower Zodiac, and therefore he is ready to "ascend" to the Milky Way and its "Door", Orion. From Orion "it goes to" Auriga to reach the Swan-Christ. Auriga is represented without horses and with his head looking back: it is like saying that Auriga does not know, he cannot, and he doesn't want to go through the Path. The Magdalen and John, on the other hand, are already close to the Swan-Christ.
The Risen One will ask twice to Peter if he loves him spiritually (*agapao)* and the third time (resigned) if he loves him in a brotherly way, and Peter will respond three times that he loves him in a brotherly way (*fileo*), which is soul love.
The Risen One will then have to "limit" his possibility of action on Peter (who with his "*fileo*", limited himself on his own), and therefore he will give him three levels of assignment, which are reducing more and more. The first one will be "worthy" of the *agapao*, to feed the little lambs, which means to offer his spiritual love as nourishment for the little Children that ascended to the Path of Perfection. Now that he went through the Dark Zodiac (with the fishing), he will go through the Milky Way starting from Auriga which corresponds to the Lamb-Aries-Head (Cefa), and he will take care of the Children of the Perfect Ones. Peter will have to donate the brotherly love he claims to have for the Jesus so that it will transform within him into *agapao.*
Then there will be the "take care of my sheep", which means to lead the souls that have Faith. He therefore descended to the planetary level. These souls are the image of the People of Israel, the part that still needs a Shepard. He is called to be the safe and wise guide to those souls who are still on the path of growth but who are still pure like the little lambs.
Lastly, there will be the "feed the sheep", which means to nourish the ones that are still outside of the path of Initiation, but who have the Faith. He can nourish them, the ones who are particularly weak in the inside and who still need "unrefined" food.
Let's remember that the calf is the animal whose blood used to be offered to the high priest on the day of the great fast (or day of "penance") in the holy space of the temple to atone and therefore purify the one who needed to be propitiated. In the specific case, the blood of the calf purified the subject from his own sins and the ones of his family. To this, follows the blood of the ram (the male sheep) to purify the mistakes of the people (community connected by the blood and the territory). Third, the blood of a buck would be offered (male goat from which we get "scapegoat") for the sins of the nation (ethnic group with a cultural homogeneity). Finally, a last buck on which they would put (destined) the sins of Israel, would be sent into the desert, which means the oblivion (this is the "+1").

[1889] Also "conduct" the sheep.

[1890] Image of the People of Israel, the part that still needs a Shepard. He is called to become a safe and wise guide for the disciples who are on a path of perfection but who are no longer as pure as little lambs.

17. The third time[1891] he tells (*lego*) him: "Simon of John, do you spiritually love me?" The Peter was hurt (labour pains)[1892] because he said (*lego*) to him for the third time: "Do you love me in a brotherly way?" And he says (*lego*) to him: "Lord, you know all the things: you have in clarity[1893] that I love you in a brotherly way". (The Jesus) says (*lego*) to him: "Feed my sheep". [1894]

18. Amen, Amen[1895] I say to you: when you were young[1896], you used to wrap yourself[1897] and you would go[1898] wherever you wanted to[1899]; but when you will get old[1900], you will

---

[1891] This reminds us of the triple denial of Peter. Jesus wants to help him correct the mistake of denial.

[1892] For the birth of the Child of the Perfection, who is yet to be born. Now the Jesus "descended" to the level of Peter, so now the labour pains begin within Peter. Let's pay attention to the fact that it is "the" Peter who has labour pains, and not Simon of John.

[1893] Peter comprehends his inner level, the *fileo*.

[1894] The ones who are outside of the path of Initiation, but who have Faith. He can nourish them, the ones who are especially weak inside and who still need "unrefined" food. At the end, Peter will prove himself to be able only of this last nourishment.
The Christ acted at first by "gift", giving Peter the possibility to ascend to Perfection. Having not overcome the tests, the Peter stays in the Sanctity ("of John-seventh step). This "last" final task of Peter: conduct the ones who are still "outside" of the Spirit to get in touch with the spiritual realities.

[1895] It is a universal truth.

[1896] It represents the development of the third Child, the "Father" aspect of the Child, the Spirit Man. The Peter was this just for a minute.

[1897] This is indicating the fact that he is "young", which means "born" in the freedom, and he can define himself.

[1898] In the zodiacal dimension. The path of the Peter is this one: from the Holiest Trinity (the lambs to "feed") he "descends" at the planetary level (the sheep to feed), to then ascend again to the Zodiacal level (the sheep to take care of).

[1899] Causing his stubbornness and impetuousness.

[1900] From the Greek *gherasko*, which indicates the maturing of the fruit. This event is in the future, since he did not appropriately replied in the present to ascend to the Spirit Man, and therefore losing the freedom that he had just achieved (the being "young").
The verb also means "to be in the threshold of the snake", which is the Zodiacal Uroboro that still has power over Peter. The Peter will enter in the skin of the snake, both as snake like Uroboro, and also Snake as the constellation that comes to life from the Scorpio and goes up to the Eagle, and then stops in front of the Eagle and Swan. To enter in the Perfection, we need to be willing to be "turned inside out", and therefore we need to get out of each end every egoism.

lay your hand[1901], and others will gird to you and they will create (*poieo*) to you what you do not want[1902].

19. And he said (*eipon*) this meaning with which death he would have glorified the God[1903]. And having said (*eipon*) this, he tells him: "Follow me[1904]!".

20. Turning around[1905] the Peter sees (*blepo*)[1906] the disciple united to the Jesus, the one who Jesus spiritually[1907] loved, who also looked up in the commonality (*deipnon*) on his chest[1908], and he tells[1909] him: "Lord, who is the one who delivers you[1910]".

21. Seeing (*idein*)[1911] this, the Peter says to the Jesus: "Lord, and what about him?"

1901 The Spiritual Self; which indicates the moment in which the Peter "gives up" to the Above that grabs on to him, to the Grace, for intercession from which he will be saved by the Zodiacal luciferic snake. To lay ones hands can be seen as opening the arms to then be crucified.

1902 Finally he will follow the will of the Father (up to the cross), and he will give up his impetuousness.

1903 The holiest Trinity, who calls us to Perfection.

1904 He still needs to follow the guidance of the Jesus: he is free to do so, to "obey" the Spirit. This is what is being asked to him to activate the Grace that will save him. Let's remember that in 13,36 Jesus told him: "*Where I go, you do not have the strength to follow me: but you will follow me later*".

1905 From *epistrefo*, connected to the axis, the bone that allows us to move our head, and therefore indicates our condition of free choice. His "block" corresponds to the "screeching of the teeth of the teeth", when Ahriman takes away from us every freedom, then making us slaves to the matter. With this, Peter ascends one step of consciousness.

1906 The soul vision, without complete and full consciousness.

1907 Now the Peter sees the human example of the spiritual love.

1908 After the polarity between John (who is now being characterized by the fact that he put his head on Jesus' heart) and Judas, there now is a polarity between John who "stays" and Peter who needs to follow. The Apostles represent the inner circulatory system. After the Holy Spirit foreshadowed them, they will be sent all over the Earth to train and baptize. They represent the new blood, the oxygenated blood full of life that the lungs oxygenated and that are distributing it in the whole body, in all the nations.

1909 The uncontrolled reaction, impetuousness.

1910 It is interesting to note how John the Evangelist is never cited by his name but only through the periphrasis of his gesture at the Last Supper. Within it we can grasp the fact that John put his spiritual ear on the heart of the Jesus and he grasped the "divine secret" of the cosmic love. Only who has completed all of their inner work can hear this way. John hears his spiritual Name: he is ready to be reborn, he become Verb.

1911 This seeing is *idein*, the grasping of the forces and laws of the logos.

22. The Jesus tells him: "If I want him to remain ardent[1912] until I come[1913], what is that to you? You follow me[1914]!".

23. Therefore this verb came out, towards the brothers, that the disciple, that one, does not reach the depth of death[1915]; but the Jesus did not tell (*eipon*) him: "He does not reach the depth of death", instead he said "If I want him to stay ardent[1916] until I come, what is that to you?"

OTHER EPILOGUE

24. This is the disciple, the one who testifies around these thing and the one who wrote these things, and we know[1917] that his testimony is true[1918].

25. And there are more thing, that the Jesus created (*poieo*), and if they would be written one at a time, I think the world itself could not comprehend[1919] the books[1920] to write.

[1912] We should also add "in the Manu", the seventh disciple present in the nightly fishing. This expression comes from the Greek word *meno*, which resounds with *menos*, which is the heat/passion of the soul as a principle of life and force, and also with *manu* (which is also found in the Latin word, *manere*). John went through the path of Time-soul, of the Light-heat, and of the Life (of the Manu).

[1913] In His return, in His Second Coming, in His new Presence in which we are called to rise up (in the first, He "descended" amongst us).

[1914] Jesus does not reply to the question since the destiny of the other one depends on Him and does not involve Peter. The invite to follow him is now being repeated with more emphasis. Peter needs to follow Jesus, which means he needs to develop the conscious I am, and not follow another disciple, even if this was John. In a macrocosmic sense, Peter-Orion needs to ascend (follow) up to the John-Eagle, and there he will rejoice because of the closeness with the Swan-Christ.

[1915] In the completeness of the Initiation. The "brothers", the ones who are on the sixth step, perceive this, that John-Lazarus would not have completed the Initiation.

[1916] Being ardent is the sixth virtue that the heart is called to develop to reach the goal of love. The virtues are: appreciation, compassion, forgiveness, humility, understanding, daring, and they correspond to the six petals of the chakra of the heart to develop.

OTHER EPILOGUE

[1917] It is the community who accepts the testimony of the John.

[1918] Since he was and is in the Love of the Christ.

[1919] Also "understand".

[1920] As Book of the Life, experiences of the I. what the Christ brought to us is higher than all the path that men can go through (and write) to reach the Father through Him. The Gospel is therefore only a part of that the Jesus did: but it is enough to understand the meaning, to comprehend the Love of God for Man and the Path that has been opened to us to go back to the Father.

DICTIONARY OF THE MAIN NAMES

AND TERMS OF THE NEW TESTAMENT

A

AB: In Hebrew **father,** more precisely in the sentimental sense (affection) of **dad.**

ABBA: like AB.

ABRAHAM: in Israel, he represents the principle of the **Spirit Man** (the transformation of the physical brain took place within him to develop a relationship with the Spirit without any images and external perceptions).

ADAMO: from the Hebrew **Adham**, which means "God in the blood" and also "man's desire towards God". This term also has other meanings: **adamantine** which means "transparent or of a diamond" reference to the "first" Adam (zodiacal) created in the image and liking of God, "**man extracted by the red soil"** (the "second" Adam formed by the "first" Adam in contrast to his future transformation in "green man" or "man of light"), **destined to the love** (*ad-amor*, the "third" Adam, us), and therefore **man.** The "third" Adam also means *a-mort*, which means "without death", destined to win over death and therefore destine to immortality.

ALABASTER: from the Copt **albobeisti,** where "al" means "stone", "bo" means "hair", "be" means "sepulcher", "sti" means "unguent, fragrant oil", and therefore the **stone receptaclefor the fragrant oil of the hair for the one who is in the sepulcher.**

ALEXANDER: from the Greek **alexo** (protect) and **aner** (Enlightened), means the **protector of the Enlightened ones** (also the ones who turn to the mysteries of the Light).

ANALEMMA: Greek word which means "**support**" or also "**solar clock**". The analemma is one of the movements that the Sun (solar analemma) makes in the sky, and it is a movement of a lemniskate. If during the year we photograph the Sun every day at the same time, we will see how it goes through a very tight "vertical" figure eight. This figure is the symbol of harmony amongst the expansive and contractive processes, and of how we go from one to the other. This re-established the metamorphic connection between above and below, between God and the man. It opened up the Path by going through the metamorphic transformation. From *analemma* we have *analepsis*, which means "**Ascension,**" or also "repairing of the amistakes". From what we just said, the Risen One presents himself to the Apostles speaking about Faith (virtue of the soul) in the solar dimension, and the Apostles perceive by Grace a sort of expansion of His Being up to the sphere of the Father of Holiest Trinity. They see

the “point” of the Jesus Christ-Sun expand like a center of a lemniskate that unites in the Christ the Sky and the Earth. The solar analemma projects itself in the cosmic analemma, in which it is no longer the Sun to go through it, but the Christ himself. In this way, the Apostles also grasp the redemption of the Heavens operated by the Risen One. Let’s remember that the *analemma* also means **the word** (*lemma*) as a name-nume (therefore in its aspect Holy Spirit) **which is being raised** (ana) to a higher dimension. The Holy Spirit within us is located in the solar dimension, and therefore from Holy Spirit to Father, from Sun to Cosmos…

ANDREW: from the Greek **andreia** which means virility, **courage**. It is the virtue of the *aner,* the enlightened man (who already reach Enlightenment). In the text it is mentioned with capital “U”. It corresponds to the Latin word “*vir”*.

AMEN: see TRUTH and JESUS.

ANTI-CHAKRA: negative chakra activated by the Initiation. These organs inspire the worlds of the Evil (machines, virtual realities, drugs, GMO, etc..).

APOSTLES.

- SPIRITUAL APOSTLES: see CROWD. Their qualities have a correspondence with the Twelve terrestrial Apostles. For the true nature of the being “Apostle” see SENT ONE…
- TERRRESTRIAL APOSTLES: they are the representatives of the 12 Spiritual Apostles, and they represent Peter the Faith, Andrew the Prayer, Jacob the Justice, John the Love, Bartholomeus the Hope, Thomas the Overcoming of Doubt, Matthew the Thought, Jacob Minor the Vigilance, Thaddeus the Patience, Simeone the Order, and Judah the Suffering (his successor will be Paul, the Consciousness). They also represent the 12 Tribes of Israel, which also incarnate the 12 tasks of the Spiritual Apostles…

  The books of the Bible, like all the history that is being narrated, express mysterious figures. The story of the Maccabees is an example of this, telling the “geometry” of destiny. It is about the correspondence between the twelve sons of Jacob, at the beginning of the Old Testament, and the twelve apostles, at the beginning of the New Testament. By going from one set of twelve to the other, we go through a human system founded on the ethnic-family ties of blood, to a system in which the more different singular individualities come to reunite through a spiritual affinity. Between these two groups of twelve men, history only shows us a third, but in a veiled way and in a way that is barely perceivable: it’s the martyr figures and the heroes of the Maccabees era, the seven sons of the widow and the five sons of Mattathias. The development of the Old Testament opens and closes with a set of 12. And then again, a group of twelve, at the beginning of the terrestrial mission of the Christ, which hints to a universally human range of those events. The twelve apostles of Jesus, according to the revelation of Steiner in his cycle of seminars on the Gospel of Mark, are nothing more than the same individualities that are being incarnated at the time of the Maccabees as the seven sons of the widow and the five sons of the Mattathias. Twelve men, who represent the human quintessence, cross together the greatest threshold in history, the last one within the pre-christian humanity, all gathered in waiting. They become the first ones to line up around the Savior who became man. In the time of the Maccabees, they find themselves still completely tied to their ethnicity and blood-ties, but already then, the high force of their faith was directing them towards the full awareness of the intimacy of their individual and immortal nucleus. In the next life, "incarnated separately one from the other and grown with deep individual differences, they will be allowed to form once again a community, but this time based on the spiritual foundation of a common faith and veneration."

Rudolf Steiner describes this meaningful intertwining of destines this way: "The souls that were incorporated in the seven sons of the widow and the five sons of the Mattathias reappeared. And with these, the association of the apostles formed. They found themselves amongst the element of fishermen and simple people; but at the time in which the Judaic element rose to its culminating point, they were permeated by the awareness that this element represented a supreme force - but only a force - and that now it needed to reappear in an individualized form, to line up around the Christ. We can picture the case in which a man who is completely incredulous wanted to consider from a point of view that is exclusively artistic the fact that, at the end of the Old Testament, there is the introduction of the seven and the five; and at the beginning of the New Testament there are the twelve. Even just taking it as an artistic and architectural element, we can feel touched in front of this simplicity and artistic greatness of the biblical books, regardless of the fact that the "twelve" consist of the five sons of Mattathias and the seven sons of the widow…"

The 153 indicates a completely special mystery dominating between the two last groups of twelve that are being mentioned, separated amongst each other by only one and a half century.

ARK: The Hebrew word for ark is *tevah* which also means "word," and it has the syllable *vath* which means "the virgin daughter of Israel (the Children of the Chosen People sons of Mary-Sion-Moses) who floats on the waters (of the Work in Black so that the White dove will come which is the symbol of the Work in White)." In the Bible, the word *tevah* comes back only in the case of the basket (or bread basket) in which Moses was put by his mother and then abandoned in the current of the river Nile. So, God invites Moses to become aware of all of his energies (representatives of the animals) within himself for the inner marriage with the "virgin." Noah's Ark is our inner being, and Noah had lived 500 years when the flood happened, and 500 means "seed of cosmic life," of New Spiritual Life. We can therefore say that *tevah* means Word of God through which the son of the Virgin (the Child within us) is being saved from the waters.

ARIMATHEA: From **rama** (a city located on the top of a hill), and **theos** (God), therefore **city of the inspiring consciousness.** Let's remember that the term "CITY" indicates a chakra.

ARIES (LAMB): see CALF.

ASCENSION: see ANALEMMA.

B

BAAL: divinity of the underworlds that is in contrast to Jahve. He represents the anti-christic forces.

BALDASSARE: from the Assyrian **balats** and **usur**, which means **God protect his life** (maybe it is a reference to the Loving Vital Spirit).

BENCH (of Levi): it is the inner altar, the inner sanctum, in which we work inwardly to the Mysteries.

BAR: in Hebrew **young son** (in the spiritual sense) who will then become "*ben*", which is adult Son.

BARABBA: in Hebrew **son of Father,** therefore the third developed Child, who corresponds to the seventh step of the Persian Initiation, the one of "Father". According to the Hebrew tradition, his complete name was "Jesus Barabba". This spiritual Being was kept prisoner by Pilatus, who would impede his action for personal interests and because he was connected to incorrect Initiations. The spiritual crowd to which the Pilate talks, which was formed by fallen entities, decided to preserve the old Initiation (represented by Barabba) instead of following the Christ in the new path towards the Father. Even though in some verses it can seem this way, Barabba **is not** one of the inner Children of the Pilatus…

BOAT: from **bar-arche',** "the principle Son", and therefore the **Son of God.**

It is important to see the assonance with the word **arca,** and the word ark in Hebrew is said *tevah* which encloses the syllable *vath* which means "the virgin daughter of Israel" who represents the combination of all the created energies. Therefore, God invited Noah to become aware of all of his energies (representative of the animals) within himself for the inner wedding with the "virgin". Noah's ark is our inner being, and Noah had lived 500 years when the flood happened, and 500 means "seed of cosmic life", of New Spiritual Life.

LITTLE BOAT: which was **developed individually by the Son of God.** It also represents conscious "navigation" of the seminal fluid, through which the spinal fluid, flows towards the cerebrum-spinal fluid, and therefore is the changing state of consciousness, the "bringing back together of the waters"… It corresponds to the Hebrew Merkaba.

BARNABA: means **son of the consolation.**

BARTIMEO: means **son who honors,** and therefore of the forces of Venus. He represents the solar spiritual I (since Venus "looks" at the Sun).

BARTOLOMEUS: in Hebrew **son of the courageous.**

BAT: in Hebrew **daughter.**

BAPTISM OF WATER: it is a Baptism of purification that opens our mind to the memory of our divine origin. It is the Baptism of John the Baptist.

BAPTISM OF FIRE: thanks to this Baptism, we receive the force of the Christ to "be in the world" and operate the spiritual evolution of the lower Kingdoms, freeing them from the Darkness.

BAPTIST: from the Greek **baptizein**, which means the **one who immerses**, who baptizes.

BELIEVE: there is a big difference between having faith and believing. The faith a virtuous motion of the soul towards an objective that is believed to be full of value, therefore it is towards something or someone. The believing is the next step with which we unite with that thing, we enter it. Since we love ourselves first, from the moment we enter this entity, we begin to love it. To believe in God, in the Christ, implies to love him, and therefore that allows Him to love us as well. The process that will take us to John begins: the disciple that He spiritually loved. With the faith, God can only show us His benevolence; but with believing he can gift us His Love.

BEN: in Hebrew **son of**… (ex: Jesu Ben Pandira), in a carnal sense.

BERENICE: from the Greek word **fero** (harbor) and **nike** (victory), which means **bearer (female) of the victory.**

BETHANY: in Aramaic is means both **house of discomfort** and **house of the healing** (where the discomfort would get healed), and it corresponds to the **Vital Loving Spirit** in which the Therapist acts. Let's remember that the term "house" represents the "subtle" element, supersensitive, of the physical body. In this case, it becomes the combination of subtle forces that operate in the healing, and therefore the forces of the Therapist, of the Loving Vital Spirit. In Mark (11,1) it is said that Bethphage and Bethany were near Jerusalem and near the Mount of Olive Trees. In Mark (14,3), it is said that in Bethany scented oil gets poured on the Jesus. Additionally, it was the city where Mary, Martha and Lazarus lived. Also, it was the location of the Ascension of the Jesus. For all of these reasons, we can connect it to the Loving Vital Spirit. Together with Jerusalem, Bethphage and Bethlehem form the "tetrahedron" of the inner Light.

BETHPHAGE: in Aramaic it means "**house of the unripe figs**" (and therefore the location where they can complete their maturation). See also HOUSE and BETHANY. It represents the forces that act subtly around the spiritual disciple who is not yet "mature", which means that he hasn't internalized them yet. Spiritually it represents the **Spiritual Self**. Together with Jerusalem, Bethany and Bethlehem form the "tetrahedron" of the inner Light.

BETH: in Hebrew **house** (see HOUSE).

BETHESDA: at first sight it means "ditch, crease, crevice". It was north of the temple (therefore between Earth and Water, in the quality of the "cold) and it separated a new neighborhood from the rest of the city. Bethesda can be translated as "house of the grace or compassion", and it was beyond the valley (the Ditch) of KIDRON that runs along the oriental part of the wall of the Old Jerusalem. It separated the Mount of the Temple from the Mount of the Olive Trees.

BETHLEHEM: in Aramaic it means "**house of the Bread**" and it corresponds to the **Spirit Man** (given the relationship between the "Bread" and this spiritual Limb). It can also mean "house of the word received from Above that gives us live". Together with Jerusalem, Bethany and Bethphage forms the "tetrahedron" of the inner Light, and it represents the upper vertex of it.

BETHSAIDA: literally Bethsaida in Aramaic means "house of fish", and also of the "Merciful". It represents the constellation of **Virgo** (look at the spiritual Map of the Sea of Galilee). It also represents the strict, conservative, and formal interpretation of the Scriptures, which bring the Light of Truth, to those who live by them, and it becomes dimmed by the darkness of the intellectual-materialistic thoughts (see also SCRIBES). It is the Light of Virgo or the dead light of the scribes, that with the first multiplication of the bread and fish becomes transformed into Life. We can understand the double meaning: the constellation of Pisces, that in contrast to Virgo, finds within it its "house".

BLIND: the one who, because of an excess of egoism (of luciferic matrix), **only sees himself…** In Hebrew, blind is said *iwer* which, pronounced *aor*, means "tunic of skin", which is the skin with which Adam covered himself after the Fall. See also EYE.

BOATSWAIN: see FISHERMEN.

BONIFACIO: from the Latin word **boni fatum**, which means **from the good destiny.**

BUCK (LITTLE MALE GOAT): see CALF.

C

CALF: The calf is the animal whose blood used to be offered to the high priest on the day of the great fast (or day of the penances) within the holy setting of the temple that was sprinkled and therefore purified the one who needed to be circumcised. In the specific case, the blood of the calf purified the subject from his own sins and the ones of his family. After this, we have the blood of the ram (male sheep) to purify the mistakes of the people (community connected by blood and territory). Third, there would be the offering of the blood of the buck (the male goat, from which we have "scapegoat) for the sins of the nation (ethnicity with a cultural homogeneity). Lastly, one last buck would be sent out into the desert, which is oblivion, with all the sins of Israel placed on its back (destined). This is the "+1".

CAPERNAUM: means "**village of Naum"** or "**village of the consolation**", and it was the village on Lake Genezareth where the Jesus lived in the three years of his public life. It corresponds to the forces of Cancer. The last syllable "**aum**" from the Latin "Capharnaum", in Sanskrit, represents the Hindu' Trinity. It was Peter's village in which he probably lived in an octagonal house.

CANA: It means to "acquire": in Cana, we acquire the forces for the completion that the married woman represents.

CAPE: The Jewish people were dressed with three base clothing: the **slip**, which was a thin shirt, close-fitting and more or less long; the **tunic** (or **vest)** which was wide, pleated and long (to the feet); and the **cape** or gown/toga, or **overdress**, with a semi arch form. Spiritually, the slip corresponds to the **"subtle" etheric body**, the tunic **the raw etheric body,** and the cape the **astral body.** The **I** was represented by the headdress of the priests (or the hood of the cape).

CHAKRA: the subtle centers of the man. See also CITY and, for their healing, GOSPELS.

CHILD: this term refers to the fruit that is born within us from the union of the right rational-empirical-masculine side and the left intuitive-creative-feminine side. From the union right-left, another union is added which is the one of the above-head-sky with the below-metabolism-earth. From these unions, "the child (the is masculine and child is feminine)" is born to indicate that is neither masculine or feminine. Mainly, we have three children: the Spiritual Self (the principle Holy Spirit within us that is born from the transformation of the astral body), the Loving Vital Spirit (the Son within us who is born from the etheric transformation) and the Spirit Man (the Father within us that comes to life from the transformation of the physical body).

CHOSEN ONES: the ones who were **chosen amongst the chosen ones**: which means the ones who entered the **Kingdom** (see Kingdom). They form the Chosen People, the People of God, or the Sons of Israel.

CHOSEN PEOPLE: this expression refers to the men who follow the Christic impulse, **the ones who are in the Kingdom,** that are "from God". It is also indicated as **Sons of Israel,** where the term "Israel" is also a synonym, or like "People of God". Jesus came to save these lost sons but, thanks to the **Baptism of Fire** (see), the ones who are outside, thanks to the strength of Faith, can enter in the Kingdom.

CHRISTIAN: from Latin, it means **follower of Christ.**

CHRIST: depending on the context:

1. **"the" Christ**: the principle Son of the Holiest Trinity united with the principle Father and Holy Spirit of the Holiest Trinity (which is the divine that is "within" Him);
2. **Christ:** the Principle Son of the Holiest Trinity.

CHRISTOPHER: from Greek **Kristos** (Christ) and **foros** (bearer), **bearer of Christ.**

CIRCUMCISED: **Title** that would distinguish the **ones initiated into the Mysteries** in Egypt. Moses imposed circumcision on all the Jewish People (firstborn) so that they would form a **population of initiated ones** (Chosen Ones). With the circumcision, the Child would be dedicated to the spiritual path. It represents the "pruning" of the flesh (of the tree of life) which will allow oneto penetrate the inner path, and which will bring the inner wedding. The "tunic of skin" that is being taken off, represents the tunic of skin with which Adam and Eve were dressed with after the expulsion from Paradise. The three phases of the ceremony (cutting, naked skin, the suction done by the priest, who by doing this connects the soul with the blood) will find their "+1" in the blood that Jesus will gift at the Passion by becoming the "circumcision of the world" (respectively: the flagellation, the emptying of the subtle bodies and the sponge of vinegar). Circumcision would happen by using a small STONE.

CITY: the cities represent the spiritual forces connected to the **chakras**, in which the respective crowds act (see CROWD).

CLOTHES: the slip (shroud) represents the subtle etheric, the tunic (chiton) represents the raw etheric, while the cape (imation) represents the astral, and the headgear represents the I. The generic term "clothes" refers to the tunic…

CLOUD: from the Greek **nefele,** from **nefos,** which also means **swarm, flock, multitude.** We can see how the cloud is like a **crowd,** which is so elevated that it is "veiled", and it is only grasped as an indistinct cloud. The hypothesis of its elevated spiritual level is confirmed by the fact that it is associated with the Christ, who will "come with the clouds", which means with His troops/ crowd, "and every eye [physical and spiritual] will see Him" (Ap 1,7). The entering of man's consciousness in this cloud, the being able to grasp with clarity, corresponds to the reaching of the sphere of the Glory.

CRYING: As a soul manifestation of the **astral predominance** on the etheric body. This happens within the man after the **banishing** from the Terrestrial Paradise that happened because of the **luciferic sin.** The root of the word tear is the same as "dragon". The tears purify us from the dragon within us.

CURE: **to take care** (like nurses do) and not **to heal.**

CYRUS: Latinized from Persian, it means **king or owner; Cyrus the Great** represents the current of **union of the Solar** (represented by **Pythagoras**) **and lunar** (represented by the prophet **Daniel**) **mysteries.** These three individualities, who would meet up at Cyrus' court, presented themselves and then they reincarnated in the **three Magi**, who were the disciples of Zarathustra (see JESUS).

CLARITY (or CLARIFICATION): represents the old "throwing lights" on things with the third soul eye. It is the prelude to a more recent discretion, the DISCERNMENT (see DISCERNMENT..).

COIL: The term coil (in Greek *speria)* indicates both the snake coils that surround a center and also the circular coils that surround the base of the pillars. This corresponds to the forces of the Snake-Kundalini that surround the sacrum and the spinal cord. The ancient Kings-priests where surrounded by people who supported them in their spiritual work. These people, these "coils", then became the cohorts. Pilate, in his ancient initiatic process, became a Son of the Snake (like many of the ones who had power back then), and he would gather around himself his soldiers, his warriors, his "coils". The soldiers of the governor represent the spiritual forces that he achieved and that allow him to act in a magical way against the Jesus.

CORAZIN: on Lake Genezareth it represents the constellation of **Leo** (see the spiritual map of the Sea of Galilee). It also represents the fanaticism of adherence to the oral religious tradition (see also PHARISEES). Therefore, it hosts the loss of enthusiasm and inner participation with the communication and transmission through the spiritual truths, the dead force of the Heat (which is present as a force of Life in what is alive in the Spirit).

CROWN: represents the connection between the head-thought and the Gethsemane-halo-love (see GETHSEMANE). The King, the Groom, the Enlightened One, has the crown (of the Holy Spirit). The crown is made of gold, which means it is connected to the solar forces (connected to the Spiritual Self or Holy Spirit within us), and it is adorned with precious stones (which symbolize the Zodiac). Therefore it can correspond to the Cherubic Zodiac that takes us to the Serafinic-Gethsemane.

CROWD: FROM THE Greek "ochlos" which comes from "echo" which means "to have", understood as a "vehicle", which means the crowd "has", "holds" a spiritual force to be the vehicle that is carrying out an action of "mercurial" type. In Latin, it means "crowd in movement".

Spiritually, it means a combination of **beings** in their etheric and soul component that is ordered according the spiritual forces. The crowds mentioned in the Gospels were connected to the spirituality of the Old Testament, and therefore the luciferic process of the Fall. They need to be tamed (from the Jesus Christ) so that they can freely recognize the Good News, and they can put themselves at the service of the Christ and therefore of the re-ascending humanity. The

PLEROMA is the combination of **entities;** the LEGION is the negative of the crowd with a spiritual-soul nature (step of suitors).

In the Gospels, there are many crowds being mentioned:

1. TUMULTUOUS CROWD: the pubertal crowd of the daughter of Giaro (passage of the Hemorrhage) (see **Mt 9,23).** It is a crowd with an astral nature. **The flute players** are the spiritual-soul entities that, acting in the larynx, activate it…
2. MULTITUDE: the components of the crowd singularly considered and not yet active…
3. THE CROWD OF THE TRIBE OF THE PEOPLE: it is the specific crowd connected to each people; it can have a luciferic or ahrimanic nature (Mt 24,30)…
4. THE CROWD OF THE BAPTIST: The Baptist acted as a Group Soul on the 12 and on Jesus, by strengthening them and bringing them forces in his crowd, in collaborating with the miracles. The action of this crowd extends itself from the spiritual plane to the physical plane, but to then be poured in the physical, it needs to be recalled by the Jesus…
5. THE CROWD WITHIN OURSELVES (to be disturbed within ourselves): It happens when the Jesus "is disturbed within himself" in front of the sepulcher of Lazarus. It means to know how to call within ourselves one of the crowds…
6. CROWDS CONNECTED TO THE PLANETARY HIERARCHIES (of the single planets): amongst these we find the CROWD OF THE SOLAR CROWN (in Mc 6,50): Jesus walks on the waters. In the same passage, the wind represents the CROWD OF THE SOLAR DISC (Lucifer)…
7. ETHERIC CROWD: emanation of the Third Hierarchy (elementary beings). **They do not exist on their own,** but as an emanation of the Hierarchies of the planets. They come from the sphere from Saturn to the Sun (as an emanation). Nowadays, an example of their action is when the Spirit of Time declares the "fullness of the time" and the lemmings kill themselves in the sea…
8. CROWD OF THE SPIRITS OF THE CYCLICAL PERIODS: **they do not exist on their own**, but as an action of the Hierarchies of the planets. Forces connected to the Spirits of the cyclical periods that can me commanded up to the point where they form a crowd. It manifests in the phenomena that accompanied the death in the cross of the Jesus…
9. CROWDS OF THE DARKNESS: it comes from the external layers of the Earth. They are the "coils" of the Passion. We can find to which layer of the Earth they belong to (action of the Pilatus, of the guardians, of the priests, of the custodians, etc.).
10. CROWD OF THE SPIRITUAL APOSTLES (Mc 3,13-14; ,32): the Twelve Entities that the Jesus calls with his own will, "Apostles", so that "they will be with him" to send them as Spirit Guides as his tools. They represent the renewed crown of the 12 Bodhisattva, of which He is the center (Mc 3,32)…
11. CROWD OF THE CHRIST (Mc 9,7; Ap 1,7): see CLOUD…

When a crowd is “being let go” (from the Greek **afiemi** which also means “to put in the light”) from the Jesus, it is being put in a condition that in the ancient times corresponded to the one of who **would be set free from a previous condition of slavery.** An additional meaning to this type of setting free is **“being consecrated”.**

D

DANIEL: from the Hebrew **Dani’el**, which means **divine judge**. He represented the **lunar mysteries**, and he reincarnated in one of the three Magi.

DARIO: Greek form of the Persian form, it means **the one who maintains the good.**

DAVIDE: from the Hebrew **Dawidh**, which means the **loved one, the beloved.**

DAY: it represents the experience of the I (of one of its incarnations or one permeation), and also the unitary aspect of one chakra (the combination of the hours-see HOUR)…

DEAF: the deaf does not listen the voice of the Spirit, he does not open up to the meeting with the Son…

DEMON (Plural demons): spiritual entity in which the Greeks saw a personal genius, an intermediary entity between man and Gods.

DEVIL (plural devils): the devil, the entity of Evil.

DEVIL: literally “spirit of dispersion”.

DISCIPLE: literally “Child” (therefore initiate) who learns with the mind. It also means “a young one born”.

DISCERNMENT: use of the conscious spiritual powers (today the thought that opens up to the Spirit). This took place of the old clairvoyance of the third soul eye, that would “throw the light” on the things, that we are now called to comprehend; see also CLARITY.

DOG: animal that represents the dark-luciferic forces of the Sun. It also is the name of a constellation in which inside of it there is the brightest star of the whole cosmos: Sirius (Lucifer) with its dwarf black twin star (Ahriman). The “external” Sun gets closer to this constellation in the middle of summer (summer heat wave), which means when he is also manifesting the maximum of his luciferic Forces. In Hebrew, dog is said *kaleb*, which is a word that comes from *kol*: the totality. It’s anagram is *kebel* which means the connection, the chain. Therefore, the dog, the forces of the Obstacle, the Cerberus of Dante’s hell, is the last dark aspect to overcome to free the fallen man and bring him back to the splendor of his Incorruptible Body of Light.

DONKEY: It’s an old image of the man’s immortality who, under various forms, he carries on his back. It is “present” (in reality under the aspect star) to the birth of the Nathanic Jesus:

therefore be takes the immortal that become mortal. The donkey represents the animal that "has ears to listen" the divine word, in this image it finds a correspondence in the rabbit or Easter hare.

DUST: in an esoteric sense, the term "dust" indicates the (human) condition in which we are in a "neutral" situation between Good and Evil. In other words, that we keep one foot in two stirrups. This brings us back to the phrase: the Kingdom of God is for the ones who listen to my words and *puts them into practice"*. To shake the dust meant to break every relation with one who is "lukewarm/aloof" towards God.

E

EAGLE: in the Gospels, eagles are only mentioned once, and precisely in the verse: "*wherever the fallen body will be, there the eagles will meet"*. This body is the Incorruptible Body within us, in which the matter entered and thickened. The eagle represents the force and the spiritual consciousness, it is the bird that flies the highest and therefore it is the bearer of the cosmic thoughts. "wherever" means "in every location", and therefore in every spiritual plane in which the man will elevate his Incorruptible Body and there, around him, the cosmic thoughts will gather, which are thoughts brought by the Archangel Michael, the one who gifts us the substance of the pure thoughts.

It is a belief that the eagle lays three eggs, but then she throws the third one out of the nest so she won't be too debilitated to feed three birds. The three eggs can represent the three loves that we "brood" within us: love for God, for the other and for the world. The third love is the one we need to let go of to spiritually develop ourselves. Once we have received the forces, we can then also help the world to evolve. The prototype of this Body death/resurrection is the Jesus Christ and "wherever this Body will be" means in each man that will operate this Work), there, there will be the forces (eagles) that will take him away from death to resurrect. The first man that will follow this path will be John the evangelist (who is represented by the eagle.

Birds are animals that did not descend in the strict animal form. They are not souls that came down here for inferior functions; instead, they transcend from that condition by going up towards the above.

Let's remember that the throat, with the collarbone (little keys that close the path to the entrance to the east door of the terrestrial Heaven, which is a door guarded by the Cherub with the rotating and flaming sword and which Jesus gifted to Peter) will keep going with the arms (in Hebrew *Sichem* which means "aim", "goal") and then the hand, which represent the force and the consciousness of the eagle within us: the Guardian (female) of the Door of the Gods, of our higher triad. For the alchemists, this is the Work in White. It is the image of force and consciousness. See also SEFIROT.

EAR: the ears are the third organ to perceive, to listen. The feet are the organ for the Earth, the kidneys for the inner voice, the ear for the voice of God. Thanks to them, the man can maintain a vertical position and ascend from the horizontal animalistic position that belongs to the "un-accomplished" man, that of the vertical "accomplished" man. Thanks to the ear, the man learns to talk, which means that he takes on the capability of the Word. The inner ear (cochlea) corresponds to the head and its function is equilibrium and verticality, and within it there is wisdom and intelligence. The medium ear (cavity and eardrum) is connected to the median part of the body, the area of inner transformation. The external ear (ear canal and auricle) welcomes the external information in its complete immobility.

EASTER: It means "transition" and it reminds us of the exiting of the Chosen People from Egyptian slavery. In Hebrew it is *pesah,* which is "getting out of the trap" (*pah),* and this exit-transition is done with the letter *taw* which means "cross". In the Easter of the Exodus, the Son of man is born, "he transitions or goes through", with the Easter of the Christ, the Son of God is born. See MOSES.

EFREM: from the Hebrew **Ephrajim**, which means **that brings fruit.**

ELIA: from the Hebrew **El (**God) and **Yah** (God), which means **God is God** (it is like a "divine God", "God", maybe it is a reference to the Holiest Trinity).

ELISABETH: from the Hebrew **El** (God) and **sebha** (oath), which means **God is my oath.** Also **El-Isa-Beth, the House of the divine Isis.**

EMANUELE: from the Hebrew **Im-manu-el**, which means **God is with us,** or also the **divine Manu**, the Solar Oracle of the ancient Atlantis, who acted as a bridge between the man and the Christ-Sun. It was the secret name of the Salomonic Jesus, the Teacher Jesus, in which the I of Zarathustra (see JESUS) would act. In the course of the millenniums, it is the reference to the Chosen People.

ENLIGHTENED: from the Greek **aner**, the groom of the inner wedding. When it is "straight", it represents the further step, the initiate..

ENON: (in Greek *Ainon*) means "springs", the "rebirth". Others say that it means "the Springs". The "territory with many springs" (*Enon*) was located on the oriental shore of the place of crossing of the Jordan, which corresponded to the spiritual world. For what we said microcosmically, it corresponds to the space behind the heart: the spiritual heart where many waters of life pour out.

ERECT ONESELF: to put oneself in the consciousness of the I.

ESSENS: religious cult formed by the **elite of the Pharisees**, which means **priests.** The initiation foresaw three years of novitiate, in which the novice would receive as symbols a cape, a curve hatchet, a white tunic (and maybe the apron). The three levels were: **Free**, who were at service of the higher levels, **Practical**, who still had a social and family life (see JOSEPH**),** and the **Contemplative,** who dedicated themselves completely to meditation. They would recognize the spiritual Hierarchies and the secret of the name of the Angels. They would venerate two mortal creatures (which means incarnated): Elxai (or Jacob, who corresponds to Ahura Mazda of the Persians and to Osiris of the Egyptians) as the principle of Good, and Yesseus (or Esau, who corresponds to Ahriman and Typhoon) as the principle of Evil. (see also MARTHA)

EUNUCH: From the Greek **eunuchos, guardian** of the virginity of the Bride, and therefore of the **purity of the soul.** The archetype of the eunuch is the **Archangel Michael**, Paladin of Mary.

EVE: from the Hebrew **Heva**, which means **mother of the living ones** (maybe referring to Bios).

EYE: it indicates the necessary death for the process of resurrection. After the tests of the Opera in Balck (wedding with the Mother), the eyes of the ones who overcame the tests are ready for the divine vision (see also BLIND).

F

FAITH: there is a big difference between having faith and believing. Faith is a virtuous motion of the soul towards an objective that is believed to be full of value, therefore it is "towards" someone or something. To believe is the next step in which we unite with that thing, we enter it. Since we love ourselves first, from the moment in which we enter this entity, we start to love it. To believe in God, in the Christ, implies the complete adhesion of His Word, to love him, and this allows Him to love us. Therefore, the process that will bring us to the step of John begins: of the disciple that He spiritually loved. With the faith, God can only show us His benevolence; with believing he can gift us His love. It is interesting to see how John never says the word "faith" in his Gospel, but only "believing".

FAST: reduction of terrestrial nutrition to help the connection with the Light-divine Word, which becomes our nourishment.

FATHER: it has different meanings:

1. **The Celestial:** he is the principle Father of the Holiest Trinity; it is the Father of the perfect ones;
2. **Who is in the skies:** he is the Principle Father of the Holy Trinity, Adonai, he is the Father of humanity;
3. **The one in the secret (occult):** he is the Principle Father within us: the Spirit Man;
4. **Thief and murderer from the beginning:** he is the Principle Father of Evil: Lucifer and Ahriman;

5. **Biological:** the dad.

FEAR: feeling that comes from the comprehension of the greatness of God.

FEET: they represent the kingdom of Earth, the *Malkut,* the terrestrial Kingdom and therefore the Mother, the Virgin Mother, the Black Madonna, the Mother of every terrestrial existence. This is why in the spiritual symbology they are represented as "wounded" and therefore they need to be healed. Eve was also bitten by a snake on the foot. The wound represents the "fake" of the foot and it is the other "half" of the wound on the head represented by the fontanel. This is because the man is created in the liking and image of God, which is the Zodiacal Man or First Adam, and he is represented by the zodiacal circle which was then "cut" between Aries-head and Pisces-feet, therefore losing the "likeness" with the Creator.

The feet represent the contact between divine will and humanity, and they indicate the descending within the man of a higher level of consciousness to which the man is called to ascend, even through all of the difficulties of acting in the soul. From this, the episode of the unction of the feet from Mary, and the Washing of the Feet with the Jesus completely purifies the Apostles and heals the wound that came from the Fall. Magdalen will also try to touch him by the feet on Easter Sunday but the Risen one will prevent her from doing so since after healing his feet and descending in the womb of Mother Earth, he needs to ascend to the Father to complete the spiritual wedding between Mother earth and Father sky.

FIG: it corresponds to the tree of Bodhi, the tree of the initiation of the Buddha. It is also symbol of the Egyptian-Chaldean initiation for its connection with the forces of the Moon which are softened through the fertilizing love of bees. The ripe/mature fig becomes the highest step of the old initiation (see also BETHPHAGE). From the spiritual composition of the word (in Greek **skye**) we understand that in an old sense, the "fig" represented the **esoteric process for the inner wedding**[1921]; in a renewed sense (post-Golgotha) the "fig" represents the **manifestation of the renewal of the spiritual forces of Kundalini**[1922]**.** This corresponds to the process of **Transfiguration,** an event in which the transformation of the old initiatic path begins thanks to Jesus. Let's remember that R. Steiner indicates that the Transfiguration is the continuation, by Jesus, of the actions of the Buddha (enlightened under the "old" fig). The transformation of the fig, once renewed, becomes the olive tree (see OLIVE TREE) by "going through" the VINE (see Vine).

Botanically, the fig is a moracea, and therefore a plant that is deeply connected to the forces of the Moon. This is visible in two other characteristics (sap, bark, type of fruit, shape of the leaf).

[1921] In the inner cave (S) two forces unite (Y) here where we are (K) and the solar force appears which remains in the heart (E).

[1922] The logical thought (S) enters the therapy brought by the snakes transformed into forces of light who go back to the caduceus (Y) bringing the decision and the capability for the action (KE).

So, we have a memory of the Jahvetic Initiation, since Jahve is a Spirit by the Solar Form who acted through the Moon to connect the Jewish People to the spiritual world. One last interesting aspect of the fig is given by its gelatinous sap which reminds us of the "waters of below" that are not yet purified by the Light. Lastly, in nature the fig is not sweet, but thanks to the process of caprification done by wasps, it develops a sweet taste, which is the sugars that are connected to hydrogen, and therefore the Spirit. The process of caprification corresponds to the transition between egotistical love to altruistic love. It is interesting to learn that this process was historically practiced for the first time in Jericho, which is the city that represents the most dark, egotistical point of humanity (see Mc 10,46). It is interesting to see how the word "fig" comes from the Latin "ficus" and it means liver. From this, we get the connection between this organ and the Light that it can accumulate in relation to the spiritual work that has been done. The fig-liver can relate to the desires of the world or the one of the spirit: the Jesus will curse the first one of these two.

FISH: symbol of what lives in our **subconscious** and that needs to be brought to consciousness, from which the various miracles of fishing. Its **scales** represent the ahrimanic aspect; its foul smelling **insides** represent the luciferic aspect. Its being "with no NECK" represent the lack of word, the Logos. Let's remember that they were created by God on the fifth day (therefore they are less evolved), while the other animals were created on the sixth day. See also SCORPIO.

FISHERMEN (or BOATSWAINS): The ones who assisted the priests in the Hebrew ritual of baptism. They had the function to pull out from the water the ones being baptized with certain nets (so that they wouldn't drown). Their job was to guide the soul of the initiate in the astral regions (from which comes the name "boatswain").

FLESH: This word has deep and complex meanings. From the Greek **sarx**, it has several meanings: "flesh", "man", "human nature", "corrupted nature", "mortal life" and also "king", "queen", "strength", "sovereign ruler". If we follow the spiritual meaning of each letter that make up this word, we find: S (within us, in the cave from which we enter), A (beginning, the primordial beginning), R (the Father, the highest aspect), X (the casket, the coffin, that is below). Therefore, the "flesh" is the **tool for the manifestation of a divine principle.**

In Hebrew, flesh is said *basar* and it means "primordial earth" and the word has in the middle the syllable *sin* which means 300, which is the number of movement, of the dynamism: the 3 (which is the ternary principle of God that overcomes the luciferic duality) descended on Earth (*basar*) as a seed for the changing of the flesh of man, to achieve the last marriage, the inner marriage. The flesh becomes the location for the complete fulfillment, of one of the most intimate unions with God.

Always in Hebrew, we find that *basar* comes from *basorah*: the good News/Novel, the Gospel. Lastly, *basar* is the abbreviated form of *beresit*, the "principle" of the Genesis, and therefore *basar* represents the Christic Principle that manifests itself, while *beresit* is the unmanifested Principle.

FLUTE (FLUTE PLAYER): the flute is the physical transposition of the larynx, and this organ transforms itself with **puberty.** Therefore they are the **entities** that preside over this transformation (see CROWD).

G

GABRIEL: From the Hebrew **gabar** (to have strength) and **el** (God), which means **God is strong, or the fortitude of God.**

GALILEE: it means **hybrid location**, with no blood related connection; it corresponds to the forces of the Father.

GASPARE: from the ancient Iranian **gazbar**, which means **bearer of treasure** (maybe in reference to the Spirit Man, the "treasure" of the matter).

GEENA: topographically, it was a cliff right outside of Jerusalem where waste would be thrown off, and also the bodies of dead animals. A fire was always burning and emanating a vile smell. For this image, it represents hell.

It also represents one of the rivers of the terrestrial Heaven. Precisely *Guibon*, the second spring of the main river of Heaven, the river that comes from God and brings life to all the creatures. *Guibon* also means "womb", the matrix of fire that purifies the man, who is forged by it, so that he can have the purified river of life flowing through him along his spinal cord. The first spring, the highest one, is *Pison,* the manifestation, the face. No one can descend in it if they first did not reach the I Am. Jesus will be the one to descend in it to free Adam and bring back the flesh in his vocation of Incorruptible Body. The third river is Chiddechel, the forth river is the Euphrates.

GENEZARETH: village that gives the name to the lake (or sea). It was the ground of Genner-Kinereth, which has been sacred from time immemorial to the god Ciniro-Adonis: seed of the grain that dies in the earth and then resurrects.

GEROLAMO: From the Greek **ieros** (sacred) and **onoma** (name), which means **sacred name**; or the **one who sanctifies the name,** who reached the Higher I.

GETHSEMANE: physically it is located East of Jerusalem, where the Sun-Spirit rises. It means (from the spiritual composition of the word): **the earth (physical location) where we expand to God. This place is within ourselves, and there the divine forces appear (luminous) and we can grasp them. The Mother Sophia gifts us here the beginning for a new connection with the mind of God, the Logos.** From what we just said, it represents the aura of life that surrounds the pituitary gland, from which we have the word "halo", which means "crown", like the highest one of the Sephirot (Keter, see SEPHIROT). Therefore, it represents the renewal, in a Christian sense, of the higher dimension to which we enter through the Crown (see). Exoterically, it means "olive press", therefore the place (of consciousness) where the oil is made, where we work for the Christic Initiation (see OIL). This is the "place" of consciousness in which the man can freely decide whether to take within him the chalice of Evil and pain of the world to transform it into Good. **The halo** corresponds to the reaching of the Seraphinic Zodiac, the dimension of love that we reach after "exiting" the chakra with 1000 petals at the top of the head, which corresponds to Saturn (the last planet of the Zodiac), and after the elevation of the consciousness beyond the physical body, image of the Cherubic Zodiac (see chapter *Spiritual vision of the geography of the Palestine)*, through the 12 "points" of the crown. Therefore a "spherical cap" forms which unites the 12 mounts in a thirteenth mount. This is also represented in the shape of the royal crowns. Almost at the top is BETHANY, where the resurrection of Lazarus happened, and also the Ascension happened. East of there, a road took to JERICHO and on the west side, another road would take to JERUSALEM through CEDRON.

GIONATA: It means **gift of God.**

GLORY: This term refers to the **higher union with the divine.** Precisely it indicates the **synergy between the clairaudience** (which allows us to perceive the music of the spheres and listen to the inner word), which rises within us from the interaction between our Loving Vital Spirit and the astral body, and the **clairvoyance** (which allows us to grasp the higher soul reality and therefore gift our transformed soul part), which is born from the action of our Spirit Man in the astral body.

GOD: the creating Principle. Depending if he is being mentioned with an article or without, it can indicate:

1. **"the" God**: the creating Principle of the Holiest Trinity, the One who generated the whole Universe;
2. **God**: the creating Principle of the Holy Trinity, the one who created our evolutionary solar system (from the Zodiac to us).

GOLGOTHA: from the Hebrew *Gulgolet* which means "location of the cranium". To be more exact, it means the "liberation from the exile", and in the man it corresponds to the head having the chakra with 1000 petals on top, which is the spiritual center that connects us to the zodiacal sphere, the Father. Inside, we have the thalamus (or "optical chambers") as the expression of the last inner wedding between right side (Father-wisdom) and left side (Mother-intelligence) of the brain, under there is the pituitary gland (the fruit of union) that leans on the Turkish saddle: the Grail cup within us.

The word Golgotha also refers to the city of Golgi situated in Cipro in front of Syria. This last one represents the star Sirius, which is the double macrocosmic saddle of the forces of Lucifer and Ahriman. In the element square, Cipro is at the same level as Crete and therefore corresponds to the middle axis between the above (element Earth and Water) and the below (element Air and Fire), and therefore representing the mercurial element. Cipro represents the aspect “east” of the clay and therefore the michaelian door, what the alchemists called the “dry path”, the path that directly takes you to the spirit going through death and resurrection. Therefore, it is the antagonist (in the good) of Syria-Sirius0Evil, and it represents the forced transition for the macrocosmic Initiation. In a microcosmic initiation, we are on the top of the head, in the chakra with 1000 petals, in the area of the babies’ dimple or fontanelle.

GOSPELS: from the Greek *evangelion*, which means “the good news”, intended as the announcement of the Resurrection of the Jesus Christ. The four canonical Gospels represent the main Christic initiatic currents: Saint Matthew represents the Gnosis, which resounds with the sphere of Saturn, the “door” for the Higher Spiritual World, and therefore the Preparation to the Christic Initiation. Saint Mark, who “sees” the resurrection of the daughter of Jairus and records as the main event the Transfiguration-Enlightenment, represents the current of the light, of the Sophia, of Abel. Saint Luke, the only evangelist to “see” the resurrection of the Son of the widow of Nain, represents the current of the Chosen People, of Manu, of Set, and that this “son” incarnates. This is why Luke uses a lot of parables, which are teachings that are appropriate to all levels of consciousness, all the members of the Chosen People. Saint John, the only one who “sees” the resurrection of Lazarus, represents the current of the Rosicrucians, of Cain, the individuality that lived in Lazarus-John.

All of this is reflected in the therapeutic value of the four Gospels Mark indicates the healing of the seven chakras in their etheric aspects; Luke indicates the healing of the chakras in their soul aspect; John indicates the healing of the chakras in their spiritual aspect…

GREGORY: from the Greek **gregoreo,** which means **the one who watches/monitors.**

H

HAIR: Hair represents the spiritual force that permeates man. Let’s remember that since they are placed on the top of the head, they represent the “olive trees” of the Garden of the Olive trees, which is the Serafinic Zodiacal dimension. From the Hebrew *sear*, they are the “principle”, the “principle planted in the spring of the being”. The Hebrew term also indicates the fear in front of the divine vision.

HAND: the hand in Hebrew is *yada,* and it represents the knowing, but it also means “I love”. This knowing is marriage; it is spiritual love. In the sense of the tri-articulation of the whole arm, it represents the Holy Spirit (while the forearm represents the Son and the upper arm represents the Father). In the Psalm tradition, the right hand represents the Holy Spirit that enlivens, and the left hand represents the Son that structures, molds, shapes. The hands put together represent the union of the force that structures with the knowledge that enlivens.

The fingers of the hand also have a precise meaning: thumb-Venus-head; index finger-Jupiter-gallbladder; middle finger-Saturn-spleen/pancreas; ring finger-Sun-liver; pinky-Mercury-heart.

HARLOT: from the Greek **pornes**, which indicates the **neophyte** reality, the initiate, the one (female) who resounds with the step of the Crow, in the Persian Initiation…

TO HEAL: from an illness, from a **biological** evil, therefore often it is **ahrimanic.**

TO HEAL: to free from the action of an unclean spirit (mostly luciferic), therefore it is a healing in the spiritual plane.

HEROD: Herod means **son of Eros or heroic son.**

HERODIAS: from **eros and diade** (the generating principle), which means **the multiplying principle of the Eros,** and therefore it represents the **luciferic presence in the soul** (it is a woman).

HOSANNA: the spiritual composition of the word (the original version is *hosannan*) has the following meaning: **the spiritual entity that descends and makes itself available to us through a vortex that brings us towards the Earth to conjoin with it, in our dark inner part. This is the beginning of the Logos within us, and now the action of the Logos starts within us.**

HOUR (indication of): the hour represents **an aspect of the chakra,** and to be precise the single "petals" (see DAY). When the hour is being indicated, or the moment (evening, morning) in which something happens, we are indicating **which macrocosmic zodiacal force** is acting through the Jesus. Since the zodiacal forces are brought to earth by the Christ, which aspect of the Christ is acting is being indicated, **and not the time of the day, which is completely different from the list that you are about to read..** The relationships are the ones that follow, and they are highlighted by the **articles** in front of the time:

- The first hour (6.00-7.59): ARIES;
- The second hour (8.00-9.59): TAURUS;
- The third hour (10.00-11.59): GEMINI;
- The fourth hour (12.00-13.59): CANCER;
- The fifth hour (14.00-15.59): LEO;
- The sixth hour (16.00-17.59):VIRGO;
- The seventh hour (18.00-19.59): LIBRA
- The eighth hour (20.00-21.59): SCORPIO;
- The ninth hour (22.00-23.59): SAGITARIUS;
- The tenth hour (24.00-1.59): CAPRICORN

- The eleventh hour (2.00-3.59): AQUARIUS;
- The twelfth hour (4.00-5.59): PISCES.

At sunrise (time 6), the Luminous Zodiac begins, the Mystical Lamb, the part of the Zodiac that is already made conscious within us, and it is ready for the sacrifice to redeem the part of us that is still not conscious, dark.

At sunset (time 18), the Dark Zodiac begins (the Virgin Sophia), the part of us that we still need to make conscious. The dark Zodiac is formed by 153 stars, from which comes the number of the miraculous fishing.

There also was a spiritual rhythm to the calculation of time, in which every 9 days there was a going through all of the 12 zodiacal constellations, and therefore each constellation "lasted" 18 hours (like the time between the capturing of the Jesus and his death: the time of the darkness-Scorpio). The events of the Passion, according to this esoteric rhythm, result in being articulated this way: Thursday from 3 to 21 acts in Libra (represented by the linen on the hips of the Last Supper); Thursday from 21 to Friday at 15 acts in Scorpio (represented by Judah and death); Friday from 15 to Saturday at 9 acts in Sagittarius (represented by the meeting with Ahriman in the darkness); Saturday from 9 to Sunday at 3 acts in Capricorn (represented by the new Christmas, the birth of the new Adam); Sunday at 3 until the 21 acts in Aquarius (represented by the ascending to the sky of the Jesus as Man-Angel); Sunday from 21 to Monday at 15 the Pisces act (represented by the eating of the fish at the meeting with the Eleven).

Lastly, "hour" **without the article** indicates the hour of the day (first hour from 6.00 to 6.59, second hour from 7.00 to 7.59, etc.)...

HOUSE: as a "residence", a word that comes from "*abito*" (in Italian residence is "*abitazione*", and clothes is "*abito*"). Since the *abito* (clothes) cover and protect the physical body, "house" is the **combination of the subtle bodies** of the man, starting from the etheric body. From *abito*, we have "*abitudine*" which is Italian for habit, which is the characteristic of the etheric body, or "*abito mental*" which is Italian for mindset, as the form of our thoughts (of an astral-etheric nature). The old styles of clothes would exalt the forms of the subtle bodies and would help the flow. Let's remember that the tunic (in Italian it's *casacca, casa-acca*), which is something that covers us up to the neck, protects our whole body. See also CLOTHING.

"House" comes from the Latin word ***domus***, which is the "house of God". In Jesus' case, the "house" represents the retiring into his higher dimensions, surrounded by the Twelve (or some of them), or by who He would invite by Grace into this higher dimension. It is the "breath" of the Jesus who is on Earth and then "goes back" to His "house", and it corresponds to the return of the Spirit of the man, who ascends during the night into the soul-spiritual worlds and descends in the terrestrial conscious sphere during the day.

ISAAC: from the Hebrew **Yi** (God) and **zahaq** (to smile), which means **the one who God smiles upon;** it represents the **Loving Vital Spirit** in Israel.

ISRAEL (HOUSE OF ISRAEL): this definition refers to the Chosen People, the ones who enter the Kingdom.

J

JACOB: from the Hebrew **Jaakob**, which means **God's follower.** In Israel, it represents the **Spiritual Self.**

JAMES: the spiritual step of "James" has a teacher, **Moses,** and he represents the initiate in the mysteries of the Time (connected to the three inner planets). This level is in the spiritual line of the virtue of **justice.** Amongst the Apostles, James Minor (the Salomonic brother of the Jesus) represents the **individualized I,** while James Major (son of Zebedee) represents the access to the **solar spiritual I.**

JESUS: It has multiple meanings depending on the context. On its own, it means **God is salvation.**

1. **"the" Jesus**: Jesus when **he manifests the principle Christ** (he is the one that gives initiations-miracles); he teaches through the universal spirit with **Amen** (individual truth, or referred to the Holy Trinity) and **Amen Amen** (universal truth, or in the Holiest Trinity- see TRUTH)..
2. **Jesus:** the union of **the two Jesus** (after 12 years) and within whom the Christ will descend at the Jordan; he teaches through the **Sophia.**
3. **"Teacher" Jesus (Didaskalos,** which is "the One who teaches to the Children", from the connection with the Latin word **discipulus, (**see DISCIPLE): Jesus as **preceptor,** the I of Zarathustra in Jesus that **teaches**. This aspect resounds with the **Father**, and the Father elaborated all of the thoughts relating to the spiritual evolution of man; He teaches and **instructs**, that means he **builds, he reinforces the I** (I-nstruct, "he builds the I").
4. **Rhabbi** (see), **Teacher Jesus (Epistata), Savior:** the purified soul (*Nirmanakaya)* of the Buddha in Jesus who **preaches**; in his pure aspect of **Nathanic soul, he preaches through the Sophia and the Logos.**
5. **Jesus "himself":** Jesus (second point) as a **prophet** and as irradiating the Light of the Incorruptible Body, the Spirit Man (Mt 17,8)..
6. **Jesus Christ: the Lord of the Karma,** this from the Golgotha on…

7. **"the" Jesus "alone":** the Jesus with the Christ within him without the presence of the Father (Mc 9,7), which means within the Loving Vital Spirit…
8. **Jesus "alone":** Jesus without the Father and with the presence of the purified soul within him (*Nirmanakaya)* of the Buddha, acting as Spiritual Self (Lc 9,36)..
9. **"The Lord" Jesus:** the Risen One, united forever to the Entity of the Christ…

JEREMIAH: From the Hebrew **Yermeyah,** which means **God has struck** (with misfortunes), or **God's exaltation.**

JERUSALEM: it is a Hebrew word, but it is also esotherically considered Greek from **ieros** (sacred) and **lemma** (word received from above), and therefore **sacred word.** Together with Bethphage, Bethany and Bethlehem, it forms the "tetrahedron" of the Inner Light. Differently from the near by villages (see Bethlehem, Bethany, Bethphage), it is not a "house", and therefore it does not bring the "subtle" aspects. Therefore, it represents the ordinary I, the sacred Word fixed in human forms that becomes dead (represented by Scribes and Pharisees).

JOACHIM: from the Hebrew **Yohaquim,** it means **God makes us strong.**

JOHN: From the Hebrew **Johaman,** which means **Gift of God, or also God had mercy.** It is the name of the bearer of the Initiation in the I. It represents the bowing down, the radiating of God in the man.

JONAH: prophet who spent three days of Initiation inside the whale. This is the experience of three days of dark, after which the man receives the inner Sign. It is no longer an era of teacher, prophets or sibyls, today the Spirit begins talking to us starting from within us. The "sign" is the fact that Jonah is being "thrown up" by the fish, and he reached the seashore (the imaginative consciousness). The throwing up is a gesture from which from the metabolism. From the longings, we go up to the head, the consciousness, and therefore it corresponds to the purification of the Kundalini, the old luciferic initiation. To this ahrimanic and luciferic generation, it will be "given" to be in the storm, to enter the fish, etc., and therefore the test will be given to them to purify themselves. The whale represents the animalistic holding entities of the feminine primigenital forces (the Black Mother) present in our depths, the parts that need to be redeemed to then unite to them in an initiatic marriage. This will be possible with the Golgotha, the "sign" given by Jesus to all of humanity, who opened the door for everyone to go back to the House of the Father.

JORDAN: from the Hebrew **jor** and **dan** , which mean **flows near Dan** (one of the 12 Tribes and an ancient Biblical city); also the **flowing.** It represents the forces of the I that flow through man along his spinal cord. The Jordan connects the waters of below (amniotic fluid-womb) with the ones of above (Dead Sea-head).. In the man, the waters of below no longer reflect the ones of above, and therefore they flow towards death. As the divine seed reawakens within us, the wound of the fall (FOOT) closes up and the flux gets reversed (see hemorrhage), and we start to participate in the Cosmic Life. Jesus will also immerse himself in the sphere of what is still incomplete to re-ascend immediately. He goes down Adam's path again, he descends in the shadow-feminine-darkness side that he needs to marry so that it can be accomplished. The expression "on this side of the Jordan" represents the whole man with his consciousness and therefore his esoteric transposition, the Chosen People. From this we also have "on the other side of the Jordan" which represents the human condition of one who is outside of the Chosen People.

JOSEPH: from the Hebrew **Yosephyah**, which means **God sends more children.** From the Hebrew Yosef or the Aramaic Iose, meaning **the one who grows in God. The "Nathanic" Joseph was an Essene disciple** who probably reached a high level of initiation, and therefore had the external symbols of the hammer and wooden hatchet for a long time. From this came the exoteric belief that he was a woodworker in his practical life. It is nice to remember that he was considered an art teacher, and in the light of what we just said, this expression can refer to a teacher of the spiritual arts. The fact that he gets married "when he is old" can make us think that he reached the third step of Initiation (Contemplative), and that he "accepted" the familiar life (second step). See ESSENS.

JOSEPH OF ARIMATHEA: let's remember that Joseph is the name that is given to the ones who "grow in God". He was an initiate in Arimathea, a word that means "*rama*" (city located on the hill), and "*theos*" (God), therefore *city,* or place, *of the inspiring consciousness.* Joseph of Arimathea is represented with a turban on his head: the crowd to which he was always connected, the crowd that connects him to the union between Bride and Groom in the dimension of the Infinite One..

JUDAH: from the Hebrew **Jehudah,** which means **zealot (supporter) of God and praise of God.**

K

KIDNEYS: they are the symbol of force and fragility. What was conquered in the lower human sphere, now becomes the seed for the upper sphere since they control the genital sphere, and at the same time, they open the upper path to the Word. They are the organs of the intuitive hearing. They preside over the transition from water to blood (that then transmutes into Spirit), and the transition from salt to fire that turns into Light.

KIDRON: valley or ditch that runs along the east part of the wall of Old Jerusalem and separated the Mount of the Temple from the Mount of the Olive Trees.

KINGDOM: at the origin, the **Malkut,** the Earth (see SEPHIROT). All that the human I can consciously experience. In the initiatic path, the disciple expands more and more what he is able to experience up to the **Kingdom of the Skies** (see), which belongs to the Chosen People (see).

KINGDOM OF THE SKIES: today, the spiritual dimension that belongs to the **Son of God, the Cherubic Zodiac** towards which the Christ brought the Path to humanity to enter (see SEPHIROT). It belongs to the Chosen People (see), which means everyone who has Faith in Jesus Christ.

KUNDALINI: old name of the reawakening of the initiatic forces along the spinal cord (see PATH). It represents the reawakening of the "snake of fire", of the forces of **Lucifer** within us that give us magical capabilities, but subjugate our consciousness. They deprive us of our freedom. This is represented by the snake placed on the head of the Pharaoh (who received this awakening).

KNEE: The knee represents different aspects of the man. It is the eye that looks at the future (in Italian *gin-occhio, occhio* means eye), the kneecap is the actual "seed" of the brain that the man will develop in the evolutionary phase called "future Venus". The word knee in Hebrew is *baruk,* and the word blessing is *Baraka*. Therefore, saying knee and saying blessing is the same thing. The knee is connected to the constellation of Capricorn, which is ruled by Saturn who rules the head. From this we have to get on one's knees and put the head on the floor between the knees (a practice used in Islam).

L

LAZARUS: from the Hebrew **Eleazar,** which means **assisted by God.**

LAW: old pre-Christian form of relationship with the Divine, based on the **blind obedience** to the revealed precepts. The Law would put order through external practices as a consequence of the Fall within us. **The Law has been overcome** thanks to Jesus Christ, who transformed it into **Grace and Truth.** This means that the "new order" consists of going back to God consciously and in Freedom (daughter of the new Truth) and Love (taking us to the Grace). By doing so, we can form a new community of Love, the Celestial Jerusalem of the Apocalypse.

LEBANON: It means "incense", which is the wood that burns to purify the astral body (soul) of the man.

LEGION: It is a negative crowd with a soul-spiritual nature (see Mc 5,11-21).

LEGS: the legs represent within us the forces of libido, and only the man who can dominate those forces becomes able to fully go through the path of inner transformation. This force is externally represented by the horse.

LEPROUS: spiritual **characterization** that indicates one **who was possessed by Lucifer.**

LEVITES: the tribe of the descendants of Levi, who needed to serve in the religious ceremonies.

LIMP: It is the second step (Mercury) of Initiation. The limp refers to one who finds it hard to go from filial love to spiritual love… It represent the one who has yet to marry himself in his wholeness but he has begun to take the step towards his "verticalization", the conquering of the 12 dorsal vertebrae (see SNAKE).

LITTLE: the "littles" (see Mc 9,12) are the Upper Limbs of the man in gestation, the Spiritual Limbs, which receive their "seed" from the Holy Trinity, and then they are "gestated" from the Marian Force that transforms our soul. Finally, they "are born" as Children of the Spirit (see John 1,13; John 3,3; John 12,36).

M

MAGDALEN: **woman of Magdala.** The Magdalen is a little bit like the mother of the alchemists since she achieved within herself the Great Opera: the transformation of the "putrid waters" into waters of Life (represented by the unction with the oil on the head of the Jesus). In Christian esotericism, she is represented by the Black Madonna.

MAGDALA: In Hebrew it is said *migedal* which means **tower,** but it also contains the root *meged* which means "the best". It is a city on the Sea of Galilee, and it is represented by the **constellation Taurus-THROAT.**

MAN: there are various ways to say "man" in the Gospels. Precisely:

- **Anthropos,** the man in his ordinary, on the path towards the Spirit. Sometimes this term is also being used to indicate Spiritual Guides of the spiritual spheres.
- **Aner,** the "groom", the Enlightened (translated as the "enlightened man").
- **Plousios,** (associated with Anthropos), the rich man, the one who is on the initiatic path up to the "Father" (most elevated step). It represents the one who is entering the Kingdom…

MARKUS: from the Latin **marticus,** which means **sacred to Mars.**

MARY: from the Hebrew **mar** (drop) and **yam** (sea), which means **drop of the sea.** It was the **spiritual title given to the little girls that were raised and educated in the Temple** so that they would be ready for the wedding and birth under the guidance of the Priests, so that the birth would happen in a state of darkened consciousness (like a dream), and therefore the spouses would not get caught in the luciferic passion. From this union, particularly elevated souls would descend. This event was synonymous with **virginity**, and this term means the complete harmonic and hierarchical agreement between the Spirit, Soul, and the Body of the person. We find different Marys in the Gospel who would take as their middle name (Cleopha, Salome,

Magdalen, etc.), their father's name, or their husband's name, or the name of the place of Initiation. **Mary, Mother of Jesus, is the archetype of all the Marys.** Therefore, she is called only Mary. In her case, the birth happened directly, thanks to the Spirit.

MARTHA: from the Aramaic **Martha,** it means **mistress/owner.** In the Essen initiation, the creating forces of Nature (the Angels) also included two "mortal" (which means incarnated) male creatures: Elxai and Yesseus (the Jewish People Jacob and Esau'), who symbolically represented the principle of Good and Evil. Elxai comes from the El-Hai (Living God), and Yesseus from Yesod, the negative principle of the Kabbalah. These two incarnated entities correspond to the feminine Martha and Marthana (or Mathranita). The name Martha represents **a title that indicates a role in becoming a positive tool of the Creation.** This will find its metamorphosis, **its higher title,** in **Mary.**

According to some ancient Christian traditions, the hemorrhaging woman was Martha, and therefore she knew very well which potent forces of life act within Jesus.

MATTHEW: from the Hebrew **math** (dono) and **yah** (God), which means **gift of God.**

MELCHIOR: from the Hebrew **melki'or** , which means **my king is light** (maybe in reference to the Spiritual Self, the "King", the Higher I).

MEMORY: from the Greek **mnemeion,** usually translated as "sepulcher", but in reality it indicates a state of consciousness of one who remembers his divine origin, and within it the presence of the Christ. The memory also represents the experience of the inner wedding that "activates"in our head the Light of the pituitary gland, the gland that represents the Light of the Grail within us, and which is the "spring" of Light of the third eye, the chakra of Sophia, of Jupiter. Let's remember that the center of the memory in the brain is anatomically found in the parts of the brain that are called **thalamus**, and therefore in the "thalamus" of the inner wedding. In **Hebrew,** the word "memory" is equal to "male", and this means the one who becomes "male-aner" within himself, what he "remembers" of his inner skies, of his divine origin. The word "sepulcher" also has a deeper meaning. This word also refers to one of the consequences of the process of the etherization of the blood. With this process, the blood current is rhythmically modified so that the etheric body gets out of the "sepulcher" in which it is enclosed, in the head. The impulse comes to life from the heart-Sun, after which the impulse of the Christ is welcomed.

MICHAEL: from the Hebrew **mi-kha-el,** which means **Who is like God?** Before the Golgotha, it is the face of Jahve, and then he ascends to the rank of the Face of the Christ.

MISTAKES: they are connected to the etheric body in relationship to the Fall from the etheric body to the physical-material body. They are mainly connected to the etheric brain. We do wrong when we interpret the things of the materialistic world. We overcome this by "changing mind" with the experience of the Baptism of Water.

MOSES: from the Hebrew **Masciah,** which means **saved by the waters.** Moses represents the initiation of the minor Mysteries (mysteries of the Time). Within him, the wisdom of Zarathustra acted since he donated to Moses his purified etheric body full of cosmic images. With the Exodus from Egypt, he purified the Hebrew people from the influences of the religion of Baal which was established in Egypt. See also EASTER.

MOUNT: generically, in a microcosmic sense, **the neck and the head,** or better the etheric force that supports the head, the consciousness… The term "Mount" is also used to indicate the ascending path that the disciples are called to take to reach the top. This path is articulated in **seven steps** (from "the Mountain with seven cliffs"). The seventh cliff corresponds to the soul sphere of Saturn, and also to the hierarchy of the **Thrones,** another term used in the Gospels.

In the Sacred Writings, the mountain represents the sphere higher than the terrestrial one, the sphere of the inspiring consciousness, the lower Devachan. In the Gospels, the Jesus urges us to have the faith that moves mountains, which are the obstacles to the direct spiritual vision. Therefore, we are in front of a double meaning: region of the Spirit, and obstacle of the complete vision of the Spirit. In the Apocalypse (Verse 8,8), the mountain is materialism that prevents us from grasping the spiritual reality. It is the sphere of the "physical-sensory" perception, which prevents us from grasping the higher reality. The seven mountains are the barrier that we need to overcome to go from the sensitive world to the suprasensitive world. Not only Rome, but also Prague is built on seven mountains, and Prague means "threshold".

MOUNT OF THE OLIVE TREEES: see GETHSEMANE.

MULTITUDE: **the crowd not yet aggregated** (see CROWD).

MUTE: the mute does not pronounce the Logos-Son. He is blocked in the development of the eightfold path, in the path of compassion, in the propaedeutic force to the development of love…

MUSTARD: a really big plant born from an extremely small seed. The word comes from the Egyptian and Greek *senapes*, assonant with the word synapsis, which means "connection". The mustard, in this light, appears as the representative of the inner force that connects us to the Spirit.

N

NAME: if a name is simple, it indicates the person in his/her ordinary consciousness, or a place in its ordinary terrestrial condition. If there is an article in front of it, it indicates the higher aspect of the person or the place. If it is repeated twice, it activates the forces of transformation present in that person or place…

NATHANAEL: it means the "divine Nathan", which is the priestly line (represented by Nathan) renewed in the connection with God (let's remember that the "Nathanic" Jesus descends from Nathan).

NATHANIC SOUL: Part of the soul of Adam which stayed in the spiritual worlds at the moment of Adam's Fall. It is bearer of the seeds of the three Upper Limbs of the man. These three aspects will incarnate into the John the Baptist, in Mariam, and in Jesus.

NAZARETH: it means **the germinating one, the blooming one, or the flower.** It is near the ancient city of Kefer (Keter, see SEPHIROT), Jonah's homeland. It is on an upland 140 km North of Jerusalem. It was the headquarters of the disciples of **Nazaratos**, an incarnation of Zarathustra of 600 B.C. Zarathustra then descended on the Salomonic Jesus, in which He brought back the wisdom of the mysteries to the corrupted side of the current of David.

NECK: from the Hebrew *savar* it means "the divine bait that catches the man to take him to the light". Analogous to this, we have the word "nape" (*oref*) which means "freedom from the tunic of skin". To have a "shaved nape" means to not allow to be caught by the divine lure, to be healed and to which the wings of a bird-eagle cannot lift up. See also THROAT and SEFIROT.

NEOPHYTE: the word comes from the Greek **neofyton,** which is "**new plant",** but the neophytes in the Gospels are indicated with the term **telonios,** which is usually translated as"publican". In reality, it indicates "**the one who works on his inner transformation to reach his spiritual goal".** It represents the one (masculine or feminine, see HARLOT) who has accomplished the first step in the Mysteries, but he is not yet a disciple, and therefore it represents the first step of Initiation, which resounds with the Crow of the ancient Persian Initiation...

NET: the combination of the spiritual links and connections of a reality.

NICODEMUS: from the Greek *nike* (victory) and *demos* (people), the "winner of the people", the one who has reached the **sixth initiatic step** (after the "name of the people", the fifth step), which means to have reached the dimension of "Son" connected to Jupiter. The Nicodemus of the Gospels was a Pharisee (see). He was an archon (in Greek *archon*), who was one of the chief magistrates of the Sanhedrin. For these considerations, he was more than an Enlightened One (*aner);* he was almost an Initiate. His initiation was completed by the Christ "in the night" (which means in the "subtle" planes) to open him up to the mysteries of the Light. Together with Joseph of Arimathea, he was the owner of the upper room where Jesus celebrated the Easter. In contrase, the Nicolaitanes of the Apocalypse (they are a group, without the individual I) are won (*nike*) by the mass (*laos*) by what is agitated in an unconscious way within the man. In Nicodemus (he is an individual, an individual I), the forces of freedom that are present in the man are the ones that win the ego over. The Greek language does not support the different interpretations that we find in the group-individual aspect.

NOAH: from the Hebrew **Noah,** it means **calm,** rest.

NUMBERS: the Hebrew alphabet foresaw that each letter corresponded to a number, therefore numbers and letters could be read in a crossed manner. Let's look at the Hebrew names and numbers:

- The number 1 is the Father of all full numbers. Before time and before creation, for long eons, only these two numbers existed: 0 (the Empty Chaos) and 1 (God who generates all of the other things, all of the infinite numbers). There was a time in which the infinite (figure eight) also "lived" inside the number 1. Even though they cohabited, the number 1 is its opposite, which filled it up first. It represents the Omnipotent God. The number 1 is The Only One, from which all the other numbers come. It is the Plotinian One.
- In Hebrew the 2 is *beth* which means "house", a word that indicates the principle of receptivity, which is like the "you" created before receiving the principle of the creating "I". The first house of the man is the Mother.
- In Hebrew the 3 is *gimel* which means "camel", a word that indicates the principle of joining, of uniting, of the dynamic movement in the sphere of the principles. It is connected to Venus, the planet of love.
- In Hebrew the 4 is *dalet* which means "door" and it indicates matter, the resistance, the death, the test, the matrix on this plane of principles. It is connected to Jupiter.
- In Hebrew the 5 is *he* which means "window" and it indicates the seed of life, the Son principle, the breath of existence put in the sphere of the principles that "enters" through the "window". It is connected to the constellation of Aries.
- In Hebrew the 6 is *waw* which means "hook", "hanger", a word that indicates union, the fecundation in the plane of the principles. It is connected to the constellation of Taurus.
- In Hebrew the 7 is *zayin* which means "weapon" and it indicates the principle of disappearance, of death, of the nothingness, but also of the return, the rebirth. It is connected to the constellation of Gemini.
- In Hebrew the 8 is *het* which means "fencing, sheepfold, gate, delineation", a word that indicates the principle of the barrier, opening, resurrection, return, rebirth of the world of the principles. It is connected to the constellation of Cancer.
- In Hebrew the 9 is *tet* which means "uterus", a word that indicates the principle of the perfection of the created and the feminine fulfillment. It is connected to the constellation of Leo.
- In Hebrew the 10 is the *yod* which means "hand", "active hand" which is the original creating potency, the Father Principle that acts in the plane of incarnation.

- In Hebrew the 11 is the *kaf* which means "hand", "active grabbing hand" which is the "secret value", the cycle of the repeated terrestrial lives in the plane of the incarnation. It is connected to Mars.
- In Hebrew the 12 is *lamed* which means "goad for the ox" where the ox represents the whole cosmos and the Bull/ox (from which the whole cosmos/world originates) is goaded to activate itself. Humanly, it is the capability to transform the reality and continue the creating opera. The 10 (which is the *yod*, which is the original creating potency, the Principle Father in the plane of incarnation) unites with the 2 (*beth.* The principle of receptivity, like the created "you" receives the principle of the creating "I"). It is connected to Libra.
- In Hebrew the 13th letter is the 40 and it is *mem* which means "water", "waves", "the flow (of water and time)". It indicates how the matter, the resistance, the death, the matrix, the test gets to the plane of the terrestrial incarnation. It is the Mother of Scorpio, and it used to be represented like a mother with many breasts (with a reference to the Milky Way where the dead live). It is connected to Scorpio (constellation from which the Milky Way comes). *AChaD* in Hebrew means "unity" and it is equal to 13 (A=1+Ch+8+D=4). The word "Love", *Ahebah,* also has the same number (A=1+H=5+B=2+H=5). In a cabalistic sense, we can say that AChaD=AHBH.
- In Hebrew the 14th letter is the 50 which is *nun* which means "fish". It indicates how the seed of life, the breath of existence, reaches the plane of the terrestrial incarnation, and it is the foundation of the existence in this world. With the 50 we enter in a new quality of time (the "old" time lasts from 1 to 49). The 50 belongs to the 8th day, the one of the revelation of the Spirit, and it is the highest resonance with the Resurrection.
- In Hebrew the 15th letter is the 60 and it is *samek* which means "snake". It indicates the union, the fecundation in the plane of the terrestrial incarnation. It also is the birth of the man.
- In Hebrew the 16th letter is the 70 which is *hain (or ahin),* which means "eye" and "fountain, spring of live water". It indicates the principle of time which flows from what is hidden. It also indicates the disappearance, the death, the nothingness, but also the return, the rebirth in the plane of the terrestrial incarnation.
- In Hebrew the 17th letter is the 50 and the 80 which is *peh* which means "mouth" meant in relationship to a border, with a limit between inside and outside. This word indicates a barrier, opening, resurrection, return, rebirth, in the plane of the terrestrial incarnation. It is connected to the constellation of Capricorn.
- In Hebrew the 18th letter is the 90 which is *tzade (or sade)* which means "part" or "capturing animals" or "a just man", like the one who captures the fish (in the

subconscious) or pulls out the man from the waters and takes him to dry land, which means to save him. The word also indicates the perfection of the created and the feminine fulfillment in the plane of the terrestrial incarnation. It is connected to Mercury.

- In Hebrew the 19th letter is the 100 and it is *qof* which means "eye of a needle". As we arrived to the one hundred, in the cosmic plane, a new life begins. This word indicates original creating potency, beginning of a new life, the Principle Father in His cosmic dimension. It is connected to Aquarius.
- In Hebrew the 20th letter is the 200 and it is *res* which means "head". It indicates the receptivity on the cosmic plane, which is the "you" created received the "I" cosmic creating. It is connected to the constellation of Pisces.
- In Hebrew the 21st letter is the 300 and in Hebrew the 20th letter is 200. It is *s'in* which means "tooth. It indicates movement, dynamism on the cosmic plane. As a bone it corresponds to Saturn meant as the door of the spiritual nourishment. The paths of knowledge are 32: like the teeth.
- In Hebrew the 22nd letter is the 400 which is *taw* which means "sign", "cross". It indicates matter, the resistance, the death, the test, the matrix on the cosmic plane.

With the 400, the 22 letters of the Hebrew alphabet end.

- In Hebrew the 500 is the *kaf* which means "eye of the needle". It indicates how the seed of life, the breath of existence works on the cosmic plane.
- In Hebrew the 1000 is *raf* which means "doctor". It indicates the unity that is reacquired through healing, with the Opera in red. From this the name of the healing archangel, Raphael.

O

OIL: it is the fruit of the Olive tree (see OLIVE TREE), and therefore it represents what we can offer to the spiritual world from within, like the Light-Truth and Warmth-Love. It represents the transformation of the water-sap in fire, and therefore the soul connected to the Spirit, to achieve the gift from the Holy Spirit…

OIL LAMP: also "torch" or "reflected light" (lunar type). It represents the inner light that each and every man possesses, but it gets turned on by the inner work. It is a gift of the Spirit. It represents the forces of the Spiritual Self born by the transformation of one's own soul. This transformation happens in the mysteries of the Light. It also represents the "horn" which is the organ to perceive the Spirit. It comes to life through the transformation of the lower bodies. The Jewish people perceived the Spirit through the force of blood. Now everything changes; the

Messianic "horn" completes his mission in the person of Jesus Christ. From a seed born in a family, it becomes a seed of the People, and lastly seed for the whole of humanity.

OLIVE TREE: esoterically, the olive tree represents the transformation of the circulation of the forces called "fig" (see FIG). From the spiritual composition of the Greek word **elaios,** we understand that the olive tree represents (after Golgotha) **the force of the Logos that gifts us the strength to reach all of our evolutionary goals[1923]...**

P

PARABOLA: expressive form in the form of images. For the ones who develop the *sense of the image,* the parabola is the spring of infinite conceptual interpretations.

PARACLETE: comes from *parakleo* which means "person called to stay close, to assist, to provide aid, to intercede"; like the judge in the judgment. The Jesus points out "another" Paraclete because this is the second Paraclete, the Spirit of the Truth of the next verse. The redeemed Lucifer, after Golgotha, will be the fourth Paraclete, the "plus one", the "inner" Paraclete that will descend at Pentecost. Lucifer was the one to "veil" the Truth, and now, returning to the service of the Father, he gives truth back to the man.

1. The **first Paraclete** (which is the "lawyer" or "intercessor") is Mary the Helper, who assists the soul in its path of redemption.
2. The **second Paraclete** is Jesus himself, the "external" Soother; "*Come to me, all of you who are tired and oppressed, and I will renew you*" (Mt 11,28).
3. The **third Paraclete** is the Spirit of Truth that Jesus breathed on his disciples the evening of Easter and he said, "*Receive the Holy Spirit*", almost begging them to accept His gift (John 14,16).
4. The **fourth Paraclete, the "plus one"** is the redeemed Lucifer who will descend at the Pentecost on Mariam (**the first Paraclete),** on the disciples that ascended to the step of Jesus (**the second Paraclete),** on which the Risen One had already blown His Spirit (the **third Paraclete).**

In the vision of the Opera, **the Spirit of Truth** is the Spirit of the Spirit of God, which is the Spirit created from man in the process of complete spiritualization of his own humanity. **It is not the Paraclete Spirit (redeemed Lucifer), and it is not the Son of man,** since this is the Jesus himself as a true man. This is the Spirit that He will blow on the disciples on Easter Sunday. This created Spirit is the combination of all the faculties and qualities that he, as a man, attracted to

---

[1923] The occult movement of the Word (E) is inserted in the thought that confronts itself with the world and dominates the forces of the Earth (L) to bring them back towards the etheric life (A) and soul (I). As we are transformed this way, we can descend to free the fallen Adam within us (O) and bring back the whole conscious thought (S).

himself, by tapping into his divine part, the Father within Him, and which he made his own by developing them and putting them into practice. This Spirit is also the Holy Spirit: the Holy Spirit within us.

To be more precise, the **third Paraclete** is the Risen Incorruptible Body and it is articulated in three aspects: the Holy Spirit (John 14,26) which is the Way; the Spirit of Truth (John 14,17) which is the Truth; and the Holy of the God (John 6,69) which is the Life.

PATH: The "path" in the Gospels represents the spiritual path. According to the situation, it can also represent the old paths (see FIRE), or the new paths (see VINE and OIL).

In a general sense, the path moves along the spinal cord, along the so-called "**sacred path**", which is the path on the sides of the spinal cord that the kidneys go down, from the area of the ears in the embryo, to reach their final destination. Examining the spinal cord, we can see how it is formed (from the upper part to the lower part) by 7 cervical vertebrae (the number which resounds with the mysteries of Time, with the path of the inwardness-thought-**Sophia**); the 12 dorsal vertebrae with the relating 12 pairs of ribs (the number which resounds with the mysteries of the Light of the heart-Sun-**Manu**, which we are called to get in touch with); the 10 vertebrae between the lumbar ones (5) and the sacral ones (5) which resounds with the number of the man, the 10 "divided" between the fallen part and the redeemed part (from which comes the symbol of the man in the star with five points, pointing towards the above or the below); finishing with the 4 vertebrae of the coccyx, that represent the number of matter (and therefore the path of the will-**Rosicrucian** that confronts the matter, and through the fallen man -the 5- gets to the Solar I Am- the 10 and the 12). So, we now have reached a total of 33 vertebrae, and by considering the fact that some say there are 33, and some say there are 34 (some do not have clear defined borders), we can hypothesize that they are 33.3, the Christic number.

The spinal cord is crossed by the spinal canal (except the 4 coccyx vertebra), which represent the "river" on which the "little boat" (see) flows, uniting the water "above" (the cerebro-spinal liquid) with the ones "below" (the seminal fluid). The cord ends in the sacrum, in which we find the sacred place within us, the "temple" of the will, the perineum (Greek name that means "around the temple"). In the Slavic language, the sacrum is said "tendril", to indicate the development of the new lunar path of the wine (see VINE).

Above the spinal cord, there is the cerebellum, which is the "hook" for the higher consciousness, the path for the memory (see).

PAUL: from the Latin **Paulus,** which means **little.**

PEACE: it indicates the condition in which the Christ acts within us, up to the physical body. The feet are conjoined at the head and the unity is re-established. This bears fruit, and these fruit are the condition of peace. This fruit-Word contains the new seeds that will be sown, and they will multiply according to the indication given by God to Adam. Let's remember that in Hebrew it is said *salom,* which means "accomplishment/fulfillment".

PHARISEES: **inner cult of Judaism off those who practice a strict and formal adherence to the law,** and who believed they had the **supremacy in the interpretation of the Writings**, since they affirmed that this science was being passed on from ancient times to the cult itself. They believed in immortality (**reincarnation**), in rewards for good work and in punishment for evil, all of this in the next life. **Pharisee** means **separated**, which is a term that corresponds to the "hidden" or "in private" of the Gospels. **Paolo and Nicodemus** were part of them, in their degenerated aspect, and they were the representatives for the **ahrimanic powers** that would oppose the Jesus. Their religious fanaticism to the oral tradition would bring them to be without inner Heat that is brought by the enthusiasm and the love for spiritual realities.

PHILIP: from the Greek word **filos** (friend) and **ippos** (horse); it means **horse lover,** and therefore of the forces of thought (which the horse symbolizes).

PIETRO/PETER: from the Greek **petros,** which means **stone** (see), and Tthe only Apostle in which Jesus changed his name. The level of "Pietro" represents the man who "enters" in the Chosen People, and it is connected to the element **Earth (**see JOHN, JACOB, ANDREW).

PIOUS WOMEN: Jesus always invites everyone who surrounds him to a higher level of comprehension of the aboveground matters. The first level of comprehension should belong to the APOSTLES, the second one to the chief PRIESTS (or Pharisees and Sadducees), the third one to the ROMANS. A fourth level added up to these three, a "+1", was given to the Pious Women. They are disciples (and therefore they correspond to the Apostles), they are priestly (connected to the lineage of Abel, and therefore the priests), they are Romans (since the wife of Pilate was amongst them). For these reasons, they will be the ones who will grasp the range of the action of the Christ within the Jesus, and they will be the first ones to meet him after the crucifixion.

PLEROMA: a combination of **spiritual entities** that collaborate for the fulfillment of a specific project.

PRIESTS: they belong to the tribe of Levi. Their task is to prepare the Chosen People for the "holy birth" (the virginal birth of the Jesus) and the "holy death", which means to welcome the resurrection of the Jesus Christ.

TO PROCEED: verb that indicates the action of the Father. From the Father, the evolution **proceeds** through the Principle Son and Holy Spirit, first from the Holiest Trinity and then the Holy Trinity, bringing with it the impulse of the Father. See also to SEND.

TO PRONOUNCE: it is the act in which the Jesus places a **purifying** virtue of all the bodies in what he is affirming. Often, to pronounce, refers to the **past,** to the accomplished experiences or the ancient relationship with the Spirit.

R

RAPHAEL: from the Hebrew **rapha** (to heal) and **el** (God), it means **God heals.**

REBECCA: from the Hebrew **ribhqab** (rope), meaning **woman that keeps a man close for his servitude.**

RESURRECT: the action through which we go back to living and **we enter the Eternal Life.**

RESUSCITATE: The action through which **we bring someone back to life.**

RABBI: In Hebrew it means **good teacher** (in reference to the aspect of the *nirmanakaya* of the Buddha present in the Nathanic Jesus, who expresses himself through his compassion). He expresses himself through parables (see). Rabbi comes from the Hebrew *rab* which means **multitude, greatness, lordship, the principality.**

ROMANS: they represent the maximum fall and the estrangement of the man from his spiritual origin. The job of the Romans was to suppress every relationship with the spiritual world. The emperors would acquire powers coming from the initiations by force through their conquering of of the headquarters of the Mysteries.

S

SADDUCEES: **Hebrew cult that did not believe in reincarnation.** They believed that the Good should have been accomplished for **the love of the good itself** (Greek philosophical doctrine) and for the other, and not for the desire of reward or penance. They particularly defended the **human free will.** They followed the written tradition and therefore the Pentateuch, **and they refused the oral tradition.** For all of these reasons, they often were in conflict with the Pharisees (see). They represent an **ahrimanic** aspect of opposition to the Jesus Christ.

SALIVA: saliva has a strong purifying and healing power. It comes from the syllable "sal", but also "health", "salvation", "Savior". In Hebrew, to spit is *yaroq* which basically is equal to *yereq*, the greenery, the green of life, of light, of eternity.

Opposite to the saliva-light, we have to s"pit on someone's face", and a consequence of this gesture is the non-light that goes against the one who showed his adversity through this gesture. Spiritually, he is punished with leprosy. "To spit on the ground" was also an exorcism against the evil spirits.

SALT: the salt represents the I, the spirit, present in everything even if in an invisible form. The salt is formed thanks to the collaboration between alkaline substances (terrestrial representatives of the forces of the Virgo), and halogen substances (representative of the Pisces), and therefore of the axis Pisces-Virgo, the therapeutic axis of the Zodiac. The ones who are in between "Pisces and Virgo", and therefore the Chosen People who follow the Christ to redeem the Cosmos, are the "salt" of the world itself, the ones who are in the world but not of the world.

The salt presides in the cells of the wedding between light and darkness so that all of the darkness can be transformed into Light.

The word "salt" in Hebrew is formed by the same three letters that form the word "bread"; it is like saying that they have the same energy. The kidneys preside over the transition of water to blood (which transmutes into Spirit), and the salt into fire (which transmutes into Light). The salt gives flavor to all food, which means it brings the divine message in the terrestrial nutrition. The salt is the engine of the fulfillment of the opera within us.

SANHEDRIN: the highest Hebrew board that administered public affairs and justice. Amongst its highest components there were the archons (in Greek *archon*), like Nicodemus (which means "the victory, the overcoming of the forces connected to the people").

SARA: from the Hebrew Sarah, which means princess.

SATAN: From the Greek Satanas, which means enemy, adversary, oppose. Corresponds to Ahriman, the prince of the Darkness.

SATURDAY: it is the Saturday, the Hebrew *sabbat* which means "day of the Graces". This is the day of the "re-ascension" to the Father, and Jesus at the beginning of His Mission acts by "leaning" on the force of this day of prayer, of grace and of giving thanks.

SAY: "to say" is the way of communication that takes place in the ordinary consciousness, of the present.

SCREECHING OF THE TEETH: the Greek term is *brugmos ton odonton. Brugmos* means "screeching of the teeth", and adding the term *odus* indicates the central bodies of the vertebrae, which in Greek are said "*denti*" (teeth). The expression means the screeching of the teeth of the vertebrae. This is a metaphor for the hardening of the cervical vertebrae that is caused by an excess of the current of the nerves which have been ahrimanized (materialistic thinking). This indicates the blockage of individual freedom and of the possibility to go through the brainstem (the lower consciousness) to the cerebellum (the higher consciousness), from the Consciousness Soul to the Higher I. This is due to the dead, ahrimanic thoughts that descend in the brain.

SCRIBES: Hebrew cult of custodians of the written tradition. They possessed the external knowledge without the living participation, and therefore that became luciferic (as a knowledge that is closed within itself). They represented the fall of the Light of thought (the vital force of the Light) in the darkness of intellectualism.

SEA: represents the **soul sphere** and its depths (with the relating "fishing"), and represents the **unconscious world** that we are called to bring to consciousness. The sea shores of the Sea of Galilee represent the 12 constellations, with their 12 "seas" (Tiberias, Magdala, etc.).

TO SEND: to be "sent" indicates a **delineated task** towards a lower dimension. The "sent" is one of the **executors of a more extended task,** he undergoes the Sent (see SENT). It represents the Holy Spirit aspect of the process of manifestation of the spiritual tasks. An example of this is the John Baptist (and the whole Nathanic Soul). See also PROCEED.

SENT (or APOSTLE): The Sent one is the **Christ,** who has a task in the Holiest Trinity and he was sent in the Holy Trinity to support the Principle Son, the Logos (in the Jesus). The sent one is **plenipotentiary for his task.** To send also means "to put someone on the Path". See also PROCEED and SEND…

SEPHIROT: combination of the 10 aspects of God and creation. They are the cornerstone of the elaboration of the Hebrew mystical doctrines regarding the secret aspect of the created, and it refers to the secret forces of the cosmos. Literally, *sefirah* (plural *sefirot)* means "calculation, numeration". The Sephirot can be defined as the levels through which God acts in the created. They are ten in number. The Sephirot have their own names: Keter (crown), the highest one and the one closes to God corresponding to the dimension of the Seraphinic Zodiac; Binah (science or knowledge, intellect-Saturn) and Chochman or Hokman (Wisdom- Cherubic Zodiac) on a lower level; Gevurah or Geburah (Force- Mars) and Khesed or Hesed (Mercy- Jupiter) on the third level; Tiferet (Beauty-Sun) on the fourth level; Hod (Glory- Mercury) and Netzah (Eternity or victory- Venus) on the fifth level; Yesod (Foundation- Moon) on the sixth level; and Malkut (Kingdom-Earth), the closest one to man.

These are the names that are most frequently used. Sometime, Gevurah is called *Din* (judgment) or *Pachad* (fear). Khesed can be called *Gedullah* (greatnedd), and Tiferet *Rakhamin* (mercy). The Sephirot are represented according to a scheme called the "Tree of Life". Additionally, there is an "eleventh" (even though it is not properly named) Sephira: Daath which is between Binah, Hokmah and Hesed and it represents the gap, which is the gap between Man and God. At the center, there is the spine of the balance which, from Keter through Tiferet and Yesod, reaches Malkut. On the left and right of Keter there are to other spines that start: the one of the Grace, through Chockmah, Chesed and Netzah. The one of the severity re-ascending through Hod, Gevurah and Binah. The 10 Sephirot are connected to each other with 22 paths, which are associated with the letters of the Hebrew alphabet. Various authors have different ways of representing these associations. The most common one is the one that makes the aleph start from Keter in direction to Chockmah and it ends with the Tau that is between Yesod and Malkut. The combined 22 paths with the 10 Sephirot form the 32 intelligences of God. There are some studies of research about the cosmic correspondences: for example, Gedullah can be associated with Abraham, Gevurah with Isaac, and Tiferet with Jacob. All of the components of the cosmos have their correspondences: Tiferet is the Sun, Yesod is the Moon, Malkut is the Earth, and so on. The 22 paths are also associated with the letters of the Hebrew alphabet, the tarot cards, the zodiacal signs, the planets and elements, etc. The existence of these associations goes back to the Gnosis and a magical vision of the universe in which every part is connected to one another. What is not knowable is what is beyond the highest Sephirot, which is the Highest that, since it is immeasurable, cannot be perceived by the man.

The path of re-ascension of the man begins from Malkut-Earth, and rises up by conquering the qualities of the first 4 lower Sephirot (Malkut, Yesod, Hod, and Netzah). The alchemists call this first step “Opera in Black”. If we leave Malkut out, a triangle forms with the vertex towards the below that corresponds in the man to the metabolism, and the axis is formed by the 5 sacral vertebrae and the 5 lumbar vertebrae. These 10 vertebrae represent the unconscious part within us and therefore, to face this work, the man was given the Law through Moses. Then, we rise to the Sea of Tiberias that represents the first projection of the Zodiac within us, and we go up through the 12 dorsal vertebrae, image of the 12 Apostles and of the “little chamber” of Our Father: from the Law we rise up in Freedom. The alchemist called this second step “Opera in White”.

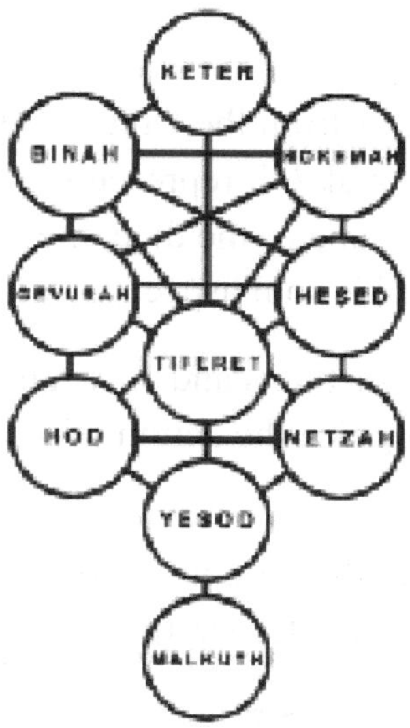

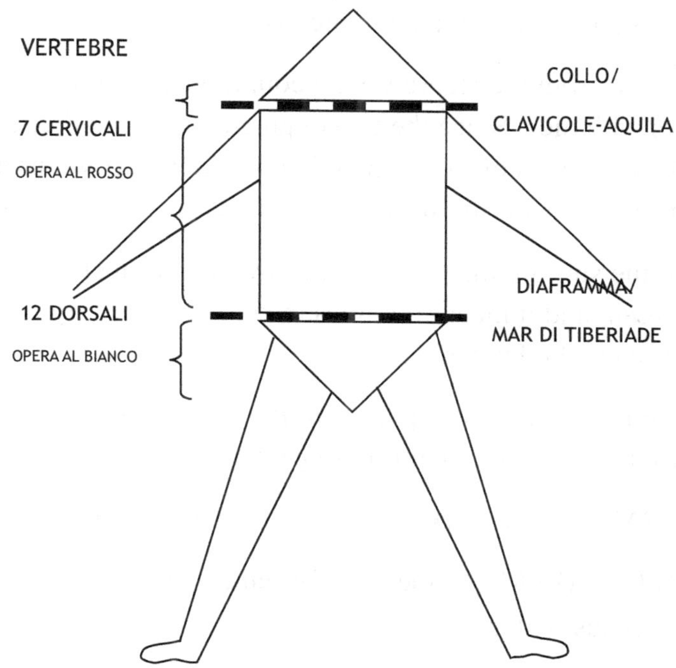

Here we fins the transfiguration (which is the Enlightenment of the solar plexus) and then we reach the NECK-COLLARBONE where our EAGLE will be able to start to fly. Therefore, we have gone through the **7 Cervical vertebrae,** and we enter in the Head-memory-sepulcher through the rebirth to the Father. The alchemists called this third step “Opera in Red” (the blood that flows out from the beheading of the Baptist and the blood that the Jesus will spill for us).

SERVANT: servant is the one who is aware that he has a mission to fulfill. It is reaching the solar step of initiation.

SHEEP: the **Right/Just,** the ones who follow the Shepherd with Faith. They are the components of the Chosen People (see) in their highest aspect.

SHOES (or TO UNTIE THE STRINGS OF THE SHOES/SANDALS):In the Hebrew law, when a husband would die without having children, his brother had the right/duty to marry the widow, so that children could be born and there could be descendants. This was represented by wearing sandals. The fact that the Baptist declared he was not worthy of wearing sandals, and not even with loosening the latchet of Jesus' sandals, means that John was not the true Groom, the Messiah. See also JORDAN and CHOSEN PEOPLE.

SHROUD: literally the cloth of linen that represents the last veil placed in front of the manifestation of the Incorruptible Body, and therefore the terrestrial light (luminosity) that represents the Fall of the Cosmic Life. With the estrangement of the young man in Mk 14,51 and then the Resurrection, the Shroud is abandoned, which means that the Body of Light resurrects (Incorruptible Body or Phantom). In the first case, it is freed; in the second one, it has the strength to go through that which is material.

SIMON: from the Hebrew Shimeon, it means God has granted, or from the Greek, it is one who plays with dice. Since the two opposite faces of a dice always equal 7, it represents the initiation in the mysteries of Time, in which we do not arrive through the cube of the dice, the form which represents the Earth. In Simon Peter's case, "Simon" represents his soul aspect.

SIN: the sins are the faults caused by the physical body with its instincts and cravings. In Hebrew it is *hata,* and it means "to miss the target". The target is to recognize the action of the Son that takes us to the Father.

TO SIT DOWN: To stop the will in the lower limbs to bring it to the thought, in the consciousness, and therefore to gather oneself, to hold oneself to work secretly (to meditate).

SMIRME: means **myrrh,** the transformation of the physical body in Spirit Man.

SON OF THE MAN: the transformation of the astral body into the Spiritual Self (or Higher I). It is the Jesus within us.

SON OF GOD: the combination of the Loving Vital Spirit (transformation of the etheric body) and the Spirit Man (transformation of the physical body).

SNAKE: it represents the force of Lucifer and his presence within us in the spinal cord. Moses raised the snake in the desert to indicate that the first 10 vertebrae (sacral and lumbar) have been formed in the Mosaic Law. The other 12 vertebrae (dorsal) can be connected to the 12 Apostles and to the conscious work of the meeting/wedding within us (see LIMP). SNAKES, SCORPIO AND PISCES represent the forces of the Obstacle that are present within us, in our subconscious, in our unfulfilled sphere.

SQUARE: in the urban setting it represents a hollow, empty "organ", but it is sunny and luminous. The aspect of the "hollow organ" recalls the **luciferic forces, and for the luminous aspect it recalls their purification.** In Mc 6,56, it is in the square that the salvation takes place, the purification from the luciferic forces. The square is the **place in which the purification takes place,** if the one who can purify is present. In the squares, through the rational confrontation, the sentient soul and the ego that divides men, would be overcome and purified.

In a microcosmic sense, the squares of the region of Genezareth (of Gemini) are the concavity of the pulmonary apex (the lungs represents the rational-affective soul), where the lymphatic vessels of the **subclavicle** enter. This corresponds to the point of strength of the lungs which, in their function, purified the blood (astral) by bringing air-Light.

In an iconographic sense, this point corresponds to the **Sistine Madonna** of Raphael, at the point where the Child leans his head on the Mother.

In an esoteric sense, these points correspond to the rise of the **two Wings of Michael**, connected to two currents of Initiation pre-Golgotha (silver left wing) and post-Golgotha (gold right wing).

STEPHAN: from the Greek *stephanos* (crown), which means crowned. He will be the first Christian martyr.

STONE: esoterically, the **eternal reality of thoughts.** If positive, it becomes a truth, a thought to build on: **the transformed thought made alive.** If negative, it is a **dead thought,** crystallized. In Hebrew, **stone** is said *even, a* word formed by *av,* the Father, and *ben* the Son. It is a symbol of the man in whom the reawakening of the consciousness happened, and therefore he confronted himself with the angular-Christ stone. The reawakened man become the Son of the Father. Also CIRCUMCISION would happened with a small stone.

SWORD: the sword can be the tongue, a *mantram, or* a magical formula of protection. It was the knife that was used for sacrifices. A religious object, not a military one. In an esoteric sense, it represents the tongue, and connected to it, the human thought that can be directed to terrestrial things or celestial things (like the two edges of the sword, where one looks at the Earth and one looks at the sky). The Greek term is *machaira,* which reminds us of the Sanskrit *Makara*, which means "sea monster", and it is also the name of the sign of Capricorn, the sign that is the "door" of the Darkness and Evil, and which is represented as a being with a fish tail.

For the Jewish People, the sword is the image of the divine Name, the tree of the knowledge with its manifestations of light and non-light (Good and Evil). The man that overcomes this antipathy, will not be hurt by either edge of the sword, and he will reach the perfect likeness with God. Where the two "edges" unite (spiritual and terrestrial logic), there the action of Michael manifests... see also TONGUE, THROAT, NECK.

SYNAGOGUE: esoterically, it represents the place where the soul forces gather.

SYROPHOENICIAN: it represents the constellation of the Dog, the headquarters of the star Sirius, the double star formed by the most luminous star of the cosmos and the darkest one. It represents the cosmic headquarters of the Entities of Lucifer and Ahriman, karmically connected in a "double system". In a moral sense, it also represents the sensual types of sins.

T

TABOR: it is the Hebrew name of "the umbilical cord", which is of the center of the world, of the chakra with 10 petals of the solar plexus. Literally, it is the "beginning of good", which is the tree of the knowledge or of the "emergency of the light". From this chakra, Jesus will descend in order to ascend to the one with 12 petals of the heart.

TEMPLE: there are various "temples". The main one, the temple of Jerusalem, represents the forehead between the temples, therefore the chakra with two petals, the so called "third-eye". The second one is in Samaria/heart, and the third one in Galilee/perineum. In general, the temple is the place in which the spiritual forces find manifestation…

The Greek language uses two terms for "temple". They are "*hiero and naos*". "*Hiero*" is the most sacred part of ourselves, the *sancta santorum,* where we are in our I Am, and therefore in perpetual communion with the Christ. The "*naos*" is the external temple, the first one which, during the exodus of the Jewish people, rose in the desert, and therefore represents the Tent for the Alliance/Covenant.

The TEMPLE of Jerusalem was placed on a large trapezoidal platform that was about 5000 square meters, and upon it there was the true Temple. The temple was formed by three parts: the Holy of Holies (Saint of Saints) where only the High Priest could enter once a year on the day of the Yom Kippur, or Day of Penance. On the east side, there was the room of the Saint (Holy) where there were the sacred objects for the cult (menorah, bread for the offering, altar of the incense). At the extreme east, there was a sort of porch with a huge altar for the sacrifices and for the basin for the purification of the priests. Here, animals would be offered (that would be killed in another part of the temple), and this area was open to the priests and the followers (believers). Even farther east, there was the area where the women could worship Jahve'. Starting from far away, the sequence of "getting closer" was: the pagans (under death penalty if they would get closer), the Israeli women, the Israeli men, the priests, and the High Priest. Everything was facing east to indicate the divine action coming from this direction. Even the ancestors had come into Palestine from the east. Everything was under the control of the High Priest who was assisted by 8 priests and a police force. The Levites were responsible for the music, the chants, and the cleaning. The Levites and the "ordinary" priests served the Temple for only 8 weeks of the year, and therefore implemented taking turns amongst the 12 tribes. Inside, there was a particular coin that was being active.

THOMAS: from the Aramaic t'oma', which means twin.

THROAT: the throat, with the collarbones (small keys that close the path to enter the eastern door of the terrestrial Paradise which is guarded by the Cherub with the flaming and rotating sword, and which Jesus gifted the keys to Peter), which will continue with the arms (in Hebrew *Sichem* which means "goal", "aim") and up until the hands, represents the force and consciousness of the EAGLE within us. See also NECK, TONGUE, SWORD.

THRONE: it corresponds to the top of the mountains of Gethsemane (GETHSEMANE), the seventh cliff, the sphere of Saturn, in which the Hierarchy of the Thrones has its cosmic headquarters. From here, we can grasp the 12 mounts of Gethsemane and the 12 Tribes of the Chosen People (see CHOSEN PEOPLE). See Mt 19,28.

TIMEO: from the Greek, the one who appreciates/appraises.

TONGUE: it is the image of the SWORD, the Opera in Red of the alchemists, of the fire that no longer destroys, but instead frees. The complex tongue-throat-sword is the freedom of the last aspect of freedom, which is the realization of the Verb within us. The tongue is the metamorphosis of the forces of the heart of the previous incarnation (and the saliva is the one of the blood).

TRUTH: corresponds to the **Amen** which comes from the Sanskrit **Aum,** the sacred syllable that represents the Trinity. When it is recalled only once, the Amen represents a partial truth, referring to a situation or a group of people. When it is repeated twice, it indicates a universal truth.

U

TO UTTER: when the Jesus utters, he connects what he is saying in a "vertical" dimension, towards the **Spirit.** This modality opens to the **future,** for a new manifestation.

V

VEAL: the veal is the animal whose blood used to be offered to the High Priest on the day of fasting (or Day of the Penance), within the sacred place of the temple to atone and therefore purify the one who was about to be offered. In the specific case of the blood of the veal, the blood would purify the subject from his own sins and his family's sins. The blood of the ram (male sheep) follows to purify the mistakes of the people (community connected by blood and by territory). The third one, the blood of a buck (male goat from which come scapegoat) would be offered for the sins of the nation (ethnicity with cultural homogeneity). Finally, a last buck, upon which the sins of Israel would be placed, would be sent into the desert, which is the oblivion (this is the "+1").

VERB or LOGOS: Principle Son of the Holy Trinity.

VINEGAR: "Vinegar", in Greek , is said *oxos*. The esoteric meaning of this word is "what penetrates in the deepest part of darkness". The Jesus is able to completely incarnate the principle Christ within him. In the esoteric sense, post-Golgotha, *oxos* means "the decision to descend in the underworlds to free Adam and go back to the Father to transform all of this in a spiritual logic that is comprehensible for the humanity". This is the comprehension of the Event of Golgotha.

The vinegar represents the closing of the cycle represented by the water: water is both the foundation of life, the purification, and also the memory. The action of the Jesus begins with the wedding of Cana (water into wine - from the terrestrial memory to the cosmic one), and then it continues ascending up to the Last Supper (wine into Blood, from cosmic memory to alliance with God) to arrive at the vinegar. It is a sacred drink used by the Egyptian priests to "extract" the soul of the deceased by putting a swab drenched in vinegar in his mouth. The vinegar also has a notorious therapeutic aspect. Vinegar is the so-called "mother", a sort of vegetable placenta from which generation and nourishment comes. We can find a parallel between man/spiritual nutrition through religiousness/God, between embryo/spiritual nutrition through the placenta/ mother and between vinegar/its sustenance through the "mother"/ Life as a divine gift. The mother of the vinegar becomes a tool to support all of the nutritive processes of the man, from the biological one (it is also physically similar to the placenta) to the spiritual one. The alchemists considered vinegar (in his mother) the quintessence (or Philosopher's Stone), which is the essence that gives life to the four elements (from which the name was written INRI). The dying Jesus becomes the Lord of Life. For the alchemists, the term "Philosopher's Stone" refers to the Incorruptible Body.

VINE: from the spiritual composition of the Greek word *ampelos,* we understand that the vine represents, in an ancient sense, the work in Nature as the door to the Heavens that expands us to bring the force of the Sun (Spiritual Self) within us[1924]. In a renewed sense after Golgotha, it means the force born from the development within us of the moral ether, that brings us to the state of virginity of the soul, and that allows the work of inner Purification, which allows the forces of the Word-Logos to act to gift us the capability of confronting ourselves with the world

---

1924 The Contact with Nature (M) begins (A) that brings us to the Heavens (P) to expand (E) ourselves up to the Sun (L) to then bring everything back down (O) within ourselves (S).

and controlling the anti-evolutionary forces within us, so that we can descend to the underworld and free our fallen Adam and bring him back to the sphere of the Logos[1925].

VINEYARD: the terrestrial existence, where we can work to achieve the Kingdom. It also indicates the Earth. The grapes are the man that mature within it. In the parable of the evil vine growers, it represents both the Cosmos and the Man.

W

WIDOW: from the Latin word *vidua*, it means the one who is lacking/deprived. In esoteric terms, the being "widow" represents the soul (the "Mother") deprived of the Spirit (the Groom or the "Father"). The soul who is a prey to sin regresses to the animal-human sphere of the sixth day of the creation, and becomes a slave of its instincts and impulses. It is no longer "married" to the spiritual sphere, and its son ("the son of the widow") dies, or she dies (see "let the dead bury the dead").

In an initiatic sense, the term "widow" can also be seen as a center, or a current of the Mysteries in which the Spirit no longer acts. Let's remember that in the late Egyptian Initiation ("Father" Osiris/"Mother" Isis), the initiates, who were spiritual "sons" of the lunar current of Isis, experienced how God retired from the spiritual worlds to descend on Earth. Therefore, they were filled with pain, and they were called the "Sons of the Widow" (see R.Steiner *Parfisal and Amfortas*). In the course of today's cultural era, the Father retires and the soul remains a "widow", which means it needs to learn to find within herself the Light of truth to be able to guide herself on her own. The revelation from Above retires and the man is called to determine himself on his own. This is the spiritual current of Mani (or Manes), and it is a higher current than the one of the Rosicrucians. It is the current that re-ascends to Set, and therefore Adam himself, the uncorrupted Adam. It is the current of the "Son", of E-manu-el.

This is the case of the widow of Nain, where Nain is a distortion of the term "Sais", which is the Egyptian initiatic center in which the current of Manu acted. Sais is the great solar initiate of Atlantis. To be precise, this current (Sais) was an the extremely particular current, and its initiates would develop completely the initiation at the next incarnation. This was the incarnation of the Child (the fruit of the Initiation) who was "dead" (Lc 7,11), and he was made "reborn" from the Christ who gave him His initiation. This Child became a great entity at the service of the Christ.

WORD: it mainly has three meaning:

1925 The new etheric body (A) brings the virginity of the soul (M) in which Mary acts who wins the snake within us (P) and therefore allowing us to develop the Logos (E) that gift the capability of winning the world over (L) to our thought, to then descend in the Underworld and free the fallen Adam (O) and bring the Logos (S).

1. As **Logos,** combination of the connections between the essences of things, **evolutionary Law** of the Cosmos present in the mind of God. It is the Principle Son of the Holy Trinity. See also VERB.

2. As **Rema,** which is the **single aspect** of the Verb-Logos, the single essence united with the evolutionary law, and from which we can re-ascend to God and the laws of the Cosmos. From this meaning we have **teorema (theorem)**, which is the "word of God" that is rationally demonstrable.

3. As **Lemma**, which means **word received from Above** (as a revelation or Grace) or it represents the "peel", **the external involucre of a spiritual truth** that allows one to catch a glimpse of its content (it is the **name-nume,** the spiritual essence of the thing).

Z

ZACHARIA: Of Hebrew origin, it means God remembered.

SUGGESTED BOOKS FOR A DEEPER UNDERSTANDING

Rudolf Steiner (ed. Antropophysics)

- *The Initiation;*
- *On the Path of Initiation;*
- *Theosophy;*
- *Occult Science;*
- *Spiritual Hierarchies;*
- *The Temple Legend and the Golden Legend;*
- *The Gospel of Matthew;*
- *The Gospel of Mark;*
- *The Gospel of Luke;*
- *The Gospel of John;*
- *The Gospel of John in relation to the other three and especially with the Gospel of Luke;*
- *The Fifth Gospel*
- *From Jesus to Christ;*
- *Christ and the Human Soul;*
- *How to find the Christ again?*
- *Our Father.*

Other Authors:

The Seven Miracles, The Twelve I Am, and The "three plus One" in the Gospel of John, by Enzo Nastati;

The Apocryphal Gospels, Einaudi tascabili;

The Dawn of the Revelation, Valentin Tomberg, ed. Estrella d'Oriente;

The Son of the Man, Valentin Tomberg, ed. Estrella d'Oriente;

Caesars and Apostles, Emil Bock, ed. F.lli Bocca;

The Passion according to Katharina Emmerick, Clemens M. Brentano, ed. Tilopa;

Elia, Lazarus and John, Adolf Areenson, ed. Antroposophy;

The Spear of Destiny, Trevor Ravenscroft, ed. Mediterranean.

The Nature of Substance, R. Hausckha, ed. Antoposphy;

The Symbolism of the Human Body, Annick de Souzenelle, ed. Servitium;

Biblical Numerology, Nereo Villa, www.esonet.org.

The translation from Greek has been done through these following editions:

Novum Testamentum graece et latine, curis elaboratum Gianfranco Nolli, Libreria Editrice Vaticana, 2001.

Novum Testamentum graece et latine, apparatu critico instructum edidit Augustinus Merk S.J., edito nona, Romae sumptibus pontificii instituti biblici, 1964;

Codice sinaitico (Internet).

Abbreviations used for the biblical references:

Gn Genesis; **Lv** Leviticus; **Nm** Numbers; **Dt** Deuteronomy; **Gs** Joshua; **Rt** Rut; **Sam** Samuel; **Rg** King; **Cr** Chronicles; **Esd** Esdra; **Ne** Neemia; **Tb** Tobias; **Ex** Exodus; **Gdt** Giuditta; **Est** Ester; **Mac** Maccabees; **Gb** Giobbe; **Ps** Psalms; **Prv** Proverbs; **Qo** Qoelet; **Ct** Chant of the Chants; **Sap** Wisdom; **Sir** Siracide; **Is** Isaia; **Jr** Jeremiah; **Lam** Lamentations; **Bar** Baruc; **Ez** Ezekiel; **Dn** Daniel; **Os** Osea; **Gl** Gioele; **Am** Amos; **Abd** Abdia; **Gio** Giona; **Mic** Michea; **Na** Naum; **Ab** Abacuc; **So** Zephania; **Ag** Haggai; **Zch** Zaccaria; **Ml** Malachia; **Mt** Matthew; **Mc** Mark; **Lc** Luke; **Gv** John; **A** Atti; **Rm** Letters to the Romans; **Cor** Letter to the Corinthians; **Gal** Letter to Galatians; **Ef** Letter to the Ephesians; **Fil** Letter to the Philippians; **Col** Letter to the Coliseums; **Th** Lettera ai Thessalonians; **Tm** Letter to Timothy; **Tt** Letter to Titus; **Fm** Letter to Philemon; **Hb** Letter to the Jewish People; **Gc** Letter to Jacob; **P** Letter of Pietro; **1Gv** Letter of John; **Gd** Lettera di Judah; **Ap** Apocalypse.